The Life of Field Marshal Lord Roberts

FIGURE 1 *Lieutenant-General Sir Frederick Roberts. The bold and successful victor of the Second Afghan War painted by W.W. Owless suitably accoutred and wearing his Afghan poshteen (sheepskin) (courtesy of the Royal Artillery Institution).*

The Life of Field Marshal Lord Roberts

RODNEY ATWOOD

Bloomsbury Academic
An imprint of Bloomsbury Publishing Plc

B L O O M S B U R Y

LONDON • NEW DELHI • NEW YORK • SYDNEY

Bloomsbury Academic

An imprint of Bloomsbury Publishing Plc

50 Bedford Square   1385 Broadway
London   New York
WC1B 3DP   NY 10018
UK   USA

www.bloomsbury.com

BLOOMSBURY and the Diana logo are trademarks of Bloomsbury Publishing Plc

First published 2015

British Library Cataloguing-in-Publication Data
A catalogue record for this book is available from the British Library.

ISBN: HB: 978-1-78093-676-5
PB: 978-1-78093-629-1
ePDF: 978-1-78093-707-6
ePub: 978-1-78093-811-0

Library of Congress Cataloging-in-Publication Data
Atwood, Rodney.
The life of Field Marshal Lord Roberts / Rodney Atwood.
pages cm
Includes bibliographical references and index.
ISBN 978-1-78093-676-5 (hardback) — ISBN 978-1-78093-629-1 (pbk.) —
ISBN 978-1-78093-811-0 (epub) — ISBN 978-1-78093-707-6 (epdf) 1. Roberts, Frederick
Sleigh Roberts, Earl, 1832–1914. 2. Great Britain—History, Military—19th century.
3. Marshals—Great Britain—Biography. I. Title.
DA68.32.R6A89 2014
355.0092—dc23
[B]
2014021252

Typeset by RefineCatch Limited, Bungay, Suffolk
Printed and bound in Great Britain

CONTENTS

LIST OF MAPS

LIST OF ILLUSTRATIONS

ACKNOWLEDGEMENTS

I gratefully acknowledge permission for the use of documents: H.M. The Queen for the 2nd Duke of Cambridge's papers; Sir Richard Carew-Pole for the papers of Sir Reginald Pole-Carew; Andrew Rawlinson for the Rawlinson papers at the National Army Museum; Mr Leo Amery for the Amery papers and 5th Viscount Esher for the Esher papers, both at Churchill College Archives; the National Library of Wales for the Hills-Johnes letters; the Trustees of the Liddell Hart Centre for Military Archives for the use of the Hamilton, Lyttelton, Maurice and De Lisle papers; the University of Sussex Library for extracts from Kipling's correspondence; the National Army Museum for several invaluable collections; the British Library Board for India Office papers and additional manuscripts.

I have been researching the life of Field Marshal Earl Roberts since autumn, 2003. My two earlier books, *The March to Kandahar: Roberts in Afghanistan* and *Roberts and Kitchener in South Africa* described his major wars in detail. I refer to this work and to articles written in a few notes. None of my writing could have been undertaken without the help and encouragement of many; over ten years the list of debts is a long one: Charles Aikenhead; Roger Ayers; Stephen Badsey; Shane Bartley; Jacqueline Beaumont; Ian Beckett; Christopher Brice; Angela Brown; Jane Burgess; Allison Derrett; Pip Dodd; Ken Gilligan; the late Douglas Goddard; Richard Goldsborough; Mrs Alexandra Gray for use of the Maude papers; Penny Hatfield; Tony Heathcote; Keith Jeffery; Rob Johnson; Ian Jones; Alastair Massie; Stephen Miller; Michael Pentreath; Karen O'Rourke; Sebastian Puncher; Paul Ramsey; Eliza Riedi; the late Bryan Robson; John Sheaf; Andy Smith; Edward Spiers; Roger Stearn; Kate Swann; Charles Toase; Peter Trew; the late Will Townend; Julian Walton; Adam Williams of Tonbridge for allowing me to use the papers of his grandfather, Private Arthur Haddock; Professor Andre Wessels; Edmund Yorke and my daughter for drawing the maps.

I owe particular thanks to Professor Jeremy Black who reviewed my earlier volumes and recommended me to Bloomsbury, and to Claire Lipscomb, Emma Goode and Jonathan Ingoldby.

Without the help and encouragement of Peter Boyden and Keith Surridge, none of my books would have been completed. Their patience, good sense, knowledge and guidance has been invaluable, and saved me numerous mistakes and infelicities. Those that remain are entirely my responsibility.

My loving thanks to my wife who has patiently endured sharing her husband's waking hours with a Victorian field marshal, his family and friends (and enemies) for more than ten years.

NOTES ON USAGE AND NOTE ABBREVIATIONS

I have used some abbreviations such as 'QMG' for quartermaster-general. In the East India Company and Indian Armies before the end of the nineteenth century, there were three divisions corresponding to the three presidencies, Bengal, Madras and Bombay. I have kept with traditional, i.e. contemporary usage. I use 'Mutiny' for the events of 1857 in India.

'Bobs' = Roberts papers at the National Army Museum, NAM1971-01-23

Dolaucothi = Hills-Johnes letters at the National Library of Wales, Aberystwyth

Elsmie-Stewart = G.R. Elsmie, *Field Marshal Sir Donald Stewart: An Account of his Life, mainly in his own Words* (London, 1903)

Forty-One Years = Field-Marshal Lord Roberts of Kandahar, *Forty-One Years in India from Subaltern to Commander-in-Chief* (one volume edition 1898)

Hamilton = papers of General Sir Ian Hamilton at the Liddell Hart Archives, King's College, London

James = David James, *Lord Roberts* (London, 1954)

JSAHR = *Journal of the Society for Army Historical Research*

K = The Kitchener papers PRO30/57 at the National Archives

Letters = *Letters written during the Indian Mutiny by Fred. Roberts. Afterwards Field-Marshall Earl Roberts, with a preface by his daughter Countess Roberts* (1924)

Low = Charles Rathbone Low, *Major-General Sir Frederick S. Roberts: a Memoir* (London, 1883)

NAM = National Army Museum

ODNB = H.C.G. Matthew and Brian Harrison, ed., *Oxford Dictionary of National Biography: from the Earliest Times to the Year 2000* (60 vols. Oxford, 2004)

Rawly = Rawlinson papers at the National Army Museum, NAM 7212-6 and 5201-33-7

Robson-India = Brian Robson, ed., *Roberts in India: the Military Papers of Field Marshal Lord Roberts 1876–1893*, Army Records Society (Stroud, 1993).

Robson-Kabul = Brian Robson, *The Road to Kabul: The Second Afghan War, 1878–1881* (Staplehurst, 2003)

SOTQ = *Soldiers of the Queen: Journal of the Victorian Military Society*

TH = Leo Amery, ed., *The Times History of the War in South Africa*, 7 vols (1900–1909)

CHAPTER ONE

A visit to Lord Roberts

In late years I saw much of [Lord Roberts]. It was a high privilege to know so single-minded a man and so noble-hearted a soldier. His love of his country was a passion. His constant thoughts were directed to the welfare of England and the security of the Empire . . .

REGINALD, 2ND VISCOUNT ESHER

In my opinion Gen[era]l Roberts is in all public matters the most dangerous & unscrupulous man I have ever known.

COLONEL HENRY HANNA

You are not going, I hope, to leave the destiny of the British Empire to prigs and pedants.

BENJAMIN DISRAELI TO THE HOUSE OF COMMONS, 5 FEBRUARY 1863

It is 1908. Edward VII is on the throne. He is also Emperor of India and head of a global empire. The Liberal Prime Minister Sir Henry Campbell-Bannerman is soon to make way for Mr Herbert Asquith. The Secretary of the Board of Trade, Mr Winston Churchill, will shortly wed Miss Clementine Hozier at St Margaret's, Westminster. A new law will introduce old-age pensions on 1 January, 1909. The fledgling Automobile Association will put up the first road signs. Wilbur and Orville Wright are to demonstrate their new heavier-than-air machines in Europe.

For men and women who have travelled the British Empire, it is but a short rail journey from London to Ascot, home of the well-known racecourse and of the famous imperial hero, Field Marshal Earl Roberts of Waterford, Kandahar and Pretoria. Fifty years earlier, in 1858, Roberts returned from

India as a young Indian Mutiny hero and Victoria Cross winner. Now in his seventies, he is renowned as 'Bobs Bahadur', 'Bobs the hero' of the Second Afghan War, author of the best-selling autobiography *Forty-One Years in India*, friend of Rudyard Kipling, commander-in-chief successively in India, Ireland, South Africa and England, the only man to hold the Victoria Cross, the Order of Merit and the Garter.

His house 'Englemere' was purchased and refurbished with the £100,000 which Lord Salisbury's Unionist government awarded him after he had turned the tide of war in South Africa in a few short months in 1900. 'Englemere' takes its name from a large pond lying on the boundary of the ancient manor of Winfield. The surrounding wild, sandy heath and forest had been converted from the time of Queen Anne for hunting and then racing. The discovery of mineral water in a chalybeate spring added to Ascot's attraction. When Englemere was first built after 1817, the races were drawing the rich to the area. From 1875 it was the home of Sir Robert Henry Meade, groom in waiting to the Prince of Wales and from 1892 Under Secretary of State for the Colonies. Sir Robert died without heirs in 1897. In 1903 Lord Roberts with his wife and two unmarried daughters moved in, for two years as tenants and then as owners.

The London and South Western Railway runs partly through the grounds. A footpath runs from Ascot station beside the railway and thence to the house.[1] Approaching the classical white walls, standing above the trimmed lawns, and then entering the house, visitors could see that the field marshal had, in the words of a local newspaper, entirely 're-built Englemere with the exception of the billiard room'.[2] The welcome from the field marshal and his family is warm, and for those who have eyes and ears there is much of interest. When John Morley, the Liberal Secretary of State for India visits, he finds the house 'all full of Afghan things, weapons, pictures, flags, etc. – and we talked Afghanistan all day long. He made me feel much at home on the frontier with his good soldierly way of talking'. This is generous as Morley has been an opponent of imperial adventures and regards 'the Jingo' as 'the devil incarnate'.[3]

In the grounds is 'the camp', a replica of a Boer War *laager* with tents, guns and other weaponry. It resembles the encampment of Piet Cronje, which Roberts captured with 4,000 fighting Boers in February, 1900.

Roberts and his wife Nora, Countess Roberts, are devout Christians. Every morning the staff, including five cooks, assemble, and the field marshal reads family prayers 'in the simple old fashion'. One frequent visitor, the politician and journalist Leo Amery, is impressed by the old soldier's simple faith and kindness to swallows in his outbuildings.[4]

Nora Roberts has seconded her husband's career for many years. By 1908, she no longer enjoys robust health. Their elder daughter Aileen is often seen at her father's side at public events and social engagements, while the younger Edwina answers her parents' many letters. Roberts receives more each day than he can read, let alone answer.[5] The old soldier is, however, alert and active. Despite his small stature, five-feet-four-inches, he is ramrod straight whether in the saddle or out of it, his back erect, his gait purposeful.[6] His face is reddened by years in the Indian sun, contrasting with his white whiskers. His expressive blue eyes twinkle with humour. One is sightless, although this is not well known.[7]

Inside, the entrance hall opens onto fine public rooms and a ballroom, with offices and service rooms beyond. In the hall is a dramatic painting of the attack on the Peiwar Kotal in Afghanistan in November 1878, showing the dawn charge of the 5th Gurkhas supported by the 92nd Highlanders.[8] The wide, curved staircase leads up to the library and Roberts's study. One frequent visitor was Reginald Brett, 2nd Viscount Esher, courtier and War Office reformer. Esher first met Roberts in November 1880 when he returned from victories in Afghanistan. Esher finds him looking active and neat in his country clothes: 'in mind [he] is as young as he was at 30'.[9] In his study Roberts has two portraits, one of his idol when a young officer, the hero of Delhi, John Nicholson; the other of his son Freddie, fatally wounded at Colenso in South Africa trying to rescue guns under Boer fire. The death of Freddie, beloved only son, was a terrible blow to a close-knit family.[10]

There are visitors from India as well as England. When a Maharajah arrived – most likely Pertab Singh of Jodhpur – he brought two elephants who lumbered up the drive and were laagered at 'the camp'.[11] Another old friend from Roberts's India days is William MacNabb. MacNabbs have been in the Bengal Medical Service since 1778. He and his daughter Dorothy drove over from Binfield to join a lunch party which included Sir Hugh and Lady Gough. Sir Hugh was a comrade of Roberts in the 1857 Mutiny. It is forty-nine years to the day since Roberts and Gough were in a running fight outside Cawnpore. No wonder Sir Hugh proposes a toast to that memory. The lunch gathering is good-natured, Aileen Roberts being 'chaffed' by her father, and she and her sister Edwina teasing their mother. The girls show Dorothy MacNabb mementoes including a casket presented to the Field Marshal, signatures at a press dinner, among them Rudyard Kipling's, and the flag which Piet Cronje flew over his laager, 'just a piece torn off a shirt hemmed at one edge, but white enough to be used for the surrender of Paardeberg. Also a silk flag made for him [Roberts] by Lady R. which he flew over recaptured Kimberley, Bloemfontein & Pretoria'.[12]

Roberts's life is intensely busy. Visits to public occasions, debates in the House of Lords, inspections of bodies of soldiers, campaigning for universal military service as President of the National Service League, gathering evidence on Britain's vulnerability to invasion, writing to *The Times* – he is constantly in the public eye. In December 1911 *The Strand Magazine* asked: 'Who are the Ten Greatest Men Now Alive?' and placed the inventor Edison first, the writer Kipling second and Roberts seventh.[13] This owes something to his reputation as one of the Empire's two leading soldiers, but much to his skill with the pen, warmth of personality and showmanship. He is astute at exploiting his press and personal contacts, but his memory for names endeared him to soldiers of all ranks. In his memoirs Major-General Sir George Younghusband remembered their first meeting forty years before at Kabul in the bitterly cold winter of 1879–80. Roberts and his men withstood siege and assault by Afghan forces. The 800-strong elite Corps of Guides paraded to receive gallantry awards. Behind the rearmost line stood Younghusband, newest joined subaltern. Roberts strode along the regiment's front rank, glanced over it and then spotted the newcomer.

'Who is that new officer?' he asked the colonel.

'That's Younghusband, just joined from the 17th Foot.'

'Call him up, I should like to make his acquaintance.'

So Younghusband was hustled forth by the adjutant, and stood before the great man.

'How do you do? Glad to meet you. You are a lucky young fellow to have joined such a splendid regiment. Goodbye, good luck.'

Years afterward, shortly before the 1914 war, the younger man was gazing at the opulent things in Asprey's window in Bond Street when a gentleman in a top hat passed him. Younghusband did not look round, but in a moment there was a tap on his shoulder.

'Hullo! Younghusband. How are you?'

It was Lord Roberts. He had not seen him for seven years.

'How are the old Guides? Going strong as ever? By the way, did you win the regimental [polo] tournament? I saw you got through the semi-finals.'

Lord Roberts recognised him after seven years, knew his regiment, and even that it had been playing in a polo tournament. Such was the secret of his appeal to so many.[14] To those closer to him such as his military secretary for many years, Colonel Neville Chamberlain, the tie of affection was stronger: 'we on the Chief's staff just loved him, and we would have done anything for him'.[15] To those who know him less well, an admiring and patriotic public, Roberts is a living embodiment of the last half century of Empire, a character from *Boy's Own* in action at so many of his country's battles, the 'hero of innumerable adventures . . . lived from the cradle to the grave within the four corners of the King's, or Queen's, Regulations . . . his heart . . . always full of romance . . .'[16] Born before the accession of Queen Victoria, the son of an East India Company officer and his second wife, an Irish background in common with so many of Britain's soldiers, Roberts was a small and delicate child. He nearly died from 'brain fever' which cost him the sight of an eye. The vigorous, 'red-faced little man' of Kipling's poem, sitting upright in the saddle, was a later development of ambition and determination. He was commissioned into the Bengal Artillery, and was serving in the Punjab when the Sepoy Mutiny broke out at Meerut. He had just met John Nicholson, who was at the forefront of the British counter-offensive against Delhi.[17] Roberts served at the siege of Delhi, the relief of Lucknow; the pursuit of rebel forces; he witnessed the bloody revenge exacted for crimes both real and imagined. He won the Victoria Cross in hand-to-hand fighting. On his return to Ireland on sick leave he married Nora Bews, seven years his junior. They were together for fifty-five years.

The advance of his career, after the Mutiny, Roberts owed in large part to his father, who advised that he remain on the staff, at the centre of command, the operational heart of the Indian Army. He also owed it to his own diligence, organisational skills, intelligence and ambition. He served under Lt-General Sir Robert Napier in Abyssinia in 1868. Later, as Indian Army commander-in-chief, Napier appointed him quartermaster general. He was Roberts's first important patron after his father. His second was Lord Lytton, Disraeli's new viceroy, who arrived in India the year that Napier left, 1876. Command in the field in the Second Afghan War of 1878–80 was his making. Roberts entered it as an unknown substantive colonel. He emerged as a hero in both India and Britain. His march from Kabul to Kandahar and victory over Ayub Khan's army restored the reputation of British arms and enabled Lytton's successor, Lord Ripon, to withdraw British forces from Afghanistan while achieving the strategic goal of making that country a buffer to defend India. His career never looked back.

After a brief South African interlude, Roberts took command of the Madras Army, and for five years initiated measures that he developed further as commander-in-chief, India. His final step in India he owed to his third patron, Lord Randolph Churchill. Roberts's warning about the probable failure in battle in the Sudan of a smart Indian regiment came true. It confirmed Churchill's judgement already formed by correspondence and then meeting.[18]

As Indian Army commander-in-chief, Roberts was hugely influential. He worked well with successive viceroys and with their advisors, the military members of their council; he increased the number of Gurkha regiments and other 'martial races' of the north; he pressed for forts and railways to strengthen North-West Frontier defences. He championed soldiers' welfare and took a keen interest in military hospitals. His wife began Indian Army Nursing.[19] A man of his time, an unabashed imperialist, he accepted the superiority of European races and civilisation. He loved India, but it was *British* India. He understood the secret of British rule: prestige and bluff rather than bayonets alone: 'An army of two hundred thousand men could not hold an Empire of three hundred million unless most of the subjects acquiesced in the Government's rule . . .'[20]

As the foremost of 'the Indians' Roberts became a hero to compete with 'our only general', Garnet Wolseley, leader of 'the Africans' and strategic spokesman for the Home Army. The rivalry between these two and their followers has been much debated.[21] It was less important than the struggle of army reformers to remove the arch conservative commander-in-chief, the Duke of Cambridge, Queen Victoria's cousin.

Roberts returned from India in 1893. Following Cambridge's retirement in 1895, the 'Africans' held sway at the War Office. Roberts succeeded Wolseley as Irish commander-in-chief. Would it prove a backwater in which to finish his career? He still longed for command in the field.[22] He established a link with the army's rising star of the Sudan war, Lord Kitchener: his son Freddie had served as ADC to 'K' against the dervishes. Following the defeats of 'Black Week', Lord Salisbury's government appointed Roberts to command, with Kitchener as chief of staff. About to sail for South Africa, he (and the public) learnt that he had just lost his son in battle. A wave of sympathy strengthened the army for its counter-offensive. 'This is not the time for any of us who can work to remain idle,' wrote Colonel Eddie Stanley, begging for a post.[23] In the British advance in February 1900, Roberts's strategic masterstroke reversed the tide of Boer success.[24]

His ability to deal with the insurgency that followed was less sure. Nonetheless, Lord Salisbury's ministry, grateful for his success, rewarded him on his return with £100,000, the Order of the Garter and the commander-in-chief's position at Whitehall. From the War Office, he wrote encouragingly to Kitchener, chasing Boer commandos, and sent out his protégé Ian Hamilton as chief of staff. Hamilton's victory on the stony hillside at Rooiwal in the western Transvaal helped convince Boer leaders to seek peace.

The South African war had revealed the British Army's shortcomings. Roberts and the Secretary of State for War undertook much-needed reforms, especially in army education. The most necessary reform, however, of War Office organisation, would mean abolishing Roberts's position. This he understood, albeit imperfectly, but when he was removed by Lord Esher's War Office Reconstitution Committee, it came as a shock. Roberts's able team of subordinates was also sacked. Nonetheless, in the years ahead many of those he inspired, 'the Roberts kindergarten', played an active role in preparing the British Army for 1914.[25]

Roberts did not grieve long, nor store up resentment.[26] At the time of our visit, he is President of the National Service League, pressing for training to prepare Britain for the war with Germany which he felt was inevitable. He is a tireless propagandist and speaker. Is his campaign a good cause, critics ask. Admiral 'Jacky' Fisher and the 'blue water' school hold that the Royal Navy is the bulwark of Britain's defences. Neither political party will support the League. The radical press accuses the old field marshal of scare-mongering.[27]

Roberts still watches closely events in India. He writes to the viceroy, Lord Minto, once his ADC in Afghanistan. Minto's ADC travels to Ascot to seek Roberts's help and advice.[28] Is he sufficiently up-to-date? Do his memories of British rule as he knew it mislead him? India is undergoing 'an immensely complex process' of political change; the Indian National Congress is establishing itself in Indian political life.[29] Secretary of State Morley, who consults him, writes: 'Lord Roberts is always a good friend of mine in every way, but he claims to know Indian affairs and Indian people better than anybody, and in a certain sense his claim may be true, but he still hangs on the Mutiny time without consciousness of the hundred changes that are sweeping over the stage.'[30]

So how should one approach the life of this famous field marshal? He has been lucky. He followed his father to India, which is in Lord Curzon's words 'the first nursery of soldiers in the British Empire'.[31] He has patrons who advance him. Like all heroes, he is in the right place at the right time. One does not become a field marshal only by fighting in the front rank, as Roberts did in 1857, or being kind to young officers, or even welcoming distinguished visitors and wooing the nation's press. Critics judge he has been ruthless in advancing his career and views.[32] He and his followers wish to ensure that his version of events is well known.[33] He collects like a magpie; his extensive papers are a revealing treasure trove, in some respects amplifying, in others casting doubt on events narrated in his autobiography *Forty-One Years in India*. His experience with journalists is illuminating. Early in the Second Afghan War he discovered that newspapermen could damn a man. He removed one only to find that others attacked his measures with such a vengeance that he sought to resign his command in the midst of the campaign. Fortunately he was convinced otherwise. On his famous march to Kandahar, he took reporters with him. General Luther Vaughan of *The Times* commented 'perhaps [Roberts] was not displeased that the brave deeds of his army would now be chronicled in the leading newspaper of the world'.[34] Following the war, Charles Rathbone Low, already Garnet Wolseley's biographer, saw potential for good sales in Roberts's life. His memoir contains a wealth of useful material, but criticism is not part of it, although Low opposed the 'forward school' of which Roberts was a spokesman.[35] He wrote: '[My book] has been compiled from the Blue Books and official despatches, and from personal reminiscences supplied in conversation and by correspondence with Sir Frederick Roberts, who himself revised the entire work, chapter by chapter.'[36] As an ambitious officer, Roberts had his enemies, among them advocates of 'masterly inactivity', a view of Indian defence contrary to his. Colonel Henry Hanna was one. Even before his three-volume history of the Second Afghan War appeared in 1899–1910, he had published *Lord Roberts in War*[37] to show that Roberts's victories had been the working of subordinates or of chance, and his 'forward school' views on Indian defence were suspect. Two years later Roberts answered him with *Forty-One Years in India*. No better source can be found for the picture of 'Bobs Bahadur', the unassuming hero of the Indian Mutiny and the Second Afghan War. As the *Newcastle Leader* said: 'The appearance of this long expected book will be welcome to every Englishman who can appreciate the responsibilities of empire, and who prizes the record of splendid public services. It abounds in attractions for the lover of exciting incident and adventure, while the thoughtful politician will find abundant material for reflection.'[38] So convincing is it that large sections of subsequent biographies were a distillation of *Forty-One Years*.[39] Roberts continued to ensure, even posthumously, that his life was told in tableaux that he set out. His friend George Forrest, son of a Victoria Cross winner, historian and biographer, briefly sketched the life in 1901; he then wrote a complete new biography 'enabling the reader to form his own judgement of this great soldier by a clear presentation of his services in three main events in the annals of England: the Indian mutiny, the Second Afghan War, and the Boer War'.[40] Roberts readily loaned the author his papers. His own death on the Western Front shortly before publication added to the work's timeliness. At the start of that terrible conflict, his sacrifice was an object lesson.[41] With Roberts's passing, his elder daughter intended to take a biography in hand, writing to Winston Churchill and Arthur Balfour[42] and assembling a slim but useful volume of his Indian Mutiny letters.[43] Alas! the 2nd Countess Roberts died in 1944 without completing the intended work of filial piety. In that year, during a second Great War, a history of *British Soldiers* trumpeted the success at Kandahar and repeated a long-held belief of Roberts's admirers: 'Above all, he was loved by the men he led. There probably never has been a more popular general in the British army . . .'[44] The memoirs of Roberts's leading protégé, General Sir Ian Hamilton's *Listening for the Drums*, depicted a man of easy temper and good humour, moral and physical courage, prepared to take risks in war. 'When Sir Fred got into the saddle and bullets were in the air [wrote Hamilton] he became, as Lord Randolph Churchill said three years later when he pressed for his appointment as C.-in-C. in India, "the first soldier of his age".'[45] Dissenting from this view was Sir John Fortescue, author of the famous history of the British Army and Redvers Buller's fellow Devonian, who may have helped that unfortunate general in facing the questions of the Elgin Commission following his South African debacle.[46] Fortescue's dismissive account of Roberts appears in W.R. Inge's *The Post Victorians*.[47] His opinion of the Indian Army and its famous commanders are of a piece. The generals were 'mostly corrupt' and 'imbecile'; transport arrangements were 'most defective, true to the Indian type'. Roberts could scarcely have learnt anything from the Mutiny for 'the campaign was carried on in such a careless and casual fashion as to furnish the worst possible schooling for a young officer'. Of the march to Kandahar, 'there was no particular danger or difficulty . . .'[48]

    The Post-Victorians appeared in the year of Fortescue's death. Future biographers ignored it. When David James wrote the last major account of the Field Marshal's life in the 1950s, Roberts's younger daughter, the 3rd Countess Roberts, supplied papers and leaned over his shoulder. His Roberts is Chaucer's 'verray, parfit gentil knyght': gallant soldier, tactician and strategist, family man, Indian Army reformer, servant of his country.[49] James performed one singular disservice to future historians: 'Incidentally, while going through the papers I (by arrangement) destroyed those of no permanent value . . .' Among these were Roberts's letters to his wife, which would have been invaluable to biographers.[50]

    The picture of Roberts appeared complete, and as the field marshal would have wished. Ensuing decades, however, saw the end of Empire and the debunking of heroes. The South African Rayne Kruger in his popular history of the South African war wrote of Roberts's return to London with Boer commandos still at large: 'no general has ever been so over-rated in England's history, or any country so gulled'.[51] In his *The Boer War*, Thomas Pakenham penned a brilliant sketch of Roberts: 'pusher' and self-advertiser', 'inspiring articles about himself', 'cultivating the female relations of British politicians' in India.[52] The book, wrote John Gooch in the *English Historical Review*, 'forces us to revise some of our judgements on the leading military figures of the day'. Redvers Buller was rehabilitated, Roberts guilty of an impatience that 'landed him in a series of administrative blunders'.[53]

To admirers there still remained Afghanistan. In the 1980s, however, William Trousdale condemned Roberts there. He edited the diaries of Roberts's chief of staff and then brigade commander, Charles Metcalfe MacGregor, printing sections which MacGregor's wife had suppressed when she published her husband's posthumous *Life and Opinions*.[54] Trousdale argued that MacGregor and Roberts depended upon each other in the Indian Army's careerist infighting, and that MacGregor knew enough to destroy Roberts. Trousdale brings into the foreground Roberts's hangings of Afghans, which he omitted from *Forty-One Years in India*.[55]

Could this celebrated general truly be a hollow man? Given so many favourable accounts, often by eye witnesses and participants, Pakenham's story was bound to be disputed. Edward Spiers's study of the late Victorian Army[56] sought a balance. He noted how in South Africa Roberts issued new tactical instructions using the lessons of earlier defeats. Pakenham had used a vast array of manuscript sources to counter the judgements of Leo Amery's *Times History of the War in South Africa* against Redvers Buller. 'Yet, in seeking to rehabilitate Buller's reputation, he largely relies upon Buller's evidence before the Royal Commission on the South African War headed by Lord Elgin (which other scholars have seen and have not regarded as mitigating their criticisms of Buller's generalship).'[57]

In Brian Robson's *The Road to Kabul: the 2nd Afghan War*, Roberts reappears as an outstanding general: 'Of his great qualities as a commander there can be no doubt . . . probably the ablest British commander in the field since Wellington.'[58] In their book on the South African War, Dennis Judd and Keith Surridge[59] note the importance of Roberts's victory at Paardeberg, coming on the Boers' special day, the anniversary of Majuba.[60] A favourable recent account is by a South African, Leopold Scholtz: '[His] war plan proves Roberts as one of the foremost military brains of his time . . . His plan evokes much admiration because of its subtlety and its indirect approach.'[61]

The biographer of Roberts thus finds a career marked by controversy. The traveller to Englemere in 1908 will meet a popular imperial figure, a link with half-a-century of history. He symbolises British rule in India. A paramount power had to retain a reputation for military invincibility; defeats had swiftly to be reversed.[62] Twice in Afghanistan and once in South Africa, Roberts did this. Thus, despite the controversies – the Afghan hangings, his ambition, his favouritism, failure to end the war in South Africa – Roberts is the object of widespread admiration bordering for some on hero worship. In November 1914, aged eighty-two, he gamely journeyed to the Western Front to visit Indian soldiers and died from pneumonia. When news reached battalions marching to battle, they could scarce believe that 'Bobs, the idol of the army' was dead.[63] Wrote one soldier: 'No man deserved better of his country or had done more gallant and unselfish work during his whole life.'[64] Another admirer, Francis Oliver, remembered Roberts's 'unflagging devotion – up till the very day of his death – to what he regarded as his duty'. He quotes a German newspaper following the old hero's passing: 'Lord Roberts was an honourable and, through his renown, a dangerous enemy ... personally an extraordinarily brave enemy. Before such a man we lower our swords, to raise them again for new blows dealt with the joy of conflict.'[65] The modern reader hardly thinks of 'the joy of conflict' when he contemplates the trenches of November, 1914. Roberts was a man of another age to be seen against the Victorian and Edwardian Empire in which he served and led.

CHAPTER TWO

Irish and Indian beginnings

Tis Ireland gives England her soldiers, her generals too.

GEORGE MEREDITH

. . . little men have . . . a happy knack of seizing opportunities and obtaining advantages.

HAROLD F.B. WHEELER, *LORD ROBERTS*

The pursuit of commerce brought us to India . . . our own selfish purposes, and our national love of aggrandizement keeps us there, and has induced us to lavish the best blood of England in fighting our way to supreme sovereignty over an empire vaster than that of Aurangzeb . . .

C.R. LOW, *MAJOR-GENERAL SIR FREDERICK ROBERTS*

Frederick Roberts was born at Cawnpore in India on 30 September, 1832. His parents were Lt-Colonel Abraham Roberts, commanding the 1st European Regiment in the Army of the East India Company, and his second wife, Isabella. Like Kipling's hero Kimball O'Hara, Frederick Roberts was both Irish and 'Indian' (or more accurately Anglo-Indian). The Roberts family had been settled for some generations in County Waterford, Ireland, when in the 1740s John Roberts married Mary, daughter of Major Sautelle, a French Protestant refugee who fought under William III at the Boyne. Their son, Rev. John Roberts, married on 23 January 1771, Anne, daughter of Rev. Abraham Sandys of Dublin. Among their children was Abraham, father of the subject of this biography, born at Waterford on 11 April 1784.[1]

British rule never wholly quenched the fire of Irish nationalism. Yet throughout the nineteenth century Irishmen were found all over the Empire and especially in its army. British and Irish identities were interwoven before

1918 and the fight for independence.[2] If an Anglo-Irishman is (in Brendan Behan's words) a Protestant with a horse, then both Abraham and Frederick Roberts belonged to these ranks. Irish landed families sent their sons to be commissioned in the British Army.[3] Irishmen sustained the Empire as administrators, soldiers, clergy, merchants and writers. Sons of the Anglo-Irish gentry and professional middle classes counted those stalwart heroes, the three Lawrence brothers.[4]

Abraham Roberts[5] entered the British Army in July 1801, aged seventeen, first in the Waterford Militia and then the 48th Regiment of Foot. The Peace of Amiens, leading to temporary economies in the army, induced him to join the Indian Service, which had then every prospect of active service. It provided a congenial home for able young officers with insufficient means to afford life in a British Army mess. Sons of the Irish gentry were pushed towards a military career by the smallness of their estates.[6] On 1 January 1803, Abraham Roberts was gazetted an ensign in the Army of the Honourable East India Company, on the Bengal Establishment. There were two British forces in India: troops of the Crown and the East India Company's three armies, largely native sepoys (Persian *sipahi* = soldier) officered by the British with a minority of European regiments. Clive's victory at Plassey in 1757 with a small force, mainly sepoys, against a motley mediaeval host of 50,000, some of whose generals had been bribed, opened northern India to conquest and changed British destiny in India from trade to Empire. British victories culminating in the defeat of the Mahrattas in 1818 established hegemony, bringing British rule as far as the River Sutlej.[7]

In 1805 Abraham Roberts served against the Mahrattas, and in 1806 against the marauding Pindaris. In December 1814, although only a subaltern, he commanded his regiment, the 13th Native Infantry, in battle. A letter from the adjutant-general praised his superior Major Richards for maintaining his position 'against superior numbers for an entire day' and giving 'conspicuous proofs of his judgement, coolness, and deliberate valour'. Abraham Roberts claimed a share of this praise, based on 'the applause which Major Richards bestowed in a subsequent dispatch on Lieutenant Roberts whose name he had omitted in his first report'. The governor-general 'extended to that officer the assurance of his favourable consideration'.[8] Further service included employment in the Public Works Department. Governor-General Lord Amherst's letter dated 2 February 1828 graciously thanked him for accommodating his party during the previous hot season; another confirmed that he was 'a zealous, diligent, and correct functionary, exercising a salutary control over subordinates in the Department of Public works', but also deprived him of a part of his salary and made no promises of further promotion.[9]

For his work in charge of the Famine Fund in Rohilcund, he was awarded by the governor-general a handsome piece of inscribed plate. He was promoted captain on 27 August 1822, major on 24 September 1826 and lieutenant-colonel 28 September 1831. He commanded the East India

Company's 1st (Bengal) European Regiment and was complimented in 1833 for its fine performance.[10]

Abraham Roberts's early domestic arrangements would have been unthinkable to his son's generation. By then memsahibs were numerous and intimacy with Indian women frowned upon. It was not so in the early 1800s. Abraham Roberts's first three children were all born to an Indian woman. William, born in February 1809, was baptised at Delhi in May 1810, and served in the army of the ruler of Oudh. The second, Anne, was born in August 1811, and baptised at Meerut in October 1812. The third, John, who became a devout Muslim known as Chote Sahib (literally 'little Lord'), manufactured gun carriages in Oude. Eleven years after William's birth, Abraham married at Noidapore, on 20 April 1820, Frances Isabella, the daughter of a Bengal civil servant. They had three children, two girls – Frances or Fanny Eliza and Maria Isabella – and a son who became Major-General George Ricketts Roberts. This half-brother of Frederick Roberts served on the Bengal Staff Corps of the Indian Army, and lived until 1915 when he died at Richmond in Surrey. He is not mentioned in Roberts's *Forty-One Years in India*.[11] Frances Isabella died on 14 May 1827, aged only twenty-four. On 2 August 1830, Abraham married again. Isabella, daughter of Abraham Bunbury of County Tipperary, was the widow of his close friend Major Hamilton George Maxwell. Maxwell had died on 17 June that year. The groom of this new marriage was forty-four, his bride twenty-six. The marriage took place at Secrole, a suburb of Benares. Geoffrey Moorhouse's claim that Isabella's mother was a Rajput is incorrect. Her ancestry was Scots.[12]

Isabella had a boy and a girl from her first marriage. From this second there were two children, Frederick and a daughter, Harriet, a cripple, to whom her brother was devoted, sending her many of his early letters. In 1834 the Robertses travelled home to England, Abraham's first leave for nearly thirty years.[13] He settled his wife, five children and two stepchildren at The Mall in Clifton.[14] Clifton was built in the late eighteenth and early nineteenth century as a rival to Bath, but instead became a prosperous Bristol suburb and a centre like Cheltenham for Anglo-Indians.[15] The Mall, with six giant attached Ionic columns in the centre of a long terrace was built as the Clifton Hotel and Assembly Rooms in 1806–11.[16] The 1841 census shows Isabella Roberts at number 35, The Mall, Clifton, and with her were Fred, as his family called him, aged eight, Harriet seven, Innes Eliza Maxwell aged thirteen, Isabella's daughter by her first marriage and Isabella's mother Christian Bunbury. Innes Eliza was to wed John Davis Sherston of Evercreech in 1851, starting an important family connection. In 1877 John Davis Sherston bought Evercreech House and was to live there with his wife and family until his death in 1897. His elder brother John or 'Jack' was in the army and served with Roberts in India.[17]

Abraham Roberts's biographer describes Isabella as a woman not easy to know from her limited correspondence, full of complaints and glad to bundle her stepdaughters, Frances and Maria, back to India to live with their father. Father tried to conciliate his new wife, writing in his letters that the girls think of her affectionately, apparently to no avail.[18] Both girls eventually married soldiers.

There is nothing of her alleged difficult nature in Frederick Roberts's letters or memoirs, and his daughter writes of her as 'evidently a woman of character and intelligence'.[19] Family tradition was that 'struggling with ill-health and the cares of a large family', she did her best for the children, especially a small and delicate Fred nicknamed by his sisters Sir Timothy Valiant.[20] In India he nearly died from an attack of 'brain fever'; when he was given up by the doctors, his father saved his life by resorting to a curious remedy. Indian hill-women at work in the fields leave their babies by a stream and induce sleep by arranging for a gentle and continuous flow of water over their heads. He applied a similar soporific to the son, but the illness cost him the sight of his right eye.[21]

In 1838, on the outbreak of the First Afghan War, Abraham Roberts was placed in command of the 4th Brigade of the Army of the Indus, which invaded Afghanistan through Scinde and the Bolan Pass. In later life Fred Roberts told of the children crowding round their mother to hear Father's letters read, and of how stories of Afghans and fighting were woven into his early memories. The British sought to replace Amir Dost Mohammed at Kabul with their candidate Shah Shuja. When the Army of the Indus occupied Kabul in summer 1839, Abraham Roberts was appointed to command Shah Shuja's force. This was not a satisfying experience. Shah Shuja's men never became effective, and British officers resented service with them. Roberts was bypassed by the political envoy Macnaghten. He was anxious at the scattering of Indian troops in 'penny packet' outposts; he feared for precarious lines of communication; and was dismayed at the indefensible cantonment outside Kabul where Macnaghten stationed the brigade left to garrison Kabul. Macnaghten was displeased, and replaced Roberts with the more amenable Brigadier Anquetil. Roberts returned to India. Anquetil's appointment was his death sentence, for he and most of his men perished in the snows in the disastrous retreat in January 1842.[22]

Abraham Roberts's granddaughter, Aileen, writing in the preface to her father's Indian Mutiny letters, quoted Abraham Roberts himself: "I am not wiser than my neighbours, but where my suggestions in regard to precaution were neglected we have suffered . . . I spoke the truth, and was thought an alarmist. Our rulers have much to answer for."[23] Fred Roberts was to benefit from his father's experience and wise advice when he reached Kabul.

With Abraham abroad, Fred attributed his early education to his mother. How greatly had he profited by her choice of schools. He first attended Miss Carpenter's, Long Ashton, from 1838 to 1840. For the following two years he was a pupil at Monsieur Desprez's at Clifton. Then in 1842 he went to school at Hampton on the river Thames. The school, Hill House, was run with a matron's assistance by Mr Mills, who had been a master in the Royal Navy. He had sixteen boarders. It was primarily a commercial and practical school, but if Roberts's reminiscences and his mother's choice can be relied upon, it did its most distinguished pupil proud in three years, 1842–5. He described Mills's system as excellent training of body and mind. Many years afterwards, on 20 March 1907, he returned to Hampton with his elder daughter to open a rifle range. He spoke with affection of his first visit sixty-five years earlier, travelling from Clifton with his mother. He said he owed much to the school: 'no better commercial and practical school could have been wished for . . . Mr Mills was not only a scholar and a master, but he had been in the Navy and taught all his boys to swim and row'. Rowing was in two boats he had built, named after his daughters, Fanny and Eliza. Mills gave those guilty of misdemeanours the choice between a prolonged task or a flogging; behind this, said Roberts, lay the desire to inspire a capacity for quick decision and the development of character. This is almost Gradgrind, and would not convince modern educationalists. The school no longer stood when Roberts spoke. In 1853 Mr Mills gave it up, and sold the house to a Captain Archer. In 1902 the Southwark and Vauxhall Water Company purchased and demolished it to make way for filter beds.[24]

In September 1845, Fred Roberts entered Eton, on whose playing fields the Battle of Waterloo had allegedly been won and where, George Orwell affirmed, opening battles of subsequent wars have been lost.[25] Mother's ambition, according to the family, placed him there, but Father's becoming colonel of the 48th Native Infantry in February 1844 provided funds.[26] He supported his wife's aim that Fred enter one of the professions or the Church: 'If Freddy is clever I hope he will not think of the Army,' he wrote.[27] The family was not rich, and the costs of Eton may have been a sacrifice. Fred's half-brother, George Ricketts Roberts, was posted to the Bengal Infantry as a cadet, presumably stupid enough for the army and without a mother to plead for his education.

Eton had not the pre-eminence it gained later, and boys often attended for one or two years only. Edward Hawtrey was a reforming headmaster, 'a scholar of liberal views', from 1840 supported by Provost Hodgson. Buildings, food, teaching – all needed change for the better after the long reign of the flogger Keate and conservative Provost Goodall. It was said the inmates of a gaol were better fed than the scholars of Eton, although Oppidans (fee-payers, not scholars), of whom Roberts was one, could supplement their diet. While Roberts attended the College, the chapel was restored, a sanatorium and library built, the assistant masters given more scope and the diet improved.[28] Fred Roberts entered a house run by a 'Dame' rather than a housemaster, by coincidence a Mrs Roberts. There was in those days no centralised entry or examination, and he went into the fourth form by age. His tutor was the Rev. John Eyre Yonge, the son of an Eton 'beak', a scholar at both Eton and King's College, Cambridge. Holding a King's fellowship did not prevent him becoming an assistant master at his old school from 1840 until 1875. Fred Roberts mentioned neither his tutor nor the Dame in future life, although he grew keen to identify his name with

Eton and send his son there. His only distinction was to win a prize for mathematics. Mathematics, not part of the formal curriculum until 1851, could be taken as an extra. The prize was probably offered by the mathematics master. It is an interesting sidelight on Roberts that either his father or mother thought the subject sufficiently important to pay extra for its study. For a Royal Engineer or Gunner officer its usefulness is obvious, but the whole point of his attending Eton was to *avoid* a military career.[29] His parents were presumably leaving career choices open.

In later life, Roberts often visited Eton. In 1881 he told the boys that for those intending to enter the army the studies and sports there were the best training; that Wellington by his famous saying 'meant that bodily vigour, power of endurance, courage, and rapidity of decision are produced by the manly games which are fostered here'. There is no record of the future 'pocket Wellington' excelling at manly games any more than the great duke, although in 1897 the College erected a neo-Jacobean arcade which recorded among its famous sons its two most famous field marshals.[30] In 1911, when Roberts's portrait was unveiled at the school, he told the audience that his stay there was 'very short – much shorter than I wished it to be'.[31] The *Eton Chronicle* on his death admitted that 'Lord Roberts owed little to Eton', while adding that the College owed much to him for the example he set.[32]

In July 1846 he left Eton, perhaps an admission of failure to preserve him from a military career, as he was to enter Sandhurst. He joined the Royal Military College on 19 January 1847. He was fourteen years and three months, the age of most of his classmates, and stood 5 feet 4 inches. He had come second in the entrance examination. This took the form of an interview to discover whether the candidate had mastered basic arithmetic and algebra, English and Latin, whether he could speak without impediment and was without physical disability.[33] Sandhurst had been founded by Colonel John Le Marchant in 1802 to improve officer training in the wars against revolutionary France. In 1847 cadets still wore swallow-tailed scarlet coats and, on parade, heavy, brass-fronted shakos. Under the indifferent regime of Sir George Scovell, governor from 1837 to 1857, there were barely 200 attending, bullying was endemic and rioting in the local Yorktown was customary.[34] Young Fred had told his family that he had decided for a military career: 'I had quite made up my mind to be a soldier, I had never thought of any other profession.' This was perhaps because he knew not how awful Sandhurst was, but he did have the facility throughout life for looking on the bright side. He attended until 30 June 1848, long enough to take three of the six 'steps' – civil service examinations in the various subjects – which would gain him a commission without purchase. One friend of these years, the future explorer and geologist Henry Godwin-Austen, for whom the mountain K2 is named, left a brief memory of Roberts:

> Lord Roberts must have been a little over 14 when he entered the R.M.C. in January 1847. I followed him there a year later, and he left not very

long after to go to Addiscombe. Although he was my senior at the College
and in years, we made friends, and I saw a good deal of him before he left.
I can well remember the day when he told me he was to go on to
Addiscombe, and even the very spot on the College front where we were
talking together at the time. Eventually we obtained our commissions in
the same month – December, 1851 – Roberts in the Bengal Artillery, I in
the 24th Foot, now the South Wales Borderers. We next met at Peshawar
in 1855.[35]

Roberts did better in mathematics than French, fortification and military
drawing; he advanced to Cadet Lance-Corporal by 1 May 1848; and he
won two decorations of merit, one of them a termly prize for German. He
was 'withdrawn by his Friends', presumably those who had entered him, in
his case his parents.[36] Abraham Roberts had written 'that he was acquainted
with no one in the Queen's Service, whereas, should the boy transfer to the
other Army, he would be serving under leaders well known to him'.[37] Not
only his father's contacts, but also money decided his future. The Queen's
Army was too expensive. In the East India Company's an officer could live
comfortably on his pay. Fred wrote to his father in October 1848, and his
dutiful letter makes the situation clear:

> Many thanks for your very kind letter and also for the sovereign which I
> received yesterday. I will try and make it last as long as possible. Some
> time ago my dearest Father I decided on the Army as the profession I
> should like the best, and would certainly prefer the Queen's Service to
> going to India, but still as you say in the Queen's Service I may go to India
> for a number of years, and then come home and be put on half-pay. I do
> not think I should like the Church or the law – Civil engineering is the
> only (one?) but if you and mamma think I should not be able to get on, I
> would not for anything be in it . . . If you and Mamma wish me to go to
> Addiscombe, I will go there willingly, and after all the advantages you
> have given me by the best education I should be ashamed of myself were
> I not to get the Engineers . . .[38]

When he left Sandhurst the lieutenant-governor wrote to his father:
'Gentleman Cadet Roberts was going on so well that I am sorry his career
to a Commission in the Queen's Army is cut short, and can only wish him
success in the Company's Forces.' The lieutenant-governor was well aware
of the pecuniary advantages of the Indian Service, having a son in the East
India Company cavalry then serving as an assistant political agent.[39]

Before Addiscombe, there was time to fill. His place at the East India
Company's Military Seminary[40] was not available until 1 February 1850.
Young Fred attended Stoton's School or Military Academy in Wimbledon,
well known as a 'crammer'. After Mills Academy, Eton and Sandhurst, and
with his father's 'interest', it seems improbable that he needed 'cramming'.

Stoton's School was a continuation of one started by the Rev. Thomas Lancaster at Eagle House in the High Street, a fine Jacobean building of 1613. In 1850 it was run by William Stoton assisted by the Rev. J.M. Brackenbury. There is however no record of Fred's studies there.[41]

He entered Addiscombe in February 1850, spurred on by his father's promise of £100 and a gold watch if he passed into the engineers and £50 for the artillery. The entry procedure was not severe. His father obtained the nomination of Major General Caulfield, an East Company director and like Abraham Roberts a former Bengal Army soldier.[42] The lieutenant-governor of Sandhurst testified that his 'conduct and progress in study were both very good'. On the forms Roberts listed Eton and Sandhurst as his schools, omitting Mills's Academy and lesser institutions; he described his education as 'mathematical and classical'. The surgeons who examined him on 27 February 1847 attested that he was 'without deformity and had perfect use of his limbs'; more remarkably, as he was blind in one eye, they found his sight and hearing to be 'perfect'. General Caulfield testified that 'his family, character and connections' made him a fit person for the appointment of gentleman cadet.[43]

Addiscombe[44] had been founded in 1809 when the East India Company bought a fine eighteenth-century house. Cadets at the time of Roberts's entry were aged between fifteen and eighteen; there were 150 in residence divided equally between two years. Families paid fees of £50 a term, but these were subsidised. To the original mansion, which in Roberts's day had become an administrative block, more land and buildings were added: barracks, a drawing and lecture hall, a hospital, a dining hall, a sand-modelling hall, a gymnasium, a bake-house, dairy, laundry and brewhouse. Initially only aspiring engineer and artillery officers attended Addiscombe, but from 1827 candidates for the infantry joined them.[45]

Roberts studied the 'sciences of Mathematics, Fortification, Natural Philosophy, and Chemistry; the Hindustani, Latin and French languages . . . the art of Civil, Military, and Lithographic Drawing and Surveying . . . the construction of the several gun-carriages and mortar-beds used in the Artillery service'. The emphasis was on arcane mathematics and rather meagre Hindustani. Military training was insufficient. The academy's scholastic reports consistently record cadets making 'great' or 'very great' progress, indicating, as the historian Peter Stanley remarks, 'either curiously uniform achievement or remarkably feeble teaching'.[46] One of its historians described it as 'not a true military college at all, but a militarised public school', although in its training not greatly different from Woolwich and Sandhurst.[47]

The regime was spartan. Cadets wore uniform throughout the day. Reveille was at 6 a.m., chapel at 6.30 and there followed an hour's work before breakfast at 8 a.m. The food was substantial but plain. An hour for lunch also included football. Football at Addiscombe was unsupervised and virtually without rules. It was unlikely Roberts played much, which, given his size, was fortunate. He was in indifferent health throughout, and suffered from a heart complaint so 'that at times he had sherry by his bedside at night to revive him', somewhat at odds with the general regime. His school reports show that he did well, maintaining good spirits and cheerfulness. In his personal appearance he took particular care, and to his dapper appearance he added a loathing for cats.[48] Roberts, like Winston Churchill, overcame indifferent health in boyhood and teenage years to develop a robust stamina that served him well later.

Among Roberts's contemporaries during the four terms spent at Addiscombe were Elliott Brownlow, commissioned into the Bengal Engineers and killed at Lucknow in 1857; the future Colonel Lambert of the 1st Bengal Fusiliers; and Aeneas Perkins, who qualified as an engineer and served under his old Addiscombe friend throughout the Second Afghan War. The latter two, with Roberts, were members of a party of six who 'chummed' together and had a fund in common which was placed at the disposal of the fortunate member who got leave to London from Saturday to Monday. His longest-lasting Addiscombe friend was James or 'Jemmy' Hills (later Hills-Johnes after a favourable marriage). Like Roberts he had been born in India. He attended the Edinburgh Academy, the Military College of Edinburgh and Edinburgh University College before joining Addiscombe. He was eleven months' Roberts's junior, commissioned in 1853 into the same Bengal Artillery; both served at Delhi in 1857, were wounded there, won the Victoria Cross, served in Abyssinia in 1868 and at Kabul in 1879–80. In 1881, both received the thanks of Parliament for their services.[49]

Roberts was circumspect in what he wrote later of Addiscombe. Sensibly he did not speak of fitness of curriculum or teaching, but of pride which its graduates must feel at attending a school which sent forth distinguished men, 'not only soldiers, but administrators – who throughout their glorious careers did their duty with that singleness of heart and honesty of purpose for which the Anglo-Indian official is so justly conspicuous, and which have gained for Englishmen the respect and confidence of the people of India'.[50] Perhaps J.M. Bourne puts his finger on what made Company men recall their days at the seminary:

> No account of Addiscombe would be complete which ignored the power of nostalgia, the appeal of the white gates, the tall walnut and chestnut trees, the level green lawn, the sunken study court with the turret clock over the arcade, the endless drill, the smell of boot polish and gun-oil, the feel of the cold, dark dormitories and the cheap uniform, the memory of the languid summer afternoons of Hindustani or "swat" (mathematics).[51]

While evidence for Roberts's education is sketchy, there is enough to show he was no fool and that, unlike other able soldiers such as Henry Rawlinson and Henry Wilson whose schooldays were a washout, he gained from the institutions attended. He passed out ninth in his batch of qualifying cadets, sufficient for the artillery. He could claim his father's £50. On 12 December 1851, he was gazetted a second lieutenant in the Bengal Artillery.[52] He was to be known throughout life as a 'lucky' general, and his luck began early. The East India Company's army was divided between the three presidencies, Bombay, Madras and Bengal. The Bengal army was the largest and offered the greater opportunities for fighting and promotion. Roberts's joining it was a natural course, following his father, yet from it his success flowed. Without this choice he would not have been in the Punjab at the outset of the Mutiny, he would not have seen at close hand the actions of John Nicholson, Herbert Edwards and Neville Chamberlain, from which he learnt so much. Nor would there have been opportunities to distinguish himself on the staff and win the Victoria Cross.

On 20 February 1852 he sailed from Southampton in the P&O steamship *Ripon*, bound for Egypt; the Suez Canal had not yet been built. Leaving was a wrench, despite his boarding experience. He wrote to his mother: 'I am indeed away from your kind care, and entirely depending on myself for all my future actions, a fact which I can hardly realise, but I will ever remember your last few words to me, and when in any difficulty think of you, and with God's blessing I shall succeed.'[53] He travelled by the overland route with changes at Alexandria, Cairo, Suez and for the Bombay passengers, Aden. From Alexandria he continued in a mastless canal boat for ten hours, then in a steamer for sixteen hours to reach Cairo. There passengers put up at Shepherd's Hotel for a couple of days. This was Roberts's first experience of an eastern city with its crowded streets and bazaars. From Cairo his party crossed the desert 'in a conveyance closely resembling a bathing-machine, which accommodated six people and was drawn by four mules'. At Suez he took passage in the *Oriental*, which had its double complement of passengers owing to the previous steamer breaking down. The heat in the Red Sea was very trying to the 'Griffins' as newcomers were called. An experienced officer remembered thirty years later Roberts remarking: 'I don't know how we shall ever be able to fight in India if it is as hot as this.'[54] On 1 April they reached Calcutta.

Roberts's memories of the first experience of India contrast with the cheerful quality of his usual writing. At Calcutta, three of the four officers put up with friends or were taken to barracks. He, the fourth, was told to stay at a hotel. That evening he met a fellow soldier who was returning to England because his health had been so affected by the climate. When he reported the next day to the arsenal and base at Dum Dum, he found a small garrison and only one other subaltern, rather than a large cheery party. His first days in India were not joyous ones. Very different was the account by his younger friend and future colleague, Mortimer Durand, who arrived at Calcutta two decades later and described 'the picturesque lanes of Howrah swarming with graceful women and delightful little brown children, like copper images', the cool verandahs of European bungalows with their cane chairs, the Bengal countryside brought out in a blaze of green and colourful flowers by monsoon rains. Durand did note less pleasant sensations: prickly heat which afflicted newcomers and for which the answer was a cold bath and black carbolic soap; the corpses which floated down the Hooghly River and had to be pushed back into the stream by useful native servants with long bamboo sticks. Durand's impressions were colourful. In time Roberts came to love the smells, sounds and sights of India, but at first all was gloom.[55]

As an aspiring man of action, his timing was unfortunate. He arrived too late for the Sikh Wars, and was not sent to Burma. His first action was to be against Indian rebels in 1857.

He found the four months at Dum Dum dreary and dispiriting.[56] Perhaps this was because he did not enjoy the charms of a native *bibi*. In 1858 Colonel Garnet Wolseley, then aged twenty-five, had confessed to his mother that he was managing to console himself with an attractive 'Eastern princess' who answered 'all the purposes of a wife without any of the bother'.[57] Roberts and Wolseley were alike in their Irish origins, their ambition and their mothers' influence, but in this they differed. In his correspondence, Roberts appears as a dutiful son with a conventional Christian faith. From a young age he was keen to get on, and not to let time slip away. He was to overcome loneliness, partly by a life of intense activity and partly by his marriage. His nature was attuned to a close-knit family by both upbringing and character. His mother had been a strong influence. In India his father stepped into this role. The four months at Dum Dum seemed four years, and his spirits lifted only when Abraham Roberts arranged for his son to join him as an ADC. This journey before railways spread across India took nearly three months, the last part in a palankin or *doolie* which was carried by four men in relays throughout the night when it was cool enough to travel, and then in a hired buggy. On this final stage Roberts and his companion, a cousin in the Survey Department, encountered two English ladies, each with two children and an *ayah*. They were on their way from Simla, and had been abandoned by their bearers. Roberts and his cousin persuaded the ladies to join them in the buggy and their own bearers to take the ladies' baggage. They made their way to Mian Mir, the military cantonment of Lahore. One of the ladies was the wife of Lieutenant Donald Stewart of the 9th Bengal Infantry. From this early act of kindness and sociability, the Stewarts became Roberts's close friends, and Donald Stewart played a propitious role in his career.[58]

Early in November 1852, the young officer reached Peshawar. The division stationed there was the largest in India, holding a strategic post thirty miles from the Khyber Pass. The walled city, five miles in circumference, lay in the Peshawar Valley's irregular amphitheatre, shut in by hills on every side but one. The British had acquired the Punjab with Peshawar in 1849 after the Second Sikh War. In its cantonment, European and native troops crowded together into a perimeter 1,200 yards by 800, guarded by a cordon of sentries and strong piquets against raids by border tribes. 'No one was

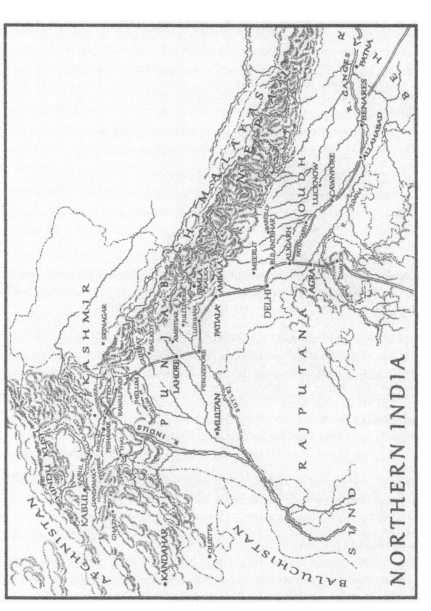

MAP 1 *Northern India*

allowed to venture beyond the line of sentries when the sun had set, and even in broad daylight it was not safe to go any distance from the station.'[59] For an adventurous officer, this was an improvement on Dum Dum, but its charm for Roberts lay in the presence of his father in command:

> It was a great advantage as well as a great pleasure to me to be with my father at this time. I had left India an infant, and I had no recollection of him until I was twelve years old, at which time he came home on leave. Even then I saw very little of him, as I was at school during the greater part of his sojourn in England, thus we met at Peshawar almost as strangers. We did not, however, long remain so; his affectionate greeting soon put an end to any feeling of shyness on my part, and the genial and kindly spirit which enabled him to enter into and sympathise with the feelings and aspirations of men younger than himself, rendered the year I spent with him at Peshawar one of the brightest and happiest of my early life.

Abraham Roberts, then in his sixty-ninth year, had acting rank of major-general. His son wrote proudly of the encomiums his father won for his diligence and activity.[60] Abraham impressed upon him the importance of preserving the health of European troops and recommended a policy of conciliation towards the frontier tribes and the Afghans.[61]

Soon after passing the necessary language qualification, Fred joined the 1st Peshawar Mountain Battery. Here his activity and smartness in learning and carrying out his duties procured him the coveted 'jacket' of the Bengal gunners, and at the end of 1854 he was posted to the 1st troop, 2nd brigade, Bengal Horse Artillery. There was nothing yet to distinguish him from other smart young officers, save fatherly influence. On field days he served as orderly officer to Major Brind of the Bengal Artillery, in Brind's words 'being then conspicuous as ever for energy and ready appreciation of field operations'.[62] In 1855 his fellow cadet from Sandhurst, Henry Godwin-Austen, joined him. Godwin-Austen wrote later: 'Thus it came about that for over a year I saw a great deal of Bobs. It was in his company that I made my first acquaintance with the frontier we were both destined to know so well in after years.' Already Roberts's seriousness in pursuing his profession was known. Godwin-Austen noted: 'It was there that Roberts laid the foundation in the handling of troops for which in after years he was destined to be famous.'[63]

Roberts was not continually at Peshawar. Several attacks of fever compelled him to take leave in the mountain air of Kashmir. He also visited Simla, British India's summer capital, and here met Colonel Arthur Becher, quartermaster general of the Bengal Army. The QMG's department in India then handled not only supply but also intelligence and operations. It was the brain of the army, to use a later phrase. Roberts's alertness and ambition may have impressed Becher, but friendship with his father was the likely reason for his expressing a hope that one day the young officer would join the department. Roberts reckoned this a turning point of his career: the opportunity came more quickly than expected. Peter Lumsden, the DAQMG[64] serving with the Peshawar Division, joined a party surveying Kashmir in early 1856, and Roberts took his place. The appointment was not confirmed because he had not passed the necessary examination in Hindustani. With the help of 'the best *Munshi* [teacher] in Peshawar' he achieved this qualification. In January 1857, with Lumsden sent to Kandahar as part of an embassy, he again took his place.[65]

Abraham Roberts had retired because of ill health in December 1853. His frail state meant his son had permission to accompany him as far as Rawalpindi. By the time they reached Attock, Abraham had so improved from the change of climate that Fred decided he was fit enough to continue his journey unaccompanied. He returned to rejoin his battery in an expedition against the Jowakis, but by the time he reached Peshawar, the fighting was over.[66] Abraham returned to Waterford; in 1864 he moved to Clifton, Bristol. He had stayed in India long enough to have his policy of an Afghan accord implemented by Lieutenant-Colonel Herbert Edwardes. Edwardes became commissioner of Peshawar in autumn 1853, after the brutal murder of his predecessor, Lieutenant-Colonel Frederick Mackeson, by a fanatic from the Swat valley.[67] Edwardes was one of Sir Henry Lawrence's young men, a brilliant frontier officer. A short Anglo-Persian War caused by Persian forces occupying Herat, a breach of a treaty of 1814, forced Persia to evacuate Herat and promise to interfere no more in Afghan affairs.[68] This victory ensured Dost Mohamed of Kabul would acquire Herat, thanks to the British. In March 1856 he signed an agreement with British India, receiving subsidies and arms in return for friendship.

A more substantial treaty followed on 1 January 1857. Edwardes arranged that the chief commissioner of the Punjab, Sir John Lawrence, would undertake the negotiations. The Amir was invited to meet Lawrence and pitched his camp at the mouth of the Khyber Pass, Lawrence setting his on the plain near Jamrud. Among the troops accompanying Lawrence was a troop of Horse Artillery including Lieutenant Fred Roberts, 'so I was in the midst of it all'.[69] The Anglo-Indian force over 7,000 strong lined the road for more than a mile, and Edwardes recorded that their strength and soldierly appearance inspired the Amir and his followers with admiration.[70] The agreed terms confirmed the previous treaty and bound Dost to keep up regular troops in return for a monthly subsidy of 100,000 rupees and a gift of 4,000 muskets. He would inform the Indian government of any Persian overtures, and allow British officers to visit parts of Afghanistan. When he had signed, the Amir said to those assembled: 'I have made an alliance with the British Government, and, happen what may, I will keep it faithfully till death.'

In his memoirs Roberts proudly claimed this as fulfilment of a policy advocated by his father, who had argued for rapprochement with Dost and had befriended Afghans such as Mahomed Usman Khan, former *wazir* or prime minister. Mahomed Usman remained in exile in India and his son provided the British with excellent service as commandant of the Khyber Rifles.[71] The treaty healed the wounds left by the First Afghan War and ensured that in 1857 the Afghan ruler did not intervene against the British when their rule in northern India hung by a thread.[72] Its consequences were momentous. The Punjab was to be the firm base from which the British launched their counter-offensive against the mutineers.[73] Afghans urged Dost to raise the cry of '*Jihad*' and exploit the Raj's hour of danger. Dr Henry Bellew, serving with a British delegation at Kandahar at the time, said Dost had only to give the word and the Punjab would be lost. Dost never gave that word.[74]

The despatch of this British mission to Kandahar in fulfilment of the terms of the treaty gave Roberts his opportunity to serve on the QMG's staff. The mission included the DAQMG Peter Lumsden. For a second time Roberts was appointed in his absence. He now had the required language qualification, and staff service was to make his career. Towards the end of April 1857 he was ordered to report on the capabilities of a hill, Cherat, as a sanatorium for European soldiers. The Peshawar garrison suffered badly from cholera. During the day he surveyed the hill and searched for water, returning each evening to the plain where he had pitched his tent. One evening he found there a second tent, that of the local deputy commissioner, Lieutenant-Colonel John Nicholson. That night they dined together, and Nicholson made a remarkable impression on Roberts. 'I have never seen anyone like him,' Roberts wrote. 'He was the beau-ideal of a soldier and a gentleman.'[75] Nicholson had come from Bannu where in two years he had brought order and respect for laws among people, in Herbert Edwardes's words, 'the most ignorant, depraved and bloodthirsty in the Punjab'. His methods were direct and often brutal, marked by contempt for red tape and brevity in communication. Roberts would soon serve under Nicholson.[76]

Roberts returned to Peshawar at the end of April as the weather began to heat up. As a DAQMG he moved into a better house than he had hitherto been able to afford. He and his house-mate, an engineer officer, were making themselves comfortable when they heard shocking news. Sepoy regiments at Meerut had mutinied, murdered Europeans, both soldiers and civilians, burnt houses and freed prisoners from the gaol. They had then marched to Delhi where mutiny spread. British rule in India was about to face its greatest test.

CHAPTER THREE

1857

It was not a time for tenderness – for mercy – even for justice.

SIR JOHN KAYE

All confidence in the native army is at an end, and only the most decided measures and strenuous exertions will save India now.

FRED ROBERTS, 14 MAY 1857

[We] heard one morning as they were all shaving that a 'little fellow called Roberts' had captured single-handed a rebel Standard and was coming through the camp . . . his mounted Orderly carried the Colour behind him. We cheered him with the lather on our faces.

COLONEL WEMYSS FEILDEN[1]

Roberts attributed his rise in the army to obtaining as a young officer a post in the QMG's Department at the heart of planning, operations and intelligence.[2] In early 1857 he became the DAQMG of the Peshawar Division. In April of that year during an inspection parade, Sir John Lawrence sent over his private secretary to offer a post in the Public Works Department. Roberts was tempted, but 'having got a footing in the Department' he decided to stay in this most advantageous position to come to the notice of leaders who counted.[3]

The immediate cause of the sepoy rising of 1857 was the introduction of the new Enfield rifle. Its paper cartridge was greased to permit ease of loading, and the soldier had to bite off the top of the cartridge and then pour powder down the barrel. Unfortunately, government contractors supplied tallow from slaughtered cattle and pigs as lubricant, anathema to Hindus and Muslims respectively.[4] By January 1857, rumours about the cartridges spread, as consignments of the new rifles reached musketry depots in India and detachments from selected native regiments underwent training. The threat to caste and religious purity found the sepoys already estranged by other measures: the arrogance and insensitivity of the British including many of their officers; the proselytising of missionaries; the spread of railways and the electric telegraph; the General Service Enlistment Act of 1856 which required Bengal Army recruits to cross 'the black sea' to places such as Burma. Hugely important was Governor-General Dalhousie's decision to depose the King of Oudh and annex his territories to British India, and this had a direct bearing on the Roberts family. Disturbing indeed was the effect that annexation had upon the native Bengal Army, for Oudh 'was the great nursery of the sepoys'. They had been a privileged class. Now all was changed. 'I used to be a great man when I went home,' lamented one Oudh soldier. 'The rest of the village rose when I approached. Now the lowest puff their pipes in my face.'[5] If the sepoys were to rebel, 1857 was a good year: native troops numbered 257,000 to 36,000 Europeans, six European regiments being away serving in the Crimean and Persian Wars.[6]

There were warnings of trouble ahead, outbreaks of incendiarism and the mysterious circulation of *chupattis*, those ubiquitous Indian loaves of unleavened bread. A district officer asked a chupatti-laden messenger what they meant. The reply was that when a *malik* or chief required a service he distributed these, and all who partook were 'pledged to obey the order, whenever it might come and whatever it might be'. 'What was the nature of the order in the present case?' Came the answer: 'We don't know yet.'[7] Chupattis were crossing the north-western provinces at the rate of 100 miles in twenty-four hours. On 29 March at Barrackpore, a sepoy of the 34th Native Infantry, Mangal Pandy, ran amock on the parade square and tried to incite the regiment. He was overpowered, tried and executed. The outbreak came at Meerut in May, touched off by the arrest, sentencing and imprisonment of eighty-five *sowars* (troopers) of the 3rd Bengal Light Cavalry who had refused the new cartridges. On the 10th, Sunday evening, the sepoys rose, joined by the *badmashes* of the town. The prisoners were freed, Europeans including women were murdered, bungalows set alight, native shopkeepers attacked and their premises looted. The mutinous sepoys then set off for the capital, Delhi. When the Mutineers arrived, the Delhi native troops joined them. Houses were burnt, civilians murdered, and those British officers and women who could, escaped. The sepoys secured the 82-year-old King of Delhi, Bahadur Shah, 'the last Mughal', as symbol and figurehead of revolt. In an act of great coolness, Lieutenant George Willoughby blew up the garrison magazine with an explosion that shook the city. In another desperate act of courage, the telegraph master at Delhi sent a message headed 'to all stations in the Punjab' telling of the revolt and its spreading.[8]

At this point Roberts takes up his tale. His account of the Mutiny is in three places: his contemporary letters[9] which his daughter edited for a book of 1924;[10] the first volume of *Forty-One Years in India*; and subsequent correspondence and speeches, for his interest in 1857 continued throughout his life. He hoped to convey to future generations what he saw as the heroism of that year, as well as correct errors and misconceptions about, for example, the death of William Hodson or hoisting the flag on the Lucknow mess-house.[11] *Forty-One Years* was shaped by his developing views and by knowledge which he lacked as a young subaltern. His contemporary letters have a freshness and youthful openness. They tell of his anger at sepoy atrocities and desire for revenge, of his ambition and his pleasure at rewards. His admiration for men of action and for firm measures influenced his career, and he never forgot the experience and lessons as he saw them. His biographer, G.W. Forrest, in 1914 counted the Mutiny among the three main events of his life. Forrest himself wrote his account of 1857[12] with the help of Roberts who 'kindly described to me on the theatre of their enactment the principal operations of the siege of Delhi'.[13]

The British debated at the time whether the rising was spontaneous or came from a carefully hatched conspiracy. Historians today overwhelmingly point to the former.[14] The circulation of chupattis and the Mutiny's timing, at the height of the hot season when European troops were at greatest disadvantage, pointed to a plot. Roberts had no hesitation: 'The cartridges have been, I believe, at the bottom of the whole affair and that a general rise was anticipated and preconcerted by the native Army there is little doubt . . .'[15] He affirmed this view in the chapter of his autobiography which begins with two questions, 'What brought about the Mutiny?' and 'Is there any chance of a similar rising occurring again?' While admitting various causes, he states that feelings of 'dissatisfaction and restless suspicion' gave an opportunity to three chief movers, the Mogul Bahadur Shah, the deposed ex-King of Oudh and most notably Nana Sahib, dispossessed heir to the Mahratta king or *peshwa*.[16] Once the Mutiny was under way, it quickly became a popular revolt in a broad band of territory across northern India from the borders of Rajputana in the west to Patna in Bihar in the east. Peasants in particular joined. Young Roberts saw the rebellion's popularity. Advancing in late September from Delhi to Agra he told his mother:

> What nonsense *The Times* talks about the mutiny being confined to the Army. In this district there never was an Army. Some 60 sepoys formed the Garrison, and yet it has behaved as bad if not worse than any other. With scarcely an exception, all the Police and Native Civil Authorities joined at the very commencement, and the many independent Rajahs raised their Standards against us. Every villager tore down European houses and robbed their property.[17]

Yet without divisions among the Mutineers and Indian support, the British could scarcely have held India. The Bombay and Madras Armies were almost untouched by Mutiny.[18] The Gurkhas and Sikhs lent martial support in increasing numbers. The majority of princes remained loyal. Merchants and bankers like the Seths passed on intelligence. Most important was holding the Punjab. Dost Mohammed, despite the appeals to Muslim Afghans to support their co-religionists, remained true to his treaty with the British. He was receiving a lakh of rupees a month.[19] The British, freed from a threat from the north-west, brought the Punjab under strict control, and made it the firm base for a counter-offensive towards Delhi. Roberts was a participant in this important campaign. His services in 1857 may be divided into four phases: action in the Punjab, the siege of Delhi, the relief of Lucknow and mopping up. In the last phase he won the Victoria Cross. In General Sir Hugh Rose's later campaign against Tantia Topi and the Rani of Jhansi he had no part.

On 11 May Roberts was dining in the Peshawar officers' mess when a telegraph signaller rushed in 'breathless with excitement'. The telegraph from Delhi 'to all stations in the Punjab' brought news of the outbreak. Senior officers ran to the commissioner's bungalow to tell Herbert Edwardes and John Nicholson. They summoned Brigadier Sydney Cotton, Peshawar brigade commander, and despatched a rider to Kohat with a call to Neville Chamberlain to join them with all speed. At daybreak the following morning Edwardes, Nicholson, Chamberlain and Cotton held a council of war at which Roberts took minutes.[20] 'It was a meeting fraught with mighty consequences, for on the counsels of the assembled officers rested, in a measure, the destinies not only of the Punjaub [*sic*], but of the entire [sub-continent].'[21] Hesitation and irresolution would have been fatal, Roberts later wrote. European troops were greatly outnumbered. Intercepted letters seized by Edwardes's orders showed the extent of disloyalty. Measures were quickly resolved: to appeal for support to chiefs and people along the frontier; organise a Movable Column of reliable troops; secure the key fort of Attock with its ferry across the Indus; disperse as far as possible disloyal Hindustani regiments.[22] 'We have some good men on this Frontier – Edwardes, Nicholson, Cotton, Chamberlain, etc,' Roberts told his mother and that he was 'in high glee at the thoughts of service, but most sincerely wish it were in a better cause, and not against our own soldiers.' He would work hard and 'no doubt, get on'.[23] Roberts was among British India's most decisive leaders: it was 'a military education to serve amidst such men'.[24] His admiration for Nicholson continued: 'about the best man in India'.[25] The 64th Native Infantry was dispersed, the sepoys at Peshawar were disarmed, those at Nowshera not long after. Officers of the native regiments swore the loyalty of their men, but were overridden. European troops and guns were skilfully disposed on the parade ground and four of the five regular native regiments laid down their arms. The subadar-major and 250 men of the 51st who deserted were rounded up by the border Afridis and returned. All were tried by court-martial and the subadar-major hanged in the presence of the whole garrison. When news arrived of the mutiny of the 55th Native Infantry at Hoti Mardan, Nicholson was despatched with a column of troops. The

Mutineers fled into the hills, but not before 120 had been killed and a similar number captured. Spottiswoode, their colonel, committed suicide from the disgrace.[26]

While Nicholson, Edwardes and others carried out ruthless but necessary measures, Roberts travelled to Rawalpindi to join Neville Chamberlain in command of the Movable Column. He was thrilled to be appointed QMG, really Chamberlain's chief staff officer, a remarkable post for one so young, writing to his mother: *'I am going as Quartermaster-General! Hurrah!!!'*[27] The heat was increasing, and he was fearful the troops would be knocked down by it. The column comprised irregular mounted Sikhs and Punjabis and two European regiments, and was preceded by the elite Corps of Guides under Captain Henry Daly. The Guides had been formed after the conquest of the Punjab on Sir Henry Lawrence's recommendation and were the first regiment to wear khaki.[28] Roberts took with him 'only just enough kit for a hot-weather march, and left everything standing in my house just as it was, little thinking that I should never return to it or be quartered in Peshawar again'.[29] While delighted at the opportunities for service and promotion, he was animated by rage at news of atrocities; to his mother he called the sepoys 'horrible blackguards', to his father he wrote: 'the Sepoys all thought so faithful and true, nasty scoundrels they have shown themselves at heart to be worse than even our enemies. No Sikh or Afghan ever abused and killed our women and children as these wretches have done'.[30]

Elsewhere rebellion spread: at Meerut the European troops entrenched themselves as the district descended into disorder; at Umballa and Jullundur native troops were on the verge of mutiny; at Ferozepore it had occurred; at Lahore Sir John Lawrence the commissioner had disarmed the sepoys, and urged the commander-in-chief, General Sir George Anson at Simla, to make Delhi his objective as the rebellion's key point. At the time the young Roberts regarded Anson as 'a most dilatory, undecided C[ommander]-in-Chief'. In *Forty-One Years* with time to ponder the travails of command he spoke well of him.[31]

The troops marched 'along the road [south], disarming regiments and executing mutineers':

> The death that seems to have the most effect is being blown from a gun. It is rather a horrible sight, but in these times we cannot be particular. Drum Head Courts-Martial are the order of the day in every station, and had they begun this regime a little earlier, one half of the destruction and mutiny would have been saved.[32]

At Mian Mir, the cantonment outside Lahore, he was warned on the night of 8 June that the men of the 35th Native Infantry intended to revolt at daybreak and had already loaded their muskets in preparation. He woke Chamberlain who ordered the officers to fall in the men, the arms were examined and two found to be loaded. A drumhead court-martial was held composed of native officers. The two offenders were found guilty and blown from the mouths of cannon, 'a terrible sight and one likely to haunt the beholder for many a long day'.[33] While revenge became uppermost in British minds that fateful year, Roberts would have seen another policy in effect: trust and friendship for the Sikhs and border tribes. In the 1850s the policy of Henry and John Lawrence had been to conciliate the people of the Punjab. Roberts emphasised in his autobiography the anxiety over which side the Maharaja of Patiala and the Rajas of Jhind and Nabha would take. If they aided the Mutineers, British communications between Delhi and the Punjab would be imperilled. Roberts tells of the deputy commissioner of Umballa seeking an interview with the maharajah and asking:

'Maharajah, *sahib,* answer me one question: Are you for us or against us?'

The reply: 'As long as I live I am yours, but you know I have enemies in my own country . . . What do you want done?'

The deputy commissioner requested the maharajah to send troops to keep open the Grand Trunk Road, the great artery running across northern India. The maharajah agreed on the understanding that Europeans should soon be sent to help, for he knew that his men would remain loyal 'as long as there was no doubt of our ultimate success'.[34] Punjabi loyalty, a key to British success, was based on shrewd calculation of probable British victory as well as hostility to the Moguls.[35] The Sepoys wished to elevate the last Mogul. In the Punjab 34,000 new troops were raised, and to Delhi there marched seven battalions of infantry, three regiments of cavalry, a corps of sappers and miners and two siege trains.[36]

On 11 June Roberts bragged to his mother: 'I have plenty of work [with the Movable Column]. Chamberlain has no other staff, and I am Quartermaster-General! Brigade Major!! And, until yesterday, Commissariat Officer!!! The General [father] would, I am sure, be amused and astonished seeing me at the desk all day, writing, writing incessantly.' He had to be first at campsites to mark out the ground. His only bother was not getting enough sleep at night. At halts, he wrote: 'I generally snooze on the ground beside my horse.'[37]

Roberts and the Movable Column marched to Jullundhur. There on 22 June, Chamberlain was ordered to join the force at Delhi. Nicholson assumed command, to the satisfaction of Roberts who continued to work hard and thus 'gained the entire confidence of his chief'. Roberts told his biographer Low that he was the one who effected the passage of troops and stores at a rising River Beas.[38] At Phillour Nicholson arranged the disarming of two suspect native regiments. The Column was ordered to return to Lahore. Hearing that artillery officers were urgently required at Delhi, Roberts applied for permission to resign his appointment and join his regiment, the Bengal Artillery, there. Nicholson at first would not consent, but so ardently did the young officer argue his cause that he answered: 'Well,

Roberts, your loss I can't replace, both personally and publicly I regret your going, but, at the same time, you have more chance of getting on before Delhi.' That evening they dined together. At dawn, Roberts left in a mail cart with two others, one of whom was to be killed and the other maimed for life by an ankle wound. His kit was a small bundle – 'saddle and tooth brush', he told his parents – his servants to follow with horses, tents and other belongings. Nearing Delhi they heard the sound of guns and saw dead sepoys on the road. On 28 June they arrived and joined the besiegers on the historic Ridge. His father's old staff officer, Henry Norman, later a distinguished field marshal, invited him to share his tent, and with no bed Roberts threw himself to the ground under the canvas and slept.[39]

Arrival at Delhi began the second phase of his Mutiny service. British troops had been besieging the capital since early June. Anson, the commander-in-chief, advancing from Ambala, died of cholera on 27 May. His successor, General Sir Henry Barnard, pushed on through dust and heat to rendezvous with the Meerut column of General Hewitt and Brigadier Archdale Wilson. Evidence of rebel atrocities met en route were answered by the burning of villages and hangings 'until every tree was covered with scoundrels hanging from every branch', wrote one subaltern.[40] On 8 June in an engagement five miles north-west of Delhi, the rebels were driven back and the British occupied the Ridge, a narrow outcrop of rock running north-south for about two and a half miles. Its highest point was no more than sixty feet above the plain. Its southern end was surrounded on three sides by the suburbs of Delhi. 'This was the weak point of our defence,' wrote Roberts, 'a succession of houses and walled gardens, from which the rebels constantly threatened our flank.' To defend this position, a battery of three eighteen-pounders and an infantry guard were placed on the low height, with a cavalry piquet and two Horse Artillery guns immediately below. The ground in front of the Ridge was covered with old buildings, enclosed gardens and clumps of trees, which afforded shelter to the enemy in their sorties. Behind rose the sixteen-foot-high walls of Delhi with gates, bastions and ramparts; beyond, the city with its towers, domes and minarets, its complex network of lanes and alleys.[41]

The besiegers were too weak to attack the city's ten-mile walled perimeter and massive gates, but too strong to be driven away. The 'British' force was only one-third European; it included fierce little Gurkhas and hardy tribesmen from the borders of north-west India. Supporting the fighting soldiers were others. 'For every British soldier in the field there were twenty Indian "followers", official or unofficial, providing all the logistic services without which an army could not function in India . . .'[42]

The Mutineers were soon reinforced to a strength of 30,000.[43] The sepoys elevated Bahadur Shah as their figurehead. He appointed royal princes to high command, conferring the office of commander-in-chief upon his eldest son, Mirza Moghul. Letters to various rajahs urged them to march at once upon Delhi with their forces to join the insurgents. However, the unpaid sepoys constantly quarrelled with their commanders, plundered shops and shot

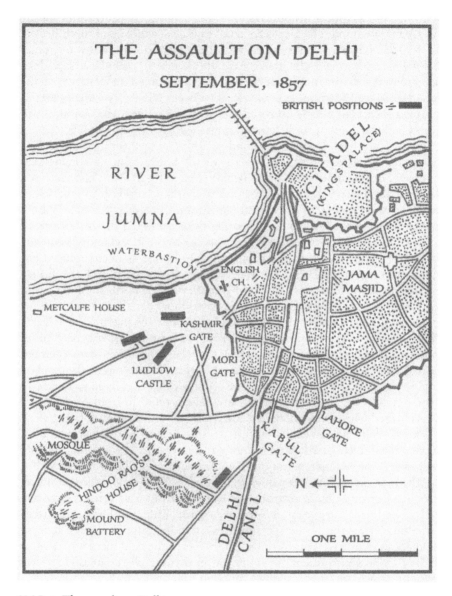

MAP 2 *The assault on Delhi*

shopkeepers. They made frequent sorties against the Ridge, but not under Mirza Moghul who was no leader. On 23 June, the anniversary of Clive's victory of Plassy, astrologers were summoned and consulted their almanacs as to whether the Mutineers would triumph. The enigmatic reply was that 'great disturbances would last for a year'.[44] The British beat off that day's sortie. Then a large body of reinforcements arrived, commanded by Muhammad Bakht Khan, a sturdy man with a barrel-like chest and large stomach. He had served forty years and been a senior native officer in a field artillery battery in the Afghan War. His commanding personality and the badly-needed money which he brought persuaded the king to appoint him to lead the army.[45] He exercised his authority with great zest and improved discipline, but was resented by the royal princes and unable to impose sufficient unity of command to assault the Ridge and drive the British away. Indiscipline and divided leadership weakened sepoy cohesion. Conversely they may have enjoyed the services of a renegade British sergeant-major directing their artillery.[46]

The British had similar difficulties. Barnard succumbed to cholera. His successor General Reed was 'more fit for an invalid couch' than command, and Brigadier Archdale Wilson took over within a fortnight. He strengthened defences, improved discipline and sanitation and sent working parties to burn or bury corpses. This was not a moment too soon as the monsoon brought debilitating sickness, especially the dreaded cholera. Wilson could not attack the city, however: his troops were too few, his guns outmatched, and ammunition so short that camp followers received two annas apiece for each enemy roundshot retrieved.[47]

Roberts wrote in his autobiography that he awoke on 29 June 'full of excitement'. Letters to his mother breathe anticipation: 'what I want more than any other is the *Victoria Cross*. Oh! If I can only manage that, how jolly I should be'.[48] He found himself among friends – 'Jemmy' Hills from Addiscombe, Edwin Johnson, another Bengal Horse Artillery man, and Donald Stewart, whose wife he had helped on the journey to the Punjab. To them he was 'Little Bobs'.[49] Stewart had reached Delhi after a remarkable ride from Aligarh, where his regiment, the 9th Bengal Native Infantry, had mutinied, and then from Agra, whence he brought despatches.[50] The man whose tent Roberts shared, Henry Norman, became one of the most remarkable military administrators of British India. Although he and Roberts later disagreed over army reform, they were bound together by remembered fellowship-in-arms and then by service to the Empire.[51] Norman wrote: 'Few comrades were ever more together than Edwin Johnson, Donald Stewart, Fred Roberts and myself . . . We were all quite confident of success, and never doubted that our assault of Delhi would be successful, if delivered after a bombardment from the siege guns and mortars . . .'[52]

Roberts became artillery DAQMG, thus rejoining his regiment.[53] He was in constant action. Delhi was the fulcrum of rebellion, identified by Governor-General Canning and Punjab High Commissioner Sir John Lawrence as the key to victory.

In the afternoon of 3 July the rebels combined an attack on the Ridge with an attempt to fall on the British rear. Roberts accompanied a mixed column of foot, horse and guns on 4 July to intercept the enemy. The action was fought in great heat, several British soldiers dying from sunstroke. The Mutineers were driven back, giving up plunder and some artillery wagons and ammunition.[54]

On 9 July rebel cavalry made a determined raid on British lines. A troop of inexperienced men of the 6th Dragoon Guards (Carabineers) turned and fled leaving only three or four to fight. 'Jemmy' Hills's battery moved forward to plug the gap. He charged single-handed to give his gunners time to unlimber. A collision with two of the enemy sent Hills and his horse flying; he was ridden over, and three sowars turned to finish him off. Wounded, he fought first with sword and then with fists when his sword was wrenched from his hand. He was saved from almost certain death by Major Tombs, his battery commander. Both Hills and Tombs received the Victoria Cross. They gave the gunners time to come into action, repulsing the enemy.[55]

On 14 July, with Neville Chamberlain, Roberts took part in repelling another enemy sortie. Among Roberts's heroes, Chamberlain was 'a dashing, gallant fellow', second only to Nicholson. 'Whenever the fire was hottest there he was sure to be, and I, thinking his invitation to go along with him was perhaps intended for the rest of the day, did not like leaving him.' Roberts received

> a shot in the back, just where my waist-belt goes. Most fortunately, thro' God's mercy, I had a small leather pouch on my belt. The bullet went just thro' the middle of this, thro' my trousers and shirt, and made a small hole in my back ... Altho' we could not, I believe, have been under heavier fire ... from the excitement, I suppose I quite forgot about the chance of being hit, and when I got this awful crack on my back for a second did not know what it was.

Feeling faint, he dismounted, assisted by two men sent by an officer who thought his wound fatal. He told his mother the pouch saved his life; the bullet just missed the spine, 'so I suffer hardly any pain. Am I not a lucky fellow, my own Mother, and has not God been merciful to me, I can never be sufficiently thankful'.[56] Nine days later he was writing to his mother again about the Victoria Cross.

Before he wrote this letter, news of the Cawnpore massacre reached the British outside Delhi. On 25 June, after nearly three weeks' siege, General Sir Hugh Wheeler accepted Nana Sahib's terms of a safe passage to Calcutta for his men, women and children. There followed the ambush and massacre of nearly all the officers and men as they embarked at the Satichaura Ghat on the River Ganges; and subsequently and even more infamous, that of the women and children, their numbers swelled to 200. The bodies were thrown down a well in the courtyard where they had been held. British soldiers arriving found torn pieces of children's clothing, locks of hair, tattered remains of Bibles and prayer-books. They were incensed, and vowed revenge. Already Colonel James Neill's column had been hanging Indians indiscriminately, and now vengeance became widespread.[57] Roberts shared in the anguished reaction. 'Nothing has ever happened in the world like this . . . I would undergo cheerfully any privation, any amount of work, living in the hopes of a *revenge* on these cruel murderers. This feeling is shared by every European in the Camp.'[58] First, however, Delhi had to be taken.

British spies who regularly entered the city estimated by the second week in August that Mutineers' numbers had fallen, morale was low, the rebels were 'much disturbed and distressed from lack of pay'. Wilson was still overcome by doubt and thought of abandoning Delhi. The British lacked sufficient heavy guns. In mid-August the situation was transformed: Roberts's hero John Nicholson arrived from the Punjab followed by his Movable Column, bringing numbers on the Ridge to 10,000. When the all-important siege train from Ferozepore came slowly down the Grand Trunk Road, long lines of bullocks dragging the guns that would open breaches in Delhi's walls, Nicholson asked Roberts to accompany him with a force to frustrate an attempted enemy interception. The doctors refused permission as his wound was not sufficiently healed. Nicholson was completely successful. On 4 September the siege train, thirty-two howitzers and heavy mortars and over 100 bullock carts of ammunition, arrived at the Ridge.[59] 'Immediately on his return' wrote Roberts to his mother, '[Nicholson] came to see me and spoke so kindly and said he wanted me to be well for the grand business, and that I might rely on his never leaving me behind, that I felt quite happy again. Nicholson is really the only Commander that we have here, now that Chamberlain is laid up, and, in my opinion, he is superior to him . . . He is very kind to me . . . a true friend . . .' Roberts had drawn a map of the local country to help Nicholson's venture.[60]

Wilson still delayed, but on 7 September a council of war brought matters to a head. It says much for Roberts that the formidable Nicholson confided in him. 'Delhi must be taken,' Nicholson said, 'and it is absolutely essential that this should be done at once; and if Wilson hesitates longer, I intend to propose at to-day's meeting that he should be superseded.' Roberts pointed out that as this would place Nicholson in command others would oppose. Nicholson answered:

I have not overlooked that fact. I shall make it perfectly clear that, under the circumstances, I could not possibly accept the command myself, and I shall propose that it be given to [Colonel George] Campbell of the 52nd; I am prepared to serve under him for the time being, so no one can ever accuse me of being influenced by personal motives.

At the council Wilson's doubts were overcome.[61] Batteries were constructed to blast breaches in the city walls. Roberts was assigned to number two battery, commanding the two right-hand guns, bringing fire onto the Kashmir bastion and the adjoining wall. The gunners stayed at their posts without cease, firing night and day, the Mutineers replying with guns brought into the open, with rockets and with 'a perfect storm of musketry'. On 13 September Wilson issued orders for attack at daybreak the next morning. The batteries had opened the necessary breaches. Nicholson, visiting Roberts's battery, said: 'I must shake hands with you fellows; you have done your best to make my work easy to-morrow.'[62] There were four columns, with a fifth held in reserve, the whole under Nicholson's command. He would lead the first column to attack the Kashmir and Water bastions. His Afghan orderly Muhammad Hayat Khan would carry a green standard to mark his position. Muhammad Hayat's father had saved Nicholson's life on the Frontier, and when he was killed in a border feud, the son had attached himself to the Ulsterman.[63] He was later to serve with Roberts.

'Once Delhi falls, the reaction will be felt all over the country,' Roberts confidently told his mother.[64] Just after midnight the men fell in, the chaplains said prayers and the regiments marched to their places. The sun was already high, however, when Nicholson gave the signal. Besieging batteries dramatically fell silent, and with a cheer the front ranks climbed over the parapets and ran forward. 'Since war was ever known, I fancy no assault took place as ours did,' Roberts wrote. 'Our men went off beautifully like a pack of hounds.'[65] The fate of the Mutiny hung on victory at Delhi. Engineers blew in the Kashmir Gate for one column while two others fought through the breaches and cleared ramparts. Meeting in open ground beyond, they separated to attack different sectors of the city. Nicholson's column advanced and captured the Kabul Gate and hoisted British colours, 'but near the Lahore Gate the road became so narrow only 2 men could go abreast [for 200 yards], and down this heavy guns were playing with grape, besides heavy musketry from the neighbouring houses. Down went the men. At the head poor Nicholson fell mortally wounded . . .' A determined counter-attack pushed back the fourth column from the suburbs outside the Kabul Gate. The enemy's heavy guns fired grapeshot at Brigadier Hope Grant's cavalry, waiting to exploit success. Nicholson had been shot through the chest by a sepoy on the roof of one of the houses along the narrow lane. A Bengal Fusiliers sergeant dragged him into a small recess under the wall. Here he refused to be moved, saying he would stay until Delhi had been taken. Eventually he was carried back to the Kabul Gate and placed in a *doolie*, a conveyance for the wounded. Two doolie-bearers were ordered to take him to the field hospital beyond Delhi Ridge, but they abandoned him by the side of the street.

Roberts, no longer required at his battery, had been with Wilson performing staff duties. Increasingly gloomy reports arrived – of the 4th column's failure, of Nicholson having fallen, of Hope Grant and Tombs both dead, this last report false. Wilson sent Roberts to investigate. Roberts did not tell the full story of his last meeting with Nicholson until he wrote *Forty-One Years*, but to his father shortly afterwards he wrote: 'Our best officer by ten thousand times, poor Nicholson, I had just seen put in a doolie [by the Kashmir Gate] with death on his face.' Dismounting to give help, he found that 'but for the pallor of his face, always colourless, there was no sign of the agony he must have been enduring. On my expressing a hope that he was not seriously wounded, he said: "I am dying: there is no chance for me." Roberts collected four bearers under a sergeant of the 61st Foot and told them to take Nicholson direct to the field hospital. He went on with his task for Wilson, ascertained that Hope Grant and Tombs were unhurt, and returned to report.[66] To his mother he wrote: 'General Nicholson is, I am afraid, mortally wounded. He led his Column like no other man could, and in him we lose our best Officer.'[67]

Liquor shops had been left open, men got drunk, others could not find their regiments, and all were exhausted by the hard work of the previous days. The advance halted. Roberts 'dropped off and never awoke till sunset'. Then he and Lieutenant Lang were able to advance with a small force of British and Sikhs to capture the Burn bastion and Lahore Gate. Shopkeepers showed them the way up Chandni Chouk, the main street of the old city, without seeing a soul.[68] Rebels and shopkeepers alike were hiding indoors.

The attackers subdued the city after six days of fierce house-to-house fighting and nearly a thousand dead. The battle was marked by random massacres of sepoys and civilians, held responsible for the murder of Europeans four months before. The British found 'ladies bonnets, flowers, all sort of things you find the blackguards had stolen'. Roberts told his mother, 'Yesterday on one battery I found a portmanteau with "Miss Jennings" on it. Her Father was the Clergyman here. She was an extremely pretty girl, and was murdered coming out of Church on the 11th May.'[69] Wilson had ordered his men to give 'no quarter' to the Mutineers, but also 'to spare all women and children that may come in their way'.[70] Roberts followed the latter part of these orders, telling his mother on 16 September: 'I was just in time this morning to save the lives of 2 poor Native women. They were both wounded and had concealed themselves in a little house. Another hour, and both I believe would have died from exhaustion; when I gave them some water they were so grateful, for they seemed to expect I should kill them.'[71] The British then advanced to the Mogul's Palace, blowing in the gate and killing the few sepoys within. On the night of the 21st the staff dined within the palace walls, 'at which we drank the health of our Gracious Queen, and also proposed that of General Wilson as the Conqueror of Delhi'.[72]

Roberts never saw Nicholson again. On 23 September he died, protected from visitors by Muhammad Hayat and knowing Delhi had fallen. At his funeral the savage Pathan horsemen who had followed him from the Frontier threw themselves to the ground and wept.[73] Sir John Lawrence wrote: 'We have lost many good and true soldiers, but none to compare with John Nicholson . . . May he rest in peace . . . He was a glorious soldier.'[74] Donald Stewart wrote that his loss was deplored by the whole army.[75] His memory remained an inspiration to his friends, Neville Chamberlain, Herbert Edwardes, Frederick Roberts and Muhammed Hayat.

'I have been most favourably mentioned in Despatches, and may get a *Brevet Majority*!!' wrote Roberts, full of optimism. He aspired to promotion and reassured his father that his health was good. 'Nothing seems to knock me up, and this is the chief thing. Do you think Major Fred. Roberts will do?'[76] He knew, however, that Henry Norman had done even better work. It is possible to exaggerate Roberts's role. Norman's *Narrative of the Campaign of the Delhi Army* praises the courage of Lieutenant 'Jemmy' Hills defending his guns and winning the Victoria Cross, but only mentions Roberts for the slight wound on 14 July.[77]

The capture of Delhi was a decisive blow. Roberts wrote in his memoirs of 'these gallant few [who] stormed in the face of day a strong fortress defended by 30,000 desperate men'. Three of the four regiments he praised most were not British: the Sirmur Gurkhas, the Guides and the 1st Punjab Infantry.[78] Roberts contrasted the heroism and loyalty of the Gurkhas, Sikhs and Punjabis with the Bengal sepoys' treachery, but his memoirs were selective, for there were also disloyal Sikhs. Those in the 10th Punjab Infantry plotted to kill their officers, seize the fort at Dera Ismail Khan, re-arm the 39th Bengal Native Infantry, which had been disbanded, and march on Delhi.[79]

Roberts's remaining Mutiny service was a denouement, but a stirring one. Wilson detached a Movable Column of 2,600 men under Lt-Col. Greathed of the 8th (King's) to clear the neighbouring Doab of the enemy and march on Cawnpore and Lucknow. Roberts described Greathed as 'a muff of a fellow . . . who knows nothing'. He was attached to the column in the QMG's Department.[80] His duties required him to go forward to mark out each encampment, to procure intelligence of enemy movements and act as a staff officer during the fighting. Yet at Bolundshur both he and Norman, also on the staff, managed to be near the forefront, joining the 9th Lancers in a charge as well as fulfilling his duties by bringing orders to place a battery.[81] He had another close escape. A sepoy took deliberate aim from a window a few feet away, but Roberts's mount – 'a favourite horse of poor General Nicholson's' which he had bought – reared at that moment and took the bullet intended for its rider. 'Lucky his head was in the way or I should have caught it,' he told his mother on his twenty-fifth birthday. Earlier a roundshot had passed beneath his legs.[82] At Allyghur on 5 October he was again to the front with Hugh Gough's squadron of Hodson's Horse, circling the town and coming at it from the far side. To relieve European families surrounded by insurgents at Agra, Greathed's column covered 46 miles in thirty hours. Roberts 'marked out the ground for encamping, then started off to enquire news about mutineers, all civil and military authorities in the fort assured me from latest intelligence the rebels had fled'. He had returned to camp, when they were surprised by roundshot whizzing through their tents and a cavalry attack on both flanks. Once again he was in the heat of fighting, his pistol missed fire and he had barely time to draw his sword and knock an enemy on the head. Enemy horsemen fled. He joined the Punjab cavalry and 9th

Lancers in hot pursuit for 10 miles, taking twelve guns, all the enemy baggage and camp equipage.[83] He was again mentioned in despatches, but the intelligence failure was partly his. The chief fault was the Agra authorities'. Norman defended Roberts: 'The most astonishing part of the whole affair was the utter want of information ... [the enemy] advanced to the attack past many villages without one word of correct information reaching the Agra authorities, who, indeed, that very morning, received intelligence directly opposed to the truth.'[84]

On 18 October Brigadier Hope Grant took command, Roberts joining his staff. He pushed on rapidly, firstly for Cawnpore and then to relieve Sir James Outram at Lucknow. They reached Cawnpore on the 26th where orders came from the newly arrived ccommander-in-chief Sir Colin Campbell, who would soon join them. Reinforcements were reaching India from the China expedition and from Britain.[85] At Cawnpore the column saw the scene of the infamous massacre and Roberts reflected again to his mother: 'Oh, mother, looking at these horrible sights makes one feel very very sad – no wonder we all feel glad to kill these sepoys.'[86] Campbell and his chief of staff Sir William Mansfield reached Cawnpore on 3 November, and decided on Lucknow as their objective.

Whereas Cawnpore became a symbol of tragedy, Lucknow was one of heroic resistance. Sir Henry Lawrence had been besieged in its Residency from 1 July and died of his wounds three days later. The Residency was stronger than Cawnpore, with 1,700 combatants and 1,300 civilians. Lawrence's wise measures enabled the garrison to resist until help came. In the first relief the column of Generals Havelock and Outram fought their way into the Residency. Casualties so weakened the column that they could not evacuate the civilians, and in turn were besieged by superior numbers.[87] As Campbell's force advanced, Roberts told his father that they would fight their way in and bring out the civilians: 'all the Intelligence Department is in my hands. In my wildest dreams I never thought of what was so soon to happen, and when next I write I hope to tell you that I am in the Department permanently'. He and Norman again shared a tent. 'Sir Colin has a great opinion of [Norman], and he certainly is one of the finest fellows in India.' Roberts was head of the QMG's department of Hope Grant's division, but Campbell was employing him, and he aspired to remain with headquarters.[88]

Campbell chose a flanking approach to the Residency. The march began on 12 November, and lay through walled gardens and parks surrounding large buildings packed with the enemy. The force quickly seized the Dilkusha Palace with its park, driving the enemy downhill to the Martiniere, which was taken with barely a fight. A number of Roberts's friends were killed in an enemy counter-attack; he reflected to his mother: 'It makes one very sad seeing all these fine fellows knocked over. I have lost so many friends during the last 6 months, and at times can't help feeling very very miserable.'[89]

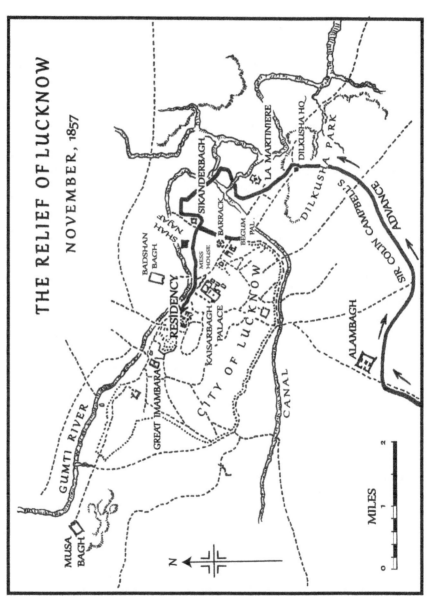

MAP 3 *The relief of Lucknow*

He had not long to repine, for after a halt until the 15th to prepare for the final advance, Campbell gave him a vital task.

The night before the attack, it was found out all the rifle ammunition had been left behind at Alambagh. I was ordered to take 300 camels and a guard of 150 cavalry and bring all that was available. I started at 8.00 p.m. a horrid dark night, across country, finding my course entirely by compass and stars when visible. By daylight in the morning I returned all safe . . .

Escorting him were the squadrons of two friends, Lieutenants Hugh Gough and George Younghusband. He had just time for a hasty breakfast before he was ordered to lead the column towards its objective, the Secunderbagh, a strongly walled enclosure 150 yards square, like a fortified castle.[90] Campbell was careful of his men's lives, using artillery to open a breach in the walls; but roundshot could not silence musketry 'from every inch of the building'. Highlanders and Sikhs were ordered to storm it. The slaughter was dreadful, nearly 2,000 sepoys on the ground dead and dying. 'I never saw such a sight,' Roberts wrote;

They were literally in heaps, and when I went in were a heaving mass, some dead, but most wounded and unable to get up from the crush. How so many got crowded together I can't understand. You had to *walk over them* to cross the court[yard]. They showed their hatred even while dying, cursed us and said: 'If we could only stand, we would kill you.'[91]

He told his mother they then advanced 'quietly' after this bloody and decisive blow, but in fact two more enemy strongholds had to be taken: the Shah Najeef, a domed mosque pounded by the Naval Brigade's guns and then taken by the Highlanders; and the Mess House or 'Happy Palace' stormed by a force led by Captain Garnet Wolseley.[92] The column then opened communications with the garrison, Outram and Havelock coming out to meet their rescuers, Roberts and Norman accompanying Campbell and entering the Residency. In the following days the wounded and the women and children were evacuated.[93] Campbell then withdrew to Cawnpore and on 30 November sent the rescued survivors on steamers to Calcutta.

In camp at Cawnpore Roberts pondered the campaign. He had been mentioned 'very handsomely' in official Delhi despatches.[94] 'I always longed for service and would not have missed being thro' these past six months for all I hope ever to possess. Few have been lucky eno' to get off so easily as I have.' He and Norman were 'both very anxious about *Medals*. One should be given for Delhi alone, and another for other parts of India'. He had received one slight wound, was sorry about the army's losses, but pleased he had given Sir Colin Campbell satisfaction as 'he is a rather particular old gentleman'. Backdated pay for promotion to lieutenant would enable him to clear his debts, 'so I hope darling Mother [he wrote] to save a little money during the next 2 or 3 years, and then go home to see all you dear ones'.[95] To his sister Harriet, on the last day of 1857, he wrote, '[Y]our brother Fred, Harriet darling, has no end of ambition, besides soldiers should make up their minds to work with their life's best blood at such a crisis to restore peace and order, and show these rascally Musalmans [*sic*] that, with God's help, Englishmen will still be masters of India.'[96] He was looking forward to meeting his half-brother Hamilton Maxwell, his mother's son by her first marriage, who had been commissioned and was already in India.[97] To Harriet he wrote 'how jolly and happy I have been the last day or two' meeting a family friend who gave him lunch and 'nice accounts of you all' at Waterford. Roberts now longed to leave India, thoughts of his family foremost in his mind, but in January he won the crowning glory, the Victoria Cross, for his future career.

Campbell's force waited for transport to return from conveying the women, children and sick, and then marched towards Fatehgarh. Roberts was ordered to accompany the 3rd brigade of Hope Grant's division to repair the suspension bridge over the Kali Nadi stream, partly destroyed a few days previously. By the morning of 2 January repairs were complete. The rebels appeared and opened fire; the British fired back, the troops crossed and by 3 p.m. were ready. Infantry and guns advanced on the village of Khudaganj just beyond the stream, and cavalry followed in two lines led by Hope Grant. Roberts was in the first line. He spotted two sepoys making off with a regimental standard, pursued and overtook them, and wrenching the colour from one, cut him down. The other put his musket close to Roberts's face and fired; it missed fire, the sepoy fled and Roberts carried away his trophy. He next came to the aid of a sowar engaging a sepoy with musket and bayonet. He rode straight at the sepoy, and with one sword stroke slashed him across the face, killing him instantly. Roberts understated the event: 'I accompanied the first line and in the scrimmage captured a very pretty standard! which I will send home to adorn Suir View [Waterford family home] the first opportunity I get, a great piece of luck my getting it was it not?'[98] The pursuit captured fourteen enemy guns and 'quite took away the rebels' pluck'. During the night they deserted Fatehgarh leaving the Ganges bridges and the gun-carriage factory intact.[99]

The historian Peter Stanley belittles Roberts's VC as being won in 'a militarily pointless act',[100] but in the 1850s standards were highly regarded. His action, however, scarcely compares with his friend Jemmy Hills's: protecting his battery until it could deploy and continuing to fight with bare hands although wounded, he was indeed 'worthy of the highest honour for distinguished bravery and gallantry'.[101] Roberts had showed courage and quick thinking, but was lucky to have been constantly under the eyes of senior commanders. The citation begins, 'repeated gallantry in the field'. His exultant letter when he was recommended contrasts with his self-deprecatory account of the deed:

> My own Mother, I have such a piece of news for you. I have been recommended for the '*Victoria Cross*' ... Is this not glorious? How

pleased it will make the General [father]. *Such a Medal* to wear with '*For Valour*' scrolled on it. How proud I shall be, darling Mother, when I show it to you – better than all the other Medals put together.[102]

Campbell now wished to turn his forces towards Rohilkand, but Governor-General Canning thought otherwise. 'Every eye is upon Oudh,' he wrote, 'as it was upon Delhi.'[103] Campbell assembled some 25,000 men to lead against an enemy reckoned at 100,000. Roberts was kept busy marking out respective brigades' camps, these vastly increased by the siege train, countless ammunition carts, each drawn by five bullocks, supply carts carrying food and fodder for these bullocks and the innumerable camp followers. He cannot have failed to notice the delays and slowness caused by this great train. To deal with small towns and their garrisons between him and his objective, Lucknow, Campbell sent out 'flying columns'. On 23 February, Roberts accompanied one of these under Hope Grant against Mianganj, a small fortified town on the old Cawnpore-Lucknow road, where 2,000 enemy were ensconced. The town was stormed. The next day Roberts supervised razing of the town's walls and nearby houses. He described what happened next to his sister Harriet. When he went into Mianganj, nearly all the houses had been burnt, except in one corner. As he approached, a very old man met him and said,

> ... for God's sake don't burn the only property I have in the world. Yesterday morning I have five sons. See, here are three of them [dead], the other two fled away, and I don't know whether they have shared the same fate and are dead, or whether they may have escaped. None of us ever bore arms against your Government. We are all labourers. Ever since the rebellion took place, I have prayed for your success, and if all my sons are killed, I shall still pray for you, for I know under any other rule we have nothing but oppression and tyranny to expect.

Roberts had not the heart to burn the man's house. Going a little farther, he came on three women watching the dead bodies of their husbands, none of them Sepoys. The sight made him wish most sincerely that 'this horrid war was at an end ... it does make one melancholy to come across accidents such as I have related'.[104] Captain Oliver Jones, RN, recounted this story and praised Roberts's 'cheering and unaffected kindness and hospitality' in camp.[105]

On 2 March Campbell's British Army was outside Lucknow, Roberts accompanying the commander-in-chief on his reconnaissance. Campbell's careful tactics saved lives but allowed thousands of sepoys to escape, prolonging the campaign.[106] At midnight on 22 March, Roberts set off with Hope Grant and a mixed brigade to Kursi, a small town twenty-five miles distant, in his last Mutiny action. 'Our success was great,' he wrote. 'The villagers in the neighbourhood gave such good information that I was able to lead the Column on the flank of the rascals as they were making off.

Consequently, we captured all their guns and killed several, with the loss of two very dear friends of mine . . .'[107]

Roberts's health now gave way, and he was ordered by doctors to return to England. On 1 April, the sixth anniversary of his arrival in India, he handed over his post of DAQMG to Garnet Wolseley (although they did not meet). On 3 May he embarked on a P&O steamer at Calcutta. Sir Hugh Rose, Campbell's successor, still had to subjugate the rest of Oudh, Rohilkand and much of Central India.

General Sir Edward Hamley, strategist and historian, later wrote: 'For a soldier of Roberts's quality nothing could have been more fortunate than the succession of events . . .' It was a most valuable training for future command.[108] In less than a year, he had seen harrowing sights enough for a lifetime and been within inches of death. Today he would be a candidate for a prolonged course of post-traumatic stress therapy. Yet he went on, apparently unscathed, to a career of continued danger, lacking neither moral nor physical courage. His Christian faith and belief in the British mission sustained him. He sought to avenge the massacres of English women and children. He was now committed to a lifelong military career. Tired as he was of fighting, he told his father, he would not choose any other profession. Colin Campbell had said to Roberts that it was wrong for staff officers to rush on ahead. Seeing the young officer's rueful smile he added, '[Even] were it one of my best Staff Officers in India (and as such I consider you, my dear Roberts).' 'So father,' he wrote, 'it has been worth all your money and trouble spent on your son . . . When you were in India, I was young and giddy. I am different now, and if I live, hope to be a General, K.C.B. and all sorts of things.'[109]

CHAPTER FOUR

Marriage and staff service

[The Englishwoman in India] is called upon, year after year, to face that pitiless destroyer of youth and beauty – the Punjab hot weather. She learns to know all the horror hidden in that dread word – cholera . . .

MAUD DIVER, *THE ENGLISHWOMAN IN INDIA*

Bobs was told yesterday that the Chief had selected him for the Lushai Expedition . . . He is of course delighted, as it will ensure him the C.B. and the Deputyship [QMG] whenever it becomes vacant . . .

COLONEL DONALD STEWART TO HIS WIFE

Roberts . . . had a quite extraordinary knack of finding himself in the thick of the action . . .

CHARLES ALLEN, *GOD'S TERRORISTS*

The most important event of Roberts's leave was his marriage. Yet we know almost nothing of his wooing. It appears from a letter to his crippled sister Harriet, to whom he was devoted, that he intended to marry. He had written: 'You must look out for some nice girl with "blue eyes and yellow hair" . . . for me, Harriet dearest, who will console me for having to return [after my leave] to the gorgeous East.'[1] Conscious he might be promoted, he purchased clothes in London and told Harriet: 'Major Fred Roberts must cut a dash, you know.' His confidence marked the change from the homesick young man who had reached India six years before. He crossed to Waterford in Ireland where his family were living, his father 'well and strong for a man of seventy-four' and his mother 'almost as young and quite as beautiful' as when he had left her.[2]

He hunted that winter with the Curraghmore Hounds. When spring came, a young man's fancy turned to love. Lady Roberts's obituary many years later simply tells us that Waterford was a regimental headquarters and the playing of the band made the drill ground a fashionable promenade for chaperoned young men and women.[3] Nora Henrietta Bews was the tenth and youngest child of John Bews, retired 73rd Regiment officer[4] and Constabulary paymaster, by then deceased, living with a married sister at 'Landscape' on Passage Road not far from 'Suir View', Roberts's parents' home.[5] Accounts of the Mutiny battles reaching Britain in 1857–8 made the army heroic. An aura surrounded a man with the Victoria Cross. Yet as a soldier's daughter Nora needed less convincing than those respectable middle classes who looked down on the army. Did the elder Robertses guide the engagement to a daughter of a family of similar background? Did the young officer confide in Nora Bews his hopes and ambitions? Did she see great expectations in this diminutive but virile Mutiny hero? We do not know, but he made a good choice. They were married at St Patrick's church, a fine eighteenth-century building next to the barracks, on 17 May 1859. 'The beautiful bride' as a local newspaper described her in an account entitled 'Marriage in High Life', wore a white satin dress and a rich Limerick lace veil. Her four bridesmaids and the groom's best men came from the immediate family, and a brother-in-law gave the bride away. The importance of Abraham Roberts's family in Waterford society was emphasised by the presence of the Chancellor of the Cathedral, Reverend R. H. Ryland, a local figure of note, to perform the ceremony; 'several of the rank and fashion of our city and neighbourhood' in the congregation; and 'a large proportion of the lower classes' thronging the church in and out to gawp at their betters, offer loud applause when the bride and groom emerged and receive largesse 'in the shape of good silver'.[6]

He was twenty-seven and she twenty. The marriage lasted fifty-five years. She supported him through thick and thin. Despite mutterings of 'petticoat government' when she appeared to interfere in patronage in India, her personality complemented his and provided warm support for the young officers whom he gathered about him. Although later the pain of childbearing, the loss of three of six children and the hot sun of India took the flush of youth from Nora's cheeks, early photographs[7] show a comely enough young woman. In the winter of 1862–3, Lieutenant Owen Burne, on the viceroy's staff, recorded, 'Fred Roberts [who] joined us as a Deputy Quartermaster-General ... had come to Simla to join the Headquarters Staff with a charming bride, who proved a great accession to our select circle, as being not only handsome, but full of goodness and brightness.'[8]

On 8 June their Scottish honeymoon was interrupted by a summons to Buckingham Palace, where the Queen presented the Victoria Cross to fifteen recipients.[9] Roberts applied for a three months' extension of leave so 'that my wife should be spared the great heat of a journey to India in July, the hottest month of the year in the Red Sea'.[10] Came back the answer, that taking the extension would cost him his position in the QMG's Department.

They decided to return to India and embarked on 27 June, a good comment on how their marriage worked. It was, said the captain of their ship, 'the hottest trip he had ever made', and twice he turned the vessel about to steam into the wind to revive some of the passengers 'who were almost suffocated'. They passed the wreck of another P&O steamer which had struck a coral reef in dead of night; the passengers had been rescued from a different reef after eighty hours, but officers and crew were still on the spot rescuing baggage and mail. After passing Aden they encountered the monsoon, then at its height, and in the Bay of Bengal 'something very nearly akin to a cyclone'. The ship broke its rudder, the coal was almost gone, so in the River Hughli approaching Calcutta the engines stopped operating and they were at the mercy of the tide until a pilot brig appeared. They then steamed upriver to Calcutta, docking on 30 July. Such was Nora Roberts's introduction to life with an imperial hero.[11]

Further trials awaited the young couple. Roberts had an attack of 'Peshawar fever', but was ordered to join Brigadier-General Sir Robert Napier at Morar, 'one of the hottest places in India in August'. There followed a 100-mile journey in a *dak-gharri*, a wagon which Kipling described as having 'the violent winnowing motion of the sifter of a threshing machine – imagine being shaken for eight hours with two minutes breaks at half-hour intervals'.[12] Then, unexpectedly, he was ordered back to Calcutta, and left his wife with relations of his at a little cantonment. At Calcutta he received fresh orders, to organise and take charge of the large camp for the progress which Lord Canning was to make through Oudh, the north-west provinces and the Punjab to meet and reward loyal chiefs. He had to collect tents from the arsenal at Allahabad, and make all ready at Cawnpore for Canning's arrival on 15 October.[13]

Canning's journey was intended to declare changes made in British rule. On 1 November, 1858, while Roberts was on leave, East India Company rule had been abolished. Henceforward India would be governed in the name of the Crown. The Government of India Act of 1858 appointed a secretary of state for India, who was henceforth to direct policy and was only a telegraph line away from Calcutta and Simla. A Council of India of fifteen 'old India hands' gave advice. The governor-general gained the title viceroy. In 1861 his Executive Council was expanded; members took on a portfolio of responsibility. The commander-in-chief was an extraordinary member, but often did not attend. The military member, appointed since 1834 to give the army's point of view, took charge of the Military Department. As he was the governor-general's prime military advisor, there was future scope for conflict between two senior soldiers. The Legislative Council established by Dalhousie in 1853 was expanded and now counted Indian members. There was a badly needed reform of finances. A deficit partly built up by the costs of the Mutiny disappeared by 1864.

The reforms of Bentinck (governor-general 1828–35) and Dalhousie (1848–56) were replaced by a spirit of authoritarian paternalism, a limited programme of peace, order, prevention of crime, public works, collection of revenue, interfering comparatively little with the people's lives.[14] The British sought to capitalise on the loyalty of the majority of princes in 1857 as a bulwark of their rule, and Canning's tour heralded a series of measures to achieve this. Canning was an enlightened viceroy who even at the height of the uprising inaugurated India's first three universities, at Calcutta, Bombay and Madras. Roberts's autobiography sketched picturesque scenes of Canning receiving the Indian princes. Wealthy estates confiscated from rebels were distributed to loyal allies.[15] Territories were guaranteed. Princes were encouraged to adopt Western measures, building roads and railways, promoting education and industry. The spread of railways and telegraph lines served a military purpose but also aided the economy and bound the country together.[16]

For a soldier the momentous change was the army reorganisation. Hugh Rose, commander-in-chief from June 1861, oversaw sweeping military reform. If the East India Company was abolished, it followed the Crown must take over its armies. Company officers were much worried about the future, but when their European soldiers were told it was intended they should be transferred to the Queen's regiments, there was 'a White Mutiny'. The 5th European Regiment at Dinapore in November 1859, fiercest in resisting, had to be surrounded and disarmed by loyal troops, one soldier executed, the unit disbanded. Widespread discontent compelled the government to permit men to take their discharge and return to Britain. Of 15,000 Europeans in Company regiments, 10,116 did so. Peter Stanley terms this 'the largest and most successful challenge to authority the British Army has ever experienced'.[17] Those who remained with the colours formed new regiments in the Queen's Army; Abraham Roberts became colonel of the 101st Regiment of Foot (The Royal Bengal Fusiliers).

East India Company officers were absorbed into the Staff Corps. This system was devised by Henry Norman, who as assistant military secretary to the Duke of Cambridge, commander-in-chief of the British Army from 1856, played a key role in the changes. Officers in the new Indian Army – composed of native soldiers – all appeared on the staff list; they would be promoted regimentally for the purpose of seniority in their units, but would be available for service with civil and military departments. A Royal Warrant dated 18 January 1861 established separate lists for the Bengal, Madras and Bombay Armies, and from the list officers could be drawn for regimental, staff and civil duties.[18] In 1860 Fred Roberts's Bengal artillery was absorbed with the Madras and Bombay artillery regiments into the British Army and he was now an officer in the Royal Artillery. He had refused command of a Royal Horse Artillery battery at Aldershot to stay on in the QMG's Department.[19] His career had advanced thanks to his father's connections. Now Sir Hugh Rose, who carried through the reforms with skill and tact against weighty opposition, announced that appointments would be no longer due to 'petticoat influence, intrigue and favouritism', and that 'patronage should go by ... merit only'.[20] Former East India Company officers, Norman, Stewart, Roberts, Edwin Johnson, Robert Napier, prospered in their new situation. But had Rose ended 'petticoat influence, intrigue and favouritism' which he denounced? In time Roberts was to be accused of all three.

Great changes affected the sepoys. The Bengal Army was completely remade, and increasingly recruited from the Punjab and North-West Frontier tribesmen. Sepoy numbers were reduced to 190,000, of whom 100,000 were in Bengal and 45,000 each in Madras and Bombay. The ratio of native to European troops was 2:1. Except for pack guns, the artillery was manned by Europeans. Native troops were brigaded with Europeans, and garrisons dispersed. The Indian Army remained divided among the three presidencies. There had long been an Indian tradition of military service as a source of honour and prestige, and the British increasingly cultivated it and regimental spirit, awarding signs of distinction such as *batta*, extra allowances for arduous service. The Order of British India rewarded long and faithful service; native soldiers received the Indian Order of Merit for conspicuous gallantry.[21]

A period of comparative peace in India followed. Except for North-West Frontier action, wars were outside the great sub-continent. Roberts had none of the opportunities enjoyed earlier by Clive, Coote, Cornwallis or Arthur Wellesley. After his death, 'Indian' soldiers like Auchinleck and Slim fought great battles. Yet he managed to serve in two frontier campaigns, Ambeyla and Lushai, and three external wars, Abyssinia, Afghanistan and Burma. The Mutiny whetted his appetite for action and fed his ambition. It profoundly affected his future. Lasting friendships with Donald Stewart, Henry Norman, Edwin Johnson, Hugh Gough and Dighton Probyn were an asset to advancement. Of Probyn Roberts told his mother, 'A very nice fellow ... we have been together the whole time.'[22] Probyn, another Mutiny VC winner, became a courtier, first an equerry, then keeper of the privy purse and privy councillor and finally comptroller of Queen Alexandra's household.

The Mutiny had failed to end British rule; but the British remembered 1857. Forty years later Roberts devoted two chapters of his autobiography to causes and prevention. Canning had stood against his countrymen's excesses, aware how much the British depended upon Indian acquiescence. The Queen shared this view, insisted that her proclamation of 1858 'should breathe feelings of generosity, benevolence and religious toleration', and promised to respect 'the rights, dignity and honour' of native princes. Pardon was offered to all who laid down arms, except murderers, although the Queen's wish that no one should be barred from office because of race or creed was not followed.[23]

Among those pardoned was Fred's Muslim half-brother, John Roberts ('Chote Sahib'). He had been a contractor manufacturing gun carriages for the Army of Oudh, in which he held the rank of colonel. He 'lived entirely in the style of Indians and was a devout Muslim who was very particular about his religious observances such as [prayers] and[fasts]'; he had married a Lucknow lady who was an Urdu poet. When Oudh was annexed and its army disbanded, to be replaced by the Oudh Irregular Force led by East India Company officers, he lost rank and contract. He wrote to his father Abraham Roberts for financial support. Abraham, with families to maintain from two English marriages, was financially pressed, but left John an annuity of sixty-two rupees a month which he drew until his death in 1892 from sunstroke. Despite some acerbic correspondence, Abraham forgave him any participation in the events of 1857. Benefiting from the pardon showed that he did not commit atrocities against Europeans.[24]

It was customary for a governor-general to tour the provinces during the cool weather. The Mutiny's aftermath meant Canning's journey was doubly important, and he made it an extensive one, beginning at Cawnpore and Lucknow, proceeding to Delhi and then into the Punjab and thence to Kashmir. Just before leaving, Roberts was offered a better paid appointment in the Revenue Survey Department, a temptation to a newly-married officer. He refused, having calculated that his best chances lay with the QMG. Colin Campbell (ennobled as Lord Clyde) had given him the first permanent vacancy, better than previous temporary appointments.[25] Canning had actually asked for a Major Garden to look after his camp. The QMG Colonel Becher, an old friend of Abraham Roberts, persuaded Campbell to state to Canning that, as Garden was his second, it would be more convenient if he took young Roberts, adding: 'Lieutenant Roberts is a particularly gentlemanlike, intelligent and agreeable young man.'[26] Family connections gave an opportunity, but Roberts had to make good. As Low, his first biographer wrote, anyone 'conversant with the details of a Viceregal progress in India, with its large body of troops, the thousands of camp followers and servants, the daily march, and the durbars, with the elaborate etiquette and attendant formalities' would know what a task he faced. The tents stored at Allahabad were on inspection found to be in a state of mildew and decay, and it was necessary to renew them almost entirely. Some 150 large tents were required for the viceroy, staff, guests and secretariat alone, and these were in duplicate. A camp of almost similar size accommodated the commander-in-chief and army headquarters with post office, telegraph and commissariat. A treasury carried jewels and other valuables to be presented to chiefs at Durbars. Elephants, camels, bullocks and bullock carts provided transport. Some 20,000 men, women and children made up the caravan, whose advance guard had usually reached the next night's camp before everyone had left the previous one twelve miles behind.[27] Roberts's young bride accompanied him, kindly welcomed by Lady Canning, and again his connections favoured him. The first halt was Lucknow, where Hope Grant commanded, residing in the Dilkusha Palace, a recent scene of fighting. He invited Roberts to bring his wife to stay with him. During the week there, he took Nora over the ground by which Campbell's column had advanced two years before. At Lucknow Canning sought to conciliate by restoring the

Taluqdars' (landowners) property rights, which he had confiscated in a proclamation of March 1858; at Cawnpore he announced that the principal of adoption according to the Indian custom was accepted again.[28] The Maharajah of Nepal and Sikh chiefs of the Punjab were given money or land in recognition of their military support in 1857.[29] The tour continued via Fategarh to Agra; here, not only were there wonderful buildings, but the princes received in Durbar made a splendid show, one on an eleven-foot-high elephant caparisoned with cloth-of-gold coverings, fascinating sights for the young couple.

The viceroy covered over 1,000 miles in six months. At the end Roberts escorted to the summer capital of Simla his wife and a baby daughter. The latter was born on 10 March at Mian Mir, the cantonment at Lahore where Nora was staying with friends.[30] On 12 November, he was gazetted captain, and thus having attained the qualifying rank was promoted to brevet-majority for Mutiny services, being a captain only one day. This promotion was not exceptional. 'But he had gained a name; it was because he had acquitted himself so well in the service of his department, that he had now been placed on the permanent establishment of the staff' and in 1863 and 1868 was to be selected for important duties.[31] One incident illustrated his wife's attitude. Hope Grant was dispatched with an expedition to China, but Clyde had not included Roberts. At dinner Clyde remarked to Nora that he had earned her gratitude by this. She replied: 'I am afraid I cannot be very grateful to you for making my husband feel I am ruining his career by standing in the way of his being sent on service. You have done your best to make him regret his marriage.' Clyde was astonished and burst out: 'Well, I'll be hanged if I can understand you women! I have done the very thing I thought you would like, and have only succeeded in making you angry. I will never try to help a woman again.'[32]

Owen Burne, Rose's military and then private secretary, described Roberts at this time as 'a slim, active fellow, full of life, quick of thought, and an exceptional organiser, to whom nothing came amiss'.[33] He was ordered to take charge of the viceroy's camp for a second tour, through Central India. The task was less, with no accompanying commander-in-chief's camp. The tour lasted into 1861, but near the end of February Roberts returned to headquarters at Simla on the instructions of Sir Hugh Rose. Hardly had he done so than his tiny daughter fell ill and died just before the age of one.[34] At the end of the year his wife was also unwell. Roberts's Delhi comrade Henry Norman wrote in the New Year wishing that 'she will recover her strength', his brother offering his house as a place to recuperate.[35] In the winters of 1861–2 and 1862–3, Roberts accompanied Rose in his tours through Central India. Rose was a stickler for high standards, but the Robertses got on well with him.

> He was very hospitable [at Simla], and having [a sister] to chaperone, my wife went out rather more than she had cared to do in previous years.

We spent a good deal of our time also at Mashobra, a lovely place in the heart of the Hills, about six miles from Simla, where the Chief had a house, which he was good enough to frequently place at our disposal . . .[36]

In the autumn of 1863 Roberts's old commander from the Punjab, Neville Chamberlain, led a force of 5,400 men, infantry, pioneers and gunners, against Muslim extremists at Sitana in the mountainous territory north-east of Peshawar on the border between Afghanistan and the Punjab, 'a most difficult and hostile country', the greater part unknown including 'the valley of Swat, peopled by the most bigoted and fanatical Mahomedans, into which we have never penetrated'.[37] In 1858 an expedition under Major-General Cotton had expelled 'Hindoostani fanatics' from their base in mountains on the fringes of the Punjab. Most were killed fighting, but a number escaped to Sitana and occupied an abandoned village, Malka. In late summer of 1863 these fanatics called on the chiefs of neighbouring tribes to 'quit the friendship of the unbelieving and join the would-be martyrs of the Faith'. Such a rising would be a serious threat to frontier stability. They had been raiding and kidnapping local people.

At the time these 'Hindoostani fanatics' were identified with the Wahhabis, a fanatical Islamic sect founded in the eighteenth century by Abdul Wahhabi. This appears to be incorrect. Sayid Ahmed of Raj Bareilly, the founder of the fanatics, was a purist in following the teachings of the Prophet, but not a follower of Wahhabi.[38] The governor-general, Canning's successor Elgin, hoped to isolate them from the local people. His secretary Colonel Henry Durand wrote: 'the overt acts of hostility which have taken place . . . impose the necessity of repressing and punishing such wanton aggressions' before trouble extended to the whole of the Hazara border tribes.[39] Chamberlain decided to take one column from Peshawar over the Umbeyla (later Ambela) Pass into the Chamla Valley, while another column cooperated from Hazara. His force was slowed by a lumbering column of bullock carts and hordes of native followers.[40] They reached the top of the pass on 20 October, too late to prevent the feared spread of trouble. All tribes in the remote Swat Valley rose, their ruler the Akhond convinced he must intervene. Among them were the Bunerwals on whose pacific intentions Chamberlain had counted. Fighting tribesmen confronting the British were estimated at 55,000. There were hand-to-hand combats at the 'Crag' and 'Eagle's Nest', truly rugged terrain, the positions captured and re-captured. In fierce fighting on 20 November, Chamberlain leading Highlanders with fixed bayonets up the 'Crag' received a wound in the arm, which obliged him to hand over command. His second-in-command was also seriously wounded. Viceroy Lord Elgin died on the same day, and his council decided to withdraw the expedition. The lieutenant-governor of the Punjab telegraphed Chamberlain authorising retirement. Sir Hugh Rose was opposed: the loss of prestige withdrawing a force of over 5,000 men would outweigh any setback in fighting save the destruction of the whole force. He wished to send 'two experienced officers of the Staff of the Army, who have seen a great deal of active service' to go up to the Umbeyla Pass and report on the situation. He chose Colonel John Adye and Major Fred Roberts. Adye was moreover a good draughtsman if topographic sketches were needed. The adjutant general recommended Roberts: his 'great merits are known'.[41] Adye as senior would carry more weight, but Roberts's friendship with Chamberlain was an asset. Their report was against withdrawal: reinforcements were arriving, and the enemy were disheartened by losses in battle.[42] The decision to continue was made by Sir William Denison, Governor of Madras, taking charge of the Indian government in place of Elgin. Rose hoped to lead the operations himself, and Roberts was detached for his now well-rehearsed task of finding a suitable campsite. General Garvock arrived with a further brigade, increasing the force to 9,000. The local commissioner negotiated with the Bunerwals to persuade them to stand apart from the fighting, and operations were resumed. On 15 December Garvock deployed his men in two brigades. The enemy with standards flying took up a position on the conical peak of one of the mountainous spurs, dominating the ridge and the village at its feet, the position strengthened with stone *sangars*. One brigade assaulted the peak directly, the other was sent to turn the right flank and storm the village of Laloo. Both succeeded in the face of the enemy's rapid musketry fire and rocks thrown down on attackers' heads. A third enemy force attacking from the Umbeyla Pass was also beaten. The following day the British advance into the Chamla Valley thrust the enemy back.

Roberts's job was to guide the batteries of mountain guns over the difficult route.[43] In the afternoon several hundred fanatical swordsmen whom Roberts termed 'ghazis' made a furious attack on the British left flank. The 23rd Punjab Native Infantry Pioneers were thrown back onto the 7th Royal Fusiliers. Although he had been sent as a staff officer rather than a fighting soldier, Roberts with a fellow officer was at the forefront, rallying the Pioneers when five of their officers fell dead or wounded. The 200 ghazis died to a man. From the heights above, the hillmen witnessed this slaughter, and dispersed under fire from British guns. The Akhond of Swat returned to his hidden valley. In the fighting the Pathans serving in the Guides, the Punjabis and Gurkhas were at home in the mountains, whereas the Sikhs and British, formidable foes on the plain, 'were helpless on the hill-side and could not keep their heads under cover'. Roberts recorded how the enemy called down from the slopes, 'Where are the *lal pagriwalas* [14th Sikhs from their red turbans] or the *goralog* [British]? They are better *shikar* [sport].'[44] Garvock boldly despatched a number of British officers to supervise tribesmen burning Malka village. This would chastise the enemy and test the Bunerwals' good faith. Colonel Reynell Taylor, commissioner of Peshawar, was in charge, with Adye, Roberts and Captain Jenkins of the Guides, an escort from that elite regiment and other officers. As a great column of smoke rose from the fires of Malka, the position of the handful of British officers with their Guides escort was unenviable, thousands of angry hillmen looking on. Reynell Taylor's calm *sangfroid* in the face of possible death was another lesson for Roberts, but it was the Bunerwals who protected them from a bad end. Less than 100, not the 2,000 requested, accompanied them, and other tribesmen threateningly gathered round them. Two Bunerwal chiefs 'behaved remarkably well and told the tribesmen they must kill them [the chiefs] before they killed the English, and if they did the whole of the Bunerwal tribe would come on them and avenge them. Another friendly chief advised them to leave Malka as soon as it was set alight as he did not like the appearance of matters, and they did.' The village was completely burnt except its mosque.[45] These flames on 22 December marked the campaign's end, and British accounts claim success. 'The spectacle,' wrote Reynell Taylor, 'of a tribe like the Buners doing our bidding and destroying the stronghold of their own allies in the war at a distant spot, with British witnesses looking on, must have been a thoroughly convincing proof to the surrounding country of the reality of our success.'[46] Nonetheless, it was the largest and fiercest fought frontier campaign to date; the losses, 238 killed and 670 wounded, were the highest inflicted on British and Indian troops in such an episode. These losses point to more than the hazards of mountain fighting. 'It would also appear that tribes fought under one of the most powerful of influences, the spirit of religious fanaticism, fanned and excited to the utmost by the Akhond of Swat.'[47] Roberts and Adye were both mentioned in despatches.[48]

British methods usually employed conciliation backed by the threat of arms. Against the 'Hindoostanee fanatics' only force was effective, but the failure to isolate them from the other tribes had nearly led to disaster.[49] Lessons were learnt. New frontier tactics emerged employing looser formations and giving more responsibility to junior commanders. 'The expedition was an admirable school for training men in outpost duty.'[50] It further stoked a young major's ambition: Roberts wrote to Rose in March, drawing attention to his services, reminding the commander-in-chief that he had been pleased with him and 'desirous of assisting in my promotion'.[51]

Roberts returned to staff duties at Peshawar and then Simla. There his wife was grateful when her sister died for the kindness shown by Mrs Donald Stewart.[52] Roberts was extremely busy and could not be with her during the day. Among his duties was the compilation of a new route-book for the Bengal presidency, published in 1865. Norman, now the viceroy's military secretary, expressing formal thanks, remarked on Roberts's 'care and ability'. Roberts himself was ill with a liver complaint throughout the whole of 1864, and was sent back to England round the Cape, the fresh breezes of a sea voyage being considered a universal panacea. The voyage was no holiday: one of the crew was attacked by smallpox and troops on board suffered from scurvy. They reached England in May 1865.[53]

Roberts did not return to India until March 1866, leaving his wife to follow. Sir William Mansfield had succeeded Rose as commander-in-chief.

Roberts served on the QMG's Department of the Allahabad division for nearly a year. His wife joined him in October 1866, and Nora's Indian education continued. Cholera was rife, and the troops were isolated in camps at varying distances from the station, to be visited by staff officers like Roberts constantly 'to get up entertainments, penny readings and the like', to distract the men and 'keep their minds occupied'. His wife accompanied him, preferring that ordeal to being at home alone. Men seen alive and well one day were dead and buried the next. In his autobiography Roberts repeated the belief that 'if once soldiers begin to think of the terrors of cholera, they are seized with panic, and many get the disease from pure fright'. On one occasion he had just rejoined his wife in their carriage after inspecting a hospital when a young officer ran up to say a corporal in whom he was much interested had died. The officer's face was blue: 'the cholera panic had evidently seized him, and I said to my wife, "He will be the next." I had no sooner reached home than I received a report of his having been seized'. Both Robertses were impressed by the work of the Allahabad chaplain, the future Bishop of Lahore.[54]

Roberts's next campaign was in Africa. Late nineteenth-century European expansion was possible partly through medical advances leading to a spectacular fall in the death rate from disease. Two British expeditions showed what a modern European army could do, even in a tropical climate: Wolseley's Ashanti Campaign in West Africa and Napier's March to Magdala, one of the best organised limited-objective operations.[55] In August 1867 Lt-General Sir Robert Napier, commander of the Bombay Army, was ordered to form a relief expedition to rescue hostages held at the Abyssinian capital, Magdala, by King Tewodros ('mad Theodore'). He was to land on the Abyssinian coast at Annesley Bay, march over 400 miles inland to Magdala and release the prisoners. The expedition had to traverse trackless and mountainous terrain before the rainy season began. Napier, a sapper and veteran of thirty-nine years' service, formed his army largely from Bombay troops with a small contingent from Britain and another from Bengal. The Bengal troops were commanded by Roberts's friend Donald Stewart with Roberts as AQMG. The new commander-in-chief Mansfield respected Roberts's keenness to take part in the expedition, and recommended him formally: 'This officer is eminently qualified for the appointment by his activity and well-known military qualities, as well as by his experience in the Quarter Master General's Department in peace and war for nearly ten years.'[56]

Roberts arranged with Stewart a special system of loading, whereby each detachment embarked complete in itself with mules and camp equipage in the same vessels. This speeded up assembly after disembarkation.[57] Judging by his autobiography, his most exciting experience happened before he sailed. He, Stewart and their wives were sharing a house at Calcutta as transports were being loaded on the Hughli. On the evening of 1 November 1867, a cyclone descended. The two couples wisely cancelled a plan to

LORD NAPIER OF MAGDALA

FIGURE 2 *General Sir Robert Napier (Napier of Magdala) was among Roberts's most important patrons, promoting him to QMG India and inspiring many of his important measures: tireless inspections, improved conditions of service, good relations with the men in the ranks and temperance to control crime (National Army Museum).*

attend the opera, as the roof of the opera house was torn off by the storm. By midnight the wind increased, the windows burst open, rain poured in and efforts by the two husbands to close the shutters failed. They dragged chests and boxes to secure the windows, but these were blown into the middle of the dining room 'like so much cardboard'. The beleaguered couples took refuge in a small room in the middle of the house and awaited the morning. The wind abated, and they emerged to a scene of desolation. Trees were torn up, the native bazaar levelled and many houses demolished. Of the transports, however, only two were damaged. Destruction had been much greater on land than on the river.[58]

An advance party had already selected Zula Bay for disembarkation, and Napier landed on 2 January 1868. The Bengal contingent followed, Roberts arriving on 9 February in the *Golconda*. He put ashore a battery of guns and mortars, of which part went no further than Senafe, the first major point inland; but his old friend James Hills took a detachment of two eight-inch mortars to Magdala. The man with whom Roberts worked most closely was Captain George Tryon, RN, whom he claims as an 'old friend and Eton schoolfellow' in his memoirs. He and Roberts worked extremely hard in a sweltering and unhealthy climate. The endless lists in Roberts's notebooks show the work of organisation, as well as details such as an elephant requiring sixty gallons of water per day, a horse or mule only six.[59] Tryon's talent for organisation, his foresight and clear-headedness, his care and his intimate knowledge of details impressed other officers, naval and military.[60] He proved a hospitable friend, to whom Roberts 'owed many a good dinner, and, what I appreciated even more, many a refreshing bath on board the *Euphrates*, a transport ... which had been fitted up for Captain Tryon and his staff'.[61] Napier with great thoroughness organised logistical support, two huge piers were laid, a railway twelve miles long constructed to the first camp, reservoirs built for water supplies and masses of materials brought from England. From India came 4,000 mules and 5,600 bullocks, these supplemented with animals purchased in Persia, Egypt and elsewhere. Over 36,000 animals were disembarked. All this is testimony to Napier's foresight, but depended upon the work of Roberts and Tryon, for everything except meat or wood for a force of over 13,000 with its bearers had to come up from Zula. For four months they laboured in intense heat with a limited water ration, but an unlimited number of scorpions. Few escaped scurvy and horrible heat boils. Napier began his advance on 25 January 1868, and by 10 April the force had reached the Magdala plateau. As Napier's force approached, Tewodros ordered 200 of his hapless Abyssinian prisoners to be thrown over a cliff, many paired in chains.[62] The final battle at Arogee just below Magdala was an anticlimax: Tewodros's master weapon, a huge mortar, blew up with its first discharge, and the advancing British and Baluchis shot the enemy to pieces. The fortress of Magdala was stormed three days later. Tewodros was found dead, having shot himself, and the captives were released. After destroying the stronghold, the force withdrew, and by 18 June had completed the return march to the coast and departed.[63] For Roberts, who always sought action, it must have been some satisfaction to receive Napier's letter affirming that he had 'received with pleasure most favourable reports regarding the able and energetic manner in which Major Roberts has carried on the duties of [his] department at Zoolla, and it has been a source of regret to the Commander-in-Chief that he has been unable to avail himself of Major Roberts's services at the front'.[64] Napier had returned on 2 June and embarked on the 10th, asking Roberts to accompany him as he proposed to give him the honour of taking his despatches to London.[65] On reaching the capital on 28 June, Roberts found a note at his London club from his old Delhi comrade, Edwin Johnson, then assistant military secretary to the Duke of Cambridge, directing him to take the despatches immediately to the Secretary of State for India. He carried them to the home of Sir Stafford and Lady Northcote, who were at dinner. Northcote read through them, and asked Roberts to take them without delay to the Duke. At Cambridge's home a servant told Roberts it was impossible to interrupt His Royal Highness in the middle of a dinner party, so Roberts sent in the despatches, but not missing a trick put his card on top. He had scarcely returned to his club when an ADC appeared with orders to bring him back. Roberts finishes the story: 'The Commander-in-Chief received me very kindly, expressing regret that I had been sent away in the first instance; and Their Royal Highnesses the Prince and Princess of Wales, who were present, were most gracious, and asked many questions about the Abyssinian Expedition.'[66] For an ambitious officer, there can hardly have been a better result to four months' hard work in scorching heat. Napier received a peerage. Abyssinia was healthy compared to West Africa, and deaths from sickness were not severe, more than half being from gastrointestinal infections and heatstroke.[67]

Roberts joined his wife and others of his family at Clifton, basking in the glory of a brevet Lt-Colonelcy and the offer from Mansfield of the post of first assistant-QMG at headquarters. This new post was specially created for him.[68] Tryon did not do so well. His health was severely tried, and for some months after his return he was an invalid, although he was to advance to flag rank.[69]

While Roberts's career was advancing, family life was difficult. The final entry in his diary of 1861 reads: 'The last day of the year which on the whole has not been a very bright one for us, losing our darling babe and the hopes of a second, and now anxious as to the fate of our third.'[70] A second baby girl had been born at Clifton in July while they were in England. Voyages to India were fated for Nora Roberts. They embarked on the SS Helvetia on 4 January 1869, the Royal Naval vessel which was to convey them having broken down. The ship was unsuitable and most uncomfortable, a gale blew the whole way to Alexandria, all three Robertses fell ill, and the baby girl caught a fatal chill. She died on board the Malabar, the regular troopship to which they transferred at Suez, and was buried in the Red Sea. Roberts wrote: 'what with the effects of the voyage and the anxiety and sorrow she had gone through, my wife was thoroughly ill when we arrived at Simla towards the end of February'.[71] They spent a quiet year at Simla; a boy was born who only lived three weeks. When David James wrote his biography of Roberts in the 1950s, the younger surviving daughter Edwina may well have given personal insights into her parents' life, for James writes: 'They had now been married ten years, yet still had no children and at times were almost in despair.'[72] Both came from large families, and this was the Victorian ideal. Then things turned right. Roberts's memoirs give a cheerful account of 1870, of the beauties of Simla, snow-capped peaks 'as far as the eye can reach', 'dark-green ilex and deodar' covered with snow and icicles in winter, 'the most gorgeous colouring' at evening as the snow turned opal, pink, scarlet and crimson in the sun's descending rays, succeeded by 'a background of deepest sapphire blue'. Night fell, he wrote, and the spectator retreated indoors 'glad to be greeted by a blazing log-fire'. The Robertses had moved into Ellerslie, a larger and warmer house than before.[73] In fairly quick succession, three children were born and survived: Aileen Mary in 1870, Frederick Hugh Sherston in 1872 and Ada Edwina Stewart in 1875. 'So faith and courage were well rewarded in the end,' wrote James. Of the Robertses' faith and courage there was no doubt, but those qualities do not produce babies, whose appearance to those who long for them can still seem a miracle.

In 1871 Nora had stayed with the Stewarts at their Simla home. Donald Stewart was unwell and she had helped his wife nurse him. He had finished 'in much better health than he had been for many years' and bought a beautiful Trichinopoly bracelet for her, 'a very small return for all their kindness and attention since I came here'. He told his wife that no one but her would have taken such trouble with a sick friend.[74]

Roberts's next task was to organise and accompany the expedition against the Lushais in the forests of Assam. He was selected by a new commander-in-chief, Napier having succeeded Mansfield. Napier was Roberts's next important patron, advanced his career and influenced his military views. He was thoughtful of his men, appreciative of Indian soldiers and a humane but firm disciplinarian. He held large-scale camps of exercise and strengthened defensive fortifications against a feared Russian threat. He encouraged temperance, thus reducing crime from drunkenness,[75] and introduced a weekly holiday for all ranks on Thursday, dubbed St Napier's day.[76] Roberts wrote warmly of him, of how Indian princes and people remembered with affection *Lat Napier Sahib*.[77] Roberts was to emulate his measures.

Stewart was then sharing a house with the Robertses. He wrote that 'Bobs ... is of course delighted' Napier had chosen him; he was in no doubt of his friend's ability to succeed and that it would secure him a CB and the post of deputy QMG. Stewart predicted: 'There will be much hard work and exposure, but little or no fighting, as these people have neither towns, villages, nor arms ...'[78] The Lushai lived in a belt of high mountain ranges north of Chittagong. From 1850 they launched a series of raids and carried off hostages. In 1868–9, they made a number of attacks on the tea-gardens in Assam. A small expedition failed to find them. Attempts to negotiate with the most powerful Lushai chief proved equally futile. Lushai tribes attacked and destroyed villages, killing coolies and a tea-planter Mr Winchester, whose six-year-old daughter was carried off. Napier, on a tour of inspection in the district, arranged frontier defences as the season was impractical for an advance; a suitable expedition would be sent when the climate permitted. On 30 June 1871, instructions were issued for this expedition of two columns, starting from Cachar and Chittagong, in cooperation with the forces of two local rajahs. Each column included 1,500 picked men from the regular native infantry, half a mountain battery with two guns and two mortars carried on elephants, and one company of sappers and miners. Some 1,400 coolies transported baggage. Political officers were subordinate to the military commanders.[79]

In September Roberts was sent to organise the columns, to be commanded respectively by Brigadiers Brownlow and Bourchier. It was excessively hot, and by the time all was ready, Roberts was reduced to little more than eight stone in weight. On 16 November he joined Bourchier at Cachar, and the force began the advance through dense and steaming forest, cutting a road sufficient for elephant transport. It took nearly nine weeks to complete the first hundred miles to the proposed base of operations. From there Roberts reconnoitred at length for the best line of advance; there was not even a jungle footpath visible, so the route had to be clearly made. Roberts wrote: 'Notwithstanding the extreme heat of the climate, and the difficult nature of the country, which was a succession of rolling hills with dense jungle and huge creepers, and intersected by numerous rivers and watercourses, a good road from six to eight feet wide was constructed, with a gradient easy enough for laden elephants to travel over.'[80] Small bands of Lushai were seen in the jungle, but evaded contact. Roberts with fifty men of the 22nd Punjabis advanced to clearings where the enemy had built stockades for storing rice and successively destroyed them. The wooded hills and oppressive heat made the ascent difficult. Whenever the Punjabis or Gurkhas drew in their piquets, the Lushai came on, sniping, and if their foes retreated, yelling and screaming. Roberts's spirits were buoyed up on New Year's Day, 1872, by the news that he had been appointed deputy QMG, and shortly afterwards by the birth of his son Freddie at Umballa on 8 January.[81] On 25 January 1872, there was the first serious action. The enemy tried to get round the column's flank to attack the unarmed coolies in the baggage train. The Gurkhas and 44th Native Infantry promptly counter-attacked and chased them up a hill, seizing a village on top. The next day Roberts was sent to destroy the village from which the attack had been launched. The way was too difficult for the elephants, who were sent back, and coolies carried the two steel guns with nine rounds for each. Fifty men each of the 22nd and 44th Bengal Native Infantry marched over three miles of difficult country, emerging at a stockade packed with armed men, a sheer mountain on one side, a steep ravine on the other. Roberts decided to turn the enemy flank by advancing along the precipitous 6,000-foot-high mountainside. This succeeded in getting round the stockade, the enemy retreating to the village. A couple of shells, the second one bursting 'with the utmost accuracy in the centre of the village, where the enemy were in a dense mass' sent them in confused flight into the forest. The bamboo houses were searched, found empty and set alight.[82] The column now made better going in higher ground, amongst fields and clearer tracks. Soon after this, news was received that Mary Winchester had been handed back to the other column. Bourchier's column pressed on to the village of the headman, and after five days reached the remote Chamfai Valley. They stayed four days. The effect of the advance on the Lushai was such that the former enemies behaved like friends. The British were shown the tomb of the chief's father, Vonolel, a famous man in those parts, while the Lushai were fascinated by revolvers, telescopes and other equipment. They expressed regret when the column left, but confronted with an unstoppable juggernaut in their own forests they had to cooperate.

Three chiefs were surrendered as hostages for future good behaviour, weapons were given up and a fine imposed of elephant tusks, goats, pigs, fowls and chiefs' necklaces. General Brownlow reported the achievement:

> The complete subjection of two powerful tribes, inhabiting upwards of sixty villages, of which twenty that resisted were attacked and destroyed; the personal submission of fifteen chiefs, and their solemn engagement on behalf of themselves and tributaries for future good behaviour; the recovery of Mary Winchester, and the liberation of upwards of 150 British subjects, who had from time to time been made captives.

Parties surveyed 3,000 square miles of territory. Casualties from fighting were trifling, seven killed and thirteen wounded; those from cholera were more serious, thirty soldiers and 118 coolies.[83] Among the dead was Roberts's orderly, 'a very smart young Gurkha'.[84] For twenty years there was peace and no further raids. The withdrawal was conducted with speed, as the onset of the rainy season threatened sickness: 'the privations were great, and the climate of Looshai most trying', said Roberts.[85] Brownlow reported:

> Lieutenant-Colonel Roberts's untiring energy and sagacity are beyond all praise; working without guides, even without map and geography, thwarted by the Looshais, whose game was to delay our progress, he seemed never at a loss. Not only in his own department was it that he exerted himself. Whether piloting the advance guard through the trackless forest, or solving a commissariat or transport difficulty, his powerful aid was willingly given.[86]

He fulfilled Stewart's expectation, receiving his CB. He concluded that the expedition was not just for retaliation, but to impress on the Lushai British power and 'to establish friendly relations of a permanent character with them . . .'[87]

As deputy QMG he rejoined army headquarters. At Simla he found his wife with the children settled in a new home, Snowdon, recently purchased. Nora Roberts had been 'at death's door' according to her husband. Their son was almost murdered by his native wet-nurse. This was unusual. Normally Ayahs were greatly attached to the children they nursed; in this case the woman had been forced into employment she did not want.[88]

In the winter of 1872–3 Roberts accompanied Napier on his tour through the Punjab and at the camp of exercise held at Hussan Abdul. 'Lord Napier of Magdala did much to improve the efficiency of the army by means of Camps of Exercise,' wrote Roberts. 'No Commander-in-Chief ever carried out inspections with more thoroughness ... On the hottest day he would toil through barrack after barrack to satisfy himself that the soldiers were properly cared for; Europeans and Natives were equally attended to ...'[89] These measures Roberts would continue. An 1864 Commission reported that mortality from sickness could be cut from 7 per cent of total strength to 2 per cent with proper precautions. About £11 million was spent on improved barracks from 1866 to 1877, and by 1882 deaths from sickness fell to below 2 per cent of strength.[90]

The 1870s saw changes in the government of India. Lord Mayo the viceroy was assassinated on 8 September 1872 on the Andaman Islands, Britain's penal settlement. His murderer was a prisoner, Shere Ali, a Muslim fanatic who had secreted a seven-inch-long kitchen knife in his clothes. Roberts's friend Donald Stewart in command on the Andamans had warned Mayo against going out at night to view the sunset.[91] Napier briefly acted as viceroy until Mayo's successor Lord Northbrook could arrive. Edwin Johnson succeeded Lumsden as Roberts's superior as QMG. In 1873 Lumsden had been on leave in England and Roberts ran his department for five months. Lumsden returned as adjutant general and Johnson joined the Indian Council in London.[92] Roberts officiated from 11 March 1874, but he was not yet a full colonel and was thus ineligible to be QMG. However, the post was kept open for him.[93] Napier clearly thought he ought to have it, as his 1874 letter to the Duke of Cambridge showed:

> [The QMG] is an appointment requiring such special qualifications and information regarding India that I have been unable to name any officer who could approach Lieut. Colonel Roberts in fitness for it ... It is embarrassing to have an officer in that high appointment who is dependent upon his Deputy, so that I have thought it better to do nothing at present, leaving Lieut. Colonel Roberts officiating for a few months, when we may expect him then to be full Colonel. I should then send his name forward instead of at present opening the question regarding his rank.[94]

In January 1874 Roberts received news of his father's death. Abraham had travelled to Windsor on 8 December 1873 to receive the GCB, but took cold in the train on the way home to Clifton, and never recovered, dying on

THE QUARTER MASTER GENERAL.

FIGURE 3 *On 1 January 1875 Roberts became QMG India with acting Major-General's rank. He showed by organising logistics for the Magdala expedition and drawing up 'The Route Book of Bengal' that he was destined for higher rank.*

the 28th.[95] Although his son's greatest successes were still to come, his father knew that his patronage had already been rewarded. Roberts told Norman after the Mutiny of his father bringing out the standard he had taken 'for every visitor, and tells them the whole story of its capture . . . he then shows the pouch through which he was wounded'.[96]

On 31 January 1875, Roberts attained the substantive rank of colonel at the age of forty-two and was confirmed in office as QMG with local rank of major-general. Napier told the viceroy he considered himself 'fortunate at the present time in being able to nominate an officer of such ability and varied experience as Colonel Frederick Roberts'.[97]

This was in time for the Prince of Wales's visit to India. His chief task in the subcontinent was to show himself to Indian princes, soldiers, peasants and workers as the incarnation of the British Raj, bringing to life a remote and abstract symbol.[98] There had shortly before been a famine in Bihar, which Northbrook sent Sir Richard Temple to deal with. Roberts assisted him. One million tons of rice were distributed from an improvised train worked by military and police officers. Some 450,000 received this support. Famine relief measures included the employment of 753,000 persons for nine months. The total cost was £6.5 million.[99] The famine proved less severe than anticipated, and Temple was criticised for his spending. This was to have an unfortunate denouement, but the success of famine measures provided a good augury for the Prince's stay.

At Delhi his visit of January 1875 was celebrated with banquets, balls, and manoeuvres. Lumsden and Roberts accompanied the Prince when he attended manoeuvres, based on the Ridge outside the city where in 1857 the British besiegers had dug in. The Prince spent an entire week in camp with the army and led his own regiment, the 10th Hussars, in a cavalry charge. He visited Delhi gaol and 'enjoyed a long conversation with an aged and notorious thug, whose life had been spared when he turned Queen's evidence, and who discussed coolly and factually some of the 250 murders which he claimed to have committed'. He was shocked by the 'disgraceful habit of officers . . . speaking of the inhabitants of India, many of them sprung from the great races, as "niggers"'.[100] His tour ended with an investiture at Allahabad on 7 March. Less than a fortnight later, Roberts's patron Napier laid down his command. He sailed from Bombay on 10 April. He was a good friend to the Robertses. To Nora he had passed the programme of his speech unveiling a statue to Outram in May 1874, inscribed with the words, 'For Mrs Roberts with best compliments, Napier of Magdala'. Roberts thanked him in a fulsome letter: 'I have always hoped to be at the head of the Quartermaster General's Department, but I never anticipated getting the appointment so soon, and I feel that my advancement is entirely owing to your Excellency's great indulgence and kind assistance.'[101]

Thanks to his father, his friends, his own talents and especially Napier, Roberts had risen steadily, if unspectacularly. He was about to enter the momentous years of his life. In November 1878, *The Times of India* described him in flattering terms as advancing first through his father's patronage to the rank of ADC; serving admirably 'as a pioneer and scout' in the QMG's Department; constantly in danger; brought forward in the Abyssinia expedition, showing 'ready tact and courteous forbearance in dealing with the naval officers upon whom the execution of details principally fell'; bearing despatches to London, 'he showed in the ease with which he accepted the role of the man of fashion, and adapted himself to the life of the courtier, dining now with Royalty, now with the Lord Mayor and the leading notables of London society, that he was as much at home in the Court as in the camp.' He had proved 'by the success which has waited upon his tenure of office' that he fully deserved the QMG's post. 'To him is mainly due the preparation of the now well-known "*Route Book of Bengal*", a work of infinite value, which lays down in precise terms the various lines of march throughout the Presidency.' The article concluded:

> scrupulously neat and natty in appearance, an excellent horseman, quick in all his movements, prompt in his decisions, sharp and peremptory in voice, he is naturally suited to command men. With comrades of his own or subordinates of every rank he is popular in the extreme. "Bobs" as his old friends call him to his face, as many others who would not so far presume, do so behind his back, is known and liked by a very wide circle in India. A thorough gentleman in thought and deed, unselfish and unsparing of personal effort when there is work to be done, his ready sympathy and cordial recognition of the efforts of others make it a pleasure to serve with him or under his orders.[102]

In the war in which he was soon to command, Roberts was to find that his promptness in decision, courage, tact, energy, ready sympathy and willingness to recognise others' efforts were to be stretched to the full. He would need all these qualities and a good measure of the famed 'Roberts luck'.

CHAPTER FIVE

War in Afghanistan

Little did I imagine, when making Lord Lytton's acquaintance, how much he would have to say in my future career.

FRED ROBERTS, *FORTY-ONE YEARS*

There never was such a stroke of luck for [news of your victory at the Peiwar Kotal] was telegraphed home on the morning of the assembling of Parliament, and must have been shouted through the streets . . .

COLONEL GEORGE COLLEY TO ROBERTS, DECEMBER 1878

God grant we may escape any more national disasters. We do not fear the [Afghan] troops, but the long communications & rough country are great difficulties, and our transport is very defective.

MORTIMER DURAND DIARY, SEPTEMBER 1879

The new viceroy, the 2nd Earl Lytton, transformed Roberts's career. He had been QMG little more than a year when Napier's command finished, and he travelled to Bombay in April 1876, to say goodbye. Roberts would also be there when Lytton landed, and his staff experience taught him to seek the notice of men in power.

> Lord Lytton received me on board the steamer which had brought him from Suez in a most friendly manner. He told me he had been greatly interested during the voyage reading a paper by me detailing the steps that would have to be taken in India in the event of a Russian Army crossing the Oxus and invading Afghanistan . . . From that moment Lord Lytton was my friend. The "Forward Policy" which I advocated was the Policy that appealed to him . . .'[1]

In this Roberts followed Napier, who had become a vigorous supporter of the 'Forward School' and ordered Roberts to prepare the paper which Lytton read.[2] Roberts overstates its importance, for Lytton had already taken his own council. Writing to the Earl of Salisbury, Secretary of State for India, just after reaching Bombay, he does not mention meeting Roberts.[3] Disraeli's government, elected in 1874, was prepared to listen sympathetically to this 'Forward School'. Lytton was a diplomat and writer rather than a politician, but his flamboyant character appealed to the Prime Minister who wanted someone with flair to proclaim Queen Victoria as Empress of India.

Lytton's first task was not Afghanistan, but this proclamation at a grand theatrical durbar outside Delhi. Victoria's new title capitalised on her son's successful tour. Roberts's previous experience of running viceregal progresses fitted him to play a major part in staging this pageant on a grand scale. The native princes' magnificent retinues made their parade led by the viceroy and Lady Lytton on a state elephant 'the most gorgeous and picturesque which has ever been seen even in the east'. Some 84,000 people, including 13,000 soldiers, watched on 1 January 1877 as the Queen was proclaimed *Kaiser-i-Hind* or Empress of India. The committee organising the durbar included Roberts, Lytton's military secretary Colonel George Colley, and Roberts's friend Owen Burne, on whom Lytton depended to brief him about Indian affairs. Burne tells us that Roberts's sterling work in preparing the event impressed Lytton sufficiently to select him for future military command, initially the Punjab Frontier Force.[4]

Roberts omitted from his memoirs the cruel background to the durbar: the worst recorded famine in Indian history. It lasted over two years, affecting most of southern India and in the second year parts of central India and the Punjab. Fever and cholera followed. Over 5 million died. Although Lytton cut relief expenditure, £11 million was disbursed from the Indian treasury and charitable funds. One good emerged: the Famine Commission under General Richard Strachey to inquire into future relief established a Famine Code, laying funds aside each year. No future famine was as bad.[5]

No matter how good Roberts's planning had been, luck played a part in his advance; for his future career might have fallen to the man who was to be his chief rival in the public's eyes, Garnet Wolseley. In 1872 the viceroy designate, Northbrook, wanted Wolseley as his military secretary; he declined. In 1873–4 the Duke of Cambridge pressed his appointment as adjutant-general in India, resisted by Napier. Wolseley may have shunned India as dominated by a reactionary clique of Mutiny generals. Instead he sought independent command against the Ashanti in West Africa.[6] Following his African triumph, Lytton wanted him for the new North-West Frontier Province, telling Salisbury on 30 July 1876: 'He has in a high degree all the qualities I most desire for this post.' It was not to be. In opposition was 'an inveterate alliance' of the Duke of Cambridge, Napier's successor Sir Frederick Haines, and other army conservatives; but Salisbury first and then Disraeli pointed out the objections. Lytton accepted these: 'He will make too

FIGURE 4 *Robert, 2nd Earl Lytton, Indian Viceroy, who launched the Second Afghan War, was another Roberts patron and 'had been coaching him in my own notions' for a year before he took the Kurram command (British Library).*

much of a splash.' It was better to have someone with excellent local knowledge, whatever an outsider's merits.[7]

Lytton then advanced Roberts who, since reaching Peshawar in 1854, had gained that local knowledge. He took a lesser position than that proposed for Wolseley; namely, command of the Punjab Frontier Force and special commissioner in the Scinde-Punjab frontier.[8] Although coming down in rank to brigadier-general, Roberts eagerly accepted the post in March 1878, embarking on an extended tour of frontier stations.[9] He was to be an ideal choice to lead one of the columns invading Afghanistan. Had Wolseley come to India, Roberts's career would have stalled.[10]

In appointing Lytton, Disraeli and Salisbury wanted a man who could act boldly and imaginatively against the Russian threat.[11] Before leaving London, Lytton had a revealing talk with Schuvalov, Russian ambassador, who read out a memorandum from Kaufman, governor of Russia's Asian provinces, proposing a division of territories in Central Asia between Russia and Britain. By the time Lytton reached Bombay, his views were clear: to build up Afghanistan with its Amir Sher Ali into a strong, stable and peaceful power as the best barrier against Russian expansion.[12]

The previous policy of successive British viceroys, John Lawrence, Mayo and Northbrook, was 'masterly inactivity'. While avoiding military disaster at Kabul, if followed rigidly this would have deprived the British of intelligence-gathering and influence. In fact, Britain had intervened in Afghan affairs, giving diplomatic support and money to Sher Ali in his fight for power in the 1860s.[13] Meanwhile, in Central Asia, Russia was on the march. In 1865 she acquired Tashkent, in 1866 Khojent, in 1867 Bokhara. The Russian driving force was General Konstantin Kaufman, veteran of war in the Caucasus, friend of Alexander II's thrusting War Minister Dimitri Milyutin and a soldier of vision and energy.[14] In 1873 Britain and Russia came to an understanding that the area south of the river Oxus was to be Afghan, and this would fall within the British sphere of influence. In the Russian Empire, however, like the British, there was a gap between policy at the centre and the 'young Turks' on the frontiers. Russian governors in central Asia were more aggressive than those in St Petersburg.

Kaufman's advance continued to Khiva in 1873 and Kokand in 1876, and he began attacks on Turkmen tribes in Merv. Northbrook had spurned the hand of friendship advanced by Sher Ali, he and his council affirming 'masterly inactivity'. Sher Ali thought it wise to adopt a warmer policy towards Russia. In India the Forward School's views were put by a friend of Roberts, Sir Henry Rawlinson, First Afghan War veteran, former diplomat, member of the India Council in London, in *England and Russia in the East*, published in 1875. Without agents in Afghanistan, the Forward School argued, the British remained in ignorance of Russian and Afghan intentions. The fear was not so much of direct invasion, but of the effects of a threatened invasion or a southward advance on India. The British, a tiny minority, ruled only by the acceptance of India's vast population. The approach of Russians

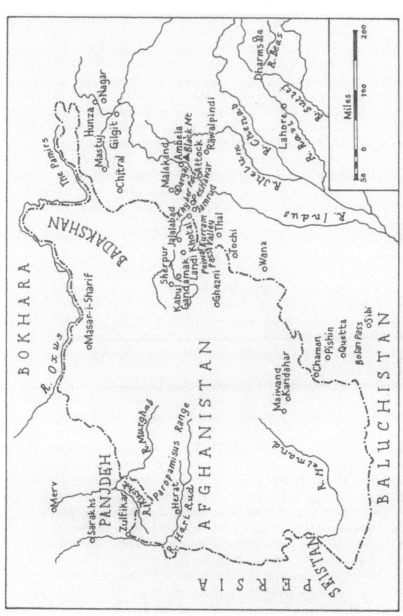

MAP 4 *Afghanistan and North-West Frontier*

or Afghans might raise that population, especially the Muslims, in revolt and make British rule untenable. In the words of J.R. Seeley's classic *The Expansion of England*, 'If the British ever had to rule India as conquerors without local allies and mass acquiescence we should assuredly be ruined financially by the mere attempt. In reality Britain would quickly withdraw'.[15] These fears were fed by the translation and publication of the Russian Colonel Terentiev's *Russia and England in the Struggle for the Markets of Central Asia*. The Indian Mutiny had failed, Terentiev maintained, because the Indians lacked a proper plan and outside support. He wrote: 'Sick to death [of British rule], the natives are now waiting for a physician from the north.' Russian military reforms after the Crimea had emphasised using fast-moving mounted columns and raising 'people's wars of insurrection'.[16]

In Britain and India, 'the Lord Lawrence School' defended 'masterly inactivity'. Lawrence feared that the disaster of the First Afghan War had been forgotten. In this he was wrong. Roberts remembered it only too well from his father's experience. But some of Lawrence's comments were to prove remarkably prescient.[17]

Lytton's first step in his frontier policy was to send troops into Quetta on the route into Afghanistan through the Bolan Pass. To Sher Ali this was a threatening reminder of the British advance to Kabul in 1838–9. Lytton and Disraeli sought to undo Northbrook's rebuff of Sher Ali by offering a defensive treaty with a British representative at Kabul or Herat. The policy might have succeeded had it not been for the Eastern Crisis of 1878 and Lytton's impatience. In the Crisis, the Russians threatened Constantinople and Disraeli dispatched the Mediterranean Fleet to Besika Bay and Indian troops to Malta.

At St Petersburg, the Tsar and his ministers agreed Kaufman's proposal that if war broke out with Britain columns from the Caucasus and Turkestan would advance on India. To reassure Sher Ali that this was not directed against him, a Russian mission was sent to Kabul headed by Major-General Stoletov, an officer well acquainted with the East.[18] The arrival of Stolietov's mission at the Afghan capital coincided with Afghan refusal of Lytton's application for a British resident there, and strengthened Lytton's suspicions that Sher Ali was plotting with the Russians. Lytton's answer was to despatch an envoy with armed escort to present an ultimatum. The timing could not have been worse. The Amir was mourning the death of his favourite son and declared heir, and yielding to 'the faithless wretch', his eldest son Yakub, as successor.[19] His reaction was bitter. Brigadier-General Neville Chamberlain and Major Louis Cavagnari with an escort from the Corps of Guides arrived at Fort Ali Masjid on the Khyber Pass with the ultimatum. The Amir's officer in command had orders to turn them back and did so. He told Cavagnari that had it not been for their friendship he would have fired upon him.[20] Chamberlain thought the rebuff justified Lytton's proposed measures, writing to his sister: 'We cannot permit Russia to be our rival in Afghanistan, and by sending this Mission she has left us no alternative but to take up the glove.'[21] Disraeli and Salisbury, bringing 'peace with honour' from the Berlin Conference, found themselves facing Afghan war. Lytton telegraphed home his Council's plan, to issue a manifesto condemning the Amir but professing friendship to the Afghan people, to send troops to occupy the Kurram Valley and seize the Khyber Pass. At a meeting on 25 October, the Cabinet agreed to the dispatch of a final ultimatum to the Amir; rejection would be followed by immediate British advance. The ultimatum of 31 October gave Sher Ali to 20 November to accept a British mission and send a full apology for the repulse of Chamberlain's mission. The deadline was extended to 30 November. Sher Ali's answer was late and deemed inadequate. War followed. Reluctantly Disraeli's Cabinet backed their impetuous Viceroy.[22]

Lytton sought advice from comparatively few. His chief advisors were Colonel George Colley, his military secretary and ablest of Garnet Wolseley's 'Ashanti ring', and Major Louis Cavagnari.[23] Excluded from this cabal was the commander-in-chief, Sir Frederick Haines, who insisted that invading columns be increased in strength, a division to advance to Kandahar and a strong reserve formed. He told the Duke of Cambridge: '[W]e shall find the Afghans much better armed and better drilled than they were when we were in contact with them years ago . . . we are bound not to despise our enemy.'[24] It was Colley who trusted the power of breech-loading rifles.

Henry Hanna, historian of the war, disliked Roberts, partly from the latter's refusal to promote him, partly from being on the opposite side of the North-West Frontier debate, partly because he saw Roberts at Kabul in 1879 ineptly wrestling with Afghan politics.[25] Hanna claimed Roberts influenced Lytton's aggression, but the truth seems to be the other way. Lytton told Sir James Stephen that Roberts 'was my own particular selection, and I had been personally coaching him in my own notions about that line of advance [the Kurram] . . . for more than a year before he got his command there'.[26]

Roberts nonetheless was fortunate in being advanced over the heads of senior men. Of three attacking columns, he commanded the smallest, intended for the Kurram Valley: 6,600 of a total of 36,000. It was, as Donald Stewart commanding 12,600 men of the Kandahar Field Force wrote, too small a force to occupy Afghanistan or interfere with the country's administration, but intended to ensure its ruler did not make friends 'with people who can damage us', namely the Russians.[27] The aim was to secure a friendly buffer. The strategic Kurram Valley outflanked the Khyber and threatened Jellalabad as well as Kabul. The roads were bad and the higher slopes never clear of snow after November. One senior officer thought the fighting with modern rifles, the Indians carrying the Snider, the British the Martini-Henry, 'will be the easiest part of the job' while 'difficulties of communication and climate will be serious'. Against Afghans armed with long-range Jezails, the Indian Army adapted to khaki. He added, 'Roberts and Stewart are both competent Officers, and when the forces have been put together and Regts are accustomed to one another, and to their new Staffs, all will go well . . .' He did not extend similar approval to Sam Browne, commander of the Peshawar Valley Field Force of 16,000 striking at the Khyber.[28] Browne's appointment was a 'job', to remove him from the viceroy's Council in favour of Neville Chamberlain.[29]

In the First Afghan War, it had been popular militias from the hill tribes, especially the Ghilzais and Kohistanis, roused by the mullahs, who had fought the British. Sher Ali had visited India in 1869 and came away convinced that unless the Afghans advanced in civilisation they would continue to be regarded (in the words of his grandson) 'as ignorant asses that they had always been'.[30] He modernised the army, obtaining from the British rifles, ammunition, other equipment and Indian NCOs to train Afghan regulars, a force of 56,000 with 379 guns. The artillery was their strongest arm.[31] Russian Colonel Grodekov, visiting Herat in 1878 ahead of the possible march of Russian columns in the Eastern Crisis, thought Sher Ali's army of good quality, but the infantry hampered by drill manuals based on English models, ill-suited to Afghan character. He reflected ironically on their belt buckles with incongruous mottoes, '1st Regiment Bengal Light Cavalry' and 'God save the Queen'.[32]

Despite Afghan modernisation, all three British columns met success.[33] Browne's captured Ali Masjid in the Khyber and reached Jalalabad. Stewart's marched through the Bolan Pass and occupied Kandahar. Roberts knew from a manual drawn up by Major Collett of the 23rd Pioneers that he faced a valley narrowing steadily from twelve miles to two, following the course of the Khurram River and dominated by mountain ranges.[34] He had taken particular care over his force. Arrangements were very backward when Roberts took charge, and the 2nd battalion of the 8th King's Regiment 'was so saturated with fever that a great portion of it was quite unfit for service'. He secured extra troops, made good the inadequate hospital provision and attempted to secure the favour of the local Turis, Shia Muslims amongst a sea of hostile Sunni. Hanna praised his 'energy, clear-headedness and practical knowledge . . . during those busy weeks of preparation'.[35] Roberts told his old friend 'Jemmy' Hills that what had made him most angry was the constant changing of his regiments and the belated replacement of a competent brigadier by Thelwall: 'Such an everlasting noodle I never came across.'[36] With Roberts as extra ADC was Lt-Colonel the Hon. G.P.H. Villiers, the viceroy's former military secretary and Lady Lytton's cousin. Taking him on campaign was a favour to the Lyttons: Villiers had been caught in adultery with a doctor's wife, there followed a nasty public divorce, damages of £2,000 were awarded, and Lady Lytton was 'in the depth of woe'. Roberts thus removed him from the public eye.[37]

Roberts received word that Afghan forces were falling back from the mountain pass, the Peiwar Kotal, and pushed forward. He was quickly disabused: far from retreating, the enemy were entrenching in a strong position and their guns outranged his light artillery. Inexperience led him to encamp within their range. The troops had to strike tents and re-pitch them further back. The young commander faced a daunting prospect: 'You never saw such a strong place, my head failed when I looked at it, it seemed hopeless to attack it in front, and the mountains on either side are successively steep, in places sheer rock, and quite unassailable.'[38] In a revealing letter composed in his earliest spare moment to his old friend Hills, we find a catalogue of fears and hopes. Haines had constantly tried to fetter him with instructions. With a quarter of the 8th King's Liverpool Regiment in hospital, he was angry that Haines would not permit an increase in his medical establishment.

Faced with such an obstacle, Roberts, Colonel Aenas Perkins of the Engineers, Colonel Gordon and an old Mutiny friend and experienced frontier veteran Major MacQueen reconnoitred. By the second evening he was almost satisfied that 'nothing could be done from the front, right or left'. He sent Major Collett quietly off to take a look at the Spingawi route (see map on p. 78), meanwhile making 'all the noise and splash I could in front'. Collett's report determined him to make a turning movement. Everyone else thought he would 'creep up the hills to our right front', and not until 5 p.m. on 1 November did he assemble his COs and unfold his plan. The enemy were equally deceived. Urging secrecy, he would lead a night flank march round the enemy's left. To disguise intentions he arranged for gun positions to be laid out in full view of the Afghans and reconnaissance parties to examine both sides of the main valley. At 9 p.m. they started, Roberts leading the 29th Native Infantry, a largely Punjabi regiment, the 5th Gurkhas and a mountain battery. The 72nd Highlanders, the 2nd Punjab Infantry, the 23rd Pioneers and four field artillery guns on elephants followed. Roberts calculated nine hours of darkness, five for marching, four for resting just short of the Kotal. Camps were left standing, fires alight. Some 500–600 native levies received orders to ascend the ridge and make a demonstration against the enemy's right. Brigadier-General Cobbe took 800 men of the 5th Punjab Infantry and 8th Liverpools and endeavoured to get within rifle range of the enemy's position on the Kotal by creeping through the wooded spurs to their right. Roberts would tell Cobbe by heliograph if his movement succeeded.

Roberts's column, impeded by huge boulders, made slow progress. Colonel Gordon was in front, and Roberts pushed forward to urge him on. He passed the Gurkhas in compact order, but found the 29th straggling in every direction. As he 'pitched into' Gordon and told him in no uncertain terms to get his men together and move more quickly, a shot was fired from the 29th's ranks, followed by another. This warning to the enemy took Roberts's breath away. Gordon's Sikh orderly whispered in his ear that there was a traitor among the Pathans of the 29th. Roberts ordered Gordon to find the culprit, and sent Gurkhas and men of the 72nd ahead. The column started again. 'It was a weary, anxious night,' wrote Roberts,' [and] to make matters worse I was not feeling very well.'

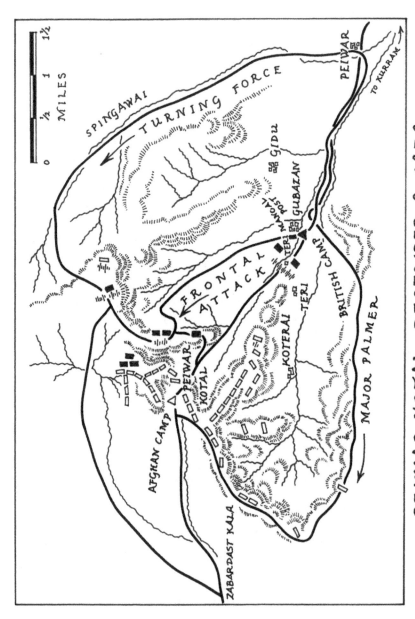

MAP 5 *Peiwar Kotal*

The slightest glimmer of dawn greeted them as they reached the final ascent of the Kotal or mountain pass. The men closed up, three companies of the 72nd and the Gurkhas, altogether 350 strong. Then they moved up the slope unobserved. At the crest enemy shots rang out. The Gurkhas dashed into the first breastwork. A tremendous volley greeted them, but on they went, followed by the 72nd. At a second breastwork the enemy made a fierce stand, but were driven out. Some of the 29th arrived, and by pressing forward British and Indians cleared the slope and reached the summit. After advancing about three-quarters of a mile, Roberts halted and formed up his men. He expected the 'noodle' Thelwall with the second wave, but he did not see him until about 1 p.m.

As soon as leading regiments had rested they advanced and gained another hill. The trees became so thick and the mountainside so precipitous it was impossible to find a way further. The Gurkhas and 72nd had taken a wrong turn. Resistance increased, and for an hour Roberts was cut off with the 29th of whom very few would fight. He despatched staff officers to bring on the lost battalions. A spent ball hit him on the hand: 'I thought it was all up.' The Afghans had rallied and mustered in strength. Eventually the Rev. J.W. Adams, who had begged to come as supernumerary ADC, was sent off in a new direction to bring on the men, and Perkins and MacQueen appeared with the 5th Punjab Infantry. After failing to find a way to the Kotal, Roberts ordered the 2nd and 29th Punjab Infantry to dig in and pushed on with the Gurkhas, 72nd, 23rd and 5th Punjab Infantry to cut the enemy's line of retreat. The threat to the Afghan escape was decisive. Enemy fire slackened and by about 4.30 p.m. it had almost ceased. Success was just in time. His force had been trudging since 9 p.m. the previous evening, had had no food and 'were all pretty well done'. They lighted fires with the plentiful wood, threw out piquets and fell asleep. Soon afterwards a messenger arrived with a note from another old friend, Hugh Gough: the 8th Foot led by Cobbe and then by their Colonel Barry-Drewe had occupied the Kotal without a shot being fired as the enemy were retreating. Gough had pursued, preventing their carrying off any guns. This was indeed good news.[39]

The next day Roberts returned to the Kotal and saw the immensely strong position taken. His men had done well, among them Subadar Major Ayeez Khan of the 5th Punjab Infantry, an outstanding native officer who died of wounds received in the fight at the first breastwork.[40] So had Roberts, leading from the front and keeping his nerve despite treachery. The initiative of Cobbe, Barry-Drewe and Gough in advancing from the left centre up to the Kotal added a second decisive blow. Roberts had been wise in keeping the unsatisfactory Thelwall and Gordon close by him. The enemy lost an estimated 300 dead and all eighteen guns. Roberts's men had twenty dead and seventy-eight wounded. Success had justified a bold operation. Only by ignoring the old truism, that no plan of attack survives contact with the enemy, could Hanna claim that 'an unexpected stroke of luck won the battle'.[41]

Roberts advanced to the Shutagardan Pass, reaching its 11,000-foot-high summit on 9 December, with a fine view of the Logar Valley. Beyond this passable route lay the Afghan capital Kabul, which Roberts thought he would have reached in less than a week given an additional 5,000 men.[42] In the event, reaching Kabul proved unnecessary in this phase. His men consolidated on the former Afghan position.

One unpleasant business was to deal with Pathans of the 29th who fired to warn the enemy or connived with them. Eighteen had deserted during the march, returned to base camp and refused point blank to return to the regiment. A court of enquiry investigated, and a general court-martial sentenced to death the man who fired the first shot. The Jemadar who tried to conceal him received seven years' imprisonment, the second shooter received two years. 'It has been a nasty business and distressed me a good deal,' wrote Roberts, 'but I feel that I am doing right in dealing firmly with the man. The Pathans need an example, several have deserted carrying off their rifles, and their heart is not in the business.'[43]

Few of his colleagues had thought an attack could succeed, but afterwards those in the Kurram Valley force were inspired 'with supreme confidence in his judgement'. Lieutenant Robertson noted how suspending his attack prevented a needless waste of life, and threatening the enemy's line of retreat 'decided the success of the day'.[44] News of the victory was telegraphed home the morning Parliament assembled to debate Lytton's policy, and newspaper boys were flourishing 'Peiwar Kotal victory' headlines as MPs assembled. 'You are quite the hero of the day back home,' Colley told Roberts. The Queen had sent her congratulations, and the viceroy's staff had forwarded it to Nora Roberts at Simla. Lytton had written to her that 'the brilliant and important victory . . . has more than justified the confidence I have always felt in your husband's military ability'.[45] The viceroy attached special importance to possession of the Kurram up to the crest of the Shutagardan Pass. 'This position completely and easily commands Cabul; there being no intervening geographical obstacle,' Lytton told the Duke of Cambridge. Sher Ali had 'made his great stand at the Peiwar, which he not unreasonably deemed impregnable', then fled from the capital which he knew to be 'at our mercy'. Lytton believed Roberts's victory rather than the advance of the other columns opened the way to success.[46]

Not all was plain sailing, as Roberts learnt from Captain Morrison of the Royal Scots. An editor of the *Civil & Military Gazette* at Lahore, Colonel Arthur Cory, had asked Morrison to be a correspondent for the paper. Cory had been attached to the Adjutant-General's Department, but retired from the Indian Army in 1877 to become chief editor and move the *Gazette* to larger premises. He had written books on the defence of India's frontier. Morrison deprecatingly replied that in the transport department, whither he was bound, he would see little of the action. 'Well,' said Cory, 'you can telegraph anything of interest and for every 10 Rupees you spend in the telegrams I'll give you 20 Rupees, but remember if you wish to keep in with this paper you must not say anything good of the column, General Roberts has behaved badly to me, and we don't want him to succeed or get a good name!' This upset Roberts sufficiently that he told Hills this 'should be published far and wide'.[47]

In Britain the war was not popular. Disraeli's defence of the Ottoman Empire in the wake of 'Bulgarian Atrocities' committed by the Turks in 1876 gave the Liberal opposition a cause. Radical MPs were seeking evidence of 'Disraeli's immoral statecraft' when Roberts entered the Khost Valley with 2,000 men, infantry, cavalry and guns. He sought to remove the Amir's rule and obtain the tribes' goodwill.[48]

The main settlement, Matun, was reached on 6 January. The next morning tribesmen massed for an attack from three sides. The British force was isolated and outnumbered. Roberts sent men of the 10th Hussars and the 5th Punjab Cavalry in a pre-emptive strike. When they came under fire from villages, infantry drove out the enemy and burnt the villages in retribution. The British took eighty-five prisoners.[49] Next day the guards on those prisoners opened fire, convinced that tribesmen were trying to release them; nine prisoners were killed and five wounded. Roberts remained in Khost until 28 January 1879, mapping and exploring, but with the onset of winter had to withdraw his force. The official he placed in charge, Sultan Jan, had to be evacuated on the day Roberts withdrew, 28 January, and he left Khost to its own devices. He attributed the trouble to local mullahs, 'a large number famous for their learning and fanaticism, had been actively engaged in raising religious prejudices against us and in calling on the people . . . to expel us from the country'. Little had been achieved except stores of cattle, sheep and grain, and knowledge of the area, at the expense of the hostility of yet another section of the Pathan tribes.[50] This should have been no surprise: his father's experience in the First Afghan War and his own at Umbeyla were both warnings.

Difficulty did not end there. Roberts found outspoken criticism in the despatches of Maurice Macpherson, war correspondent of the London *Standard*, accompanying his force. Macpherson made much of the captured tribesmen's deaths and of an alleged order to the cavalry in Khost to give no quarter. He argued that 'the Khurum field force had been cruelly treated in order that forced and objectless marches might be made, and . . . an escape from disaster was possible only through the indiscreet impatience of the enemy'.[51] Roberts's risks had been calculated, based on reconnaissance and hardly 'objectless'. Macpherson also asserted that wounded prisoners were left to writhe in agony and die as an example to the others.[52] Questions were raised in Parliament, radical MPs gave exaggerated accounts in a debate on 17 February 1879 and Roberts's despatches were sent to the Commons for scrutiny.[53] Colonel Edwin Johnson, QMG, supported his old friend. There was no alternative to opening fire, he stated, as the sentries' rifles were being seized, and 'every attention was paid to the wounded'. The regimental medical officer of the 21st Punjab Native Infantry was on the spot at once.

Surgeon Griffiths lost no time in separating dead and wounded, examining each, assisted by two other medics. 'The wounded received every care and attention,' Griffiths declared.[54]

This was a turning point in Roberts's dealings with the press. Brian Robson writes: '[He] was at pains in future to ensure that war correspondents who accompanied him were on his side.'[55] He enlisted the help of Burne and of Colley, who both had Lytton's ear, to remove Macpherson on the grounds that his despatches were false and that he had added to a telegram after Roberts had approved it. Burne told Roberts that he had simply to report Macpherson's action officially to Simla and his press pass would be cancelled. This Roberts did. He told another old friend, Martin Dillon, serving at Whitehall, that Macpherson 'proved to be an unmitigated cad', admitted changing a telegram after Roberts had approved it, had promised not to do so again, but had not kept his word.[56] Macpherson's removal prompted further trouble. *The Times of India*'s London correspondent wrote: 'the entire journalistic fraternity of London should extend their sympathy to Mr McPherson, the Standard Correspondent, whose letters were too truth-telling to suit General Roberts'. On 18 March there were questions in the House of Commons about his muzzling the press.[57]

Winter now set in with thick snow and intense cold. Roberts's men at the Peiwar made themselves snug in huts they built. Stewart at Kandahar had difficulty obtaining supplies. Sam Browne at Jalalabad was surrounded by formidable border tribes, including the merciless Ghilzais. Lytton's invasion appeared, however, to have achieved its aim: Sher Ali had fled from Kabul with the last members of Stolietov's mission. In Turkestan he appealed to the Russians, who told him to make terms. He died on 21 February. His son Yakub Khan, who had succeeded him at Kabul, opened negotiations. Cavagnari conducted these for the British. On 8 May 1879 the new Amir arrived at Sam Browne's camp at Gandamak, scene of the 44th Regiment's last stand in January, 1842, to negotiate. Agreement was reached in late May. Yakub surrendered control of foreign policy and accepted a British representative at Kabul in return for an annual subsidy of six lakhs (600,000) of rupees and guaranteed protection against foreign foes. Land was not ceded, but border districts including the Kurram Valley came under 'the protection and administrative control' of the British government, while the Khyber Pass remained in British hands.[58]

Meanwhile Roberts impressed the neighbouring clans by inviting them to witness the Queen's birthday parade of his troops on 24 May at Ali Khel. In the afternoon an impromptu rifle competition was got up. The Gordon Highlanders' regimental historian proudly recorded that Afghan marksmen found they could not match the Gordons' best shots with Martini Henry rifles. Athletic sports and a horse show were staged, at which Roberts's grey Arab charger 'Vonolel' carried off first prize. In the evenings all ranks enjoyed open-air concerts round a huge bonfire. Roberts's care for his men began to forge long-lasting comradeship with the Gordons and Gurkhas.[59]

In mid-July, Cavagnari arrived en route to Kabul with a staff of three and an escort of seventy-five men of the Corps of Guides. Roberts and a strong force accompanied him as far as the boundary just beyond Ali Khel where his Afghan escort would meet him. At a farewell dinner good wishes were exchanged. Despite Cavagnari's outward high spirits, foreboding overhung the occasion. In all minds was the fate of Alexander Burnes, British envoy murdered at Kabul in 1841. Hanna pointed out that 'never did a state of peace bear stronger resemblance to a state of war': British and Indian troops constantly on the alert, convoys strongly escorted, supplies at famine prices.[60] In London former viceroy, John Lawrence, foretold the worst: 'They will all be killed.'[61] Roberts bade Cavagnari an emotional farewell. Cavagnari proceeded to Kabul, where he took up residence on 24 July in the Bala Hissar, 'the high fortress' above the city. Roberts returned to Simla where he his wife were honoured guests at dinner at Lytton's residence. Edith Lytton noted that Haines had not written a line to Roberts to congratulate him on his victory or his knighthood awarded among honours given by Parliament. The Lyttons believed Haines to be jealous of Roberts's success.[62]

Afghan events took a dramatic turn. Cavagnari and his escort of Guides were attacked, overwhelmed and massacred on 3 September after several hours of heroic resistance against impossible odds. Jemadar Jawant Singh led the last eight Guides in a final sortie, striking down their foes before being overwhelmed. Roberts's avenging army recorded later: 'The annals of no army and no regiment can show a brighter record of bravery than has been achieved by this small band of Guides.'[63]

Subsequent investigation showed that the Amir had not planned the attack. Could he have saved Cavagnari? Yakub had sent both his son and his commander-in-chief, Daud Shah, to plead, the latter thrown from his horse by the mutinous soldiers. A mullah urged him to use his artillery or 'go and die rather than disgrace Islam'. He tore his hair and clothes, but continued to disgrace Islam. His fate was sealed by his failure: as Donald Stewart said, if Yakub could not save the embassy, he was no use as an ally.[64]

The news reached Simla via a political officer at an intermediate station. For Lytton the news was shattering. To Disraeli he wrote that day, 5 September: 'The web of policy so carefully and patiently woven has been rudely shattered. We have now to weave a fresh and, I fear, a wider one . . .'[65] To begin the weaving Roberts's column was best placed, just eighty-five miles from Kabul. Browne's and Stewart's forces were tied down in garrisons and on lines of support. Lytton was also using his most successful general; his confidence in Roberts's military ability was shown in his letter to Nora Roberts of the previous December.[66] At noon on 5 September there was a conference at the viceroy's residence, Roberts received his briefing from Lytton and from Haines, and prepared to depart. Accompanied by his wife he travelled as far as Umballa on the 7th, where they separated. Roberts wrote in his diary, 'God help her and bless her – I am travelling as fast as I can to Kurram.'[67]

He found his force assembling, desperately short of transport. It numbered 192 officers and 6,425 men, 2,558 of them British, and 6,000 camp followers.[68] Two Gatling guns the armourers attempted with limited success to make fit for action. His infantry regiments were hardened Highlanders, Gurkhas and Sikhs, and serving with the 92nd (the Gordons) was a future field marshal, George White. A brigade command was given to Lytton's military secretary, Thomas Baker, like Roberts an active and ambitious soldier. He had served in Wolseley's 'Ashanti Ring' in 1873 as QMG. Was this a 'job', a favour to Lytton? Cambridge wrote from London to protest. Baker showed himself a competent fighting leader.[69] The cavalry brigadier Massy proved a headache, 'very lazy and careless'.[70] Chief of staff, Colonel Charles MacGregor, was an intelligent and experienced veteran of the North-West Frontier. He confided in a highly critical diary which has interested historians. Among political officers was the young Mortimer Durand, son of Henry Durand, hero of the capture of Ghazni in the First Afghan War. The son had edited his father's account of the war, and Roberts had a copy with him. Native assistants were Nawab Gholam Hussein Khan, who had spent many years on the frontier, respected by Napier;[71] and Mohammed Hayat Khan, who had served with both John Nicholson and Cavagnari. These men gave Roberts their considerable experience, but he was determined not to play second fiddle to the 'politicals' including their chief Lt-Colonel E.G. Hastings.

He was joined by his old friend James Hills. Hills had served with Donald Stewart in the first phase of the war, twice mentioned in despatches. Promotion to major-general left him without a post. He eagerly joined the column. Neville Chamberlain, nephew of the general of the same name, came onto Roberts's staff. He was to remain a supporter and champion of 'the little man', defending him against Henry Hanna's 'pestilential and biased history'.[72] Howard Hensman of the Allahabad *Pioneer* and Luther Vaughan of *The Times*, a former soldier, joined Roberts. Their attitude was altogether supportive.

Roberts later reckoned the eighty-five-mile march to Kabul in the face of Afghan resistance and with transport so inadequate that only half his force could move at a time as a greater feat than the three hundred to Kandahar.[73] The 3rd Sikhs, 'a regiment always well equipped', gave up ninety of its camels. MacGregor issued orders to send on every beast able to take the road, however sick and feeble. Hussein Khan and Hayat Khan negotiated with the local tribes. Ghilzai chieftain Allud-ud-Din received a bribe of 2,000 rupees monthly and a present of 3,000.[74] The small force advanced with MacGregor complaining to his diary, but not to his commander, about 'all this blackmail paying' and 'the carelessness and happy-go-lucky style in which we do things' – 'the whole line of march was sprawling along three times as long as it need . . .'[75] Speedy revenge was what the viceroy wanted. On the 25th an attack by Mangal tribesmen was routed by Sikhs and Highlanders. Roberts had remained at Ali Khel long enough to give the impression that he did not intend an advance until the spring, while Baker advanced to establish a camp at Kushi, halfway to Kabul, hidden in a great ravine three miles long and half a mile wide. Roberts had already issued on 16 September a proclamation to the Afghan people stating that the British purpose was to punish those responsible for the murders and to strengthen the Amir's authority; those who did not oppose him had nothing to fear. Yakub had already sent two of his ministers to beg Roberts to wait, giving him time to disarm his troops and raise fresh levies. When relentless advance continued, Yakub fled from Kabul, riding through the night of 26–27 September. He pleaded for a halt. Roberts, consulting Simla, replied that British public opinion would not tolerate delay. Both he and Lytton believed rapid vengeance would demonstrate Britain's power to deal with treachery against her representatives. He also believed 'that the lesson of the Indian mutiny was to act swiftly and with resolution'.[76] The Amir was more prisoner than honoured guest.

Yakub's flight simplified things. On 1 October Roberts concentrated his force, and on the 2nd there was a 'great march of transport', he told his diary. It was still insufficient, but the day was his forty-seventh birthday, and he marked it with champagne. He issued a further proclamation: the city of Kabul would be occupied, those guilty of attacking the mission punished, anyone armed in the city or nearby would be treated as an enemy. If the Afghans resisted, they and not he would be responsible for what followed. At dawn on 5 October, troops were fired upon from the village of Koti Khel. In retaliation three villagers were killed and five captured, of whom three more were immediately shot on Roberts's orders for being in rebellion against their lawful ruler, the Amir, a specious argument.[77]

Roberts advanced again across open cultivated country, watched by groups of armed tribesmen. Early in the afternoon the vanguard reached a group of villages known as Charasiab. Ahead loomed a crescent-shaped range of hills running roughly east-west, between 700 and 1,500 feet above the plain. As part of his force was still to come up, Roberts encamped nearby. Uncharacteristically he had made a mistake not seizing the pass ahead, but he was to correct it the next morning.

At dawn the rising sun showed masses of regular troops with artillery deploying on the heights. Superior enemy numbers were in front and behind, and Brigadier Macpherson had yet to come up with an awkward mass of baggage animals. Sending a message to Macpherson to join him before dark, and a squadron of cavalry to help him fight through, Roberts resolved to attack. He made the enemy's weak point, their right flank, his target and would then roll up their line. He sent forward Brigadier Baker with 2,500 men, Highlanders, Gurkhas, Punjabis, Bengal sappers and miners, guns and the two Gatlings, retaining 1,300 men as a reserve protecting the camp. Baker split his force in two. As a feint, George White approached the Sang-i-Nawishta defile, where the enemy had concentrated their guns, assuming the main British attack would be there.[78] After fierce resistance, Baker's men seized the enemy's forward position. They then moved forward in a series of short rushes against the second position. As men were withdrawn from the defile to oppose Baker, White was able to outflank the defenders. Seeing one of the Gatlings jammed immediately and the other had no effect, White led two companies of the 92nd against a conical hill controlling the gorge through which the British must pass. He took the hilltop, but still faced overwhelming numbers. As Baker's main attack on the right diverted attention, White moved forward boldly, detaching two companies to assist Baker. Baker and White's relentless advance was too much for the Afghans, despite superior numbers. They disintegrated and fled, leaving their twenty guns to be taken.

It had been a critical action: failure or even serious hesitation would probably have meant the total destruction of Roberts's divided force. MacGregor not unfairly said that to Baker and White belonged the honours of the fight, but Hanna pointed out they and every man under their orders had 'felt the inspiring influence of their commander's indomitable courage, and unshakeable confidence in himself and them'. Roberts's relief is shown in his diary: 'Enemy assembled in large numbers early in the morning on range between Charasia and Kabul. Ordered Baker to turn them out. Great victory – captured 20 guns.'[79]

On 9 October he discovered the enemy had fled during the night. The following evening his force encamped on a ridge overlooking the city of Kabul. Remembering the lessons of the First War, Roberts had issued strict instructions against looting or 'intimacy' with Afghan women. Major Mitford of the cavalry had to intervene at one point, firing shots over the heads of camp followers attempting to pillage.[80] On the 11th Roberts rode across to Sherpur, a great parallelogram of a cantonment, 2,700 yards by 1,100, as yet incomplete. Here the British found Yakub's extensive artillery, no less than 214 guns.[81] On the 11th Roberts visited the Bala Hissar and the Residency where Cavagnari and the Guides had made their last stand. The reporter Hensman wrote:

> [W]e entered the main court of the Residency, and were soon thoroughly able to appreciate the fate of its defenders . . . The whitewashed walls are here and there bespattered with blood . . . in one room in which I went there can be no doubt fire had been used for [burning bodies]. The ashes were in the middle of the chamber, and near them were two skulls and a heap of human bones still fetid . . . a desperate struggle had taken place in this room, the blood stains on the floor and walls being clearly discernible.[82]

A mass of charred timbers was still smoking although set alight six weeks before.[83]

The young Mortimer Durand disapproved of Roberts's treating Yakub with contempt and listening to his enemies. MacGregor thought Durand going on about justice for Yakub when the bones of Cavagnari cried for vengeance and 'treating these fiends with justice of the high court kind was sickening'. MacGregor was afraid Durand and the chief political officer Lt-Colonel Hastings had shaken Roberts's determination.[84] He need not have worried.

Roberts's orders from Simla were to 'assume and exercise supreme administrative authority'. He thus had political as well as military power. Lytton appreciated that his political position at Kabul was 'undoubtedly a delicate one'; 'the character and extent of your political authority ought, in my opinion, to be properly defined and proclaimed with the least possible delay'.[85] On 12 October his whole force lined both sides of the road approaching the citadel, bands playing, swords drawn, bayonets fixed as the infantry presented arms. Roberts with his brigadiers and influential Kabuli Sirdars rode along the ranks and entered the fortress, where the Union Jack was hoisted. Roberts's earliest biographer wrote: 'Around the British commander crowded the Afghan Sirdars, ready to make any promises to their conqueror, and equally ready, as the event proved, to break them. At his side stood Musa Khan, a child eight years of age, heir-apparent of the Amir. . .'[86] The people looked on, much as they had in 1839, neither enthusiastic nor welcoming. The city was a tangle of dark, filthy, narrow streets and alleys. There were well-stocked bazaars. A foreign army with its money brought profit to the merchants.[87] For Roberts, following in his father's footsteps to the Afghan capital, this was a proud moment. George White, however, wanted retribution: 'I would have made the march through Cabul a hotter one for the people than ours has been. An Army sent to avenge the second Ambassador of ours murdered in Cabul ought to have razed it to the ground, instead of sprinkling rose water about as we are doing.'[88] Roberts was soon to show he was not a man for rose water.

CHAPTER SIX

'One equal temper of heroic hearts'

We have nearly eaten all our provisions, and if we were to get worsted, not only would the whole country be up, but we should get no supplies. I hope Bobs' luck will carry him through; but we are playing a risky game.

BRIGADIER CHARLES MACGREGOR, KABUL, OCTOBER 1879

Everything depends upon Ayub Khan being defeated without delay . . . The situation here is of the gravest.

LEPEL GRIFFIN, 27 JULY 1880

The men were veterans all, inured to fatigue and of the highest fighting quality . . .

CAPTAIN G. J. YOUNGHUSBAND

At Kabul Roberts found an extensive correspondence from the Russians, Kaufmann and Stolietov, to Sher Ali and his *wazir* (prime minister). This appeared to confirm the Amir's treachery. One damning letter told Sher Ali to treat the English 'with deceit and deception', another advised him 'to make peace openly and in secret prepare for war'.[1]

On 16 October an explosion of gunpowder in the Bala Hissar killed Captain Shafto of the Royal Artillery and fifteen Gurkhas. A second followed two hours later and then a series of smaller explosions. A young subaltern of the Coldstreams, Reginald Pole-Carew, narrowly escaped. The chief magazine holding a million rounds of ammunition, 450 tons of gunpowder and 'arms and equipment and guns without end' was close by, but did not go up.[2] This strengthened Roberts's decision to make Sherpur his base. The

Bala Hissar was marked for destruction, but dire threats were not carried out, presumably because of pressure of events. The viceroy and his council had urged this measure as a 'signal punishment'.[3]

Roberts's third proclamation read to the Sirdars was harsher than the previous two. He condemned the inhabitants of the city as rebels against the Amir assisting the murder of Cavagnari and his escort. He instituted martial law ten miles around Kabul and the death penalty for anyone carrying a weapon within five miles. Rewards were offered for the apprehension of those who had taken part in the attack or resisted the British. Razing the city as retribution would be justified, but not carried out. Instead, buildings interfering with the safety of the British force would be levelled. He would appoint a military governor 'with the consent of the Ameer [sic]'.[4]

This last was ingenuous. For Yakub had abdicated, saying he would rather be a grass-cutter in the British camp than rule at Kabul.[5] Roberts having won on the battlefield was now faced with a political vacuum. Lytton agreed by telegram to Yakub's abdication. James Hills, Roberts's old friend, became military governor of Kabul. His assistant, the frontier veteran Gholam Hassein Khan, helped interview Yakub.[6] Stewart at Kandahar thought an Afghan would have been a wiser choice 'because the Governor if a man of influence would have had his own party at any rate on his side'.[7] Roberts took into custody some of the chief men of Kabul and established two commissions. The first led by MacGregor with Surgeon-Major Bellew and Mohammed Hayat Khan, both experienced in the frontier, was to investigate those accused of the attack on the Residency and recommend punishment; the second under Brigadier Massy was to try them. The only officer at Kabul belonging to the Judge Advocate General's Department was not on either commission.[8]

Roberts urged on these commissions; it was the darkest episode in his life. Yet, given the circumstances, something of the sort was bound to happen. Colonel Edward Chapman writing from Kandahar told Hills that he and Roberts had been 'brought together singularly enough to carry [out] suitably the punishment we are to inflict'.[9] Even the viceroy's charming wife writing to Baker gloried in the contemplation of vengeance:

> I think it was a great relief when you got to Cabul, & now that one daily hears of some of the vile murderers being captured, one can lift up one's head again. I delight in the idea of the Bala Hissar being destroyed, & the more of the brutes of Cabulese who are punished for their wicked deeds the better pleased shall we be.[10]

Her husband, deeply upset at the loss of his friend Cavagnari, had given Roberts clear instructions:

> You cannot stop to pick and choose ringleaders. Every soldier of the Herati regiments is ipso facto guilty and so is every civilian, be he priest, or layman, mullah or peasant, who joined the mob of assassins. To satisfy

FIGURE 5 *Roberts and Sirdars at Kabul, winter 1879–1880. Roberts's political mistakes at Kabul stand in contrast to his fighting success. He later claimed the majority of Kabuli Sirdars were with him at Sherpur during the siege. They were, as virtual prisoners (National Army Museum).*

the conventions of English sentiment it will probably be necessary to inflict death only in execution of the verdict of some sort of judicial authority. But any such authority should be of the roughest and readiest kind such as a drumhead Court Martial. It is not justice in the ordinary sense, but retribution that you have to administer on reaching Kabul . . .'[11]

The attitude of Roberts, who had seen sepoys blown from the mouths of guns in the Punjab in 1857 and 'Pandies' strung up to trees, was clear enough. The forthright Cavagnari had spoken 'with the highest admiration of Roberts as a general & as a politician with the tribes'; they were men of the same stamp, daring to a fault, ready for war to the hilt with Afghans.[12]

Nonetheless, despite strong motives for revenge, the executions that followed were wrong. Most were unjust: clear testimony was not forthcoming, and innocent Afghans were caught in the net of vengeance. Men like MacGregor and George White, hot for revenge at first, changed their tune.[13] Roberts justified martial law by his men's need for protection, but it has never been the usage of war to shoot men for defending their homes. Hanna blamed Lytton's instructions to Roberts 'based on the assumption that every Afghan might justly be held responsible for the massacre of the British Embassy' and thus leaving their 'fatal mark on the proceedings of the military commission'.[14] Far from cowing the Kabulis the executions stirred up an Afghan hornets' nest and produced storms in the Indian press, the British newspapers and finally Parliament. MacGregor claimed to be determined not to sentence men to death unjustly, but other than condemning Roberts as 'the most bloodthirsty little beast I know' he did little enough for the victims.[15] Perhaps like so many men in a similar spot, he put his career first. The two correspondents with Roberts, Hensman of the Allahabad *Pioneer* and Vaughan of *The Times*, were not critical. Hanna claims that the former accompanied the force 'in contravention of the Government's orders', but he had been authorised.[16] Hensman took Roberts's side throughout; the army's action was just retribution.[17] Vaughan had been sent by Lord Lytton. He recorded Robert's cordial greeting: 'Perhaps Lord Lytton had written to him favourably of me, or perhaps he was not displeased that the brave deeds of his army would now be chronicled in the leading newspaper of the world.'[18] Both were true. Lytton told Roberts: 'Vaughan is ready to write up any policy of which the cue is given to him by me, or by you on my behalf. His letters to the *Times* from Kabul may have a considerable effect upon public opinion at home . . .'[19] Vaughan's memoirs were favourable. One report to *The Times* repeated Roberts's assertion of the complicity of the Amir in Cavagnari's death.[20]

British injustice rolled inexorably forward. Nominal rolls of some Afghan regiments were found, the surrounding villages cordoned off and every man whose name appeared on the rolls was detained for trial. Mohammed Hayat Khan was deputed to examine witnesses in secret and produce their depositions rather than the witnesses themselves at the trials. Thus the accused had no way of knowing how the evidence had been extracted or of cross-examining. This was contrary to the principles of British justice. Over 160 came to trial and eighty-seven were hanged on the two tall gallows Robert erected outside the city gates.[21] One officer wrote: 'I have all along been dead against the indiscriminate hanging and shooting of the common prisoners, who merely obeyed orders in fighting us, while the headmen who gave these orders were simply placed under arrest, and it is absurd to call these people "rebels" and "insurgents".'[22]

Hills believed in the guilt of one big fish: the Kotwal or chief constable. A Guides' Rissaldar who had been on leave in the city testified that he had fomented the outbreak and then had the bodies treated with contumely. In a report which seems to have been prepared to help Roberts against the press, Hills stated that under the Kotwal's orders the burial 'was carried out in a brutal way, the bodies being dragged along the ground by their legs & flung over the wall into the ditch below'. 'Chowkedar Afhiz Khan was permitted to take [Cavagnari's] body away and without doubt the Kotwal must have sanctioned its being thrown into the refuse heap under the city gallows . . .' Hills also defended the execution of a ghazi carrying 'a large Afghan knife' hidden under his left arm 'bent on taking the life of the first European he came upon.[23]

Vaughan and Hensman may have been compliant, but others were not. On 1 November *The Bombay Review* questioned: 'Is it according to the usages of war to treat as felons men who resist invasion?' On 17 November, *The Times of India*, praising an amnesty Roberts had proclaimed early that month, declared that the work of vengeance had become 'somewhat indiscriminate', and 'regretted that a good many innocent persons should have been hanged while [Roberts] was making up his mind as to their degree of guilt'. On the 21st *The Friend of India*, a prominent Calcutta journal, feared Roberts had done Britain 'serious national injury by lowering our reputation for justice in the eyes of Europe'.[24]

Meanwhile Lytton and the British government were uncertain of Afghanistan's political future. Roberts was faced with the necessity of laying in food and forage for the winter. Resistance led to his men burning villages, smashing corn-bins, seizing livestock and stores of grain.[25] This, the hangings and the dispatch of Yakub under escort to India, fuelled the campaign led by the Mullah Mushk-i-Alam to raise *jihad* under the leadership of Mohammed Jan, an able Sirdar and artillery officer. Roberts's intelligence showed that bodies of men from south, north and west were advancing to concentrate at Kabul where they would be joined by inhabitants of the city and neighbouring villages. The bold Roberts over-reached himself. He sent Brigadiers Macpherson to the north to prevent a junction and Baker to cut off the retreat. More news of a large force of Kohistanis caused him to change his orders to deal with this new threat. On the morning of 11 December, Brigadier Massy advanced with a reduced mounted force, not along the road as Roberts had directed, but across a countryside bisected with irrigation ditches.[26] Massy with barely 300 men found himself confronted by the main Afghan force of 10,000 men. Two cavalry charges ended in something akin to rout, guns bogged in ditches; Roberts arrived post-haste and nearly lost his own life, being unhorsed and rescued by a cavalry *sowar*. His muscular chaplain the Rev. J.W. Adams pulled two cavalrymen from a ditch, for which he was awarded the Victoria Cross.[27] Roberts displayed 'presence of mind and clear insight' (Hanna's words) by sending Hills to summon Brownlow and 200 Highlanders to frustrate an enemy approach on Sherpur. What saved him, however, was not his presence of mind, but Brigadier Macpherson's initiative marching to the sound of Massy's guns, striking the enemy in flank and rear, dispersing them despite their superior numbers. MacGregor rescued the lost guns. At midnight the Corps of Guides arrived as reinforcements, after a forced march of thirty miles. With them was a newly-joined subaltern, George Younghusband, who never forgot his first meeting with Roberts that critical December.[28]

On the 12th, 13th and 14th Roberts sent out his brigades to disperse the enemy, but in vain. The Afghan masses were too strong, despite a brilliant charge by Captain Vousden and ten sowars of the 5th Punjab Cavalry dispersing several hundred Afghans. Vousden received the Victoria Cross and the seven surviving sowars the Indian Order of Merit.[29] Roberts now concentrated his defences on Sherpur, allocating troops to the extensive perimeter, ordering them to conserve ammunition and rely on the bayonet if the enemy broke in. In places the walls were incomplete, and the defenders worked hard to fill gaps. He had 7,000 men along 8,000 yards. On the night of 19 December it was bitterly cold and snow began to fall. 'The Afghan hills have put on their wedding garments to celebrate the beleaguering of the Kafirs,' wrote George White.[30] Many remembered the fate of Elphinstone's brigade in the winter of 1841–2. The Afghans hoped to repeat that success. Mortimer Durand recorded 'something very like a panic' and the despair of some officers. News of the arrival of Charles Gough's brigade at nearby Lataband, signalled by heliograph, cheered everyone. It was not Roberts's nature to wait passively, but as Haines commented sagely to Cambridge after the fighting of 11–14 December: 'He has now had a lesson he will never forget'.[31]

On 22 December Afghans were seen moving out of Kabul in large numbers. Spies, especially a cavalry *rissalder*'s servant, warned of an assault planned early next morning, the signal being Mushk-i-Alam lighting a signal fire on the Asmai Heights. An attack on the south wall would be a demonstration; the main attack would be against Bemaru village and the east. Mohamed Jan had no siege artillery; Roberts's seizing the Afghan guns on his arrival now reaped its reward. Afghan scaling ladders proved too short, in places at least. Before first light on the 23rd the men stood to. The signal fire on the Asmai Heights burst forth. Hanna who was present wrote that 'men's hearts stood still with astonishment and awe'. Then Roberts's guns fired starshell followed by case shot, and the infantry massed volleys. If the Afghans had broken in by weight of numbers, the garrison might have

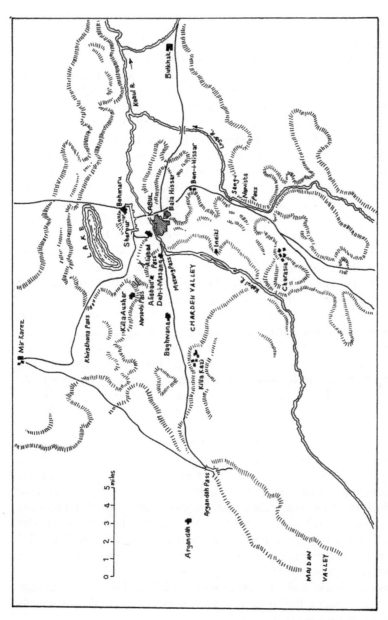

Approach to Kabul and the Chardeh Valley

MAP 6 *Approach to Kabul and the Chardeh Valley*

been destroyed. The Afghans could not breach the walls, and enfilade fire turned the defences' apparently weakest sector into a killing ground.[32] After four hours, the attack weakened. Mid-morning, Roberts seized his chance, sent out guns to enfilade the enemy and then cavalry to pursue as they fell back. Without modern artillery and faced by a resolute leader and his men, the Afghans' great effort had failed. Roberts suffered five dead and twenty-five wounded; he estimated Afghan dead at 3,000; total British and Indian losses in December had been 103 dead and 262 wounded. The Russian General Soboleff wrote later that the attack was 'a feint' to allow Mohammed Jan to draw off his forces; if true – and it seems unlikely given the life-and-death struggle – it was one of the most expensive feints in history.[33]

With the hour of danger past, Mortimer Durand in his diary had some fun at Roberts's expense: 'The Genl now estimates the enemy at 60,000 – and has officially reported to Govt "over 50,000". MacGregor says that on the 23rd "there may possibly have been 15,000". Such are the materials from wh[ich] History is made.' Whatever the odds, across the Empire men breathed relief. From his headquarters at Pretoria, Garnet Wolseley told the Duke of Cambridge: 'I have just heard by telegraph from India of General Roberts' brilliant victory at Cabul on the 23rd Dec. and was delighted to find that he was following his success up in an abler manner. I succeeded him as Sir Hope Grant's Q.M.G. in 1858 immediately after the taking of Lucknow. He was then a most promising officer.'[34]

The following morning, Christmas Eve, Brigadier Charles Gough marched into Sherpur with his 2,700 men. The Afghan thousands had gone. Mohammed Jan, the Mushk-i-Alam and Yakub's son Musa Jan newly proclaimed as Amir escaped to Ghazni. Letting Musa Khan get away was a mistake by Roberts and his staff, but not a serious one. An eight-year-old was at best a figurehead. The British reoccupied Kabul and the Bala Hissar. Not everyone was sorry. Hindu traders told of a reign of terror in the city from 15 December. Many of these feared Afghan reprisals when the British left – as they thought they must – and fled to Peshawar.[35] The Quizzilbashes of Persian descent had been spared only on taking an oath on the Koran and promising to become good Muslims.[36] The insurgents had smashed up the medical dispensary which Roberts's doctors had established. It was soon back in working order, treating over 200 patients, mainly for opthalmia and cataract.[37] James Hills had taken refuge in Sherpur, but then returned as city governor before passing the position to Sirdar Wali Mahmed Khan. He specially drew to Roberts's attention his native assistants who had 'been most willing and zealous in the performance of any duties'.[38]

On New Year's Eve Roberts's Highlanders celebrated their survival with hot whisky and water. Enthusiastic volunteer musicians took instruments from grinning bandsmen and

> marched along the frozen path in front of the barracks all the way to the Headquarters' gateway, making the night hideous with their din. At the

Staff Quarters, loud calls were for 'the General'. At length he appeared, somewhat *deshabille* indeed, but enjoying the fun, and saying good-naturedly, 'Well, the 92nd have always come to the front when I called on *them*, so I suppose I must do the same now.'[39]

One belated casualty of the fighting was the cavalry brigadier, Massy. He had been dilatory in the advance on Kabul[40] and had mishandled the action on 11 December, ignoring Roberts's instructions to stay on the road and trying to cut across country.[41] He merited removal, but some suspected Roberts was deflecting the blame for his setback in the fighting of early December.[42] Roberts submitted his account of events including Massy's version, and hoped that although he would not be employed in the field again, certainly not with him, other work might be found. Haines determined that the events of 11 December 'shew [sic] Brigadier-Massy to have been as wanting in judgment as in military appreciation'. His misconduct led to loss of life and four guns, although not to the failure of Roberts's plan. Haines refused to give Massy other employment.[43] The Duke of Cambridge, however, overturned this judgement; Massy was eventually promoted major-general to command in Ceylon.[44] Baker's belief that Massy's father had influence with the press may well have been true,[45] for a correspondent of the *Civil & Military Gazette* of 21 May 1880 wrote: 'One officer in high position assured me the other day that if the duke [of Cambridge] could have his own way, General Roberts would be shelved for good.' He claimed that an official at the War Office had declared: 'There was nothing to save Roberts ... the facts were so strongly against him.'[46] Another controversy found its way into the papers to Roberts's discredit.

Despite Massy, Roberts had again defeated the enemy, but now came the reckoning over the hangings. So confident were Roberts and Lytton that public opinion would support the desire for vengeance that little was hidden in the published despatches. Frederic Harrison, bitterest critic, author of 'Martial Law at Kabul' in the radical John Morley's *Fortnightly Review*, stated that he drew his information from Roberts's despatches and Howard Hensman's reports in the *Daily News* and *Pioneer*.[47] On 3 January Roberts received telegrams from Calcutta: one from Colley warning that the hangings had caused much excitement at home; another from Lyall, the Indian government's Foreign Secretary, disapproving of his deportation of Afghans to India. The telegram strongly warned him to avoid undue severity in dealing with insurgents and to treat them as belligerents. Both Colley and Lyall were close to Lytton; it appeared the viceroy now repented. Roberts was much upset, and talked of resigning. He asked Mortimer Durand for help.[48]

Harrison's article in the *Fortnightly Review* of December 1879 was the strongest attack in Britain.[49] In the Commons, Charles Dilke and others questioned discrepancies between Lytton's statements and Roberts's despatches.[50] The Peace Society meeting on 29 December 1879 called upon the people of Britain to repudiate 'the system of terrorism'. On advice from

Simla, Roberts prepared counter-arguments. On 3 February *The Times* published a telegram forwarded by Nora Roberts's brother-in-law J.D. Sherston of Evercreech from his son Lieutenant Jack Sherston, Roberts's ADC: 'No one executed unless convicted of attack on Residency. No soldier shot for fighting against us. Fuller explanations submitted to Government, which I am confident will be considered satisfactory.'[51] The fuller explanation was Roberts's letter read by Viscount Cranbrook, Secretary of State for India, in the Lords on 13 February, offering 'a short explanation of what has really occurred since we entered Afghanistan last September', justifying martial law and the prohibition of firearms by pleading defence of his men 'among a nation of fanatics' and denying that Afghans were 'hanged for the simple fact of their having fought against us'. This last was patently untrue. There was, however, enough truth in the rest to make it plausible. The majority of Kabuli Sirdars had, for example, been with Roberts at Sherpur during the attack, as he claimed, but they were virtual prisoners.

As Cranbrook finished reading 'there were loud cheers from both sides of the House' showing the Lords' sympathy when Roberts's force might have been destroyed. *The Times* leader declared that the letter 'sets at rest some very painful questions', that it would be 'ridiculous' to complain of the actions of a general exposed to such dangers and that the conduct of the British Army was 'merciful and generous'.[52] The advantage of a good pen enabled the government to survive the immediate storm, but did not end the difficult questions. Roberts could have been hoisted by his own correspondent: on 13 December, contrary to the claim that no one was executed without trial, Hensman reported four Maliks and four servants were shot out of hand.[53]

The Indian and British governments had backed their star general, but were seriously worried. Lytton had expected the investigation to find evidence of important men's guilt, but only the Kotwal was executed. Others hanged were small fry and not instigators.[54] At the end of January 1880 Lytton admitted: '[Roberts] is a splendid soldier; but his management of the political situation has not been altogether as judicious as I had hoped it would be; and, unfortunately, the strongest men about him have hitherto been officers destitute of political or administrative training, and incompetent to give him good advice or assistance in any but military matters.' The Indian government sent up Lepel Griffin, the experienced chief secretary to the Punjab government, to hold Roberts's hand. He had not been well served by Hastings, his chief 'political', and while Durand criticised in his diary he seems to have exercised no restraint. Roberts thought that the treacherous murder of Cavagnari and his escort and Lytton's instructions gave him *carte blanche*. It was pointless his protesting that the Afghans 'received much more consideration than was shown to the peoples of India in 1857–8'. Times had changed.[55]

It was not just Roberts's political fumbling that caused the Indian government to order Donald Stewart to march from Kandahar to Kabul where, as senior, he would take command. Kandahar had been quiet, aided by a good harvest in southern Afghanistan. Gholam Hussein Khan had transferred there as governor; 'by his wisdom and justice he had become most popular with the Afghans'.[56] Kabul was the centre of events, and there was still no political solution. Rivals for the amirship, Abdur Rahman, Sher Ali's nephew and pensionary of the Russians, and Ayub Khan, Sher Ali's son and Herati Sirdar, were on the move.[57] Stewart was unhappy leaving Major-General Primrose in charge at Kandahar, 'a very poor selection . . . neither safe nor strong I fancy', he told Hills. Primrose's Bombay troops were new to the region, ignorant of 'ways & methods of dealing with the people'.[58] Oliver St John had political authority with Primrose; the local Wali Sher Ali would succeed as ruler of Kandahar, and Stewart wanted to see him established.[59] On 30 March Stewart mustered 7,000 men and equal camp followers with six weeks' supplies, and set forth through a bleak and empty countryside. His march took place during a British general election, and unlike Roberts later, he took no newspaperman. Colonel Edward Chapman, his chief of staff, praised his chief as being 'in intellect, in experience and in judgement a head and shoulders taller than the men who had the honour of serving under him. Not great, perhaps, as a strategist or tactician, but referring every matter to principle, and determined to do his duty at whatever cost . . .' The march was carried out under stringent discipline, 'neither troops nor followers allowed to enter a village except when detailed as part of an organised foraging party'. Stewart defeated the Afghans in a major battle at Ahmed Khel on 19 April and a lesser one at Arzu on the 23rd. At Ahmed Khel, two long lines of 3,000 fanatical swordsmen out of an army of over 12,000 'seemed to spring up from the hill' and charged headlong. The shock of the attack overran advanced positions. Stewart and his staff drew swords to defend themselves, but his men rallied, the Gurkhas forming squares and shooting down the attackers. Stewart's handling of the battle was far from perfect, but Afghan fanaticism was no match for disciplined firepower. Over 800 bodies were counted, and later Afghans erected a monument to 1,100 'martyrs' on the battlefield.[60] On 1 May Stewart reached the Argandab Valley where 'Bobs came out to see me, looking very jolly and well.' He entered Kabul the next day and took command.

During the march news reached the soldiers in Afghanistan of the election. A trade recession, bad harvests, blunders in the Zulu War in South Africa and the killing of Cavagnari's embassy turned the voters against Disraeli's government and its adventurous foreign policy. Gladstone emerged from retirement late in 1879 to fight the famous Midlothian campaign. Roberts's hangings and village burnings gave him ammunition: 'Remember the rights of the savage, as we call him. Remember that the happiness of his humble home, remember that the sanctity of life in the hill villages of Afghanistan among the winter snows, are as sacred in the eye of Almighty God as are your own.'[61] Results marked a huge swing to the Liberals, who secured a majority of 137. The Queen had no wish for Gladstone to succeed her favourite, but she had to summon the Ogre to kiss hands and form a ministry. Victoria's antipathy was equalled by the soldiers'. Stewart told his wife: 'The news received from home about the elections has put a sad damper on all our spirits . . . If the Liberals gain the day, everything that is being done here may be upset.'[62] For Roberts it was more serious: Lytton and the Conservatives had been his protectors, the radical Liberals his critics. 'The result of the elections has called forth a good many d[amn]s from the soldiers here,' wrote George White. 'I fancy Sir F[rederick] R[oberts] is about as much put out by it as anyone can be.'[63] Lytton resigned on the news of the Conservative defeat. His Liberal successor was Lord Ripon. Ripon had served as under-secretary of state for India in a previous administration, disliked imperial adventures and assumed British rule of India would lead to self-government. He was acutely critical of Roberts's methods, especially the 'constant burning of villages' and unimpressed by claims that Sher Ali had been plotting with the Russians. For him, the defeat of Disraeli was a victory over the powers of darkness.[64] Stewart told his wife that there was no telling what would happen after Lytton left; it would be a great shame 'if nothing were done' for Roberts, which he feared. 'He has done great service here, taking it at the estimate of those who are least friendly to him.'[65] Would his military usefulness outweigh political mistakes and brutal measures? Stewart wrote to Ripon defending his old friend and stating that reports reaching England regarding the destruction of villages were inaccurate. He was economical with the truth.[66]

Roberts was much upset by reports of him in the press 'as a murderer', he told Colley, and greatly put out by a report in the *Daily News* of 'a want of cordiality between myself and the Generals under my command'.[67] Early in June he telegraphed to Lytton, who was awaiting his successor. 'I ask your Excellency's permission to leave Kabul. I am not required here now. It is not possible to take an interest in the work and my health is not as good as it was. I am quite happy with General Stewart but my wish to leave is so strong I trust your Lordship will approve of my doing so.'

Lytton replied wisely: 'I deeply sympathise, but as your sincere friend most strongly urge you not to leave your post till close of war . . . I feel sure your premature retirement would be generally misinterpreted to your great detriment.'[68] His was not the only encouraging voice. Stewart had tipped off Hills: 'Bobs is talking of going away on M[edical] L[eave] as advised by his doctor. He tries to be jolly and does his very best, but he can't help feeling his position and it's affecting his health. I must say I could not stay willingly if I were in his place.' Hills, seeing his old friend 'terribly down in heart & nothing would keep him here', straightway 'flashed him to "stand fast" & wrote a very cheery letter telling him he must stick to his task till the very end'.[69] Roberts's chief political officer Lepel Griffin also submitted his angry resignation at the granting of political powers to Stewart, but was dissuaded.[70]

The Roberts-Lytton exchange appeared in the most 'official' of Roberts's biographies, supervised years after his death by his younger daughter.[71] By then the rest of his career outweighed this potentially embarrassing episode. Roberts took Lytton and Hills's advice. He was soon to have the chance of a lifetime.

Even before the election and change of government, Lytton argued for withdrawal after finding a friendly Amir. This was to be Abdur Rahman, Sher Ali's nephew, son of his chief rival in the civil war of 1863–8. He had sought asylum in Samarkand and become a Russian pensioner. The British wondered, was he still 'a slave of Russia'.[72] In January he left Samarkand to raise support. He played his cards well as a champion of the Prophet against invaders, but negotiating with Lepel Griffin as the best man for the British. Lytton's foreign minister told Griffin that Abdur had both administrative and military capacity and Griffin should seek terms.[73] In April Griffin with Roberts's agreement made clear that Abdur would be their man, Yakub would not be restored, nor would the British annex Afghanistan.

For by now the war had reached an *impasse*. The British were too strong to be beaten, but their control extended only as far as their rifles and artillery reached, costs were mounting and morale in Indian regiments away from home over two years was poor. Abdur had learnt his lessons in the civil war of the 1860s, to bide his time. If the Russians would not do business he could seek help elsewhere. His combination of studied opportunism and 'iron' character support Rob Johnson's argument that there is no single Afghan 'way of war', but adaptation to circumstance.[74]

Ripon arrived at Simla on 8 June, 1880 and declared his policy on the 27th along the lines established by Griffin and Lytton. Mushk-i-Alam and the insurgent chiefs had said they would recognise a British nominee as Amir.[75] Abdur Rahman seemed to accept British terms. 'You have resigned to me Afghanistan up to the limits which were settled of old by Treaty with my noble grandfather, the Amir Dost Muhammad Khan.' He did not say which treaty, Griffin and Stewart both hoping for clarification. Ripon decided to accept Abdur, and on 20 July Stewart was told to send him money and weapons and declare acceptance of him as *de facto* ruler of northern Afghanistan. At a durbar on 22 July, he was declared Amir. Hills described the meeting:

> Sir Donald Stewart, Lepel Griffin, self & a very large gathering of officers rode out some 400 yards & met Abdur Rahman & we all went into a tent & had almost a quarter of an hour's conversation with him. I am glad this came off, for . . . it still wanted this interview to finish our work here in right good form. The Amir is a man about 45 years of age but looks older – he seems very intelligent & has a much better face than any Sirdar we have yet come across. From his speeches & his manner & acts up to date we all think we have got the best man for the Amirship & we all devoutly hope that he will be able to hold his own – his having secured the Ghilzais & Kohistanis & got the great priest Mushk-Alam on his side.[76]

At the same time local wali (or ruler) Sher Ali was installed as ruler of Kandahar; some ladies of his family and court scorned his reliance on the infidel. At Herat, Ayub Khan, brother of Yakub, mustered unbeaten Herati regiments, strong artillery and skilful military engineers. Would he threaten the settlement reached? Primrose's Kandahar garrison found gaining intelligence of enemy movements difficult, as Haines explained: 'few of the Bombay officers have any knowledge of Persian or Pashto. Then the absence of the Pathan element in the ranks of the Bombay Army cuts off a source of obtaining information which has been found valuable in Sir Donald Stewart's force'.[77]

Ripon doubted a threat: 'Ayub has cried wolf, wolf, so often, he will never come,' said the viceroy at council, but he misquoted the fable. Haines remarked: 'Ayub is the wolf, we are the heedless shepherds ... Ayub *will* come, we shall have a disaster, and I shall be hanged for it.'[78] Ayub was an able commander and looked upon by many Afghans as their champion. As Stewart prepared to evacuate Kabul, leaving the capital and captured Afghan guns to the new Amir, British intelligence failed to track Ayub's moves. At Simla there were divided councils, Ripon wanting to order Primrose at Kandahar to lead out his whole force.[79] Instead a weak brigade under Burrows, only 2,500, was sent with the Wali Sher Ali's troops. The latter deserted, another case of Afghan treachery in British eyes. A minister of the Wali, who at Kandahar entertained British officers in his own home, led them over to Ayub.

On 27 July at Maiwand, Burrows's 2,000 riflemen, 500 sabres and twelve guns faced Ayub's 8,000 regular troops, thirty-two guns, 3,000 other mounted men, with probably 15,000 tribesmen and ghazis. After more than four hours' fighting, defeat came suddenly. The British smooth-bore battery withdrew to refill its limbers. A host of Afghans rose from folds in the ground to envelope Burrows's line of battle. The brigade was overwhelmed. One hundred men of a veteran British battalion, the 66th, made a heroic stand and inflicted huge losses. Afghan casualties were said to be *beshumar* – 'countless': 1,500 regulars and double that number tribesmen. Burrows lost nearly 1,000 dead and only 168 wounded. It was news of British defeat, not Afghan losses, that rang round the Empire. A Jemadar reached Kandahar with a message that the day was lost and the whole force massacred. This story was telegraphed to London and read to the Commons that night. The survivors, however, staged a fighting although disorderly retreat, plagued mainly by thirst as Afghans stopped to loot. One party of sepoys faithfully guarded the pay chest of 13,000 silver rupees. Brigadier Brooke led out a force and withdrew the beaten brigade into Kandahar.[80]

The garrison was reasonably strong, 5,000 men and thirteen guns to defend walls of 6,000 yards. Primrose expelled the Afghan population to prevent treachery. On 8 August Ayub's main force arrived and his artillery opened a continuous bombardment. On the 13th they occupied two suburbs.[81] Across the Empire, men lamented the defeat – 'the melancholy catastrophe in Afghanistan – the most terrible which has occurred since the Mutiny'[82] – and that so small a force had been sent. An imperial riposte was necessary, to beat Ayub, restore prestige and ensure Abdur. The first anxiety of Liberal War Secretary Childers was for India: 'What however we have most to fear is the effect all over India of such serious news . . .'.[83] A British relief force from Baluchistan, the nearest approach to Kandahar, was obvious, but on 30 July 'Anglo-Indian' wrote to *The Times*:

> Surely General Stewart could spare 10,000 troops, under that magnificent fighting General Sir F. Roberts, to make a rapid march on Ghazni, and co-operate thence with the force advancing from Quetta for the relief of the garrison of Candahar? The veteran regiments which took Cabul last autumn might be trusted to do this march with equal expedition and as brilliant success. It is no use to say anything more about Abdurrahman till Ayoob has been disposed of . . . What then is Sir D. Stewart waiting for? The roads are open, and the garrison of Candahar is in deadly peril.[84]

What followed put into the shade the hangings at Kabul. News of Maiwand reached Simla on 28 July.[85] Stewart was asked whether troops should be sent from Kabul. His first instinct was doubtful, but he soon changed his mind. With his approval, Roberts proposed to Greaves, adjutant-general at Simla, leading an elite striking force while Stewart evacuated Kabul. Stewart summarised arguments to his wife on 31 July:

> [T]he present question is the relief of Candahar and the defeat of Ayub. I have a fine force ready for the work, and Bobs would go in command of it. I know it would beat Ayub into a cocked hat; but there are objections to sending a force away by itself through a country which is sure to be hostile, and we should rouse animosities, which would bring about further complications, and, perhaps, prevent our withdrawal from Cabul. Still, if the work cannot be done from the Quetta side, *our* troops must be employed, whatever the risks and inconveniences may be. Bobs is very eager to go . . .

The force Roberts would take would be nearly twice as strong as his had been. He and Lepel Griffin both supported Roberts's proposal.[86]

On the Quetta side, there were serious delays. Major-General Phayre of the Bombay Army took a fortnight to assemble transport animals to cross Baluchistan's scorching desert, and faced a tribal uprising fomented by the news of Maiwand. Expecting to start mid-August, he did not march until the 30th, and on 5 September was just drawing clear of the Khojak Pass.[87]

At Simla the dithering stopped. Ripon had been one of Roberts's hottest critics, but as viceroy he had to ensure Ayub was knocked out. Roberts's earlier victories decided him. On 29 July Haines was still considering troops being sent from England, but Ripon told his commander-in-chief that he had ordered Stewart to prepare to despatch a force.[88] On 30 July the viceroy's council confirmed the plan, and on 1 August Haines replied to a decisive Ripon note:

> After your Excellency's Minute which came to me in circulation today, I no longer doubt that a force will be despatched from Kabul to Kandahar. I am also aware that if a force is to go it will be under the command of Lt Gen Sir F. Roberts; than this, no better arrangement could be made; By virtue of his local rank in Afghanistan dated from Nov 1879, he will . . . supersede Gen Primrose . . .[89]

Ripon told Haines: 'The arrival of the Kabul force at Kandahar cannot possibly be much later than that of the Quetta Force, and it will be a moot point as to which of these Forces the honour of finishing off Ayub Khan will fall.'[90]

From this everything flowed. Some 10,148 men were selected, 2,562 British. There were 8,134 followers and drivers, and 10,800 animals. Roberts took no wheeled transport or wheeled artillery, only pack guns and animals, to speed the march. Baggage was lightened by assigning ten soldiers to a tent usually holding six, only thirty-four pounds of kit per man, one mule for each officer's things, and an additional mule to every eight officers for the mess. Thirty days' tea, sugar, rum and salt, and five days' rations per man were taken. Chapman, who had been Stewart's chief of staff on his march, took the same position, Major-General John Ross was second in command, Roberts's friend Hugh Gough commanded the cavalry. Baker, Macpherson and MacGregor commanded infantry brigades. The Indian regiments through sickness and long service were not all eager for the enterprise, but were assured that after victory they would return home promptly. Roberts himself visited the battalions to inspire them with his ardour. 'The enthusiasm which carried Sir Frederick Roberts's force with exceptional rapidity to Kandahar,' wrote Chapman, 'was an after-growth evolved by the enterprise itself, and came as a response to the unfailing spirit which animated the leader himself.' Over 160 soldiers discharged themselves from hospital to rejoin their comrades.[91] 'This is a grand thing for Bobs,' wrote Stewart to his wife. 'If there is any fighting, he can't help being successful, and his success must bring him great credit.'[92] Of the march's importance, Lepel Griffin wrote: 'I see immense & national interests at stake in this Kandahar expedition. On its success or failure the most gigantic issues may depend.'

On 3 August Ripon wrote to Roberts expressing confidence in his skill and energy. 'Remember that Ayub is your one and only objective,' he added. The Indian Foreign Secretary told him he was to treat as friends all persons not in arms and reassure the tribes.[93] On 8 August Griffin and the political officers gave a banquet for Roberts and his brigadiers. Griffin concluded his speech of good will with words from Tennyson's 'Ulysses':

> . . . we are
> One equal temper of heroic hearts
> Made weak by time and fate, but strong in will,
> To strive, to seek, to find, and not to yield.

Roberts replied, expressing confidence in his force to reach Kandahar quickly and dispose of any Afghan army he might face. He repeated this confidence in a general order to the troops.[94] At 2.45 a.m. on the 9th camp was struck and the movement began. After the long halt at Kabul the troops were not yet marching fit, and the first days in great heat over difficult ground were among the hardest.

Roberts took his publicists, Vaughan and Hensman. The crisis alone guaranteed maximum publicity, as did the unique circumstances: an army of 10,000 marched out of sight and then appeared again to win a victory that wiped out a defeat and ended a war.[95] Soboleff, the Russian commentator, wrote of the excitement among the native population in India. He thought the march 'desperate' but 'excellently carried out'. 'What was expected of General Phayre and what he undoubtedly could have done had he been possessed of more decision, General Roberts effected ... General Roberts decided on an heroic exploit, and in spite of its incredible difficulty carried it out.'[96] This was unjust to Phayre: the Khojak Pass especially proved difficult.

The march began down the beautiful Logar Valley. Seven marches took them to the great fortress of Ghazni. After Ghazni the country opened up, the regiments passed the site of Stewart's victory at Ahmed Khel with its newly erected martyrs' memorial, and the column was able to march on a broader front. This was impressive to onlookers and troops alike, and Baker thought unfriendly tribesmen were overawed by the force's obvious strength. The average daily mileage was between thirteen and fourteen. Lieutenant Eaton Travers of the Gurkhas and Brigadier MacGregor both drew attention to disorder on the march and difficulties with the baggage.[97] In a column seven miles long, rigid control was impossible, and Roberts gave speed priority. Tribesman told the marching force that Kandahar had fallen, and while discounting that, Roberts had to accept Ayub's imminent threat with his artillery.[98] Each day was bitterly cold at first, the men rising at 2.30 a.m. to strike tents, but grew increasingly hot. They were plagued by thirst, by choking sand, raised by the marching column itself, and by poor footwear. Roberts stayed with the force until after the breakfast halt, and then rode forward to choose that night's campsite. He returned to meet the columns and cheer them with news that camp was near. The regimental bands would strike up a swinging tune, and there was an effort to finish the day in good spirits. Worst sufferers in the ordeal were the poorly dressed followers, who despite midday heat felt the bitter wind sweeping across the southern Afghan plateau. On arrival there were night piquets, wood-gathering parties and cutting animal forage, so fatigue was intense. Major George White told the viceroy that both British and Indian regiments were eager to avenge Maiwand, but one soldier of each found the ordeal too much and shot himself.[99]

Captain Stratton's heliographers signalled from brigade to brigade to keep in touch. Unsung heroes of the march were Lt-Colonel Low and Major Badcock in charge of the commissariat and transport. Food was obtained as soon as camp was pitched. Low and Badcock ensured that supplies were

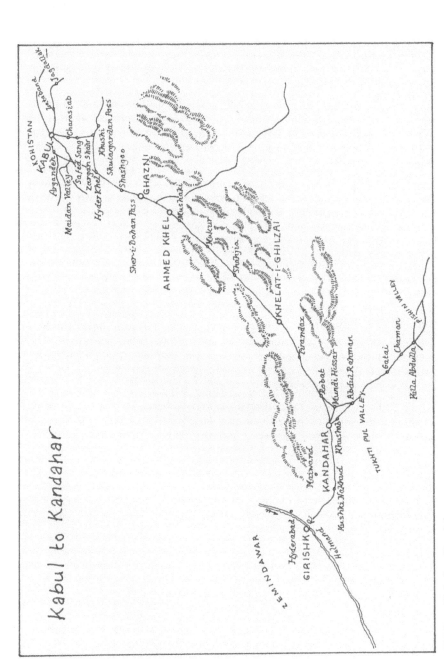

MAP 7 *Kabul to Kandahar*

replenished whenever possible; the force reached Kandahar with three days' flour in hand and flocks of sheep driven before them.[100] A special field treasure chest had been taken to ensure expenses were met. Firewood was scarce, and with the agreement of Abdur Rahman's and Mushk-I-Alam's representatives, the unfortunate local inhabitants' houses were pulled down and timbers used for cooking. Indian corn was everywhere growing and procurable, the force paying for this as well as the firewood.

The presence of Afghan representatives and absence of serious opposition enabled Roberts to force the pace. Chapman noted: 'we owe it to Abdur Rahman's efforts, or to the withdrawal of Mushk-i-alam's fanatical opposition, that the people remained to sell their grain and flour'.[101] Careful preparations were essential. The 23rd Punjab Infantry made up the road in places, as no sappers were in the column. Tins of pea soup and extra meat or rum were issued. Chapman's experience with Stewart's column was invaluable, but the speed of Roberts's march made one handicap he could not expect. Numbers of carriers and doolie-bearers were drafted in just beforehand, many of these ill-fitted to march 300 miles. Thus, 'the rear-guards [were] detained upon the road, covering and aiding the march of a weary following, pressing forward the feeble amongst the cattle, shifting loads and rendering such assistance as was required'. They left camp three hours behind the main body, and reached the next encampment shortly before sundown. Despite this, the daily pace increased to over sixteen miles between 16 and 23 August; those days, reckoned Chapman 'will be allowed to rank high in the annals of marches'.[102]

On 21 August the force learnt by heliograph of a disastrous sortie from Kandahar, resulting in the death of Brigadier Brooke, the garrison's animating spirit, and other officers. On the 22nd at Baba Kazai they found food, forage and supplies sent by the Khelat garrison. On the 23rd they reached Khelat, and a letter from Primrose gave further details of the sortie, but also news that Ayub had drawn back from close siege. Kandahar was no longer in danger. The march had achieved its first objective.

After a day's rest, they set forth again on the 25th, strengthened by the Khelat troops. Ayub's force was composed of Herati regiments, reckoned to be the best Afghan regulars, and was formidable by reason of its artillery. Burrows's force had learnt this to their cost. Roberts resolved to advance by the most direct route, and make contact by heliograph with Kandahar to learn of Ayub's intentions. He might try to elude Roberts by marching up the Argandab Valley and on to Kabul via Ghazni, there attacking Abdur. Instead, however, he fell back three miles and fortified his position.[103] Roberts was now stricken with what he told his wife and his biographer Low was a fever, but according to a medical board and the historian Brian Robson was a duodenal ulcer. A subsequent medical examination ascertained that since embarking on his advance to Kabul in autumn, 1879, he had suffered from 'a continuous pain in his chest, a feeling of weariness and occasional passing of blood per anum ... tenderness or pressure ... sickness of the stomach, and a great disinclination for food'. He was completely prostrate for four days, and forced to travel in a doolie, a conveyance for the sick. As he told his wife in a scribbled diary entry, this illness reduced him to 'such a state of mind; I saw there would be a big business here and I began to think I should not be well enough to command it'.[104] On the 27th he sent forward Hugh Gough with two regiments of cavalry and heliograph signallers. At Robat they signalled to the garrison. In reply to the question, '*Who are you?*' there flashed forth a dramatic message: '*The advanced Guard of General Roberts's force – General Gough with two regiments of Cavalry.*'[105]

At Robat, twenty miles from Kandahar, Roberts received news from Phayre that his leading brigade was still in the Khojak Pass. There would be no prompt help from that quarter.[106] As the tired but triumphant column neared Kandahar, many of the footsore being carried on pack animals found new strength and rejoined their battalions. On the morning of 31 August, two or three miles from the city, Roberts rose from his doolie, mounted his famous grey 'Vonolel' and led them in. They had covered 313 miles in twenty-three days. He signalled to Simla news of his arrival and that the Kandahar garrison were in good health. He added: 'Troops from Kabul are in famous health and spirits. The assurance of the safety of this garrison enabled comparatively short marches to be made from Khelat-i-Ghilzai, which much benefited both men and animals; the cavalry horses and artillery mules are in excellent condition, and the transport animals are, as a rule, in very fair order.' This was more than slightly rosy. The loss of animals from hard work was 733, although replacements were found on the march.[107] Some 500 men had fallen ill. He requested several thousand pairs of new boots be sent. Nine soldiers and eleven followers were dead or missing.[108]

Roberts took command as intended. His forceful character and administrative ability promptly solved one problem, as Ripon explained to Cambridge:

> Before his arrival at Kandahar we were threatened with serious difficulties in regard to the supply of grain and forage along the whole line of communication . . . and I was beginning to be really anxious, but from the moment that Genl Roberts appeared upon the scene a total change occurred, local sources of supply were tapped, order took the place of confusion, and in a very short time we were relieved from all anxiety. The contrast is really wonderful and has impressed me very much.[109]

Ayub sent letters saying he had been forced to fight at Maiwand against his will and was a man of peace. Roberts told him to give up any prisoners and surrender unconditionally.[110] He did not.

Roberts had always preceded his battles by a reconnaissance, but Hensman tells us the idea here was Chapman's.[111] He accompanied Hugh Gough's force of horse and foot. They established that Pir Paimal was held in strength, but could be taken by a flank assault. Once again Roberts's luck played its part. When Gough and his men fell back, Ayub's followers were confident they had beaten the British and could stay put. This was important; as an intercepted Russian appreciation put it:

> [T]he object of the expedition will not have been achieved if Ayub Khan's army evades battle and retires to heart . . . According to intelligence from India, the Mahommedan population of that country is greatly excited by the advantages which Ayub Khan has so far obtained over the English. In order to suppress this excitement it is necessary, at all hazards, to demolish Ayub Khan's army . . .[112]

The odds in any case were probably in favour of the Afghans standing to fight. Ayub's Herati regiments had mocked those at Kabul for losing to the *feringhis*. The fanatical ghazis who made over a third of his force had a place reserved in paradise.

The day of battle, 1 September, dawned, a beautiful clear autumn morning. The troops struck tents and breakfasted. Roberts gave his orders. Ayub's camp lay at Baba Wali behind a line of hills. An approach through the obvious pass, the Baba Wali Kotal, invited disaster. Here Roberts instructed the Bombay Regiments to make a feint and await developments. His favoured flanking attack would be round Ayub's right, protected by the villages of Gundigan, Gundimulla and Pir Paimal. The stone walls of gardens and houses made each a small fortress, orchards and enclosures providing further cover and obstacles to the advance. Ayub was a skilful general, and these places were strongly defended, walls loopholed, his formidable artillery ready.[113]

None of this was of any avail against Roberts and his elite regiments, keyed up for victory and then a quick march home. Ayub's force did not even enjoy the usual numerical superiority, at 12,800 being only slightly larger than Roberts's, which enjoyed advantages of weaponry and training. Two thirds of the 5,000 ghazis were armed with sword and spear. Even Ayub's formidable artillery was outmatched. The Afghans did not understand the fuses on captured British ammunition and consequently few shells burst.[114] British guns, especially the 40-pounders from the walls of Kandahar, opened fire. Segment shell with layers of cast iron balls around an explosive charge did great execution among massed Afghans. Lt H.L. Gardiner, the newest joined Royal Artillery subaltern, years later remembered having a clear view as the Gurkhas went into Gundimullah and were driven out. The artillery brought fire on the enemy, and Gurkhas and Gordons went in again and carried the village. As the infantry advanced, the guns, especially pack guns brought on mules, followed them through the orchards and enclosures. In fierce hand-to-hand fighting the first two villages fell to MacPherson's and Baker's brigades. Officers led from the front, and the Seaforths lost their CO, Brownlow, shot through the throat. As the Afghans abandoned their first positions, the khaki-clad British and Indian pursuers fired into them at close quarters. Roberts now ordered up MacGregor's third brigade for the final effort. Major George White played a leading role in the battle's climax.

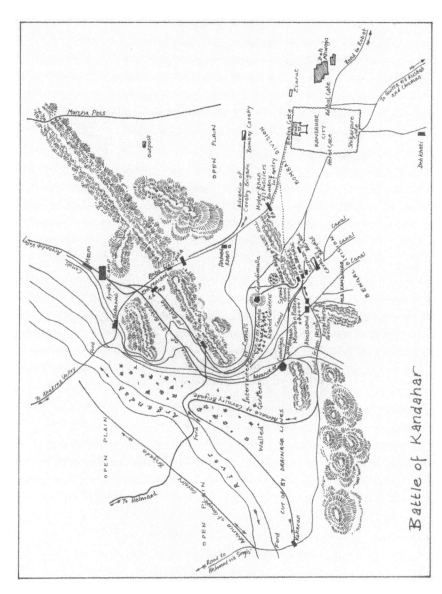

MAP 8 Battle of Kandahar

FIGURE 6 *An unusual photograph showing Afghan prisoners taken in Robert's victory outside Kandahar. Their clothes mark them as irregular Ghazis who normally fought to the death.*

He had ridden coolly up and down the lines at the start of the battle to warn his men of the Afghan guns. Now he called on the Gordons for a last effort. He advanced at their head as they and the 2nd Prince of Wales's Gurkhas raced for the enemy artillery. Gurkha Inderbir Lama placed his cap over the first gun and claimed it for his regiment. The 2nd and 3rd Sikhs overcame final enemy resistance, and all thirty-two of Ayub's pieces were taken including two captured at Maiwand.[115]

The enemy were now in full flight. Where were the cavalry? This was Roberts's one mistake. He had sent Gough west over the Argandab river, and picking his way through orchards, gardens and irrigation canals he could not cut off the retreating Afghans. The Bombay Cavalry pursued through the Baba Wali Kotal. After a short halt to replenish ammunition, the troops continued their advance and entered Ayub's camp at 1 p.m. to find it deserted except for the body of Lt Maclaine, RA, captured at Maiwand and murdered by a passing ghazi against Ayub's orders. Everything in the camp denoted confidence of victory – not a tent struck, not a saddlebag carried away, meat in cooking pots, bread half-kneaded, the *ghee*-pots out ready for a feast. Roberts estimated Afghan dead at 1,200 with equal wounded. His own were thirty-five and 213 wounded. Of these forty-three died, partly due to poor medical care. This was infuriating to Roberts, with his particular regard for field hospitals.[116] Ayub's army scattered, and he made his escape with a handful to Herat. He was, however, to recover.

To the British everywhere, the victory was in Haines's words, 'a superb event'. The viceroy sent special congratulations and predicted the march would be famous. He ordered a royal salute fired at all stations in India in celebration.[117] From Gibraltar, Napier wrote to the victor: 'I watched your march with breathless interest . . . I knew you could average fifteen miles a day, and each night I said Roberts will be so far tomorrow.' George White told his wife: 'The men are very proud of their performance & it was splendid. Sir Fredk made them a speech when it was over saying "that only they could have done it & that they had even exceeded themselves".'[118] Roberts rode to each brigade in turn and congratulated them. His admirers were quick to claim that only he could have led the march.[119] His outward cheer and boldness, his care for morale and supplies, even previous hanging of Afghans believed to have murdered the Guides enabled him to call for special exertion from British, Gurkha and Indian soldiers. With Gurkhas and Highlanders he henceforth enjoyed a unique comradeship of arms.[120]

CHAPTER SEVEN

In command at Madras

The relations that prevailed between this Government and Sir F. Roberts were simply ideal . . . by a happy accident we had for the Madras Commander-in-Chief a warrior of world wide reputation . . .

M.E. GRANT DUFF, GOVERNOR OF MADRAS

[T]he ancient military spirit had died in [the Madras sepoys] . . . they could no longer be safely pitted against warlike races.

FREDERICK ROBERTS

The forward movement of Russia on the Persian and Afghan frontier has brought her to a position when her next step must bring her into collision with England; and the Power which then recedes before the other must, from that date, take the second place in Europe and Asia.

LEPEL GRIFFIN, *THE TIMES,* 26 MAY 1884

As Roberts's men rested outside Kandahar, Stewart's withdrawal from Kabul continued, the last regiments passing through the Khyber on 13 September.[1] Ripon's biographer Gopal thought the withdrawal from Kabul and the march to Kandahar were complementary: 'The one was proof of British sincerity, the other was proof of British strength. Perfect loyalty to friends was combined with vigorous action against enemies.'[2]

The British continued to hold Kandahar for the Wali against the wishes of their new ally Abdur. A hot debate was conducted in Parliament and the letters columns of *The Times* as to whether it should be given up. The city lay astride the strategic route from Herat to the Bolan Pass. The Russian advance did not cease. In January 1881 the Russians, having built a railway forward from the Caspian, stormed Geok Tepe. When General Skobolev's men surged through a breach, no quarter was given. Some 6,500 dead were counted in the fortress, and 8,000 men, women and children were cut down trying to escape. 'The whole country was covered with corpses,' an Armenian interpreter confided to a British friend. Skobolev asserted that wholesale slaughter was a much better method of keeping the locals quiet than Roberts hanging ringleaders.[3]

Despite this, Gladstone's ministry had decided to give Kandahar to Abdur.[4] He was committed by his alliance with British India to have 'no political relations with any foreign power except the English'. The Kurram Valley, Sibi and Pishin were ceded to India. Moreover, whatever Russians in central Asia wanted, Tsar Alexander II was intent on internal reform and peace abroad. St Petersburg accepted that the Second Afghan War had reduced Afghanistan 'to a tributary of the British Empire'.[5]

This was, however, only assured once Abdur had beaten Ayub. Haines shrewdly wrote that while Roberts had won a 'superb' victory: 'I have constantly to keep the fact prominently before my colleagues that it does not finally dispose of Sirdar Mahomed Ayub Khan as a possible source of future trouble. Many a defeated man has refitted his shattered forces in Herat . . .'[6] At Herat Ayub faced a mutiny among his troops, perhaps because he had failed to lead them to victory over Roberts. Not until July 1881 did he advance and seize Kandahar. As Sher Ali's son and victor at Maiwand, he had a strong claim to Afghan loyalty and was a skilful general. Abdur however was ruthless and determined, he had the advantage of the arms and ammunition from Kabul and British subsidies, and he took the offensive. At Kandahar he led his men personally and Ayub was routed. He fled west, seeking asylum first in Persia and then in 1887 in India. Abdur, 'the Iron Amir', consolidated his rule in a series of bloody internal wars. For Britain, the Second Afghan War had secured a friendly buffer state guarding India's North-West Frontier. Abdur was bound to British India by treaty and fear of military retaliation. He and his successors kept this tie until 1919, nearly forty years. The Russians who had assisted his return were disappointed and considered this period 'a dark page' in the history of Russian diplomacy.[7] Although Roberts among others remained suspicious, Abdur with one or two wobbles stayed loyal to his alliance.[8]

Thus Roberts's march and victory proved a strategic triumph. Without the British invasion, the overthrow of Sher Ali and Yakub and success against Ayub, it is unlikely Abdur would have gained control. Although Roberts in his memoirs glossed over Abdur's help, the British understood his role assisting the march. James Hills shrewdly commented: 'Abdur Rahman . . . has done everything in his power to keep the tribes quiet who are in Roberts' patch for he wishes him to go along as fast as he can & do what he himself would have to try & do hereafter, namely knock [Ayub] out of turn.' Chapman, Roberts's chief of staff, explained that the column owed it to Abdur and the withdrawal of Mushk-I-Alam's 'fanatical opposition' that they were regularly fed. On Stewart's march, by contrast, food had been secreted, and 'we were forced to dig in the fields for buried grain'.[9] Brigadier Charles Gough wrote that the victory was 'a most fortunate thing for us as a nation, and has brought the war to a close in a complete and satisfactory manner and will also completely establish Abdul [sic] Rahman on the throne'.[10]

The price was heavy in gold, less in men. The war cost India £19.5 million, of which Britain paid £5 million. The British and Indians lost 1,850 killed in battle, the Afghans an estimated 5,000.[11]

Roberts himself was ordered on leave. His condition left him totally unfit and a medical board thought rest absolutely essential to recoup his health.[12] His wife was much relieved: 'I have been very unhappy about him lately. He has been so ill for some time that he was unable to answer even a telegram himself.'[13] Roberts travelled to Simla where Ripon lionised him, and thence to England to fame and rejoicing. Hugh Childers, the Liberal War Secretary, had already told the Duke of Cambridge: 'Mr Gladstone is writing to the Queen to the effect that he proposes that both Stewart & Roberts should be made G.C.B., that Roberts should have the Madras Command when it becomes vacant, but that nothing will be done as to either Stewart or Roberts having a step in military rank until further consideration can be had.'[14] This reward must have been unwelcome to radical critics of the 'Forward School' and Afghan hangings. Its niggardliness[15] given the spectacular success was to rankle with Roberts. In May 1883 he wrote a long letter to Lytton, upset at Hartington's belittling his march to Kabul. In February 1885, he nearly fell out with Chapman, who was disappointed not to become an ADC to the Queen and may have told friends that Roberts had depended upon him on the famous march. '[Hartington] was most unjust and ungenerous to me. He made light of everything that was done by me in Afghanistan before the march to Kandahar, and endeavoured to give me as little credit as possible for that march.' A tactful letter from Chapman cleared the air. Mollified, Roberts replied, 'What you said "privately" about the Aide-de-Campship must have gone beyond your own friends, for the officer to whom I alluded in my former letter was loud in his abuse of me, mainly in consequence of the treatment he believed you to have received at my hands. That officer I may tell you is Redvers Buller [AAG, Horse Guards].'[16] As 'Lord Lytton's General', Roberts believed he could find no favour in Liberal eyes, partly because of his view that Kandahar should not be given up.[17] Despite this, Madras was to be the first of a series of promotions.

He was fortunate it became available. In 1878–9 Edwin Johnson, military member of the Viceroy's Council and an old Delhi comrade of Roberts, was earmarked for Madras in succession to Neville Chamberlain. By September 1879 it was realised he was not suitable: his health was bad and the Military Department which he oversaw was in a terrible shape, partly shown by unsupervised overspending on the Afghan War.[18] Donald Stewart was chosen.[19] Then Stewart was switched to military member, so as to be in a position to succeed Haines when the latter retired shortly.[20] This left Madras open.

Meanwhile, in England the Robertses were celebrities and welcomed in high places. In 1868 on his last visit home he had been an unknown major. Now he was renowned. Cambridge told Haines, 'I like him much and his conversation is modest & reasonable.' He was being feasted 'in all directions. He has done wonderfully well by the modesty of his speeches which give general satisfaction'. Haines, until now not a pronounced admirer, replied that he was glad he had made a good impression. 'He is a charming fellow and one of the pleasantest travelling companions I ever met,' adding perhaps tongue in cheek, 'he falls off at sea; in fact there he collapses.'[21] In March 1881 he visited one of his old schools, Eton, to inspect the corps. He was presented with a sword of honour, one of several he received. 'So great was the enthusiasm on the occasion that the boys drew the carriage containing Sir Frederick and Lady Roberts as far as Windsor Bridge.'[22]

Etonians rejoiced; not all MPs did so. In a Commons debate of 5 May 1881, on a vote of thanks to Haines, Stewart, Roberts and other generals for Afghan services, several MPs spoke against Roberts's inclusion. Tim Healy, MP for Wexford, who viewed the war as 'needless and unjust' was thinking primarily of Ireland's oppression: 'the old system of British policy as carried out in Ireland was renewed in Afghanistan'. Sir Wilfrid Lawson, MP for Carlisle, said the British Army under Roberts had 'hanged more soldiers than they shot'. Stanhope and Childers, successive War Secretaries, defended him; the vote of thanks was passed 304 votes to 20. Stewart and Roberts received baronetcies and cash rewards.[23]

Nor did all the press salute him. After he had been dined and made a member by the Fishmongers' Company, a cartoon in the periodical *Moonshine* portrayed him as 'a purveyor of fish' and declared: 'General Roberts, his sword being perfectly useless as things go, is made free of a new business.'[24] Roberts was not long a fishmonger. On 1 March he had been appointed to take command in South Africa; it proved an abortive and frustrating journey.

In 1877 Disraeli's government had annexed the Transvaal, the Boer republic established in the interior away from interfering British missionaries and colonial governors. It was bankrupt after a disastrous war with the Pedi. The Boers had expected Gladstone on coming to office to restore their autonomy, but were disappointed. They took matters into their own hands, and in December 1880 resolved to reassert independence. The task of smashing this rebellion fell to Colley, now properly Major-General Sir George Pomeroy-Colley, governor of Natal, high commissioner for south-eastern Africa and commander-in-chief in Natal and the Transvaal. Rapidly the Boers became masters of the situation. The climax of a series of small but disastrous British defeats was Majuba, 27 February 1881. A force from various regiments seized the summit of the hill by a night march.[25] Colley's carelessness and failure to entrench seem in retrospect inexplicable. An

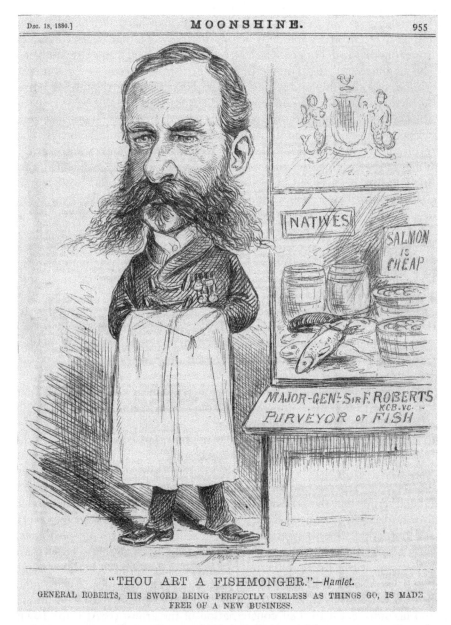

Dec. 18, 1880.] MOONSHINE. 955

"THOU ART A FISHMONGER."—*Hamlet.*

GENERAL ROBERTS, HIS SWORD BEING PERFECTLY USELESS AS THINGS GO, IS MADE FREE OF A NEW BUSINESS.

FIGURE 7 *Not all London applauded Roberts's Afghan success. When the Fishmongers Company welcomed him as guest of honour, the critical periodical* Moonshine *published this cartoon (National Army Museum).*

attacking Boer force slightly superior in numbers skirmished up the hill using every fold in the ground and routed the British. Colley was killed. So comprehensive had been his failure that he may have welcomed death, despite a recent and apparently happy marriage. He had received orders from London to put out peace feelers, but had thrown all into a last gamble.[26] This humiliating defeat pointed to many British shortcomings: poor use of ground, bad shooting and scouting, inflexible tactics. For the insular Boers the victory encouraged a contempt for the *Rooineks*.

Gladstone's second ministry was beset with troubles in Ireland. The cost of continuing the war and garrisoning the Transvaal would be heavy. The revolt, however, threatened imperial security throughout South Africa. Whigs in the Cabinet, the army and the court demanded that the affront to British arms be avenged. The radicals wanted to conciliate. While the Cabinet battled over policy, ministers would reassure public opinion by despatching an imperial hero. Roberts attributed his selection to Childers, as his son had accompanied the Kabul-Kandahar march.[27] Officially it was Kimberley, colonial secretary, who on 4 March 1881 appointed him as Colley's successor. Evelyn Wood had temporarily taken command, but the Duke of Cambridge told him: 'The Gov[ernmen]t have thought that so large a command in the Field, as that now in S.A. should be under the orders of a Lt General combining in his person the Civil & Military responsibility & they have selected Sir F. Roberts for this most important post.'[28] Roberts's Afghan reputation made him the obvious man to reassure a patriotic public. Choosing him to succeed Colley was a rebuff to Wolseley who had done the same job only a year before.[29]

Childers told Wood that it was for Roberts to clear up what Colley had left. At the same time Kimberley declared Cabinet ambivalence when he advised Roberts that, while the government 'will not relax their determination to carry on the military operations with the utmost vigour, they would rejoice should any opportunity present itself for an honourable and satisfactory settlement of the affairs of the Transvaal without further bloodshed'.[30] Liberals and radicals triumphed over Whigs. Kruger accepted Liberal terms, that the Transvaal should be an autonomous republic, under British suzerainty. London retained a veto over relations with foreign powers and bordering tribes.[31] Instructions were sent to Wood to end hostilities. With reinforcements giving him a total of 14,000, he was no keener than Roberts to accept the humiliation, but at the end of March he carried out the government's instructions and negotiated an armistice. Meanwhile, Roberts travelled by train to Dartmouth where he embarked. At Madeira he and his staff learnt to their consternation of the armistice. At Cape Town harbour on the evening of 28 March a boat with people crying 'Peace' greeted them. Roberts, furious and disappointed, would not stay in South Africa a moment longer. He and his staff took the first ship home, leaving Cape Town on 30 March.[32] Wolseley was equally angry: Wood had betrayed the 'ring' by not avenging its leading member.[33]

Officers in South Africa were enraged. Subaltern Percival Marling expressed the common feeling: 'Everyone is cursing Gladstone and the Radical Government, and Lord Kimberley, the Colonial Secretary. A more disgraceful peace was never made.' In a Roberts scrapbook is a card edged in black and inscribed, 'In memory of Honour, wife of John Bull, who died in the Transvaal and was interred at Kandahar March 1881 [the date of its return to Abdur].' It shows a banditti-looking Boer on horseback contemptuously holding a poster with Queen Victoria's head and 'Suzeraine' spelt out. British colonists who had pinned their faith on Wolseley's declaration that 'as long as the sun rose and set, the Transvaal would remain British' were also victims of the defeat. The soldiers saw them trekking over Lang's Nek with what they could save from their farms, flocks and herds, and wagons with wives and children, 'all cursing Gladstone'. They had put all their money into their farms: now they were ruined, boycotted by the exultant Boers.[34]

Roberts wrote one angry paragraph about this interlude in his memoirs: 'A peace, alas! "without honour", to which may be attributed the recent regrettable state of affairs in the Transvaal – a state of affairs which was foreseen and predicted by many at the time.'[35] The crisis of 1880–1 left deep marks. The Transvaal burghers had a stronger faith in themselves. The Royal Commission chaired by Lord Carnarvon (1879–82) to investigate and report on colonial defence believed paramountcy in southern Africa still necessary to an Empire with sea routes to India, Australia and the Far East. Relations with the Transvaal remained unstable. The London Convention of 1884 failed to resolve future tension; the appearance of the Germans in south-west Africa, disputes over Bechuanaland and the discovery of gold on the Rand increased it.[36]

Returning to England, Roberts spent three weeks in August as the guest of the German emperor at manoeuvres in Hanover and Schleswig-Holstein. Having seen the way German company officers instructed their men, he concluded that British officers could do more.[37] Childers as War Secretary was carrying through the second stage of the Cardwell reforms. Despite army opposition, the single battalion regiments were replaced by twin-battalion county regiments. One battalion would be at home training recruits, the other of seasoned men on overseas service. Flogging was abolished and NCOs granted better pay and pensions. The period with the colours was extended from six to seven or eight years if abroad. These reforms and Cardwell's earlier abolition of purchase for officers' commissions did not transform the army; it remained the poor relation of the Royal Navy. Except in times of trouble, soldiers recruited from the poorest, least educated classes were looked down upon by the respectable middle and skilled working classes.[38] Opposition to reform was serious enough that Childers wanted Roberts as QMG in succession to Wolseley, a strong man to lend service support. Hartington supported Childers, but Roberts refused.[39]

He reached Madras to take up his new command on 27 November 1881.[40] Already Cranbrook, the former Conservative Indian Secretary, had wished him 'the success in India which you deserve and Lady Roberts the comfort of seeing your health transformed by work ...'[41] Roberts was sore at not receiving his step, and was still writing to Childers in December 1882 to protest his acting rank of lieutenant-general held for nearly a year not being made permanent, especially when the Wolseyites in Egypt were being promoted.[42] Roberts's colleague as governor of Madras was Mounstuart Elphinstone Grant-Duff. He had been MP for Elgin and from 1868 Under-Secretary for Indian Affairs; he dealt with Indian business in the Commons. In opposition he resolutely attacked Disraeli's Afghan policy as 'one vast web of crime'.[43] Nonetheless, relations between the two were excellent. Grant-Duff wrote of him as 'the best and most agreeable of colleagues'.[44] This was in spite of opposing positions on amalgamation of the three presidency armies, which Grant Duff stood against. There was no conflict between Roberts and civilian members of the Madras government: 'everything was talked over in the most friendly spirit, and there never was a hitch or a vestige of a hitch'.[45]

Roberts's absurdly small staff was typical of the British and Indian Armies. Lt-Colonel George Pretyman was his military secretary; Lt Neville Chamberlain was ADC and interpreter; Subedar-Major Mahomed Abdullah was his native ADC. To these in 1884 he added Lt Ian Hamilton.[46] The 'Indian Ring' of chosen supporters was yet to form. As a Bengal soldier whose service had been at headquarters or in the north, he brought prejudices to southern India. His view that the Madras sepoys were inferior to the northern 'martial races' most likely originated in the Mutiny when Sikhs and Gurkhas joined the British force on the Ridge outside Delhi. It gained weight in the Afghan War.[47] Lytton, who reinforced Roberts's views on the northern frontier, may have had the same effect on his 'martial race' ideas. He described the Madras regiments garrisoning Calcutta in February 1879 as 'the laughing stock of the whole town'; 'a more weedy, seedy, wretched set of creatures was never seen in uniform since Falstaff organized his ragged regiments'.[48] Stewart had a similar although more moderate view of the Bombay Army: 'The Regiments are for the most part well disciplined and well trained but ... the men (with the exception of the Belooch Regiments) are certainly inferior to the warlike races found in the majority of Bengal Regiments.' Jacob's Rifles, which fought at Maiwand, he held to be 'about the worst [regiment] in the Army'.[49] There was also the alleged feebleness of the Kandahar garrison when Roberts's column arrived: 'the garrison had distinctly lost heart'.[50] This was a neo-Darwinian view: northern peoples were lighter skinned than those of the south. Nonetheless, Roberts and Stewart had evidence: the fighting qualities of Sikhs, Gurkhas and Punjabis in their Afghan victories. Modern writers have pointed to the explanation: better officer leadership on the frontier. Enterprising British officers shunned Madras and Bombay for the chance of active service in the north-west, especially as the 'martial race' premise took hold.[51] Neville Chamberlain, previous commander-in-chief at Madras, was able to defend his men. The fault of the Madras regiment's poor show at Calcutta lay with the CO who was 'addicted to intemperance [drunkenness]'. Chamberlain struggled to weed out old and inefficient officers. Some Madras regiments were isolated at small stations distant from his control and without the competition of other units to raise standards.[52] Bengal soldiers' evidence was selective. In *Forty-One Years* Roberts ignored the Sikhs among the Mutineers. The Pashtuns who fired their rifles to warn the Afghans at the Peiwar Kotal were from the martial races. Jacob's Rifles did falter at Maiwand, but the two companies involved were not from the Presidency Army proper.[53] How much did this disdainful view affect Roberts's command?

Roberts's ambition, energy and high standards did much for the Madras Army. He set about improving their shooting (called 'musketry' although soldiers carried rifles). More ammunition was issued, and the South India Rifle Association which Roberts supported held an annual competition among teams of soldiers from all stations.[54] Admitting that the Madras sappers and miners were 'a most useful, efficient body of men', he converted two infantry regiments into Pioneers on the Bengal model, one serving on the Baluchistan frontier.[55] He had improved barracks built at Trichinopoly; set up messes for recruits which bachelor sepoys could join to develop *esprit de corps*; established a small gymnasium for each regiment; began a scheme of employment for discharged Indian soldiers. To keep the Madras Army before the public and encourage fitness, he arranged that regiments marched whenever possible between stations rather than travelling by rail. He acknowledged that 'Madras soldiers are more intelligent and better educated than others.'[56] Nonetheless, he carried out the disbanding of eight Madras regiments previously agreed. He told Cambridge and Cranbrook that the standards of physique among Madras sepoys had fallen and they would not be a loss as they would be unable to face a serious enemy in battle. Also, regiments were short of men following the war and both NCOs and privates from disbanded units had volunteered to return to the colours with other regiments.[57]

Following Napier's example, he valued 'camps of exercise' to improve army readiness in the field. He based his orders for a camp of exercise of 9,000 men at Bangalore in August 1883 on regulations framed by Napier.[58] The three commanders-in-chief, Stewart, Roberts and Sir Arthur Hardinge of Bombay met there. Stewart wrote of his friend's enthusiasm: he 'inspires every one around him with a like spirit'.[59] Roberts also secured approval for establishing a Madras Army intelligence branch at Ootacamund.[60] Visiting and inspecting the Madras regiments, he tried to encourage regimental pride in their appearance.[61] He chose Ootacamund, 'the Queen of the Hill Stations' in the Nilgiri Hills, as the future headquarters: it was healthier, less expensive and as he told Cambridge 'it is the place at which the Government usually resides during the time when I was not likely to be much on tour'. Cambridge agreed, as did the Madras and Indian governments and the Indian Secretary of State.[62] At 7,228 feet, Ootacamund lay in a natural amphitheatre surrounded by hills; all about was an extensive plateau in contrast to Simla's narrow ridge; thus, as the *Imperial Gazetteer* explained: 'The outdoor life is a joyous and characteristic feature of the place. Riding, driving and all manly sports are possible.' His home was at 'Snowdon', a rambling house used earlier as a school; the large schoolroom became a ballroom.[63]

Influential in the 'martial races' debate were the conclusions of the Eden Commission,[64] assembled in early 1879 by Lytton to propose Indian Army economies. Lytton had thought victory in the Afghan conflict proved what Colley had been telling him: 'that a regiment armed with breech-loading rifles could march through Afghanistan'.[65] War exposed Indian Army weakness in organisation, personnel and equipment. The cost of running the three Presidency Armies and fighting in Afghanistan imposed a crippling financial burden on the Indian government, already hard hit by drought and famine. Lytton was convinced of the conservatism of the average military mind and that 'the average Indian officer is the most narrow-minded and bigoted of his class'.[66] He sounded out Stewart and Roberts, both Bengal soldiers, and filled the commission with those favourable to reform. Haines was opposed to change and to Roberts being chairman; as former QMG knowing army organisation intimately he was a logical choice.[67] Instead Sir Ashley Eden, lieutenant-governor of Bengal, was appointed. The commission investigated questions weighted towards the North-West Frontier threat and the belief that the Madras and Bombay armies could not cope with modern war.

Its findings roused strong feeling among opponents, foremost of whom were the Duke of Cambridge and Haines, Edwin Johnson, military member, Chamberlain and Hardinge, then commanders at Madras and Bombay, and old India hands on the council in London.[68] So angry was Johnson that he told Cambridge:

> Roberts is one of the most self seeking men I have ever come across and would override everybody & anything that stood in the way of the attainment of his ends. I hate saying all this of a man whom I have liked very greatly and who has been on such intimate & friendly relations with me for many years, but I have lost faith in him. He is a fine dashing plucky clever fellow full of Soldier like instincts – but he terribly fails in independence – would do anything or say anything which he thought would be acceptable to the reigning powers.

The reigning power had been Lytton. Johnson asserted that Roberts '*under Lord Napier* held such very different opinions from those to which he is now committed'.[69] How seriously must we take these harsh words? As QMG Johnson had had his deputy (Roberts) do most of his work for him and his running of the Military Department was hopelessly inefficient.[70]

That Roberts would do Lytton's bidding is shown by the Kabul hangings and by taking Villiers and Baker into his command. But the widely respected Stewart agreed with him on reform.[71] Since Roberts had been Napier's QMG, the British Army had been re-equipped with Martini-Henry rifles, and the hitting power of these weapons lay behind proposed economies. Better weapons required fewer men.

The Commission's work was completed and the report presented on 15 November 1879. Among 500 recommendations, the most important were to replace separate Presidency Armies with four army corps including one for the Punjab and North-West Frontier; the commander-in-chief to leave the viceroy's council and be subordinated to the military member who would administer a unified War Ministry; a general staff to be created; headquarters and the Military Department to be permanently at Simla; the number of officers in native regiments to increase, as would other ranks in both native and British regiments; and a system of reserves established. In return, ten cavalry and thirty infantry regiments would be disbanded, making annual savings of 12.5 million rupees (equivalent to £2 million). The changes would allow a force of 75,000 men and 240 guns to be mobilised on the North-West Frontier.[72]

Opponents argued that in 1857 the Madras and Bombay Armies had remained loyal, and to integrate the three presidencies invited disaster. Lytton's successor Ripon shared his views, however, and would have liked Roberts as military member to implement reform.[73] Integration of services steadily whittled away the separate armies' independence: departments of Military Accounts and Audit (1864), Remount (1876) and Ordnance (1884) were amalgamated. Transport was partially reorganised. From 1885 more followed as Roberts took command of the Indian Army. Until then the greatest changes were postponed.

An important feature of Roberts's Madras command was care for young soldiers. In his memoirs he records his repugnance witnessing a flogging parade. On this occasion, the punishment of fifty lashes was remitted pending good conduct; Roberts proudly wrote, 'their conduct was uniformly satisfactory and . . . they had become good, steady soldiers'.[74] The historian Peter Stanley points out that Roberts witnessed only one such parade, an uncommon occurrence, and sets Roberts's leniency against a background of improved conditions of service and behaviour. Habitual drunkenness virtually ceased. Roberts was following a family tradition, his father having publicly remitted a flogging in the 1820s as the condemned man had displayed great courage at the storming of an enemy stronghold.[75] Roberts issued instructions that good conduct men should be granted privileges such as passes, excuse from roll-call and irksome formalities.[76]

His thought for soldiers was partly based on the fear that newly arrived British and Irish recruits could not cope with the Indian climate. He protested against the vulnerability of short service men in his speech at the Mansion House on 14 March 1881. Only qualities entirely missing in young soldiers – discipline, *esprit de corps* and powers of endurance – had enabled British regiments to face tremendous odds and win. Cambridge, who was present and opposed Cardwell's reforms told Haines: 'We have had a great speech by Sir Frederick Roberts ... a great impression ... certainly the public have taken the subject up very warmly ...'[77] Wolseley replied to the speech intemperately in the *Nineteenth Century*; thus did the rivalry of these two first come to public notice. An article in *Blackwood's Magazine* of May 1881 stated that the military profession would applaud Roberts, not Wolseley, but short service would prevail.[78] The writer was correct. In November 1882 in 'The Present State of the Army; sequel to the Mansion House Speech' in the *Nineteenth Century* (1882), Roberts acknowledged that Childers had met his criticisms. 'This great improvement in the position of the non-commissioned officers,' he wrote, and 'increasing the length of service in the colonies and India to eight years quite reconciled me to the short service system.'[79]

On 'a shilling a day' Tommy Atkins continued to come from the unemployed, the poorest and least educated. Roberts returned to his theme of more and better recruits in 'Free Trade in the Army' (1884), bringing together proposals already sent to Cambridge, Childers, Hartington, Randolph Churchill and others.[80] 'There must, in fact, be free trade and reciprocity in the Army,' he wrote, 'by which I mean the sweeping away of many hard-and-fast rules which now unnecessarily hamper the soldier's life, from the hour of his enlistment until the day of his leaving the Army.' He called for an end to the stoppages which much reduced the soldier's pay. He wanted clear-cut terms of enlistment: either for three years, after which men would pass into the reserve and adapt to civilian life; or twelve years for long service men who would make the army their career.[81]

It would be years before improvements advocated by Roberts, Wolseley, Redvers Buller and others became practice. The Victorians had an imperial army on the cheap; reforms were aimed primarily at economies. Even in 1898 with 215,000 regular soldiers throughout the Empire, an Indian Army of 148,000 and 100,000 seamen manning the Royal Navy's ironclad ships of war, a defence budget of £40 million was only 2.5 per cent of net national product.[82]

The Russian threat continued to exercise Roberts's mind. Opponents of the Forward School quoted his statement at the end of the Second Afghan War, *the less the Afghans see of us, the less they will dislike us*.[83] News of the advance to Geok Tepe and Russian adventurism in central Asia caused him to renew his former views. From 1877 he drew up twenty papers on the Russian threat and wrote to politicians. In March 1882 he told Cambridge that in a war with Russia the British must take the offensive, for if the Russians reached India the mercenary army of sepoys would prove disloyal. He affirmed Kandahar's strategic importance; it could be rapidly connected to the extending British railways and the port of Karachi for reinforcements.[84] Disraeli had spoken imprecisely of 'the Scientific Frontier'; Roberts gave it substance: it ran along the Hindu Kush mountains from Kashmir to northern Afghanistan, before swinging south through the mountains and hills of central Afghanistan and culminated at Kandahar, its western flank protected by the Baluchistan desert.[85]

At the end of 1883 he circulated a paper, 'Is an Invasion of India by Russia possible?' Copies went to Grant-Duff, John Cowell, Dighton Probyn, Henry Rawlinson, Lord Northbrook, Charles Dilke, Lytton, Salisbury, Randolph Churchill and Childers. One found its way to Garnet Wolseley. 'Articles published anonymously in the *Quarterly Review* would not carry the same weight as if signed,' writes the historian Adrian Preston, 'but if signed they would open him to censure and disavowal by the Government. Roberts therefore decided to send his papers privately to selected strategists and politicians known to be sympathetic to his point of view.' This became his *modus operandi* on such questions. Some would have put strategic planning outside the responsibilities of the commander-in-chief of Madras.[86] His main concern was continued Russian advance in Central Asia and its onset raising rebellion in India. While the better educated Hindus would be on our side, he wrote, 'the Mahomedans [*sic*] and many other restless spirits in the country would be found against us'. Security rested 'on the prestige of the British name'; decisive activity was 'the only policy possible with Asiatics'. After Afghan disaster in 1841–2, bad news had 'spread like wildfire through the bazaars', British prestige sank and there were outbreaks at Gwalior, Lahore and Mooltan. After Maiwand a similar feeling of excitement passed through parts of the population. Persia was now pretty much in thrall to Russia, the Turkoman tribes were in her power. Kandahar had been given up. Abdur Rahman was no better than Sher Ali, taking weapons and subsidies while Russia advanced. Invasion would come via Herat and Kandahar, with threats simultaneously to Peshawar and other frontier posts. The invading army would include hosts of Persian irregulars and Turkoman light horse, armed with modern breech-loaders and trained by European officers. He advocated vigorous action on the Kandahar side, while acting defensively on the rest of the Frontier. It was vital, Roberts wrote, that Britain prepare.

Roberts acquired an ally in the radical MP Sir Charles Dilke, who received a copy of his paper in March 1884. They corresponded and agreed on defence policy on the North-West Frontier. Dilke was impressed: 'On the whole, when Sir Frederick Roberts sent me his view on the defence proposals, I was struck with the contrast between the completeness of the manner in which a defence scheme for India has been considered, and the incompleteness, to say the least of it, of all strategic plans at home.'[87]

In pointing to the Herat-Kandahar route, Roberts drew on the work of his former chief of staff, Charles MacGregor. MacGregor had identified Herat as commanding the important roads to India. Occupation of this strongest fortress between the Caspian and the Indus would give Russia control of Persian and Afghan military resources. MacGregor saw the immediate danger not as full-scale Russian invasion, but seizure of strategic points so as to paralyse British action in a future crisis or war and raise the cry of rebellion or *jihad* in India.[88]

While Roberts was at Madras, MacGregor served as QMG India. He played a major role in forging an Indian Army Intelligence Department. The Indian government suppressed his official *History of the Second Afghan War* because of its critique of Indian defence policy beyond its terms of reference. In 1884, frustrated by what he saw as the Liberal government's retrograde policy, he published *The Defence of India*. Kimberley, Liberal Secretary of State for India, said: 'I have never read anything wilder.' When the *St James's Gazette*, a Conservative paper hostile to Gladstone, published an article based upon the book, the Liberals insisted that MacGregor be formally 'cautioned' and withdraw all copies known 'to have got into the hands of unscrupulous journalists or editors'.[89] Roberts was therefore prudent to be on good terms with Grant Duff who wrote: 'I do not look upon a Russian invasion of India as an event at all likely to happen.'[90]

While Roberts pondered strategic questions and martial races, the important Indian event of these years was Ripon's Ilbert Bill, named for the legal member of his Council. This would abolish 'judicial disqualifications based on race distinctions' which prevented Indian magistrates trying Europeans. The changes would have involved few cases, but fierce and persistent agitation against the Bill sprang up among the British, especially tea and indigo planters. Roberts told Cambridge that if anything might make him support the Bill, it was the planters' vituperative and violent language aimed at Ripon. He found it difficult to understand 'how Englishmen except of the very lowest orders could have behaved so outrageously'.[91] A compromise was adopted which surrendered the principle Ripon sought: a European defendant would in all cases have the right to claim trial by a jury of which at least half the members must be European. Indians did not have a similar right, so Europeans' privileged position was maintained. Nonetheless, educated Indians appreciated and admired Ripon, and at his departure in December 1884 acclaiming crowds lined his route to Bombay. Ripon's reduction of salt tax and repeal of Lytton's Vernacular Press Act marked his Liberal spirit.[92]

Grant-Duff and Roberts were both cautious over the Ilbert Bill.[93] Roberts was unenthusiastic about an Indian political role:

> The Europeans feel that they are being gradually ousted by the natives, while the latter again will not rest satisfied with the managing Local Boards and small municipalities: in time they will claim a place and voice in the government of the country. In theory it seems impossible to object to this, but to one who knows the natives of India well, the time seems very distant, when they can be safely trusted with such power . . .[94]

He told Ripon that he could recall no government measure in thirty-two years 'which has called forth such a bitter feeling of opposition' as the Bill.[95]

Ripon's successor, the Marquis of Dufferin, an Anglo-Irish landowner and diplomat, was appointed to overcome the division Ripon's reforms had created, splitting 'the country into two camps with Natives and Anglo-Indians yelping at each other from either side of a ditch'.[96] Dufferin promised educated Indians a larger share in provincial administration, but condemned incendiary speechifying. This period of apparent peace and British serenity was one of great importance for India's future, and Ripon had been right in trying to advance the aspirations of educated Indians. The first Indian National Congress was convened in December 1885, at Bombay, by Allan Octavian Hume, former imperial civil servant[97] and Liberal critic of Lytton's government. Indians who had met in London while studying for the Bar or the Imperial Civil Service (ICS) became its first leaders.[98] Lytton's Press Act was a catalyst for national feeling; in February, 1878, a British official had written of 'a feeling of nationality, which formerly had no existence': 'the . . . Press can now, for the first time in the history of our rule, appeal to the *whole Native population* of India against their foreign rulers'.[99] The early Congress was moderate and cautiously loyal to the crown. Roberts says nothing about it in *Forty-One Years*, although much of the Indian princes whom the British were busy wooing and rewarding. Who would guess in these years where India's future lay? As an avowed imperialist who had passed as a young soldier through British India's greatest crisis, Roberts was unsympathetic to Indian national aspirations. He was to send Randolph Churchill the Rajah of Binga's pamphlet, 'Democracy not suited to India' and a memorandum opposing the growth of local self-government.[100]

In summer 1882 Roberts's oldest friend James Hills became engaged to Elizabeth, younger daughter and co-heir of John Johnes of Dolaucothi, a fine country house in Carmarthenshire. They were married on 16 September at Westminster Abbey. He took the additional surname and the arms of Johnes.[101] Roberts congratulated him on 'becoming a Benedict'.[102] 'I am quite sure that Miss Johnes is all you say,' he told the former bachelor, 'but as one of your oldest and closest friends you must allow me to say that I think the young lady is to be congratulated on getting such a good fellow for a husband.' His wife wrote to Miss Johnes: 'We have wished for a very long time that he should marry – but we could never find any one half nice enough for our friend, it is very nice to be able to think of him *now*, quite happy.' Roberts admitted to his old friend that the Ootacamund monsoon, high wind with mist and rain, had not agreed with Nora and she was far from well. They had gone to Bangalore for a change, enabling him to inspect the troops. By contrast, the girls Aileen and Edwina were thriving 'famously' and Roberts himself very fit.[103]

Until the famous march, Hills and Roberts's careers had enjoyed similar success in the Mutiny, Abyssinia and Lushai.[104] Donald Stewart had wished to send Hills as Roberts's second-in-command on the march to Kandahar, but two Bengal artillerymen could not hold those posts together. Hills lamented: 'Alas . . . as Roberts was a Bengal artilleryman & I ditto I had to remain behind.' Had Roberts left Afghanistan when he tried to resign, Hills reflected: 'I should have been the chosen com[man]der ... I felt utterly miserable for some days after the bidding Godspeed of that column.'[105] Roberts's career left Hills's far behind, but they remained firm friends. Hills as godfather played a seminal role in the life of Freddie Roberts. Freddie had gone to his preparatory school, Sunningdale. He wrote rather familiarly to 'Dear Jimmy' signing himself 'Your affectionate godson', writing as boys do about football.[106] He spent most holidays in Wales with the Hills-Johneses, going at Easter to Roberts's sister with the Sherstons in Somerset and seeing his mother who returned each summer.[107] His father prepared the way into Everard's House at Eton, writing to the housemaster on Indian defence.[108] The girls, Aileen and Edwina, were at home at Ootacamund with their parents and their governess, 'Prydie'.[109] In February 1882, Roberts's mother died at Hampton Court where she had enjoyed a 'grace and favour' apartment. His friend Childers sent his sympathy. Roberts replied: 'She lived to a good old age (83), but she had all her faculties to the last and is a great loss to me.' Childers also reassured his friend that his 'not accepting the Quartermaster-Generalship of the Army will not in the least prejudice' future advancement and 'that the day may come when your service may be given to us ... here'. Roberts replied: 'There is plenty of work for soldiers out here, and I hope I may be able to do something towards improving the Madras Army before I leave the command.'[110]

While Madras was at peace, there was war in the Sudan. In 1882 Wolseley's victory at Tel-el-Kebir gave Britain control of Egypt. In the Sudan a nationalist and Islamic revolt under the *Mahdi*, 'the chosen one', Muhammed Ahmed, rose against Egyptian rule. Major-General Charles Gordon was sent to evacuate Egyptian garrisons, but stayed at Khartoum and was besieged by the Mahdists. Britain's 'only general', Garnet Wolseley, was sent to the rescue. A combination of bad luck, poor decisions, Mahdist resistance and the harsh climate and land frustrated the ring's last campaign. In January, 1885, the Mahdists broke into Khartoum and killed Gordon. The failure was a turning point in Wolseley's career.[111] Soldiers throughout India shared in the grief at Gordon's death. To Grant Duff, Roberts wrote of his anxiety for Wolseley's scattered force. 'The Mahdi either by accident or design has played a good game. Khartoum fell into his hands just as Wolseley had committed himself by dividing his force.'[112] 'The Indians' were sure a different plan would have offered a better chance: a landing on the Sudanese coast at Suakin and a swift march across country to Khartoum, a shorter distance than the painstaking journey up the Nile in Canadian Red River boats. 'I could never understand why Wolseley insisted upon the Nile route,' Roberts told Grant-Duff.[113]

While Wolseley's force had ascended the Nile, another under General Gerald Graham did attempt to cross from Suakin to Berber, only 240 miles, but with difficulties over water supplies. Graham won two battles but strategically achieved nothing.[114] One adventurous officer later wrote that

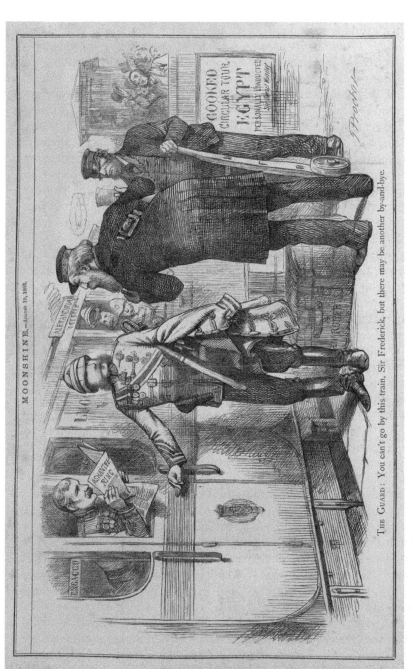

FIGURE 8 Moonshine *highlights the growing split between Roberts's 'Indians' and Garnet Wolseley's 'Ring': the Gordon Relief Expedition was the African 'Ring's last and unsuccessful campaign. Ian Hamilton thought Roberts would have succeeded (National Army Museum).*

he was sure 'Bobs' would have succeeded. 'Certain it is that Roberts would have saved Charles Gordon,' wrote that officer, Ian Hamilton. '. . . wherever the main clash was to come Roberts would have been there, in personal command.'[115] Hamilton spent six weeks' leave on the expedition, but his conviction, that Wolseley 'was not so keen to relieve Charles Gordon as to wipe the floor with Roberts's march to Kandahar', was certainly untrue.[116] His wrong and romantic views, however, point to the growth of Roberts's 'Indian ring' as rivals to Wolseley's 'Africans'. His autobiographical *Listening for the Drums* gives a memorable account of the late Victorian Army. It may have given more substance to the Wolseley–Roberts rivalry than it merits.

Hamilton first met Roberts in 1879 after an Afghan adventure: he dragged himself from his sick bed to ascend a rocky hillside and repel Afghans who had attacked a signalling party. Roberts, intrigued at the young Gordon Highlander's bold initiative, invited him to his tent to tell the tale, gave him a glass of sherry and promised to write to his father. 'The indirect sequel was Sir Fred's offer to me two and a half years later to come on his Staff,' Hamilton concluded, 'and the sherry and the letter give a useful glimpse of the secret of his popularity.'[117] Hamilton had thrived in the Gordons after an unhappy schooling, and in early 1882 was due to attend staff college. Roberts's offer intervened, he took the ADC post, and in February was promoted captain. At Ootacamund he met Lady Roberts and her daughters, Aileen and Edwina, aged eleven and seven, both full of mischief. So quickly did he fit in that Aileen remembered years later 'that Edwina looked on herself as engaged to him (aged 8 or 9) . . .'[118] Hamilton kindly told his brother: as 'little Freddy Roberts goes to Eton this term', ask a friend to take him under his wing 'and be the civil big boy towards him'.[119]

Hamilton joined other young officers, George Pretyman, Reginald Pole-Carew and Neville Chamberlain, inventor of snooker and composer of topical songs for the Christmas pantomime at Sherpur in December 1879. Roberts encouraged Hamilton's literary bent: he wrote articles for the *Madras Mail*, execrable poetry and better books.[120] As the Gordons' musketry instructor, Hamilton had absorbed the doctrine of the School of Musketry at Hythe. He had served at Majuba where the Boers totally outshot the British, and had his wrist shattered by Boer fire, leaving it crippled for life. His book *The Fighting of the Future* of 1885 envisaged that infantry sharpshooters would win battles and that cavalry charges and 'cold steel' were obsolete.[121] Roberts shared Hamilton's enthusiasm for developing good shooting. He had the rank and prestige to turn aspiration into achievement. Hamilton claimed that the revolution in musketry training originated with him. His new musketry regulations for the Indian Army were imposed two years later upon the Duke of Cambridge and the British Army followed suit.[122] For six months in 1884 Hamilton acted as Roberts's assistant military secretary, but the War Office refused to confirm the appointment, and he reverted to ADC. When he went to the Sudan, Roberts wrote to his father to say how sorry the family was to part with him: 'He has been my constant companion for more than 2 years, and like every one at Snowdon I have a great affection for him. Both socially and officially Ian has been a perfect success, he is a thorough gentleman and a first rate soldier . . .'[123]

As Roberts's five years at Madras drew to a close, British eyes in India were looking to the north-west. The viceroy invited Abdur Rahman to meet him at Rawalpindi. Lady Dufferin recorded 'a magnificent array of British uniforms – the Commander-in-Chief, Sir Donald Stewart, General Hardinge from Bombay, Sir F. Roberts from Madras, Sir Michael Biddulph the General in command here, many more officers, heaps of aides-de-camp, governors, members of Council, &c, and behind them a long line of native Princes, the Punjab chiefs'. Thirty-six tents for the viceroy's staff and guests, map-posts between them, water laid on, telephones and a post office, six extra ADCs, messengers on camels – 'that is the way we are "roughing it" in camp!' she wrote. A downpour greeted the Amir, the troops in greatcoats looking miserable. British regiments' bands escorting Abdur emphasised whose ally he was by playing Gilbert and Sullivan's 'He might have been Russian, he might have been a Prussian, but, in spite of all temptation, he is an Englishman!' The Amir did not know *HMS Pinafore*, but riposted British compliments with warnings of Afghan prejudice: 'you know my people; they are ignorant and suspicious. I cannot force them without danger, and I will not undertake responsibilities which I may not be able to discharge'. The Amir did, however, pledge his army and people to stand with the British.[124]

In April there was better weather, but bad news. In 1881 the Russians had defeated the Turkomans and in February 1884 captured Merv, the Turcomans peacefully submitting. No mountain ranges or obstacles stood between Merv and Herat.[125] A stream of intelligence during the winter of 1884–5 told of Russian pacification of Turkmenistan as a prelude to advance on Afghan territory.[126] At Pandjeh on the northern Afghan border, halfway between Merv and Herat, Russians attacked and defeated Afghan troops. Despite continued assurances from St Petersburg of pacific intent, the Russians opened a murderous fire. Over 800 Afghans were killed and the survivors fled.[127] It appeared to be the start of a Russian bid for control of northern Afghanistan. A small British detachment, the Boundary Commission, which had been sent to delimit the Russo-Afghan frontier, withdrew, but throughout spring and summer Russia and Britain prepared to fight. Gladstone felt obliged to send the navy to the Far East and 25,000 troops to Quetta. A Russian attack on Herat would mean war. Historians of Russia's Asian strategy declare that war was not part of it, but that is more obvious today than it was then.[128] General L.N. Sobolev was head of the Russian general staff's Asiatic Department and advocate of an advance on India. He provocatively published a fifteen-part series on conquerors of India.[129] Fortunately both Dufferin and Abdur kept cool heads. Abdur had no wish to be caught between the Lion and the Bear, as *Punch* cartoons showed. Dufferin observed: 'But for the accidental circumstances of the

Amir being in my camp at Rawalpindi, and the fortunate fact of his being a prince of great capacity, experience and calm judgement, the incident at Pandjeh alone ... might in itself have proved the occasion of a long and miserable war.'[130] The Russians realised that even Gladstone would fight.[131] Abdur bartered Pandjeh for Zulfiqar.

Pandjeh was not finally resolved until 1887. By that time Salisbury's Conservatives were in office and Roberts had produced another paper on Indian defence: 'What are Russia's Vulnerable Points and How have Recent Events Affected our Frontier Policy in India?' was written in May 1885 at the request of Stewart as commander-in-chief. He wanted to know where Russia could be most readily attacked. Roberts persisted in regarding the Hindu Kush as the best line of defence, but abandoned his planned advance on Herat in favour of a counter-attack. The Russians now in Merv and with new railways would get there first. To protect vulnerable British supply lines he proposed the Hazaras, who had been Britain's friends in 1878–80; they were Shia, whereas most Afghans were Sunni.[132]

Roberts would continue to follow Madras themes. What had he achieved as commander-in-chief of a scattered force composed of soldiers in whom he lacked confidence? To his former patron Napier, he had itemised his reforms, particularly improved shooting.[133] The *Madras Mail* approved most measures: he had identified himself with his army's interests and materially improved its efficiency. He had visited and inspected every unit and station at least once. The largest and most successful assembly of troops for grand manoeuvres since Lord Cornwallis's time had been held at Bangalore. Clothing material for new uniforms had proved defective 'but is being put right'. Roberts put his idea for uniform to Childers: 'for a volunteer Army such as ours, an attractive uniform is necessary; at the same time we require something like what is known as "khaki" in India, for rough work and service'.[134] The move of headquarters to Ootacamund, 'a hill where not a single soldier is quartered', was an error of judgement, concluded the *Mail*, claiming Napier and others thought so too.[135]

For the ambitious Roberts, the logical advance was to the Indian commander-in-chiefship. His key backer was Lord Randolph Churchill, Conservative politician. Churchill's support began in 1880–1. In the Commons debate on 4 September 1880, three days after Ayub's defeat, Churchill unjustly attacked Ripon for 'want of foresight, military knowledge, and caution' leading to Maiwand, and went on to praise 'the great and brilliant victory just achieved by General Roberts'. He continued: 'it was intensely gratifying to reflect that the country had still at its command skilful and intrepid generals, and could rely with confidence on its gallant soldiers.'[136] He and Roberts began corresponding in 1881.[137] At the start of 1885 he embarked on a three-month tour of India; his reputation was if anything that of a radical. He met Indian intellectuals and leaders. Meeting Roberts, however, created a deep and lasting impression.[138] R.F. Foster in his biography of Churchill attributes his subject's change from 'ostensible Riponist progressivism to a Lyttonist reaction' to the influence of Roberts, Lepel Griffin, Owen Burne and other India hands. 'Roberts's talent, decisiveness, originality and Irishness appealed to Churchill and his influence was a prominent factor in Indian policy from the time of his accession.'[139]

Roberts had already staked his claim to special insight at a first meeting with Churchill, at Allahabad in February 1885. A brigade of Indian troops was encamped there en route to Suakin to join General Graham's column in the Sudan. Lord Randolph accompanied him on an inspection. He was much struck by the men's fine appearance, which he remarked upon. Roberts replied that, fine looking as they were, he felt sure that if seriously attacked they would disgrace themselves. He wrote later, '[Lord Randolph] utterly refused to believe me and said that it was impossible such soldierly looking men could behave badly, that the Mutiny had prejudiced me against the Hindustani, and that I had no faith except in Sikhs and Gurkhas.' The denouement vindicated Roberts. At Tofrek in the Sudan on 22 March 1885, the British and Indian force was in a defended *zariba* when the Dervishes burst upon them. The 17th Bengal Native Infantry, whom Roberts and Churchill had disagreed about, fired one volley and ran. Sikhs, Royal Marines and Berkshires drove off the enemy attack in desperate fighting.[140] Roberts reminded Churchill in a letter of 15 April: 'I hear that the men quite lost their heads and fired wildly, being more dangerous to their friends than their foes.'[141]

Shortly afterwards the Conservative Unionists came into power (June 1885–February 1886). Lord Randolph became Secretary of State for India. As Donald Stewart's time of command drew to a close, men speculated on his successor. Lt-General Sir Charles Brownlow at the War Office warned Roberts of Wolseley's potential rivalry: 'you have *tout le monde* in your favour, but Wolseley is a power in the land and if he insists on it he may get it ... your best friend [Cambridge] may be glad to get him out of the way even at your expense ...' Hardinge, commander-in-chief at Bombay, had supporters, 'but God forbid that he should ever be let loose upon India with his egotistical fads & follies'.[142] Brownlow was a Bengal soldier who had served in the Umbeyla Expedition with Roberts, and the latter's fitness for command needed no proving to him. Major-General Martin Dillon at Lucknow told Cambridge: 'In public opinion at home & in India and with the Army, Sir F. Roberts stands first, and Lord R. Churchill appreciates this as do [senior?] Conservatives generally.'[143] Stewart urged Roberts 'to put all your irons into the fire *without delay* if you want to succeed me'. The Unionists gave him his best chance.[144] Lord Salisbury, Prime Minister and advocate of 'the forward policy', told Sir Henry Ponsonby, the Queen's private secretary:

> I think that Roberts has been quite the equal of Wolseley in the brilliancy of his successes, as well as in the importance of the field upon which they have been won. There is a general impression in the army that Wolseley

has had much more than his share of opportunities of distinction: & he has certainly been fully rewarded. If Roberts were to be passed over for him, a painful impression would be produced.[145]

Churchill pressed Roberts's case, Lytton supported him and Conservatives who saw Wolseley as the Liberals' man united on this cause. The Queen, busy in her own piece of royal jobbery to have her son Arthur, Duke of Connaught, appointed to Bombay, was opposed. Dufferin was unenthusiastic. After the appointment he wrote resignedly to Churchill, 'The way in which your people [the Conservatives] had run him against Wolseley made his appointment a necessity.'[146] By contrast Randolph Churchill asserted that Roberts 'was the first soldier of his age. The Russian crisis [Pandjeh] and Sir Frederick's unequalled service and experience in the theatre of possible war constituted in his eye overwhelming qualifications'. It was Lord Randolph who had convinced Salisbury and the Queen.[147] On 22 October 1885 Her Majesty gave formal approval. Roberts received local rank of general and assumed command on 28 November.[148] Grant Duff published a very fulsome tribute on Roberts's departure from Madras; the recipient, aware how differently other Liberal critics of the Afghan War had spoken of him, replied, 'it has touched me more than I can say'.[149]

CHAPTER EIGHT

Commander-in-chief, India

He became a legend in the British Army and the Indian alike . . .

P. MASON, *A MATTER OF HONOUR*

The Army, I hope under my authority, has never been jobbed . . .
Roberts will introduce a system of this sort . . .

THE DUKE OF CAMBRIDGE TO LORD DUFFERIN

The Gurkha is the bravest Asiatic I know . . . completely distinct
from all the other races in our army . . . We cannot have too
many Gurkhas . . .

LORD ROBERTS

Roberts took leave in England before beginning his new command. He spent
it profitably. He and Randolph Churchill planned the big camp of manoeuvres
which was shortly to take place.[1] Stewart had approved, and preparations
were already under way.[2] Roberts visited Florence Nightingale, who fought
a long battle for female nurses as the backbone of well-run military hospitals;
the War Office remained unenthusiastic, but in Roberts and his wife she
found a receptive audience.[3] Roberts once again followed Napier of
Magdala, who with Nightingale had planned barrack and hospital reform.[4]
Roberts also wrote to his old friend Burne on the India Council, asking that
the vacant Grand Cross of the Star of India (GCSI) be awarded to the
retiring Stewart. 'He would never ask for it himself . . .' Stewart duly received
it on 7 December.[5] Of the two long-standing friends, Stewart impressed
contemporaries with his 'sound' qualities and modest self-effacement in
contrast to Roberts, a bolder field commander and equally bold at bringing
his merits into the public eye. The Duke of Cambridge wrote to Stewart:
'I *very greatly regret* your giving up a command the duties of which you

have filled with so much tact, judgment & ability, and, if you will allow me to add, with *so much satisfaction to myself . . .*'[6] To Roberts he sent muted congratulations and a caution: 'all I would suggest is to be very prudent in council, & not to be the advocate of hasty reforms in Military Matters'. After meetings with Roberts, Cambridge admitted to Stewart: 'I doubt not, that he will prove himself a worthy successor in the post you fill.' He feared Roberts would throw himself behind the Eden Commission reforms, especially the abolition of the Madras and Bombay Armies.[7]

Major-General Martin Dillon commanding at Lucknow told Cambridge that he 'could have made no selection which would have given such satisfaction to the Army British & Native and to the Civilian element. Sir Frederick is liked and trusted'. Not all agreed. Hardinge, commander-in-chief at Bombay and senior to Roberts, was bitterly disappointed: 'Roberts assured me that he had exerted no influence to get into first place & that Lady Bobs' first thought upon hearing of his selection was that it would be my disappointment! *Il est fort celui la*! It would have been straighter to say "*Comme a la chasse*"!'[8]

His leave over, Roberts wasted no time. He reached Bombay on 24 November, spending three days with Stewart. The two friends went over the Bombay defences together and Stewart briefed Roberts on the coming camp of exercise and Burmese developments. Then Stewart embarked for England and a seat on the India Council, 'leaving the country in which he had served almost continuously for 45 years'.[9] Roberts went straight to Gwalior to see the viceroy, Dufferin, and then on to Delhi to finish preparations for the camp. He wrote to Cambridge describing the manoeuvres. Sir George Greaves commanded the northern and Sir Charles Gough the southern force. Preliminary brigade drills had begun, to be followed by the two corps commanders, Greaves and Gough, exercising their divisions one against another. The two corps would close to within 100 miles of each other. Greaves would then advance to raise the notional siege of Delhi, Gough covering the siege, seeking battle as far from the city as possible. Roberts, who knew his Indian history, explained that the plain of Panipat where they would meet was 'famous for two great battles fought in its immediate neighbourhood, one in April, 1526 by the Emperor Baber [*sic*] against Sultan Ibrahim, the other in January 1761 by Ahmed Shah against the Mahrattas'.[10] The forces would gather for a deciding contest on 14 January. In this engagement Greaves, by means of a feint, was able to mass against Gough's right and overwhelm him. Not all had gone well – too rapid an advance of cavalry killed several horses, transport needed improvement, there was a lack of good scouting – but the troops had done well. Roberts was pleased at the reaction of foreign observers. The Russians did not expect to find such an army. They noted the smartness of British and Indian cavalry and their rapidity over difficult country. Roberts rubbed points home, adding that the observers wondered 'at the obsolete pattern of our guns' and said 'it would never do for us to go to war against a European enemy without more British officers in the native regiments'.[11]

FIGURE 9 *Roberts's extensive manoeuvres on the site of famous Indian battles at Panipat were part of his measures to keep the Indian Army in a state of war readiness to repel possible incursion from the north (National Army Museum).*

After spirited work on the last two days, the 'march past' before the viceroy was spoilt as the heavens opened in a storm of thunder and lightning. Neither the commander-in-chief nor the viceroy would take shelter when the men were drenched and marching ankle-deep in mud. 'Lord Dufferin was good enough to express his entire satisfaction with the parade and the appearance of the troops.' The commander-in-chief echoed these encomiums on general orders, approving a marked improvement in fire discipline.[12]

Roberts held these manoeuvres in realistic conditions and on a grand scale. The home army had nothing like it; the first exercises on Salisbury Plain were held in 1898.[13] Comparison can be made with British-based forces. In 1892 Wolseley noted how manoeuvres in Ireland depressed him 'for they have displayed a sad amount of tactical knowledge or instinct on the part of all the Commanding Officers & Majors of Batteries. I cannot induce them to keep their commands together'. The artillery was badly handled, the infantry 'straggle all over the country in an aimless fashion strong nowhere & weak at all points'. Like Roberts, Wolseley based high standards upon experience in war.[14]

While over 35,000 men were practising war near Delhi, others were waging it in Burma. The Third Burmese War followed agitation by British merchants in Rangoon and Lower Burma for intervention to open the country to their goods. A Burmese court imposed a heavy fine on the Bombay Burmah Trading Corporation for abuse of privilege, almost certainly unjustly, and seized some of its teak. When the Burmese refused arbitration, the British issued an ultimatum. By 9 November 1885 a Burmese part refusal was met by a declaration of war.[15]

The Burma Field Force already assembled at Rangoon in Lower Burma consisted of 10,000 men in three infantry brigades, one from Bengal led by Colonel George White, two from Madras. Major-General Sir Harry Prendergast, a sapper from the Madras Army, commanded. Burmese forts at Minhla on the Irrawaddy were no match for floating batteries of 74-pounders towed up the Irrawaddy. The Burmese surrendered unconditionally on 27 November and on the 29th the British occupied Mandalay and deported King Thibaw and Queen Supiyalat. Casualties in this brief campaign were slight, primarily from cholera.

On 1 January 1886 as a New Year's present to the Queen, Burma was annexed. To the Duke of Cambridge, Dufferin wrote: 'General Prendergast certainly deserves great credit for the manner in which he has conducted the operations.'[16] In his report to Dufferin, Prendergast added: 'I deported the *Times* correspondent for transgressing the press regulations.' There broke out a prolonged insurgence against '*dacoits*' or bandits, mostly ex-servicemen. Prendergast went up to Bhamo to organise operations, leaving White in command at Mandalay. Victorian Britain's longest war ensued.[17]

In February 1886, Dufferin travelled to Burma with his wife and staff, accompanied by Roberts and his staff.[18] White organised the viceroy's formal state entry at Mandalay which 'went off without a hitch'. White was

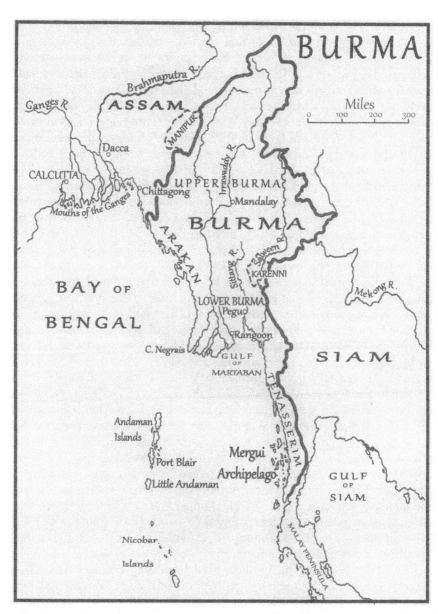

MAP 9 *Burma*

delighted to see old Simla friends again. 'Lord Roberts is looking so young, and so are all his staff except Chapman, who is looking very wretched . . .' He had been seasick.

Dufferin was impressed with White, who pointing to a sentry told him British authority reached no further than the man's rifle and bayonet.[19] Roberts was to champion White's career following his Afghan fighting. White told his wife Amy: '[Roberts] is such a pleasant little man and I have a great feeling towards him as my chief.' He had shrewdly told her that she must see Roberts when he was home between Madras and Bengal commands.[20] Roberts did not stay long: he sent Cambridge a map to show how vast Burma was and how small Prendergast's force. Police were to be raised, the country divided into districts under civil officers, but for some months troops carried out civil duties. Sir Charles Bernard, a friend of Roberts and a nephew of Lord Lawrence, was head of the civil administration. Roberts wanted centralised military control under Prendergast, answerable to him. Opinion at home was critical as Burma remained unsettled. Roberts regretted this, and told Cambridge that Prendergast had done very well and was 'very straightforward and hard working; and though not brilliant, he has more than average intelligence'.[21]

White, however, disagreed: 'General P[rendergast] is a man of *no* ability . . . singularly weak & without [judgement?]. His chief of the staff is not much better.' White thought their orders contradictory and their expeditions ill advised. He may have told Roberts this. Success had 'dropped into our hands' because the captains of the Irrawaddy Steam Flotilla Company were experts, with a magnificent fleet of river steamers and barges. White told his brother it would have been harder if the Burmese 'had been handled with energy'.[22]

Prendergast was soon in trouble from the reports of *The Times* Rangoon correspondent E.K. Moylan, whom he had deported. Moylan reported the provost marshall photographing Burmese insurgents being executed by firing squad. He published an interview with Thibaw and an exaggerated tale of disorder and looting at Mandalay. T.H. Buckle, editor of *The Times* and a friend of Randolph Churchill, pulled strings to return Moylan to Mandalay. He embarked on a bitter vendetta, first against Prendergast and the soldiers, then against civilians. He claimed to have discovered threats by the provost marshal to extract testimony from a Burmese about to be shot. This hit the press like a bombshell. Churchill wired to Dufferin that Prendergast was unfit for command.[23]

The Indian Secretary in the short-lived Liberal government (February–August 1886), Lord Kimberley, refused to extend Prendergast's service beyond March 1886. He could be retained only by Kimberley's agreement. A delighted White took his place. Prendergast was only fifty-one, but his military career was over.[24]

It was a demonstration of press power. Dufferin's protests were to no avail. Roberts does not appear to have stood up for him; perhaps it was too late, the correspondence having passed by him to the Indian Military

Department; perhaps as a Bengal soldier he felt less loyalty to a Madras sapper; in any case White would benefit. Colonel Hooper, the provost marshal, was acquitted by a court of enquiry, but to appease the howl in England he had to hand in his papers. He was granted a full colonel's pension of £1,100 in recompense.[25]

White now in command faced huge problems. Roberts asked Cambridge that he be given major-general's rank. Dufferin wrote in support: '[White] seemed not only to be a good soldier, but an intelligent man all round ... Moreover he had got to know the country thoroughly, and was on most cordial terms with the Chief Commissioner.'[26] Cambridge was obdurate; he saw Roberts's hand in pushing forward his man.[27] In July he accused Roberts of 'jobbery', but not to him; he told Dufferin: 'I greatly objected, not because Colonel White was not a good officer, but because his selection passes him over the head of 250 officers, many of whom are of great service, & some of whom are even serving at the present moment in India.'[28]

In late September 1886, Viscount Cross, Indian Secretary in Salisbury's new ministry (1886–92), wrote: 'I had a long conversation with the Duke of Cambridge about White, but he will do nothing as to military rank.' General Sir Herbert Macpherson, commander-in-chief Madras, veteran of Afghanistan, was appointed to take command in Burma. White had served with him, and the two got on well, but in October 1886, Macpherson died suddenly from fever. In view of White being a junior colonel and public opinion at home wanting reassurance, Roberts was sent. His arrival with his staff on 9 November calmed English anxieties. He was under no illusion about the nature of his task or the length of time it would take. He was careful to pay tribute to the 'two able officers at the head of affairs', White and Bernard, and to draw public attention to their achievement.[29]

White saw that Burmese soldiers who occupied Mandalay and its forts had been thrown out of work and joined 'the lawless hill-men'; both hillmen and ex-soldiers were burning villages. The people had not welcomed the British: in their easy-going way, they were loyal to a corrupt royal family. White planned to work up the two great rivers, the Irrawaddy and Chindwin, and get a firm grip of country on both banks by establishing mutually supporting military posts.[30] In December he was awarded the KCB, and travelled upriver with Roberts to Bhamo. He told his wife: 'Sir Frederick is a first-class chief to serve under. He is only too anxious to be always at work. He has both mental and bodily vigour to a degree I have never before met with in the Army. We have organised some more little campaigns.'[31] Roberts accepted White's wish not to reduce troop numbers; he issued detailed instructions to officers commanding columns; and a police force was raised, largely in India.[32] He was dissatisfied with the hospital established for European soldiers and ordered the inspector general at Rangoon to visit at once 'and arrange to relieve Surgeon Major Bennett who is now in medical charge, and is evidently quite unfit for so responsible a position'.[33] He made a point of cultivating the saffron-robed priests, whose

FIGURE 10 *Roberts and Staff in Burma. Roberts took charge in the Third Burmese War to reassure public opinion after General Sir Herbert Macpherson died. His 'young men' accompanied him: Military Secretary Pole-Carew to right front, Rawlinson in the back (National Army Museum).*

temples controlled education, and who, he insisted, 'bore us no ill-will'.[34] He told Edward Sladen, chief political officer at Mandalay, that the head priesthood constantly came to see him 'and are helping us in every way; and the people were flocking to work on the railway and entrenchments'.[35] When Roberts returned to India, White corresponded with him in 'demi-official form' although his chief was Arbuthnot at Madras, more evidence of Bengal soldiers' *modus operandi*. Villages were protected with stockades and outposts, and skirmishes continued. In November 1887 White was promoted major-general, thanks firstly to Roberts, secondly to Dufferin and thirdly to Ripon who wrote on his behalf to Cambridge.[36] 'I believe I go over about 280 Colonels [White wrote] including some who think themselves quite the pick of the bunch . . .'[37] In January 1888 it was proposed he stay another year, but Roberts was ready to give him a division, at Quetta, a frontier posting which suited his temperament; a change was desirable. He had been working extremely hard in far from ideal conditions; in Thibaw's quarters which he occupied the rain came down through cracks in the Portland cement.[38]

The Third Burmese War was a subalterns' war, with units of 120 mounted men moving through apparently endless jungle in pursuit of an elusive foe. Mounted infantry, largely organised by Major Penn Symons of the South Wales Borderers, proved their worth. It took five years to bring peace.[39] In Roberts's career, the Burma War draws scant attention, only three pages of 500 and an appendix in *Forty-One Years*. Time there was short, but issues were important: civil-military cooperation in an insurgency, establishing a police force, the power of the press, a huge country added to the Empire. Occupying an enemy capital did not end a long guerrilla war, a point which Roberts chose to ignore in South Africa.

In September 1887 both Roberts and White were at Simla, a break from Burma. It was seven years since the victory over Ayub outside Kandahar, and fifty officers attended a celebratory dinner. Roberts was in his element, saluted in toasts and showing an unusual memory for steps made by his former comrades-in-arms. He hailed George White as 'the bravest among many brave men' and predicted 'a bright professional future'; and Mortimer Durand for his appointment to 'the blue ribbon' of the Civil Service, the Foreign Secretaryship of the Indian government. Durand in his reply made the soldiers laugh by referring to political officers as 'an inconvenient and rather disagreeable species of campaign follower'.[40] The following year Ian Hamilton, close to Roberts, wrote to Lady White predicting her husband would be the next Indian commander-in-chief.[41]

The Indian government had some misfortune in 1886. Two successive military members of the viceroy's council died in quick succession.[42] The military member as the viceroy's personal advisor could throw obstacles in the way of a commander-in-chief's plans. Roberts did not look forward to working with Lt-General George Chesney, the next nominee; 'he is very clever, but he has a fashion of starting hares, and never likes running anyone's hares but his own'.[43] Roberts, a master at hare-running himself, preferred his friend Sir Charles Brownlow, but Cambridge reassured him that the allegedly radical Chesney had moderated his views. Roberts was soon thanking the commander-in-chief: 'I find [Chesney] most agreeable, and anxious to meet me in every way; his ability is undeniable and I have every reason to believe that we shall get on well together.' They were travelling together in the Punjab, the North-West Province and Oude, and meeting to discuss frontier defence.[44] Chesney, a Mutiny veteran two years older than Roberts, had achieved notoriety in 1871 when he anonymously published 'The Battle of Dorking', a vivid tale of a German surprise invasion of Britain and the destruction of British power. The two proved like-minded, agreeing on 'the martial races' and strategy against Russia. They cooperated in constructing frontier and port defences and strategic railways. In his memoirs Roberts recorded his debt.[45]

Dufferin told the Duke of Cambridge: 'We have also appointed a mobilization committee under the presidency of Sir Frederick Roberts, which is doing good work, and with our present active minded little Commander in Chief, I hope that things will gradually be got into such shape as will make us pretty safe against the Russians.'[46] Mobilisation meant improving transport, found wanting in Afghanistan. Roberts chaired the committee, but benefited from the work of Lt-Colonel W.K. Elles and Major-General Collen. Several thousand mules were purchased in readiness, and a record made of districts where animals could be obtained in war. A prize was offered for the design of a strong, light cart, and when a plan had been selected large numbers were constructed. Specialist transport officers underwent a course of instruction and had to pass an examination in loading and animal management.[47] Roberts also chaired a defence committee, and he appointed as secretary Lt-Colonel William Nicholson, veteran of Afghanistan, a Royal Engineer from the Public Works Department: 'It was in a great measure due to Colonel Nicholson's clear sighted judgment on the many knotty questions which came before us, and to his technical knowledge, that the schemes for the defence of the frontier, and for the ports of Bombay, Karachi, Calcutta, Rangoon and Madras were carried out so rapidly, thoroughly and economically as they were.' The cost was about £3.5 million.[48] Roberts continued to advocate building strategic railways and defence works: he wanted railways to Kandahar and Jalalabad, to the Zhob Valley and Pishin, thus enabling rapid deployment of troops against a Russian incursion aided by border tribesmen. Liberal and Conservative governments reduced his plans on grounds of cost.[49]

Roberts continued to praise the 'martial races' and denigrate the Madras sepoys.[50] 'From all sides complaints were heard [in Burma] that the Madras sepoy was useless, and that even against the ill-armed and unwarlike Burman it was hopeless to expect him to acquit himself creditably . . .' This appeared in Roberts's published account of his command, and is *ex post facto* justification. Lt-General Menezes, historian of the Indian Army, had no difficulty in showing that the allegedly suspect regiments, the 10th and 12th, were commanded by poor leaders; the CO and most officers of the 12th posted in just before reaching Burma and were physically unfit for active service; the CO and second-in-command of the 10th were both unfit and soon retired. Even George White, a Bengal soldier, praised six Madras regiments, while detachments of two others had shown 'conspicuous gallantry under fire'.[51] It was perverse to judge a whole regiment on a few incidents when the troops were scattered in penny packets. Martin Dillon sent the Duke of Cambridge a newspaper cutting of the deeds of the 21st Madras Infantry and 2nd Madras Cavalry in March 1886. Led by a Jemadar and an Indian soldier, the infantry with bayonets fixed had crossed a disputed bridge in the face of a force of Dacoits. Firing volleys into the thick scrub along the bank, they killed or cleared out the enemy. 'The Madras sepoy . . . only wants to see service, and to be knocked about a bit,' wrote the local commander, 'to be as good a fighting man as any else.'[52] Macpherson, commander-in-chief of the Madras Army, quoted George White to defend his men: 'I think the Madras troops have much improved since the commencement of the campaign. They have got more confidence in themselves. I also expect that the campaign will reawaken the traditions of soldierly spirit which [had] almost died out of the Madras Army of today, from the absence of active service.'[53]

On the Ridge at Delhi and in Afghanistan, however, Roberts had seen the fighting prowess of Punjabis, Sikhs and Gurkhas. When his column arrived at Kandahar in 1880, he and other Bengal soldiers documented Bombay apathy and lack of spirit.[54] He had disbanded eight Madras infantry regiments. Now, supported by Chesney, he arranged the disbanding of six more.[55] The opposite side of the coin was the increase in Gurkhas. Roberts championed these hardy, bullet-headed soldiers, whose distinguished service continues today. He was not alone: in June 1885 Stewart thought five new Gurkha regiments which he had promoted 'will be a grand acquisition'.[56] In 1885–6 recruitment was delayed both by the home government and difficulty in Nepal; Roberts advised the government to raise one of the battalions in upper Gahrwal. At the same time he sought to raise three extra Sikh battalions.[57] By 1891–2, difficulties had been solved. 'The number of Gurkha recruits we now get annually is really astonishing,' he wrote. There were thirteen Gurkha regiments and more than sufficient men 'of excellent stamp'. He attributed success to placing recruiting under one officer, Captain Vansittart of the 5th Gurkhas. He spent October to March or April at the hill station nearest to Nepal, and was so successful as to fill police corps in Burma and Assam with Gurkhas as well as the regiments.[58] Roberts's influence continued. Sir Herbert Kitchener, as commander-in-chief from 1902 to 1909, recruited an additional 6,000 Gurkhas and converted nine battalions of Madrassis into Punjabis.[59] Even today, the Indian Army recruits widely from the 'martial races'.[60] The limits of this policy were shown, however, in 1914–18: recruitment in the martial races proved too narrow for the necessary massive expansion.[61]

Roberts told Cambridge in April 1886: 'you may depend, sir, on my never losing an opportunity to press upon the Government the necessity of improving the efficiency of the Army, the importance of which no one is more alive to than I am'.[62] British and Indian troops trained intensively for operations against Russians or Afghans at large camps of exercise in the 1880s and 1890s. His newly-instituted Bengal Presidency Rifle Association encouraged shooting through competitions in regimental rifle clubs, leading to a meeting at Simla in the hot weather. Roberts offered a silver cup and 100 rupees to the best infantry and cavalry teams for volley and independent firing. Four schools of musketry were established (Roberts wanted seven). In 1892 at Attock, a field firing exercise was carried out with battle realism never before attempted, using moving targets.[63]

Roberts also ordered an increasing number of machine-guns of varied types, Nordenfeldt, Gardner and Gatling; he had tried them, without much success, in Afghanistan in 1879–80. He saw that they were an infantry weapon which would prove invaluable in gateways, ditches or weak points of fortresses.[64] Guns for the artillery were designed at home, but as a gunner, Roberts was alert to their strengths and weaknesses. After the 1886 Camp of Exercise he pressed for a better weapon than the 9-pounder. The breech-loading 12-pounder was adopted by both field artillery and horse artillery by 1885. In the cavalry camp of exercise at Meerut, however, the Horse Artillery could barely 'manoeuvre their guns with sufficient rapidity'. Roberts told Cambridge that the exercises 'proved conclusively that the new 12-p[ounde]r is far too heavy a gun for Horse Artillery'. The carriage was too complicated, and dust caused axle traversing devices to seize. A lighter 12-pounder gun was developed in 1892, the more powerful cordite replacing gunpowder, the carriage simpler, the barrel shorter. It entered service in 1894.[65]

In October 1887, he secured the appointment of Brigadier-General George Luck as the first inspector general of cavalry in India. Luck had impressed him at a cavalry camp of exercise near Rawalpindi. He told him on his inspection tours to note the qualities of officers, especially the most senior. 'We want to get the best fitted for command, and unless I am mistaken, very few men possess all the qualities required in a cavalry leader.' He wanted to improve British cavalry scouting and readiness to use firearms. 'Cavalry should be armed with the best rifle that can be conveniently carried', and it should be slung over the men's backs as soon as enemy were reported. He asked Charles Gough, an experienced cavalry general, about the lance's effectiveness, whether they should have more lancer regiments, and if lances should be for the front rank only.[66] Soldiers in both Britain and India wondered whether increasing accuracy and rate of fire of infantry and artillery weapons had rendered obsolete the *arme blanche* ('cold steel'). In 1888, Wolseley as adjutant-general created a Mounted Infantry School at Aldershot to train men from every line battalion in the army.[67] In Burma the Mounted Infantry organised by Colonel Penn Symons and riding small, hardy Burmese ponies did excellent work. Was their success in Burmese forests applicable elsewhere? Brevet-Major Percival Marling, who had transferred from infantry to cavalry and who judged that in the Sudan 'cavalry shooting was rotten', was put in command of the first Mounted Infantry School held in India, which lasted six weeks.[68]

On the urging chiefly of Roberts and George White, the Indian government established class regiments, i.e. regiments composed of men of the same race. From 1887 to 1902, twelve new battalions were raised and nine reconstituted on this system. It was argued that this produced better and happier fighting units, but there was a danger as agitation and attempts to subvert the army increased in the early 1900s: might the men of a homogeneous regiment desert together? Sikhs and Hindus were introduced into Muslim regiments, and mixed regiments were formed based on class companies.[69]

Roberts was opposed to giving Indians rank above subedar-major. Chesney for once disagreed with him, and supporting his view the Indian government, in May 1885, decided to commission Indians. Two regiments were raised and officered under this system. Much dispute ensued. In a powerful minute of 29 July 1886, Roberts opposed the scheme. He said they were good soldiers, but did not make officers, claiming 'a strong feeling among the ranks of the British Army that natives neither physically nor morally are as good soldiers as they themselves'. Chesney, however, argued in January 1888 that troublesome natives who allied themselves with the seditious vernacular press got what they wanted, whereas soldiers who remained loyal and silent received nothing. He wanted an Indian Sandhurst. Roberts strongly objected in another minute in May, posing the question what would have happened in 1857 if the sepoys had been well officered and possessed a general capable of directing an army in the field. Giving higher education to senior native officers would work against the British; such men would have better intelligence and knowledge of English, and the Russians would be sure to outbid the British in promises of pay and preferment. His views carried the day, until Chesney revived his scheme when the Bombay Army wished to start a college for the education of Indian gentlemen as a memorial to the Duke of Connaught who had just retired as Bombay commander-in-chief. Roberts once again opposed: the least warlike peoples would be selected, not the Gurkhas, Pathans and Sikhs, good soldiers, fond of manly sports, but slow to learn. Muslims would be deterred from enlisting if there were Hindu officers, and vice-versa. Recruiting would fall off. In 1890, Chesney retired as military member, plans for schools to educate native officers were dropped on grounds of expense, and Roberts returned to the debate in a minute of July 1890; he asserted that a mercenary army could turn against its paymasters, that the sepoys remained loyal when their true interests were considered, and these did not include elevating the more educated Indian to higher rank. This appeared to be the last word, for a time. Schemes for commissioning Indian officers began again under Kitchener, who knew nothing of India and did not speak the language, and

Curzon, most masterly of viceroys, who founded a school at Dehra Dun for native princes.[70] Philip Mason, historian of the Indian Army, notes the paradox: Roberts 'so warm a character in his personal relations and [who] inspired such affection among Indian troops' was swayed by his memory of the events of 1857 to oppose commissions, in contrast to Kitchener who 'never won their hearts'.[71] Indianisation began properly, but somewhat half-heartedly, under Roberts's protégé Rawlinson in the 1920s, and then proceeded apace during the Second World War.

Roberts's energy extended to mobilising and improving the armies of the native princes' states to assist the defence of India. He wooed the native princes, especially those who were good sportsmen and soldierly. Following demonstrations of princely loyalty, especially by the Nizam of Hyderabad, in 1885 at the time of Pandjeh, the Indian government sent training officers and modern weapons to prepare selected units of the princes' armies to fight beside Indian Army regiments. Roberts inspected troops of Jodhpur, Ulwar and Kashmir on his 1889 tour, and an inspector-general of imperial service troops was appointed. Kashmir, where Roberts's protégé Neville Chamberlain was military secretary, was the largest of these improved contingents.[72]

India as 'an English barracks in an Eastern Sea' was a bulwark of Empire. In the nineteenth century, Indian troops served in Abyssinia once, China and Afghanistan twice, Burma three times, on the frontier on innumerable occasions; they were deployed to Malta, Egypt and the Sudan. Roberts was aware of their ubiquity, but it was Russia against whom he prepared to lead his improved army. He was convinced of the Russian threat and tirelessly sought to convert politicians and leading soldiers to his view.[73] The Russian storming of Geok-Tepe, the seizure of Merv and the Pandjeh Incident were evidence of aggressive plans. Roberts did not always find a willing audience for increased military expenditure. The Indian government already spent 40 per cent of its revenue on the army in peace, and railways were built for strategic as well as economic purposes. In the late nineteenth century, the decline in the value of silver, on which the rupee was based, put further pressure on Indian finances. Reluctantly, the Indian government imposed income tax and increased the unpopular salt tax.[74] Roberts, criticised by Edwin Johnson and the Duke of Cambridge for seeking economies proposed by the Eden Committee, now argued for troop increases. Indian mountain batteries received an extra gun, the Bengal Army nine new infantry battalions, cavalry extra regiments and extra squadrons in existing regiments: this brought total Indian troops to 153,092. The proportion of 'martial race' troops grew from 28 to 46 per cent.[75]

The Russians continued to plan for an invasion of India, based on an assumption shared with British leaders, that military victory was not necessary to bring down the Raj, simply a brief campaign followed by an Indian rising. 'The very appearance of even a small force on the frontiers of India is sufficient to kindle a rebellion, and to ensure the overthrow of the British dominion in Hindustan,' wrote one Russian general.[76] The Russian plan which fell into British hands in 1886 envisaged a two-stage advance. A single campaign would absorb the northern provinces of Afghanistan. After a pause of two or three years to rest the army and administer the country, a second campaign would close with the capture of Kabul, Kandahar and Kashmir. 'There is no occasion to speak of a third campaign, because after our first advance the English would be in a pitiable state in India, and fifty per cent of their influence would have gone: and after our second advance the English would find themselves in the same state as they were in 1857, with this difference – that the natives would have our support.' Roberts believed that British power in India rested on prestige and military readiness. Pointing to Russian advances which brought them to the Afghan border, he asserted that Russia must be taught 'that between her and the fulfilment of her ambition lies a barrier that may not be passed – the might of imperial England'.[77]

Vital to war readiness was intelligence. The War Office's Military Intelligence Department was established by Cardwell on April Fools' Day, 1873;[78] the Admiralty followed in the 1880s. In 1876 Captain Collen, RA, had written to Roberts, then QMG, suggesting the formation of an intelligence branch. Napier and Roberts gave approval and allowed Collen extended leave to study the London department. Captain J.A.S. Colquhoun's Durand-Medal-winning essay 'On the Formation of an Intelligence Department for India' (1876) closely represented the views of Roberts and MacGregor. Colquhoun argued that the Russian threat to India and the Prussian revolution in conducting war made such an agency imperative to India's defence.[79] The Indian beginning in July 1878 was modest: three officers, three draftsmen (mapmakers) and a Persian interpreter. The Corps of Guides added intelligence-gathering to its fighting role.[80] In 1884, MacGregor as QMG took charge of the intelligence department, improved its efficiency and prepared plans to mobilise an army corps in emergency. After his death from peritonitis in February 1887, aged forty-six, Roberts was left to champion the Forward School.[81] He knew he had to tread carefully; Gladstone's government had suppressed Macgregor's work *The Defence of India* and administered a formal rebuke.

Roberts's influence depended upon several factors: his reputation from his Afghan victories, his force of character and persuasiveness, his recruitment of allies like Chesney, his certainty that he was right. Relations with the viceroy were critical: he had seen how Lytton looked down upon Haines, and how advantageous had been mutual respect at Madras with Grant Duff. Dufferin had not been keen on Roberts's appointment. He and his wife liked Sir Donald Stewart, whom Lady Dufferin termed 'always the gayest of the gay', at parties enjoying himself immensely and joining in everything.[82] Did the vicereine have reservations when Roberts opened the sports at the Delhi Review with a feat of tent-pegging (picking up a tent-peg with a lance from a galloping horse)? 'As everybody said, no other commander-in-chief in the world could have attempted such a thing ...' And perhaps no commander-in-chief should have attempted it, but he was known for his horsemanship, winning the same event at the gymkhana in May. In June 1886 Dufferin and Roberts hosted the Etonians, and as there were only sixteen Roberts asked the ladies to dine and 'made a nice little speech' which met with the vicereine's approval. Seventh February 1887 was chosen to celebrate the Queen's Golden Jubilee as June, the official date in England, would have been too hot. On the 22nd Lady Roberts held a fancy-dress ball, and made it an occasion to puff her husband's success:

> it was undoubtedly a very pretty ball [wrote the vicereine] and a very successful one. The new room is painted blue and white, and it lights up very well. On the walls were blue shields with the names of Sir Frederick's fields of battle in gold letters on them, and standing sentry in various parts of the rooms were soldiers from some of the regiments which made the great march with him. At the back of the stage was a trophy made of bayonets, a great '50' in the centre of it, and the world 'Jubilee' below. The night fortunately was fine . . .[83]

The ball was at the Robertses' house, 'Snowdon'. They had bought it in 1873–4 while he was QMG, and began to improve the building, once used as a dispensary. Lady Roberts, who was 'a really good judge' at fitting out homes, used Whiteley's of London who '[knew] how to send everything to remote parts of India'.[84] In 1887, the ballroom had just been completed, and that year Simla was particularly jolly because of the celebrations.[85]

White visited them in July the following year and told his wife: 'The Chief and Lady Roberts have been kindness itself. Sir Fred the most attentive host I have ever stayed with and Lady R. is most kind. The party consists of Sir F. Lady R their son Freddy . . . Miss Roberts . . . and a younger girl . . . It is the nicest family party possible. The children are on the nicest terms with their father and mother.' The ADCs were 'all nice & bright'.[86] White's letters speak of Lady Roberts's influence. Five days later, he wrote: '[Lady Roberts] is a prejudiced woman & nothing is too bad for those she does not like but I think she is a warm friend. One thing is very certain, that she takes too much part in Sir Fred's business and that it is generally known.' He asked his wife in replying to any letter from Lady Roberts to mention the good impression the family created. 'I think it would gratify Sir F. & Her Ladyship.'[87]

Lady Roberts shared her husband's ambition.[88] In the Second Afghan War, in early 1880 when he was in trouble after the Kabul hangings and Brigadier Massy's sacking, she established 'my headquarters while at home' at Evercreech in Somerset with her sister and brother-in-law, the Sherstons. She sought the support of the young Lord Melgund, the future viceroy, Lord Minto, against hostile newspapermen. Later from Exmouth where she had gone for 'six weeks sea-bathing and air for my chicks', she encouraged Melgund to write against a Captain Norman 'whose nasty unfair letters'

FIGURE 11 *Roberts, aides and family outside their home at Simla. The Robertses were praised as welcoming and attentive hosts. Daughters Aileen and Edwina are on either side of father with Governess 'Prydie' seated above Edwina; Nora is behind her husband's right shoulder (National Army Museum).*

appeared in *The Times*.[89] Rumours of her influence abounded and long
persisted.[90] Hugh Bixby Luard, an Indian Army medical officer, wrote:
'When I was in India, it was said that any ambitious officer who wished to
get on found it advisable to get favour from Lady Roberts at Simla, who was
supposed to have unbounded influence with [her husband], and was a
person of very strong character.' Luard modifies this:

> It was also said quite truly that Bobs never forgot his old friends and
> comrades, and took care to advance their sons in the services. My own
> belief is that he was a good judge of character, devoted solely to the
> public interest, and rarely made a bad appointment: but naturally out of
> a host of equally competent officers chose those whom he knew most
> about: and that he exercised the same discretion in considering Lady
> Roberts candidates or favourites.[91]

Letters from the future General Sir Henry Rawlinson, then a young
officer in the 60th Rifles, supplement White's. The friendship of Roberts and
Rawlinson's father, also Sir Henry, advocate of the Forward School, brought
him to Simla in April 1886. He ecstatically told his parents: 'I am now here
comfortably installed . . . The Chief and Lady Bobs have been very kind to
me and everything bids well for a good time during the next few months.
My brother A.D.C.s are a capital lot of chaps and we are all great palls [*sic*]
already. Lady Babbs [*sic*] is very nice indeed . . . she looks after us all like a
mother.' There was more of the same in May: 'Lady Roberts is very nice and
extremely kind in every way and in fact treats us all as if we were her many
sons.' She told Rawlinson's mother: 'Rawly is great fun and v. useful to us.'[92]
In August 1888, however, 'Rawly' came back from sitting exams and
wrote in a different vein:

> You may be surprised at what I am going to say, but *on no account repeat
> it*. Lady Bobs is the most impossible person to get on with for those to
> whom she takes a dislike. Personally I have no difficulty whatever she is
> always most kind to me and I have nothing whatever to complain of.
> However, people in Simla hate her; she in her position as wife of the C. in
> C. should have no prejudices whatever and ought to treat all people with
> the same amount of courtesy. This she will not however do, and if she
> hears a story (and there are many about) relating to anyone she dislikes,
> whether it be true or not, she refuses to ask them to the house and ignores
> them entirely.

He added that 'many people's backs are up' and that she had behaved badly
to Maxwell Sherston who was leaving the staff to command a troop of
cavalry. Rawlinson and staff friends thought she was doing Sir Fred 'a great
deal of harm and getting for the house a bad name'. He added that her
temper might be affected by her liver and that the best thing for 'the Chief

and his staff is for Lady R. to go home – either on account of health or to take her children'.[93]

Here are the words of a young man, exuberant at first, then overly critical. In fact, Maxwell Sherston remained on good terms with her husband.[94] As a Victorian wife with professions closed to her, Nora Roberts had few openings for ambition and talent. As a memsahib in India, she could have been drawn into frivolity and idleness.[95] The classic defence of memsahibs was made in *The Englishwoman in India*[96] by Maud Diver, herself one of them, daughter and wife of a soldier: 'The fact remains that India's heroines and martyrs far outnumber her social sinners; and it is a fact of which English men and women may justly feel proud.' Mrs Diver divided Englishwomen in India into two classes, 'devotees of work and devotees of play . . . both desperately earnest'. As one of the former, Nora Roberts comes out rather well.

The vicereine, Lady Dufferin, drew encomiums by establishing in 1885 institutional midwifery in India, founding the National Association for Supplying Female Medical Aid to the Women of India, often known as the Countess of Dufferin Fund. The Fund paid for recruiting and training women doctors, nurses and midwives to relieve Indian women's suffering from illness and child-bearing. By the time the Dufferins left India her scheme had been adopted in every province.[97] Lady Roberts's nursing scheme may have been triggered by this success; it drew inspiration from Florence Nightingale and from her own experience helping her husband in cholera camps. She herself stated: 'My first thought when Sir Frederick was made Commander-in-Chief in India was that I would do my best to get female nursing sanctioned for our soldiers, and when I came out, I wrote . . . to Government . . . 29th July, 1886.'[98] From the Irrawaddy in November 1886, Roberts had told Cambridge when praising a hospital at Rangoon: 'On these occasions, however, I always regret that there are no Lady Nurses in our Indian hospitals. The want of them is much felt, but I am glad to say that the Government have agreed to a proposal made by Lady Roberts that Ladies shall in future be employed.'[99] Until 1886 the untrained orderly was the only substitute for nurses. The Army Hospital Native Corps cleaned the wards. To remedy this, her memorandum of July 1886 called attention to many lives lost, especially through enteric (typhoid), and appealed to the Indian government to sanction employing lady nurses.[100] Her husband as a member of the Viceroy's Council could draw her plans to the attention of India's highest authority. Dufferin accepted the proposal that a number of trained nursing sisters should be brought from Britain. The Secretary of State agreed, subject to conditions. Official funds would pay for the nurses' passage to India, and their salaries while serving there. Other funds would have to be raised for passages back to Britain on health grounds, and public subscription would pay for homes for the nurses in hill stations where they might rest and recuperate during the hot weather. The 'Lady Roberts' Fund' was subscribed to by every British regiment and battery in India, and within a few months the scheme was in operation. The first nurses reached India in March 1888.[101]

Another need was for the care of young officers, convalescent after discharge from official hospitals. Many went to the hills to recover, but, lacking proper food and attention in the clubs and hotels where they stayed, some died of their illnesses. A further appeal, to the officers, led to a fund which provided wards for them at the nurses' homes and paid for nursing, either there or in the plains when the hill stations were closed in the winter.

Funds from continued appeals maintained and repaired homes in Murree and Quetta, Kasauli and Wellington, and established nurses at other stations. Lady Roberts's care and foresight in providing nurses won praise.[102] On 26 April 1892, *The Times* published a letter from a surgeon-colonel with nearly twenty-seven years' service in India stating that shortage of nurses had been the main difficulty in overcoming typhus and other illnesses. 'Now all has changed. The Government of India has a staff of most skilled and excellent lady nurses . . .'[103] In a cholera epidemic, the chief medical officer praised 'the valuable services rendered to the cholera patients by the nursing sisters . . . Nothing could exceed their attention and care . . .'[104] Although the nurses were few, they proved an important beginning. Thirty members of the Army Nursing Service were sent to India at the end of the nineteenth century and carried on the work of Lady Roberts's nurses. They formed the nucleus of the Queen Alexandra's Military Nursing Service for India, organised in 1903, with an establishment of eighty-four nursing sisters and five lady superintendents. Their duties were to nurse sick and wounded British soldiers in hospital (including the British officers of Indian units) and to instruct and supervise the ward staff of the Royal Army Medical Corps (RAMC). They also ran the hospitals where families of British troops were treated.[105]

A counter-claim is that Lady Roberts induced her husband to close down Indian Army brothels and with them 'lock hospitals'. These provided a system of inspection to prevent prostitutes passing VD (venereal disease) to soldiers.[106] That she was influential is clear; that she had the power of parliamentary statute is untrue.[107] Regimented military prostitution was revived following an 1863 Commission on the Sanitary State of the Army, which described VD as a scourge of British troops. The Cantonments Act of 1864 laid down registration of prostitutes and the Contagious Diseases Act of 1867 extended the system. However, in India missionaries and in England Quakers, the Bishop of Lichfield and Josephine Butler of the Ladies National Association sought to end it.[108] When the Madras and Bombay governments were told to suspend the Contagious Diseases Act in 1881, Madras protested, supported by Roberts. The hospitals were closed, however, and by the time Dufferin succeeded Ripon, VD was spreading. Indian authorities wished to reopen hospitals. On 17 June 1886, QMG Major-General Chapman issued a circular memorandum, which he later regretted, explaining that Roberts was anxious to do all possible to check VD, and wanted inspections and treatment whenever necessary. That year the repeal of the Contagious Diseases Act ended the system in England. In July 1887 London sent an order for its abolition in India. Both Dufferin and Roberts wanted it to continue. Roberts told the viceroy that 101 of 177 soldiers in hospital at Rawalpindi had VD, and reopening the lock hospital there should prevent such a state of affairs. VD was to be treated along with cholera, smallpox 'or any other loathsome disease'. By the Cantonment Act of 1889, hospitals were reintroduced.[109]

Trouble soon came. Alfred Dyer, a seasoned Quaker publicist, travelled to India and discovered prostitutes' tents pitched next to the regiments'. 'The tents of the Government harlots confront the troops from morning to night,' wrote Dyer. He scored a publicity coup. In 'The Infidel Government of India' he published Chapman's circular and a paper from the CO of the 2nd Battalion the Cheshire Regiment seeking additional prostitutes for his men; the CO concluded: 'Please send young and attractive women.' There was uproar in the Commons, and reformers carried a resolution that the offending laws should be repealed.[110] Dufferin wrote of 'the shrieking sisterhood' and denied that his government knew anything about obtaining pretty women for the troops. Both Roberts and Chesney said that VD cases had increased in number and virulence and new rules were needed. When Mrs Elizabeth Andrew and Dr Kate Bushnell travelled to India to investigate, they found that in large cantonments the old system was still flourishing, lock hospitals having been renamed 'voluntary venereal hospitals' and VD treated like other contagious diseases.[111]

Roberts, with other Indian soldiers and the viceroy, wanted lock hospitals to continue. So far as we can tell, Lady Roberts had no influence in this. VD remained a serious problem until its incidence fell in the twentieth century. In June 1893, Roberts's successor White wrote of MPs' attacks on measures to control VD which had 'reached alarming proportions'. Hospital admissions for VD were not far off 50 per cent of the total.[112] In the army's bloodiest frontier campaign of 1897–8, there were 948 admissions for gunshot wounds, but 1,065 for VD. At the time infection at last was falling.[113]

Another side of looking after army health and discipline was the temperance campaign. In this Roberts emulated Napier, who in his parting orders praised improved discipline as partly due to temperance; the offences of 'temperance men' compared to drinkers was in the ratio 1:40.[114] Both commanders-in-chief sought temperance rather than total abstinence; the latter was difficult to achieve. The Army Temperance Association which Roberts promoted welcomed as members 'moderate drinkers as well as total abstainers' and all religious denominations.[115] By the time he left India nearly a third of the British army stationed there were members.[116] To coincide with the Jubilee of 1887, Roberts persuaded the Viceroy's Council that clubs or regimental institutes should be established in every regiment and battery in India: 'a sufficient number of good-sized, well-lighted rooms, where soldiers can amuse themselves in a rational manner, and where they can have their supper and glass of beer with comfort and decency'.[117] These spread. In the early 1890s, when Childers, former Secretary of State for War, visited the Worcestershire Regiment's Institute at Quetta, 'there must have been four hundred to five hundred men in the different rooms'. Childers wrote: 'Sir F. Roberts has done a great deal to make these soldiers' clubs popular.[118]

Victorian army discipline could seem callous. After the abolition of flogging, a common penalty for drunkenness and similar offences was Field Punishment No. 1, known as 'crucifixion': securing the offender for two hours a day to the wheel of a cart or other fixed object. Set against this background, Roberts was not a harsh man. He reduced sentences of penal servitude, the usual punishment for serious acts of insubordination by other ranks.[119] There were comparatively few military executions, although these conducted in public as a deterrent were grim spectacles. From 1865 to 1898, some thirty-seven men were executed; under Roberts as commander-in-chief eight were put to death; in both cases roughly one a year. The execution of Private George Flaxman for the murder of Lance-Sergeant Carmody became known through Kipling's poem 'Danny Deever'.[120] To reduce temptation to violent crime, Roberts ordered the removal and storage of ammunition from the pouches of both British and Indian soldiers, a measure at first refused by the Viceroy's Council and then agreed in 1887.[121] Poor discipline was often attributable to weak leadership, as in the Royal Scots Fusiliers in Burma, 'a fine looking body of men . . . but . . . in a bad state of discipline, and requires a most carefully selected commanding officer'. Roberts felt certain the CO was not up to command: 'I don't remember hearing of any regiment having the number of Courts Martial for drunkenness, insubordination and selling kit, as the Fusiliers have had this present year, upwards of 150!' Captain Tew the paymaster had had to be cashiered, and it was imperative to find a good successor to the CO: 'I am quite sure with such material, the Royal Scots Fusiliers might be made into a grand regiment.' Usually, he tried to avoid a scandal and to save the regiment the disgrace of a court-martial, accepting an officer's resignation instead.[122]

'We believe that the feeling is universal throughout the army in India, that in the present Commander-in-Chief each soldier has a real friend,' stated *The Civil & Military Gazette* of Lahore in September 1889, 'and to have inspired such a feeling, while undoubtedly improving the discipline, *morale*, and general fitness of the troops, will be a memorial more lasting than titles.'[123] Stationing young soldiers in the cooler hills on arrival in India had proved a success; clothing had been improved; soldiers had enjoyed more liberty to smoke and 'passes' to leave barracks. Roberts worried that, in an increasingly educated population, conditions of service would discourage enlistment unless reformed.[124]

Roberts was restricted in helping the private soldier. He achieved more for officers he favoured. Both Roberts and Wolseley struggled to advance their protégés against Cambridge's principle of promotion by seniority and merit, stressing the first. Stephen Badsey writes: 'For a general to be made aware of a capable young officer and promote his career was seen as necessary and legitimate. But abuse of the practice, by a general promoting the career of a less capable officer out of "friendship" or obligation to his family and associates, was not.'[125] Did Roberts violate this principle? Cambridge told him when he sought to advance White: 'The Army as a whole is *not* benefited by causing heart burnings & dissatisfaction amongst these Officers [who are passed over] & I certainly *strongly object* to be made a party to such an arrangement.'[126] He accused Roberts of 'jobbery', but it was White to whom he most objected, and White was waging a difficult war. Roberts defended himself in a letter of August 1887: 'I am not ashamed of helping my friends so long as they deserve it, but I would not put my own brother into any place for which he was not, in my opinion, fitted. I knew that men passed over would abuse me, but I am prepared to bear the burden, rather than promote men whom I believe to be inefficient.'[127] He tried to find a post for the retiring AG of the Madras Army,[128] he sought promotion for Henry Brackenbury and Thomas Baker,[129] supported by Dufferin;[130] he recommended his former military secretary, Pretyman, as assistant to the inspector general RA; he advanced Brigadier Charles Gough to the Oude command.[131] Except for Pretyman, none of these was a member of the future 'Indian ring', and all were men who had proved their worth. Cambridge angrily opposed, but Baker got his division and Pretyman his posting. Roberts had been helped by his father and his father's friends like Becher, advanced by Napier, and he supported sons of friends similarly. The boys of Donald Stewart and the War Secretary Hugh Childers marched to Kandahar. He arranged the transfer of his old comrade Henry Norman's son from the Warwickshires to the Bengal Lancers. He sought a commission for his nephew Alex Maxwell. To Brownlow he wrote: 'It is not easy to appoint a young fellow out of his turn, but I will see if Brownlow [son] cannot be given a lift.'[132] Henry Rawlinson's son, drawn into the bosom of Roberts's military family, is a stronger case. Could the Duke of Cambridge justly criticise? From 1886 his private secretary was Captain Fitzgeorge, one of three children born to him by the actress Louisa Fairbrother whom he had wed in defiance of royal marriage law.[133]

Young Rawlinson knew of the critics, and told his parents of a poem 'A Job Lot' in September 1888 in the *Pioneer*: 'though not entirely unfounded', he wrote, 'it is a little bit too strong'. It was written 'by Kipling, a very clever cad . . . were he only a gentleman he would be quite unrivalled in the way he writes . . .'[134] This 'cad' became more famous than Roberts as symbol and spokesman of Britain's Indian Empire, although he was over thirty years younger. He left the United Service College at Westward Ho! on the north Devonshire coast to return to India, land of his birth, in October 1882, aged sixteen, and found a billet as assistant editor on *The Civil & Military Gazette* at Lahore. In November 1887, he moved to George Allen's *Pioneer* at Allahabad. At the barracks at Mian Mir outside Lahore he had befriended men of the 2nd Battalion Northumberland Fusiliers, and at Allahabad the East Surreys, 'a London recruited confederacy of skilful dog-stealers, some of them my good and loyal friends'.[135] He got closer to soldiers than any other famous writer, seeing at Mian Mir the 'dreary, dismal cantonment' 'with its baking hot weather and oven-like barracks, its boiling rainy season and marrow-chilling winter, its sorry bungalows and brackish water . . .'[136] These were the conditions that Roberts was trying to improve. Years later, in *Something of Myself*, Kipling wrote: 'the proudest moment of my young life was when I rode up Simla Mall beside [Roberts] . . . while he asked me what the men thought about their accommodation, entertainment-rooms and the like. I told him, and he thanked me as gravely as though I had been a full Colonel'.[137] Against this memory must be set his poem 'A Job Lot'. Young 'Ruddy' was not going to admire anyone uncritically, not even the hero of Kandahar. On 31 August 1888, Allen's *Pioneer* suggested Roberts's position left him in control of a 'vast patronage' which was open to abuse, and accused him of using his influence to gain Colonel Neville Chamberlain a place on Mortimer Durand's Afghan frontier mission: 'Colonel Chamberlain's professional career has been no less favoured and fortunate than remarkable for the extravagance of its rewards . . . But after all, it is not the young officer who feels himself rushed along the pleasant roads to preferment that is to be quarrelled with, but those who push him.' On 1 September, Kipling followed with the poem, headed, 'Not to be Sung at Snowdon Theatre' where amateur theatricals were performed.

> They glorified the new canteen.
> They called him 'Tommy's Pride',
> But O they said his patronage was sometimes misapplied.
>
> Perpend, retreat, refrain, reform
> O man of Kandahar,
> For even pocket-Wellingtons
> May carry things too far . . .
>
> (Chorus) We've heard it before, but we'll drink once more,
> While the Army sniffs and sobs
> For Bobs its pride, who has lately died,
> And is now succeeded by Jobs.[138]

Roberts was stung; he wrote to the Adjutant-General: '[George] Allen may make any apology he likes, but I will never forgive him. His article about Chamberlain was most uncalled for . . . I don't care a straw for fair criticism, but on this occasion Allen mistook the business altogether and the vulgar lines by Kipling were the outcome of his inappropriate attack on me.' Roberts claimed that Durand wanted Chamberlain; he was well fitted for the work and knew Kabul better than anyone.[139] On 19 September, the

Simla Herald launched a counter-attack which uncannily resembled Roberts's angry letter: that Durand chose Chamberlain who had done similar work nine years before at Kabul.[140] Perhaps Roberts's enemies sung Kipling's chorus; Major-General Granville Egerton recalled in his memoir of service with the 72nd Highlanders that the 'sobriquet attached to the pair in India of Sir Bobs and Lady Jobs, was not undeserved'; the alternative nickname reached the Wolseyites' ears and clung to Roberts and his wife.[141]

In December that year, Kipling's poem 'One Viceroy Resigns' in the style of Robert Browning, imagined Dufferin advising his successor Lansdowne about his council, and presented a clear appraisal of Roberts, not rose-tinted, but balanced:

> . . . Look to one –
> I work with him – the smallest of them all,
> White-haired, red-faced, who sat the plunging horse
> Out in the garden. He's your right-hand man,
> And dreams of tilting Wolseley from the throne,
> But while he dreams gives work we cannot buy;
> He has his Reputation – wants the Lords
> By way of Frontier Roads. Meantime, I think,
> He values very much the hand that falls
> Upon his shoulder at the Council table –
> Hates cats and knows his business . . .[142]

Horsemanship, ambition, clubbability, hatred of cats, rivalry with Wolseley, plans frustrated by treasury constraints – all in these few lines. In the next century, Kipling and Roberts would become allies in battles for the Empire.

CHAPTER NINE

From Bengal to Southampton via *Forty-One Years in India*

The establishment of an empire in India changed the context of British foreign policy, and even, to an extent shifted its foundations . . . The defence of India was now as important as that of England.

S. GOPAL, *THE VICEROYALTY OF LORD RIPON*

I'm afraid my V.C. has had to be postponed but I do hope I get the chance some day of getting it.

FREDDIE ROBERTS FROM THE SUDAN TO SIR JAMES HILLS-JOHNES

Our forces are already on their way to the border. If we wait longer our cause may be lost.

PAUL KRUGER TO MARTHINUS STEYN, 27 SEPTEMBER 1899

At the end of 1888, Roberts wrote to Cambridge asking him to place his son on a list of candidates for the 60th Rifles. 'Frederick Hugh Sherston Roberts' had passed the preliminary for Sandhurst, and would take the further exam in November when he was nearly eighteen.[1] Roberts's own parents had given him every opportunity. Now he and Nora would do the same.

Freddie had had an undistinguished time at Eton's Everard's House, 1885–7.[2] In September 1886 he was elected as a senior boy to the Debating Society. On 3 October he spoke well in a debate on the motion 'whether the ordnance were in a satisfactory condition'. The house book records: 'The debate was rather a good one, being remarkable ... the speeches of the new members were certainly above the average, those of Mr Roberts

& Mr Browning particularly so.'[3] He much enjoyed field sports, and told his godfather Hills-Johnes: 'I have been playing a great deal of fives this half, it is a very nice game. That and paperchases are the chief things this half. If I pass trials [school exams] . . . I will get into fifth form & then I won't have any more fagging.'[4] In August he told Hills-Johnes ruefully: 'I am sorry to say I have not quite passed my Preliminary [exam for Sandhurst] this time, but I only failed to pass in 2 subjects, viz Algebra and Dictation, so I will only have Mathematics and dictation to go in for in the next Examination. I can't imagine how I failed in dictation.'[5] Freddy succeeded at the second shot, but did not pass into Sandhurst, and in December told his godfather he was going to join the family in India. 'I will write to you . . . and always remember your great kindness to me, and look upon you as a second father.'[6] His time in India was spent maturing and gaining responsibility. His mother told Lady Hills-Johnes: 'it was the very thing he wanted, to give him confidence in himself and to show him the absolute necessity for hard work in every stage of existence if a man is to do any good'. For his last year there he had 'entire charge of the stables', and his management was excellent. There was another gain: 'I feel now that he knows his father as his first and most sympathetic friend and that if ever he should get into any trouble his father is the first person he would confide in.'[7]

Freddie entered Sandhurst aged eighteen and was there a year. At five-foot-eight he was taller than his father. His conduct was 'very good' and his marks in his final examination were reasonable, helped by high scores in drill and riding.[8] He told Hills-Johnes in May 1890: 'I am getting on very well with my work etc. At present my company is going through a course of musketry which is rather a grind.'[9] His father wrote to Afghan comrade T.D. Baker, now at the War Office:

I am delighted to hear that Freddy will be posted to the 60th Rifles. I have told him to get his uniform and arrange to come to India with his mother in March next. It will be a great pleasure to us all to have him with us until he is posted to the 1st Battalion. Indeed, I am almost inclined to hope that there may not be an early vacancy.[10]

His godfather presented him with his sword. His father, remembering an encouraging reward from *his* father, told Freddie to go to Rigby's in London and choose a shotgun as prize for never being late on parade.[11] Lady Roberts took their elder daughter to England to be with Freddie when he passed out, they spent Christmas together, and Aileen was presented to the Queen; her father thanked Sir John Cowell at court: 'I was most anxious that Miss Roberts should be presented to Her Majesty; indeed, it was one of the reasons why Lady Roberts took her home this winter . . .'[12] The constant involvement of Freddie's family, especially the Sherstons at Evercreech, and close friends, the Hills-Johneses, stands in contrast to Rudyard Kipling's desperately unhappy experience at 'the house of desolation' in Southsea.[13]

He joined his battalion, but soon 'managed to get leave . . . and joined father and saw three days [cavalry] manoeuvring it was awfully jolly and I enjoyed myself immensely'. He stayed with the Hugh Goughs at Mian Meer. Gough's son Charlie's regiment competed in the final of the Punjab polo tournament, but was beaten: 'there was great grief in the Gough family that night'.[14]

Polo dominated the thoughts of young officers, to the extent that polo tournaments became an obsession and the price of polo ponies rose astronomically. Trains were chartered to transport them. Polo, like pigsticking and hunting, trained men in quick thinking on horseback, but there was danger and many casualties from falls onto iron-hard ground. Between 1880 and 1914, thirty-six officers died from polo accidents; from pigsticking only two. Roberts ordered officers to wear helmets with chin-straps. There was resistance to his guidelines, and they had to be repeated.[15] Pigsticking too was useful training: to follow the wild boar's rapid twists and turns and then to face his sharp tusks needed quick wits and expert horsemanship. Indian villagers welcomed pig-sticking, for boars took over coveted patches of sugar cane into which the villagers dared not venture.[16] Roberts was a skilful horseman and keen pig-sticker and tent-pegger; so too was Freddie. A visitor from England wrote of a day's pig-sticking at Kashmir: 'The hunting party consisted of Lord Roberts and his son Fred (perhaps the two best tent-peggers in India), the two brothers of the Maharajah [of Kashmir], and several of the Commander-in-Chief's staff.' The visitor and the Maharajah watched the sport from elephants.

This visitor was Henry Spenser Wilkinson, a writer on military affairs for the *Manchester Guardian*. His series of articles on the Prussian general staff were published in 1890 as *The Brain of an Army* on the very day the Hartington Commission recommended a similar 'brain' for the British Army. He had sent a copy to Roberts, who replied kindly, but disagreed: the Prussian system was not necessarily applicable to the British Army, which gave command to a royal prince and practical control to professional soldiers.[17] That system would work well with a capable commander-in-chief, thought Roberts, not adding who that might be. Wilkinson then collaborated with the politician Sir Charles Dilke on *Imperial Defence* (1891), chiefly on naval strategy to defend the Empire. Dilke had toured the North-West Frontier with Roberts.[18] Sir Frederick Maurice, 'the second pen of Sir Garnet Wolseley' and 'the most articulate voice of the Ring', told Wilkinson that the Indian chapters which he had written would carry no weight unless he visited the frontier.[19] He determined to go, his father kindly paid, and he obtained Roberts's permission to tour as special correspondent of the *Standard*, whose editor took him on.[20] He went as an admirer, having told Dilke of Roberts's clarity of writing and thought on Russia and the North-West Frontier: 'His strategy is sound as a bell, as is best shown by the absence of any parade of it. He is evidently a very different stamp of man to Wolseley or any other of the home set, & far superior to them.'[21] Wilkinson came to a military review at Mian Mir: 'Lord Roberts was a small, spare figure. His clear-cut features and firm thin lips were the fit setting of two clear-blue, piercing eyes. In kindly moods a peculiarly gracious smile lit up his face; when he was displeased his look was stern indeed.' His kind reception made Wilkinson feel at home. No rider, he awkwardly mounted to follow Roberts observing manoeuvres, but fell off: 'I wished the earth had opened and swallowed me. The chief did not seem to mind.'[22] Roberts recognised an able correspondent, and horsemanship was not a necessary skill. He suggested Wilkinson dismount and rest and gave him some riding pointers. Wilkinson proudly told him later that he had not 'dropped off the horse again since Mian Mir'.[23] He saw the rocky, treeless terrain of the frontier over which British and Indian soldiers had fought. His admiration for Roberts grew: he wrote in his memoirs that although he had been a student of war for eighteen years, he had learnt more from a few weeks with Roberts than could be had from books:

> Little by little I became convinced that he was a great man. He had the qualities of character which mark the true commander. By the whole Indian Army he was both revered and beloved. Those feelings I shared, and in looking back over my life I find nothing that gave me more pleasure and pride than the knowledge that my affection for him was not one-sided.

Wilkinson's third child was born while he was in India, and he asked Roberts to be the godfather.[24] When he left the *Guardian,* Roberts found him a position on the *Morning Post,* at the opposite end of the political spectrum.[25] Roberts's continued friendship with the leading military intellectual influenced his own perspective; Wilkinson gave advice and support in Roberts's next war.

He also met Roberts's leading protégés. At Meerut he was a guest of Colonel William Nicholson and his wife. He found Nicholson 'one of the cleverest officers in the Army', ready with a Latin quotation from Ovid or Virgil.[26] There also he met Colonel Ian Hamilton, whose first essay on the importance of shooting Wilkinson had read. 'I was able before I left India to satisfy myself that, as Inspector-General of Musketry, he had taught the native infantry of the Indian Army to shoot better than the British infantry (over whom he had no control) and perhaps better than any infantry in the world at that time.'[27] On these two Roberts spent time, energy and correspondence seeking their promotion to colonel. Nicholson, assistant -adjutant-general at Simla, had impressed Roberts with his work for the defence committee, and at the start of 1890 he succeeded Pole-Carew as his military secretary.[28] Hamilton had served him since Ootacamund. Roberts became convinced that promotions in the Home Army were quicker than in India, and he repeatedly urged his men's case. Nicholson had served twenty-six years, in three campaigns, seen four actions and was mentioned six times in despatches. Hamilton had nearly eighteen years' and four campaigns' service, fought in three actions, been very severely wounded (his hand crippled at Majuba) and been mentioned four times in despatches. Roberts sent a chart showing others promoted quicker, and appealed to Stanhope, the Secretary of State. Lt-General Harman writing for Cambridge refused to yield on principle, and finally insisted in a letter of 1 January 1891, that Nicholson's case differed from Hamilton's and 'the substantive rank of colonel may possibly be conferred upon him at an early date'. In fact, Roberts got his way: Nicholson's substantive colonelcy was dated 1 January 1891, Hamilton's 25 November of that year.[29]

Disputes over promotions and between Roberts's followers and Wolseley's reflected the Indian Army's belief that they were the poor relation of the Home Army, perhaps a hangover from the time when commissions in the regular army outranked those of the East India Company. Roberts told Lytton in May 1883 that in the nineteenth century only six Indian Army commands had been filled by Indian officers.[30] According to Lepel Griffin, Stewart and Roberts regarded the latter's second-in-command on the march to Kandahar as an incompetent. General Ross it had to be although 'absolutely unfit, both mentally & physically ... notoriously weak, timid, vacillating'.[31] Not just generals thought the Home Army barely capable of 'penny-fights an' Aldershot it'.[32] Lt Henry Denne of the Gordon Highlanders, veterans of Kabul and Kandahar, wrote after Wolseley's victory at Tel-el-Kebir: 'Sir F. Roberts had much greater difficulties to contend with & did much more than Wolseley.'[33] Conversely, Wolseleyites thought the Indian Army hopelessly inefficient and Roberts's victories hugely overpuffed. 'All this bosh about Roberts "makes me sick and don't argue with me",' wrote Baker-Russell to Wolseley. 'Upon my honour the so called battle of Kandahar was no proper fight, but a most ill managed scramble of 16,000 disciplined troops against some 10,000 half armed savages.'[34]

While there may have been, as Adrian Preston writes, 'a deadly game of musical chairs' between Roberts and Wolseley and their followers for top jobs, the serious battle for both men was to reform the army. Both wanted to advance able subordinates; both wanted their strategic vision to predominate; both wanted more and better recruits. This is clear from the evidence submitted to the Wantage Committee, established by Edward Stanhope, Conservative War Secretary, in 1891 to examine terms and conditions of army service. Senior officers testified for a pay increase and an end or reduction to 'stoppages' for messing, barrack damages, haircuts. Only the Duke of Cambridge dissented: 'It would not be wise to add to the soldier's pay.'[35] Roberts sent evidence from a distance. He told Stanhope that he had asked men of the 2nd Seaforths what would make overseas service more popular. They confirmed mostly what George Spratt, one of four privates examined by the Committee, stated: 'I found that I did not get all my rations free, and I did not get a clear 1 [shilling] a day; and I found that the clothing was not sufficient for me to soldier in.' The rations were not fit to eat, and he sometimes had to buy his own meals. Let the soldiers have rations free, without stoppages, and the army would get the men it wanted, said Spratt.[36] Like Roberts, Wolseley argued for better pay, otherwise 'we shall always be obliged to take in "the waifs and strays" '. The Committee referred to Roberts's papers, 'Free Trade in the Army' and 'National Prosperity and its Effect on the Army' arguing for three-year enlistments followed by the chance for re-engagement. In a second paper, he argued for a scheme leading, if wished, to the soldier being able to serve twenty-one years. The Duke of Cambridge said this was 'very theoretical', but when pressed agreed that it would be right to eliminate uncertainty in the soldier's mind caused by changes in terms of service.[37] As evidence was dominated by those serving at home rather than 'Indians', the Committee endorsed the Cardwell system, did not accept Roberts's views on length of service, but did suggest improved pay and conditions.[38] Penny-pinching chancellors granted these grudgingly and belatedly. Better barracks and higher pay came slowly, recruiting remained difficult throughout the nineteenth century and critics claimed that home battalions were enlisting schoolboys.[39] Roberts stated that the average draft of men to India had declined physically. Although the army turned a proportion of 'undersized and partially-developed youngsters' into good soldiers, he noted that of 35,298 recruits to the army in 1891, 13,000 failed to come up to the modest physical standard.[40]

Wolseley's main wish was to overcome the obstacle of the Duke of Cambridge. The 'Ashanti' ring broke up before this happened. The Gordon Relief Expedition was their last campaign in the field together, not a happy one. Wolseley complained to his wife: 'they torture themselves with jealousy one of the other, and sometimes even in their dealings with me are inclined to kick over the traces'.[41] They went their own ways, Evelyn Wood and Buller finding their protégés, Brackenbury and Baker becoming 'Indians'. Strongest at the War Office, as Cambridge aged and let slip the reins, was Buller, QMG and then adjutant-general, lifting that post to a higher plane than before.[42]

In both age and seniority the 'Indians' gathered about Roberts differed: younger men, mostly captains and lieutenants in their twenties. Jack Sherston, William Nicolson, Ian Hamilton, Reginald Pole-Carew and Neville Chamberlain served in Afghanistan. Henry Rawlinson and Henry Wilson joined later. Not until South Africa did 'the Indian ring' serve together in a major war, complicated by Roberts's alliance with Kitchener and his 'Egyptians'.[43] Ian Hamilton did more than anyone to create the idea of a 'battle of the rings'. 'Wise or unwise, the die was cast,' he wrote, 'and it was to be my fate for the next twenty years to spend any surplus energy I had left after fighting the enemies of my country in fighting for my Chief against the Wolseley Ring.'[44] There were many regimental and personal loyalties in the Victorian army, but Roberts and Wolseley can hardly be said to have divided it. A tiny minority of officers belonged to the 'rings', although more were caught up in the Indian Army-vs-Queen's Army rivalry. Cambridge controlled another group. In Adrian Preston's words: 'The Duke, advised by a knot of reactionaries to keep good men out, could only propose duds: stiff martinets ... whose reputations did not reach beyond the walls of their offices.'[45] Ultimately, chief appointments – the two commanders-in-chief, adjutant-general and QMG at Horse Guards – lay in the politicians' hands. Hew Strachan writes that the 'rings' showed officers' political awareness and developed their capacity for faction and intrigue, but gave further leverage to politicians. They were not tightly knit as Hamilton and the press suggested.[46] Brackenbury became an 'Indian'. Hamilton served for six months in 1884 as Roberts's assistant military secretary; the War Office would not confirm the appointment, and Hamilton blamed Buller. Then, eager for action, he tried to join the Gordon Relief Expedition: Buller gave him a billet. Beating the Dervishes was more important than 'ring' rivalry.[47] In 1898, Hamilton returned to England after twenty-five years in India, declining the Indian QMG's post; Adjutant-General Evelyn Wood appointed him to command the musketry school at Hythe.[48]

In 1890 occurred one of those events of Preston's 'musical chairs' which may have led the 'Indians' to think their hero was sacrificed to the Home Army, but demonstrated politicians' control: namely, War Secretary Stanhope's offer and then withdrawal of the adjutant-generalship at Whitehall. Roberts's five-year term of command in India was nearing its end, being adjutant-general was a next step, possibly leading to becoming commander-in-chief at Whitehall. Behind the *volte-face* lay army politics at top level. Stanhope had wanted Roberts, 'the strongest man available for the post', to push through the Hartington Commission reforms, notably abolition of the commander-in-chief's post, a step which Cambridge would bitterly oppose. The Queen and Cambridge wanted Connaught to go to India as Roberts's successor, but Salisbury's Cabinet blocked that, not wishing another royal commander-in-chief. Wolseley might have gone instead, but he had his eyes on Aldershot; if there were a European war, the GOC Aldershot would have a leading role. With no suitable candidate, Roberts was asked to stay on for two more years, to April 1893. At the age of fifty-eight, he thus lost the adjutant-general's post, which went to the 51-year-old QMG Buller.[49] Roberts thought his treatment was shabby, and asked Lansdowne to write to the Queen that not being appointed was 'a serious disappointment': 'The Viceroy trusts that Sir Frederick's cheerful postponement of his personal interests to those of the public service will be properly appreciated ...'[50] It was not appreciated by the Liberals, for they had no commensurate post when he returned to England. Did Roberts blame Buller? They continued to correspond amicably, especially about new musketry regulations.[51]

Having worked well with Dufferin and Chesney, Roberts had to adapt in 1888 to a new viceroy and in 1891 to another military member. Dufferin's successor, Lansdowne, was also Anglo-Irish and a former Canadian governor-general, but a disillusioned Whig politician rather than diplomat. He had fallen out with Gladstone over Irish reform, and became a Unionist under Salisbury. Salisbury sent him to India.[52] He and Lady Lansdowne with two daughters and staff including his private secretary, John Ardagh, reached Bombay on 3 December 1888. Roberts was anxious about the influence of Ardagh, as an 'African': 'The announcement that Colonel Ardagh has been appointed Private Secretary to the new Viceroy has made me feel a bit low … Ardagh's selection looks to me as if Lord Wolseley may have had something to say to it.'[53] Roberts's fears were misplaced. Ardagh was a Royal Engineer who had served in the Intelligence Branch and as an instructor at Chatham, the sappers' training school. Campaigning at Tel-el-Kebir and on the Gordon Relief Expedition did not make him a member of 'the ring'. He and Roberts got on well primarily because Ardagh took his cue from his chief. Lansdowne and Roberts met in November 1889, and toured the North-West Frontier together.[54] This gave scope for Roberts to advance his ideas on the Russian threat and the defence of India. India was peaceful, with the exception of a rising in Manipur, so Lansdowne concentrated on the frontier.[55] By now Roberts was *the* expert on Central Asian strategy, his prestige increased by his extended tenure as commander-in-chief, his knowledge through preparing Indian defence papers. Even a Liberal government in power from August 1892 to June 1895 (Gladstone's last, Rosebery succeeding March 1894) could not change Lansdowne's outlook. Kimberley, the Indian Secretary, viewed him as 'a mere tool in Roberts's hands'.[56] The historian Gopal notes how Roberts got his way with the building of strategic railways.[57]

Roberts's apparent omniscience was amplified by the agreement of the new military member, Major-General Henry Brackenbury, a select Wolseyite and reckoned 'the cleverest man' in the army (Wolseley's judgement). 'Black Brack' with his 'pasty-yellow, black-mustached face' had an uncanny knack of reaching the root of a matter.[58] He had been director of intelligence in London from 1886; his department found Russian plans for an invasion of India and drew attention to British military weakness. While Roberts was working on a mobilisation scheme for India, Brackenbury prepared one for Britain.[59] In April 1891 he succeeded Chesney. He had helped to shape the London government's war strategy of amphibious operations on Russia's borders, rather than an advance into Afghanistan, and Roberts's protégés feared his appointment could not be 'either agreeable to [Roberts] or for the good of the Indian Army'.[60] From Roberts's viewpoint he proved a model colleague. This stemmed, according to Adrian Preston, from Brackenbury's conversion to 'Indian' strategy on 20 June 1891. At a meeting attended by Collen, the viceroy's military secretary, Mortimer Durand, the Foreign Secretary, Brackenbury and Roberts, the last opened the questioning: what were HM Government's strategic plans in a war against Russia? Brackenbury replied: if against Russia alone, to form a Turkish alliance and send expeditionary forces to Constantinople and elsewhere; if against France and Russia combined, to concentrate all troops for home defence. The Intelligence Department believed invasion possible since the Home Fleet would be blockading and hunting the French fleet in the Mediterranean. Roberts disagreed: the French could not embark 100,000 troops without convoy protection, for even if the Royal Navy were decoyed away, there were mines, fireships and torpedoes to wreak havoc upon unprotected wooden transports. Even if the French Army managed to land, it would be blocked at every turn by regular troops and field-works, and its cross-Channel lines of supply would be cut by the returning Home Fleet. Invasion was a convenient War Office bogey with which to rationalise its refusal to send reinforcements to India.[61] Brackenbury's biographer, Christopher Brice, suggests the 'conversion' was less dramatic, pointing out that Brackenbury deliberately accepted Roberts as the foremost Indian expert. He wrote to him before making proposals and kept quiet in council when Roberts's ideas came up. There was 'nothing except mutual admiration and respect between the two'.[62]

Russian planners with knowledge of India and their eyes on Asian frontiers continued to plot forward leaps. Colonel Terentiev and others predicted that a Russian army's approach would be fatal to British power. The Indian Army would turn on its masters. This was the fear lying behind Roberts wanting strong British reinforcements in a war. Of Roberts's plan for a pre-emptive advance to Kandahar, Brackenbury was not convinced, but he was keen to strengthen garrisons and communications on the North-West Frontier and maintain a good road through Peshawar to Chitral. He thought 30,000 British and 70,000 native troops were sufficient to repel the Russians. This assumed that Germany and Austria-Hungary would support Britain in a war, while an Anglo-Turkish attack was made through the Black Sea.[63]

In summer 1886, Brackenbury then at London had warned of General Kuropatkin's plans.[64] Following the Pandjeh Incident, British spies reported increased Russian strength in Turkestan and Bokhara. While London's Intelligence Department was the centre of strategic information and assessment, Indian intelligence watched frontier tribes' unrest, the shifting politics of Afghanistan and Persia, and Russian movements. It was vital to have information in time for Roberts's planned riposte.[65] From July 1889, Captain Francis Younghusband with a small party negotiated unsuccessfully with the Mir of Hunza and probed Russian activities in the Pamirs. His contest with Russian officers Captain Gromchevsky, Consul Petrovsky and Colonel Yanov could have been lifted from *Kim* except the Russians gave as cleverly as they got. Only after Roberts's return to England and a formal complaint by London did the Russians withdraw from the Pamirs.[66] Younghusband was another of those officers who fell under Roberts's spell: 'he had that wonderful buoyant way of carrying you along with him and lifting you up – making you feel that all things were possible'.[67] A recent appraisal of Roberts's use of intelligence to forge strategic plans judges that British India 'ended up with a best possible plan for defence, following a natural political and defensive line'. This was the one Roberts had sketched out earlier;[68] fears for internal security meant that the enemy had to be met at a natural barrier well forward of the Indian frontier; closer relations with tribesmen would assure their support, always from a position of British military strength. The Afridis on the Khyber Pass occupied the strategic key and were most likely to throw in their lot with the Russians.[69]

Under Lansdowne, there was some cooling of relations with Abdur Rahman, whose attitude towards British India 'was based on a shrewd conception of his own interests'; he was not pleased by the arrival of an English envoy in the border state of Chitral in 1893. Lansdowne proposed to send a mission to Kabul, but wanting Roberts to lead it was a mistake; Abdur never forgave him for the hangings, although his march and victory had paved Abdur's way. The Amir announced that owing to Hazara troubles and the state of his health, he could fix no date for the mission. Having delayed matters until Roberts left India, he proclaimed himself ready to receive Mortimer Durand instead. Durand entered Kabul without escort, despite memories of Burnes and Cavagnari. Following negotiations from 2 October to 16 November 1893 to remove Anglo-Afghan friction, the Amir agreed not to interfere with the Afridis, Waziris and other frontier tribes; British and Afghan commissioners marked out a common boundary. 'The Durand Line' between British India and Afghanistan still marks today's Afghan-Pakistan border. Roberts praised Durand as the only man who really understood the Amir's character and the problems of Central Asia. To the British a clear line made sense, Roberts distrusting the Amir and wanting an area in which Britain could establish a dominant position with the tribes. To the Mohmands especially, divided by the line, it was a source of bitter resentment and fear of British encroachment, and Abdur disliked it almost as much, despite an increase in his subsidy from 12 to 18 *lakhs*.[70]

The Indianisation of British strategy continued after Roberts's return to London.[71] Already, in May 1892, he told Maj-General T.D. Baker, 'Your information that the defence of India is now recognised at the War Office as of "paramount importance after that of England" is most satisfactory.'[72] Chapman, head of London intelligence, told him in April 1893 that Lord R[osebery, Prime Minister] 'expressed a great desire that you should be able to take part in any deliberations' on the situation in the Pamirs.[73] In 1902 it became official doctrine that 'in fighting for India, England would be fighting for her imperial existence'. She would be compelled 'by the necessity for maintaining her prestige to apply her main strength across the Indian frontier'. As Russia could nowhere 'put effective pressure on England except in Afghanistan', the contest must be decided there.[74] Defending India was vital, for her strength counterbalanced Britain's relative decline in population and industrial strength against Germany, Russia and the United States.[75] Britain and India's combined production figures of 1897 were nearly 20 per cent more than the United States and three and a half times Germany's.[76] Viscount Curzon shared Roberts's outlook; *The Place of India in the Empire* (1909) summarised this view: if Britain lost India 'we should sink into a third-rate power, an object of shame to ourselves and derision to the rest of mankind'; India was 'a royal piece on the chessboard of international politics'.[77]

'A question in which I am very specially interested is the selection of Lord Roberts's successor,' wrote Lansdowne in 1892. Both Roberts and Lansdowne knew that Cambridge's candidate was Buller; the objection was that neither he nor Brackenbury as military member had Indian experience. Lansdowne wrote: 'I feel no doubt myself that [George] White would be the best man for the post, and, as far as I can make out, the only objection to him is founded upon his want of seniority, but he is 57 and has plenty of experience.' He added: 'Horse Guards' prejudices ought not to prevail.'[78] White was initially a dark horse. For a time Connaught was a candidate; even Lady Roberts thought that 'he would loyally do his best to carry on whatever my husband had begun . . .'[79] Brackenbury told Buller, however, that the abilities of Connaught whom he had instructed as a young man in strategy and tactics 'were not of a high order'; he was a martinet who 'would care more about dress and the details of discipline than about keeping the army a ready instrument for war'.[80] The choice was Buller or White. The Liberals were in office from August 1892, and Campbell-Bannerman became War Secretary. He described the adjutant-general as: 'My Buller whom I back to keep his end up against them all.'[81] On 30 August Roberts wrote to the commander-in-chief:

> I was only made aware a few days ago that Your Royal Highness is in favor of Sir Redvers Buller being the next Commander in Chief in India. As you know, Sir, I have urged that whoever is appointed to that position should have recent Indian experience. This is still my opinion, but if it is impossible to find an officer with this experience, who possesses at the same time rank and other necessary qualifications, then there is no one I would rather see in my place than Sir Redvers Buller.[82]

There *was* an officer with recent Indian experience (White), but the efforts of Roberts, Lansdowne and Brackenbury would be of no avail against the combined weight of Campbell-Bannerman and the Indian Secretary Lord Kimberley. Kimberley wanted someone who was not committed to the 'Forward School'.[83] In November 1892, Campbell-Bannerman offered the post to Buller. He pondered for ten days, but despite being pressed twice to accept, he refused. Cambridge and Campbell-Bannerman were intensely disappointed.[84] Without Buller, they had no candidate. Campbell-Bannerman told Cambridge: 'I scarcely think that Your Royal Highness's suggestion of Sir A. [Archibald] Alison is practicable, as it would be an infringement of the Regulation as to age. I suspect that the real alternative is Sir G. White who we must remember is universally recommended by the Indian authorities . . .'[85] Brackenbury supported White as the only officer 'in either the British or the Indian Army who possesses the qualities required in Lord Roberts' successor'.[86] White, although encouraged by Roberts, was bemused and doubtful.[87] In September, he seemed to have reconciled himself to disappointment, telling Roberts that he could not have a better successor than Buller. He added: 'I did not think that he would leave England for any length of time . . .'[88] He was right, and thus his moment came. On 25 November he accepted the post.[89] Kimberley's hope to avoid a Forward School partisan was disappointed. White's command led to a series of frontier campaigns.[90] Cambridge's great fear was realised: the abolition of the separate Madras and Bombay Armies.[91]

Roberts marked his 1893 departure with extended tours and public dinners: occasions in which he revelled, treated almost as royalty by Indian princes as well as soldiers and politicals. In a famous pig-sticking incident at Jodhpur, he rode to help the Maharajah's brother, Sir Pertab Singh, who had been thrown from his horse by a wounded boar which he was holding at arm's length by the snout. The two together despatched the pig. Pertab Singh was 'a magnificent rider & sportsman' of the type the British admired. Although Roberts continued to associate with Indian princes, he kept his eyes open on his tours; he used the evidence to support the argument for military readiness:

> my impression is that a great change has come over India since [Lord Lawrence's] time, and that the Native press – the intercourse among chiefs and princes which railways and other means of communication have made possible – the gradual spread of education, &c, &c, are quietly but surely working against us, and that when the struggle with Russia comes, we shall find more need than ever for an efficient army.[92]

He passed on his Mutiny memories. In late March, his elder daughter, his nephew Maxwell Sherston, Percival Marling and 'a civilian who was writing a book' accompanied him on a tour on the Delhi Ridge, through the Kashmir Gate and inside the walls to the spot where John Nicholson was killed. Marling wrote: 'I don't think I ever spent a more interesting day, and it was great luck for a young fellow like me to be taken round and have the siege described most graphically by Lord Roberts, who had himself been present.'[93] The civilian was G.W. Forrest, historian and later biographer of Roberts, whom the latter encouraged in his research and writing.[94] Roberts's 'final tour of the Punjab was a triumphal procession such as few soldiers can ever have received or merited'. At Lahore the Hindu, Muslim, Sikh and European communities all presented addresses.[95] *The Times* gave its version of his achievements, romantically comparing him to 'a great Roman commander who had held the Danube [and] might have returned to the Capitol, adored by his legions', and asserting that 'he leaves behind him a sense of security which never in India before rested on so solid a foundation of military strength'.[96] There was truth in this: the army was stronger, better trained and better informed through its intelligence agents. White had written to

Roberts: 'he who succeeds you as Chief in India comes to the post very heavily handicapped. If he does what you have done for the Armies in India, & keeps up the position of the head of those Armies with the Govt. of India which you have established, I shall be agreeably surprised . . .'[97] To his brother, White wrote in a different vein

> Since I arrived at Simla there has been an outcry about Lord Roberts's touring expenses. They are now nearly five times what they were when he came here & some of his proceedings have amounted to something very near a scandal . . . Altogether he has left me as difficult a heritage as it is possible to imagine. Many of the measures he takes credit for having introduced have been kept over for me and I have stopped several of them which I have thought ill-judged. His aim has been to get name associated with endless measures. Through the agency of the press he has them cried up as 'One more great reform for Lord R'.[98]

This was the lament of a new man facing a huge task – 'an immense labour & I don't covet it', he had written[99] – complicated by the falling value of the rupee raising military costs, but carries weight. The charge of extravagance stuck, like that of 'jobbery'. In November 1900, Pandelli Ralli, London man-about-town, wrote to his friend Sir Herbert Kitchener: 'Roberts has a very bad financial reputation: his financial record in India was one of awful extravagance & you have heard of course of the famous speech he once made on an Indian frontier in which he said "that was his policy, as to the financial part of it, it was no affair of his" or words to that effect.'[100]

Roberts, accompanied by his wife and daughters, returned to London via Brindisi and Rome, and reached Victoria Station at 5 p.m. on 11 May 1893. He was greeted on a platform covered with crimson cloth, a guard of honour from the 2nd London Volunteer rifles of which he was colonel, and a distinguished gathering including Connaught, Stewart and Hugh Gough. Outside a humbler crowd gave rousing cheers.[101] The 'jobbery' was muttered, the extravagance murmured, but to many he was still the victor of Kandahar and a most distinguished British soldier. Where next? The Queen wrote: 'Lord Roberts looks extremely well, and not a day older.'[102] To a man still in his prime and the vigour of good health, aged sixty, retirement or a garrison post was unthinkable. Stewart had joined the India Office Council, Napier had become Governor of Gibraltar. In December 1891, Roberts brushed aside an offer of Malta or Halifax on the plea that he had been abroad too long.[103] He had his sights higher: the Aldershot command perhaps, and then to succeed Cambridge in *the* top job. There was also another possible pinnacle: Viceroy of India.

The *Punjab Patriot* at Lahore called for 'Lord Roberts as Viceroy' when Lansdowne retired. The *Civil & Military Gazette* claimed that 'the martial races' hoped he would return as viceroy.[104] Roberts wrote in June to Ian Hamilton, now White's military secretary, that he would like the position (so much for pleas of not serving abroad), 'but Ladyship dislikes the idea immensely, in fact I think she rather dreads it ... A few years ago the possibility of being viceroy would have elated me considerably, but now somehow I take it very quietly, and am not sure whether I would not prefer Aldershot!'[105] He doubted that Gladstone's government would appoint him, and he was right: there is no evidence of his being considered.[106] The post was offered to his old friend Henry Norman, who then withdrew on grounds of age and health. Lord Elgin accepted.[107] In June Roberts discussed career prospects with his friend Stewart; Stewart told Cambridge that Roberts was 'still desirous of being considered a candidate for the Aldershot Command. Malta & Gibraltar have no attraction for him ...' He added: 'Your R. H. Highness [sic] is quite right in thinking that "the Lady" has much to say for this determination.'[108] Campbell-Bannerman was determined against Aldershot: 'Roberts ... is a good soldier,' he told Gladstone, 'but he is an arrant jobber, and intriguer, and self-advertiser and altogether wrong in his political opinions, both British and "Indian".' Being 'wrong' in political opinions meant sharing the ideas of Unionists like Salisbury, Lytton and Lansdowne. Wolseley had written to Cambridge wanting Connaught to succeed Evelyn Wood at Aldershot, and Cambridge and Campbell-Bannerman proposed to appoint the royal duke.[109] The War Secretary told Roberts that at Aldershot he would be at the beck and call of officers at HQ, unsuitable for a former Indian commander-in-chief. The headline of the *Birmingham Mail*, 30 August 1893 reflected the feeling that 'Bobs' had been 'Shunted for a Duke'.[110] Roberts wrote to apologise for this newspaper furore; Campbell-Bannerman blamed Dilke 'who professes to be an intimate friend of Roberts, and stayed with him in India a year or two ago. Dilke is an eminent wirepuller in the Press, and in the House so far as he can. I should think it must be distasteful to Roberts, who will try to repudiate it and stop it'.[111]

So Roberts remained Britain's most eminent unemployed gentleman, and set about writing three articles on the 'Rise of Wellington' in the *Pall Mall Magazine*. As a general he placed Wellington in the front rank; as a man, not: 'there appears to be no instance in his military career of his adopting a course where his duty was opposed to his own interests ... In his case the paths of duty and of personal advancement were identical ...' As a leader of men, he won his soldiers' confidence, but not affection: 'he regarded his army in the light of a fighting machine'.[112] Roberts had help with these articles from his 'golden pen', William Nicholson, who the next year helped his speech-writing. But in 1896 Nicholson was back in India, and soon campaigning on the frontier.[113] Roberts told Hamilton that he had called on Buller. 'His manner puts you off rather, but I was determined to get on with him, and we left each other fairly good friends, I think.' Campbell-Bannerman pressed Malta on him once again: 'The Horse Guards people evidently want to get rid of me, and Buller, I hear, talks openly about the wickedness of my refusing Malta!'[114] Was this the first serious souring of relations between Roberts and the adjutant-general?

While the Liberals left him in the cold, the public could not ignore him. In December 1893, the *Pall Mall Gazette* published Kipling's poem, 'Bobs', belatedly celebrating his peerage of January 1892. Things had changed since the poet of Empire wrote 'A Job Lot'. Now 'Bobs' was the hero of the British soldier, 'the 'Pocket-Wellinton' [*sic*] who had 'elped the soldier's load'. Why did a newspaperman as shrewd as Kipling write:

Oh, he's little but he's wise,
'E's a terror for 'is size,
An' 'e—*does—not—advertise*—
   Do yer, Bobs?

Soldiers at Mian Mir and Allahabad had described 'benefits bestowed', and a few years later Kipling told Roberts: 'never did living leader of men have so many passionate worshippers among the rank and file'.[115] He knew, however, Roberts's reputation for self-advertisement; the verse was a tongue-in-cheek hit at Wolseley.

Within two years, while Roberts employed his pen and attended dinners, Campbell-Bannerman took the step that was to give him an opening. Cambridge was seventy-six, had been at the head of the army for thirty-nine years, and change was overdue. He was retired on 31 October, 1895.[116] When Rosebery as Prime Minister wrote with Campbell-Bannerman's proposal of Buller as the new top man, baiting it with Connaught's succeeding him, the Queen approved. The Liberals, however, were defeated in a Commons vote and Salisbury's Unionists[117] returned to power. Salisbury had backed Roberts for Indian commander-in-chief and his friend Lansdowne was War Secretary. Both, however, chose Wolseley to succeed Cambridge and Roberts to follow Wolseley in Ireland. If Wolseley were not available, Connaught 'would be better than Buller'. Another royal duke was the Queen's preference, and she certainly did not want Roberts, 'ruled by his wife who is a terrible jobber'; his candidature was impossible 'on account of his readiness to listen to his wife, & her notorious favouritism'.[118] Roberts's jobbery had been rather successful; the Queen was to find hers on behalf of 'dear Arthur' a frustrating business. Wolseley accepted the post with alacrity provided there would be no changes in power and responsibilities. Lansdowne warned him that things would change. This longed-for pinnacle of his professional life proved an anticlimax. The Queen was not pleased and thought that Connaught 'must not be kept out of the command-in-chief for long'. Wolseley's appointment was for five years, to 1 November 1900. He was the War Secretary's principle advisor, supervising operations, intelligence, distribution and mobilisation of troops. Buller, still adjutant-general, had discipline, education and recruiting.[119] Wolseley believed that Buller had betrayed him by his willingness to become commander-in-chief. Buller thought he was innocent of intrigue. The War Office was an unhappy place: Wolseley and Buller disliked Lansdowne. Wolseley's health and mental powers were declining. Buller and Sir Arthur Haliburton, the under-secretary, shared a mutual antipathy. According to Clinton Dawkins, Financial Secretary, 'the greater part of the energies of the leading soldiers is devoted to "putting each other in the cast" '.[120]

Wolseley claimed that Roberts was 'moving heaven and earth to get Lansdowne . . . to make him boss at the War Office', but earth and heaven were insufficient against politicians. Salisbury's ministry was firmly in control. Roberts took the Irish command, for by now even 'the Lady' realised Aldershot was not on the table. In the summer, already bound for Ireland, he tried a last letter to Lansdowne:

> There are however so many rumours of possible changes in consequence of the Duke of Cambridge's approaching retirement, rumours which it is difficult altogether to ignore, that I shall be greatly obliged if you will tell me whether I am likely to be left in Ireland. Please do not think that I am asking for or expecting anything, but if there were the least chance of my not remaining in Ireland I should not put myself to the considerable expense of sending all my worldly goods there.

Lansdowne replied, properly: 'Nothing would be nicer than having you at my side, but you must go to Dublin as arranged by my predecessor.'[121]

Sensibly Roberts then wrote to both Lansdowne and Wolseley, congratulating the latter and saying to both that although the field marshals 'may have differed on matters of detail . . . on the main question, viz: the necessity for our Army being thoroughly efficient, we are entirely agreed'. He promised that Wolseley would have 'no warmer supporter than myself' in any reforms.[122]

In May 1895, Roberts had gained his field-marshal's baton.[123] Ireland was not necessarily a dead-end, for Wolseley had moved thence to Whitehall, but like his predecessor he found insufficient challenge. He and his wife entertained regularly; his house-steward recalled, 'there were no dinners more enjoyable and merry than those given by Lady Roberts in Dublin.'[124] He set about writing his memoirs,

> urged to do so by friends, who, being interested themselves in what I was able to tell them of India as my father knew it, and as I found it and left it, persuaded me that my experience of the many and various aspects under which I have known the wonderful land of my adoption and its interesting peoples would be useful to my countrymen.[125]

He told Lady Hills-Johnes that he hoped her husband 'will institute it as one of the prizes in all the schools he has to deal with, and give it as presents to his many Godchildren! The more copies that are sold the better for me'.[126] A biography from a famous soldier would make money, would remind everyone of his fame and continued existence, and set out his views on the

Indian Empire. This was important. Action and debates on the North-West Frontier had continued. In 1894 there had been an expedition against the Waziris. In 1895 strong forces relieved a British mission besieged at Chitral. In 1897 against the Great Frontier Rising, the British would deploy the equivalent of two army corps.[127] George White's tenure of command extended the Forward School's reach. Not all agreed this was the way to pacify the frontier. Major Henry Hanna was on the opposite side. In 1895, during the debate on Chitral, Hanna published *Lord Roberts in War*.[128] He knew Roberts had occupied of late years 'the foremost place in public estimation' but 'our latest Field Marshal is neither a safe nor a consistent guide'. He attributed Roberts's victory at the Peiwar Kotal to his subordinates; pointed out that the hangings simply enraged the Kabulis; defended Brigadier Massy and condemned Roberts for asking Brigadier Charles Gough to march to his relief against forces of unknown strength.[129] Hanna should have learnt from Gough about the bungling Massy: 'there is no doubt that he is incompetent, not a single cavalry man speaks well of him', Gough had written.[130] The attack on Roberts's generalship was meant to damn his argument to retain Chitral: 'an insignificant little town 185 miles from Peshawar, and a thousand miles from any ... possible base of Russian operations against India'. His claim that Roberts scattered troops over an enormous area in small, isolated bodies hardly made sense.[131] Roberts's railways and troop increases were designed for the opposite: to mass troops for a strategic response to any Russian advance.

Roberts's admirers were furious. Hills-Johnes called it 'a very nasty book' and Sir William Lockhart sent a copy to Neville Chamberlain inscribed 'vile poison'. 'No one thought it necessary to take any notice of it,' wrote Hills-Johnes.[132] He was right. In Parliament and the letters columns of *The Times* there was debate, but no book review. In India the Forward School prevailed: British influence in Chitral was 'a matter of the first importance'. At the Royal Geographical Society, Captain Francis Younghusband, veteran of the 'Great Game', outlined with Roberts's supporting presence Chitral's role in India's security.[133] Roberts's biography, *Forty-One Years in India* was not just written to put the author's views on India, for he felt that he needed the money and pressed his publishers, Macmillan, for better terms.[134] His runaway bestseller dominated public thinking on India, whatever opponents of the Forward School might write. The newspapers were full of praise. On 9 January, five days after the book's appearance, one reviewer wrote: 'There has only been one thing to do in London this week – to go to India with Lord Roberts. No autobiography has been so run after for years, and novel-reading is in abeyance.' Roberts benefited not just from it being the year of the Queen's Diamond Jubilee, but by the Empire of India Exhibition eighteen months earlier (August–October 1895) showing the sub-continent as 'a picturesque wonderland ... glad to be ruled by Britain'.[135] The book became standard reading for young men embarking on an Indian career. The young Winston Churchill's mother sent him a copy.[136]

Another best-selling author was sent one. To Kipling Roberts wrote:

You who take and have made others take such a keen interest in our soldiers, and have brought India so near to the people of Great Britain by your jungle stories and vivid word pictures, may, perhaps, come to read the narrative of a soldier's life in India. At all events the book will serve to reassure you that you are most kindly remembered by, Yours very truly, Roberts.[137]

The two men were not yet close allies. Kipling told his former editor at Lahore, Stephen Wheeler, that he was 'amazed at the things he does *not* say.'[138] The hangings at Kabul were the obvious omission, and Kipling as a *Civil & Military Gazette* correspondent had had an intimate knowledge of Afghan affairs.[139] To Roberts, however, he sent congratulations: '. . . even I, who know, I think, every step of your career by heart, was amazed by it. The papers have been so taken up with the *matter* of the book that, so far as I have seen, they had not in the least done justice to its perfection of *technique*, and that is the side on which it appeals to me.' He wanted 'a cheap sixpenny précis. .. for barrack-reading-rooms and bookstalls'; one time-expired soldier had told Kipling they 'want to know what Bobs 'as been writing about us'.[140] There was some dissent. The *Civil & Military Gazette* criticised his espousal of the Forward School with its costs. The Rev. Kane and Colonel Fred Keyser, late Royal Fusiliers, both at Kandahar in 1880, protested to *The Times* against the story of the garrison's failure to hoist a flag on Roberts's arrival. None could be found.[141]

While commanding in Ireland, Roberts had time to visit London frequently and to keep up a copious correspondence, not just to Lansdowne at the War Office, but to George Curzon on the frontier question; to Colonel G.F.R. Henderson, the outstanding Staff College lecturer; to the Countess of Wicklow about acquiring land for an artillery range and infantry field firing; to Lytton's daughter on seeing proofs of her biography of her father: 'I look forward with sincere pleasure to reading the vindication of his far seeing policy in the account of his Indian administration.'[142] R.J. Wicksteed of Ottawa, Canada, had written asking him to name the author of the saying, 'the British Army is an Army of Lions led by asses'. Roberts thought it might have been an opponent of military service, or perhaps Daniel Defoe. 'At no time, I hope, in the military history of Great Britain,' he added, 'would the remark have been altogether applicable.'[143]

Roberts was no donkey. His summer manoeuvres of 1899 were conducted under conditions as close as possible to active service. His 'Irish Manoeuvres Circular Memorandum' of 6 July 1899 advised: 'Under the existing conditions of war, which render frontal attack over open ground impossible, reconnaissance is, perhaps, the most important of all the many duties that devolve on Commanders, and Staff and Regimental Officers.'[144] He published a collection of speeches on 'Musketry Training and Artillery Practice'.

Success would lie with 'the artillery which can bring an accurate shrapnel fire to bear upon the enemy with the greatest rapidity'.[145] To those manoeuvres, Roberts invited a special guest: Lord Kitchener of Khartoum, the newly ennobled hero of the campaign in the Sudan against the Mahdists.[146]

Kitchener, a Royal Engineer, Arabic speaker and intelligence officer in Egypt and the Sudan, became *Sirdar* or commander-in-chief of the Egyptian Army in April 1892. He longed to advance up the Nile and avenge his hero Gordon. The Mahdi died soon after Gordon's death, succeeded by his closest intimate, the Khalifa Abdulahi. In 1896 Salisbury approved an Anglo-Egyptian advance.[147] The ensuing three-year campaign was the culmination of Victorian small wars. Kitchener's deadliest weapon was the Sudan Military Railway, 'forged in the workshops of Wadi Halfa'.[148] The Khalifa trusted to the courage of his *Ansar* ('helpers') against modern firepower, the new .303 Lee-Metford, Maxims and artillery. The battle of Omdurman on 2 September 1898 was a one-sided slaughter. Dervish charges melted away in a hail of fire.[149]

Captain Henry Rawlinson, Roberts's protégé, served with Kitchener from 2 January 1898 as DAAG (deputy assistant adjutant general). He sent Roberts a series of letters describing the Sirdar at close quarters: 'I get on well with the Sirdar and like him much – he is a strong, able, hard soldier, full of energy and resource but hard as steel . . .'[150] Many soldiers sought a billet with Kitchener, and he strenuously resisted the arrival of 'medal-hunters'. On Rawlinson's urging, he agreed to take Freddie Roberts as an extra ADC. Freddie was 'a real soldier', mentioned in despatches for service on the North-West Frontier. Rawlinson told his old chief that nothing had given him greater pleasure than sending the telegram summoning Freddie.[151] Freddie served at Omdurman, and accompanied Kitchener with a select force to confront the intrepid French explorer Colonel Marchand at Fashoda. Kitchener astutely avoided a clash, and showed Marchand the helplessness of his situation. Lord Salisbury brought naval and diplomatic pressure on France, forcing a climb-down. This secured the Sudan for an Anglo-Egyptian condominium, a new form of rule with Kitchener as first governor-general.[152]

Although there was a storm over Kitchener's having the Mahdi's body dug up and thrown into the Nile,[153] the typical European view was that he had ended a regime 'more like a system of plunder than an administration'. The Austro-Hungarian consul-general in Cairo applauded Kitchener's campaign as 'a masterpiece of organisation which does great honour to England'.[154] Roberts agreed. He wrote in April 1898 to congratulate Kitchener 'on the success that has attended your operations since you commenced your advance up the Nile and the very complete blow you dealt to the Dervish Army. Nothing could have been better . . .' The Sirdar wrote a brief reply: 'The troops did splendidly . . . I am now hard at work getting the gunboats put together.'[155] Roberts was among those greeting Kitchener on his triumphant return. In December 1898, he wrote to *The Times* that the victory had been a feat of arms invaluable to Britain and shown the Sirdar to have the qualities for command: clear judgement, quick perception, common sense, tenacity of purpose and above all a talent for organisation.[156] On 25 June the following year Kitchener was introduced to the House of Lords by Roberts and Lord Cromer on his elevation to the peerage. In August, Rawlinson arranged that the two men meet in Ireland for Kitchener to see the manoeuvres. Ian Hamilton later told Sir George Arthur, Kitchener's biographer: 'In the sense in which mice help lions, [Rawlinson] and I had a hand in Lord K. coming out to South Africa with Lord Roberts.'[157]

The years of Kitchener's campaign coincided with increasing tension between Britain and the Boer republics, the Transvaal and the Orange Free State. The Jameson Raid of December 1895 sowed a harvest of Boer mistrust. Kruger armed his state with German Mauser rifles, Krupp 75-mm field guns and French Creusot 155-mm 'Long Toms'. When asked the object of his enormous armaments, he replied: 'Oh, Kaffirs, Kaffirs – and such-like objects.'[158] Kruger stood for Boer independence. Britain held this cheap. Kruger assumed Salisbury might retreat as Gladstone had done after Majuba. Salisbury's strong-willed ministry would not yield, and wrongly thought that Kruger would.[159]

British soldiers remembered Majuba and thought there would be war. For Roberts South Africa was 'unfinished business'. He and Kitchener took an instant liking to one another, and Kitchener made it clear that he would be glad to serve as Roberts's second in the field.[160] They had much in common: both were 'single-minded imperialists' in the words of a South African historian.[161] Did they discuss how to fight the Boers? Roberts had already considered plans with Captain Henry Wilson to whom Rawlinson had introduced him at a cricket match in 1893. In April 1897, he had lunched with Wilson and Major H.P. Northcott of the Intelligence Division, who presented the scheme they had been preparing 'for knocking Kruger's head off'. Wilson and Rawlinson met the next day, and agreed the latter would write to Roberts. As far as the War Office was concerned (wrote Rawlinson), if there were war in South Africa the choice for command lay between Redvers Buller and Evelyn Wood. Wolseley's health was too poor.

Roberts not being considered was later put down by Salisbury and Arthur Balfour to Wolseley's 'well-known jealousy', but it was the politicians' choice. The Cabinet feared he was too old, unacquainted with the English military system, his Indian experience unsuitable for South Africa.[162] Rawlinson assumed his hero had only to put his name forward. 'Possibly you may have already approached Lord Lansdowne on the subject [of command in South Africa],' he wrote,' if however you have not, I hope you won't think it presumptuous on my part if I were to suggest that you should do so without delay.'[163] Two days later he was delighted that Roberts would press his claims.[164] In March 1896, Roberts had already offered his services to Lansdowne in either the Sudan or South Africa, hoping that he would not be thought too old, and prepared to serve 'as a General instead of as a Field Marshal'.[165] The following month he joked: 'South African affairs look so serious that I think you will have to send a Field Marshal there!'[166] His pleas had no effect, and he did not write again about South Africa until June 1899.[167]

In summer 1898, he had been invited by St John Brodrick, the Under-Secretary of State for War, to stay near Salisbury Plain to see the largest manoeuvres yet held in Britain: 50,000 men in two armies, the Blue under Buller and the Red under Connaught. Buller was defeated in almost every encounter.[168] Brodrick quoted him saying: 'I have been making a fool of myself all day.'[169] The future Lady Milner wrote: 'I wondered what Lord Roberts thought of it all, but he was much too discreet to say anything critical on this occasion ...'[170] The manoeuvres hardly reflected new firepower: the main forces operated in squares and solid lines. By contrast Colonel Ian Hamilton sent out mobile groups who overran enemy headquarters and disrupted communications. He was admonished for his tactics.[171]

Buller in command of the First Army Corps at Aldershot was earmarked for South Africa. Salisbury's Cabinet did not even like him; he remained in command because ministers expected a climb-down by Kruger.[172] Colonial Secretary Joseph Chamberlain had sent Alfred Milner to South Africa to negotiate, but Milner would not conciliate and was prepared to run the risk of war to 'break the dominion of Afrikanerdom'. After the Bloemfontein conference collapsed on 5 June 1899, Kruger declared: 'I am not ready to hand over my country to strangers.'[173] His defensive alliance with President Marthinus Steyn of the Orange Free State nearly completed preparations. In September, Salisbury's government found war staring them in the face. 'Kruger has nipped my holiday in the bud, confound him,' Lansdowne told Roberts.[174] Belatedly he sent reinforcements to South Africa's outnumbered garrison, but it was 10,000 men from India who saved Natal from being overrun.[175] The Cabinet had been preparing an ultimatum: Kruger forestalled them on 9 October, demanding arbitration on all points of difference, withdrawal of recently landed troops and those on the frontiers, men on transports at sea not to disembark. The ultimatum's timing was crucial: before reinforcements arrived and while summer grass sustained the ponies of the Boer commandos.[176]

This expired on 11 October without British acceptance, and on the morning of the 12th Piet Joubert's force invaded Natal.[177] Mounted commandos composed of citizen soldiers – the Boers preferred 'burgher' to 'soldier' – were a formidable enemy. The two republics assembled the largest modern army yet seen in South Africa.[178] The young men, hardy, expert riders and marksmen, were supported by professional gunners, the *Staatsartillerie*, adapting modern European techniques. The British Army had an unrivalled knowledge of small wars against 'savage peoples', but had not faced modern weapons since Majuba. The squares and *zaribas* employed in the Sudan and described by Captain C.E. Callwell in his book *Small Wars* would be suicidal against magazine-fed rifles. Kruger made excellent use of spies in Cape Colony to keep himself informed of British movements. It was fortunate for Britain that Boer commanders, Joubert and Piet Cronje, were old and set in their ways, and they frittered away early advantages by failing to seize key railway junctions like De Aar. They besieged Kimberley, Ladysmith and Mafeking, instead of following Jan Smuts's urging to penetrate the British colonies on a wide front and destroy the infrastructure, thus frustrating a British counter-offensive.[179]

On 14 October Buller commanding the 1st Army Corps 40,000 strong sailed for South Africa. Ian Hamilton and Henry Rawlinson had already left on 16 September with George White to defend Natal. News of the battle of Talana near the mining town of Dundee, with the death of cousin Jack Sherston, had arrived before Freddie Roberts sailed on 21 October, also to join White. Father had been pushing doors open. In August he had written to Evelyn Wood, adjutant general, hoping he would recommend Freddie for Staff College: mentioned in despatches, Freddie took a keen interest in his profession, wrote his father, and would make a good staff officer.[180] Alas! In the exam poor Freddie fell 400 marks short of all other candidates save one. Wood was doubtful: 'I am not certain that the Commander-in-Chief will be able to knock out men in favour of those who did less well in the literary [written] examination.'[181] Wolseley did just that, selecting Freddie for a place. Wood told Roberts the good news and concluded: 'Lord Wolseley has desired me to add that it has given him much gratification to be able to meet your wishes.'[182] To Roberts's grateful letter, Wolseley replied: 'Many thanks for your note, but if your son was not to have a nomination for the S.C. who should have one? Besides he has a very good reputation of his own as a soldier.'[183] Was this more 'jobbery'? It mattered not. For Freddie a bright future beckoned.

Roberts saw a less cheerful prospect in South Africa following Buller's manoeuvres fiasco. His fear was increased when Brackenbury, now master-general of the ordnance, warned him of unpreparedness for war.[184] Buller, who knew South Africa, was gloomier. He had told Lansdowne in July that the war was 'a big thing' and it would be better if he were not commander-in-chief, but Wolseley's chief of staff. To Wolseley he expressed 'very strong objections to accepting the command . . .' Wolseley's health was not up to it, but Buller only accepted after persuasion.[185] He reached the Cape on 31October and heard the news of 'Mournful Monday', a British debacle outside Ladysmith. Two regiments had surrendered to the despised farmers. Four days later he wrote to his brother: 'I am in the tightest place I have ever been in, and the worst of it is that it is none of my creating. I don't know if I shall ever get out of it all right . . .'[186] This was not the spirit that had won the VC facing Zulu *assegais*. He divided his force in three, and abandoning a planned advance towards Bloemfontein, capital of the Orange Free State, went by sea to Natal to relieve Sir George White penned up in Ladysmith.

White, recently QMG at the War Office, hobbling on a gammy leg after a riding accident in India, failed as Buller did to live up to past performance. Buller and his defenders blamed him for being trapped with 12,000 men in Ladysmith, '*un pot de chambre*' overlooked by encircling hills.[187] Buller's tactical limitations were embodied in the British Army's principal all-arms manual, *Infantry Drill 1896* which he had issued as adjutant-general. It advocated quarter-column (i.e. dense) formations, frontal attacks, volley firing, disdain of cover.[188]

The British humiliation of 'Black Week' (10–15 December) followed. The three parts of the Army Corps were beaten: Gatacre at Stormberg, Methuen at Magersfontein and Buller at Colenso. Gatacre exhausted his force on a cross-country march without adequate scouting. Methuen sent the Highland Brigade on a night march in quarter column formation, an ideal target. They were shot to pieces by the Boers, suffering nearly 1,000 casualties.[189] At Colenso on the Tugela, Buller's 18,000 men gave him a three-to-one superiority, but he faced the determined Louis Botha, dug into a strong position, hills rising tier upon tier behind the winding Tugela River. Buller failed to note that Hlangwane was the key to the position and guns placed there could enfilade the Boers; this was spotted by several officers including Major William Birdwood from the Bengal Lancers.[190] Buller sent forward Hart's Irish Brigade to cross at Bridle Drift. Hart deployed his men in close order, but his scouts could not find the Drift or ford, and his brigade was pinned down by a crossfire from concealed riflemen. Buller especially blamed Colonel C.J. Long, for taking his two batteries of guns dangerously forward.[191] There is evidence to the contrary. Long's guns soon found the range to Fort Wyllie, one of four hills overlooking the Tugela, strongly entrenched with well-built stone walls. Their shooting continued despite Boer fire and casualties: 'there was no interruption to the rapid and accurate fire of the batteries which soon silenced the enemy's guns, and caused their rifle fire to slacken, until it became almost insignificant'. Long himself was wounded, but fire kept up until, with ammunition running low, he called for resupply.[192]

By now Hart's brigade was being withdrawn. Buller decided that any attempt by Long to reopen fire was out of the question, and stopped the wagons which were on their way from the ammunition column. He ordered the withdrawal of the supporting naval 12-pounders. Without resupply, the gunners retired into a gully. Buller's attack had broken down.

He had been in the sun, on horseback for hours, bruised by spent shrapnel. Under the strain of command, he made a fatal decision. The obvious step was to station infantry from intact brigades to cover the guns and withdraw them at nightfall. The British were in superior numbers despite losing 1,100 men. Instead, Buller called for volunteers from his staff and gunners to ride out with limbers and save the guns. Seven gunners came forward, and were joined by Captains Walter Congreve and H.N. Schofield and Lieutenant Freddie Roberts. Freddie had been assigned to White's staff, but Ladysmith being cut off he joined General Clery as a 'galloper' and was with Buller to carry messages. They hitched the horse-teams to the limbers and cantered towards the guns, half a mile distant. They were met by a storm of fire. Two guns on the left were successfully limbered up. The Boers increased fire at the other group of rescuers. Congreve 'had never seen bullets thicker even at play or field firing'. Freddie was hit three times, one a fatal wound in the stomach, and went down. Congreve with about thirty men and a doctor lay under cover in the gulley, until the fire slackened. He then ventured out, and with the doctor and a gunner got Freddie into cover where his wounds were dressed. They 'then lay in the blazing sun & without a breath of wind till 5 p.m. when the Boers surrounded us & took us prisoners.'[193] A second rescue effort broke down under Boer fire. Colonel Lawrence Parsons had retired his batteries under cover, and went to Buller, offering to range onto Long's guns and prevent the Boers carrying them away. Buller said: 'No, everything that is possible has been done, & I will not risk losing more lives.'[194] Between 2 and 3 p.m. he retired his force. The victorious Boers allowed the wounded including Freddie to be sent back in ambulance-men's care to a hospital train. Captain Henry Warre found him in great pain, but showing 'extraordinary pluck. 'Goodbye warrior, we'll meet again soon,' Freddie murmured, touching Warre's hand. When a distinguished surgeon, Frederick Treves, examined him, he was comfortable with morphine. Treves saw the case was hopeless. William Birdwood lamented: 'he is such a good dear fellow . . . loved by everyone'. He died at midnight and was buried on the afternoon of the 17th.[195]

Meanwhile, Roberts's messages to Lansdowne about South Africa had become more urgent.[196] On 22 October he offered his services if either White or Buller were incapacitated. On 8 December he made a further offer believing Buller lacked confidence in his own abilities, a belief fully supported by events. 'He seems to be overwhelmed by the magnitude of the task imposed upon him.' Lansdowne replied on the 10th, noting Gatacre's defeat but also that Buller had made no mistakes so far. The next day Roberts wrote that the force was too large for one man. On the 16th and 17th he sent further advice. By then Buller had been beaten. Newspapers carrying stories of Colenso reached British HQ in Ireland, and Roberts prepared an outspoken telegram urging radical change in strategy. As he drove to Viceregal Lodge to encipher it, Buller's arrived stating Freddie had been dangerously wounded and recommended for the VC. Roberts's telegram crossed Lansdowne's asking him to London at once and to be ready to sail for South Africa without delay. He told his wife that he would return the next night. The two sent another telegram, this time to South Africa telling their son of their pride in him and their prayers for his recovery. It was too late.[197]

FIGURE 12 *A dramatic illustration by Stanley Berkeley of the death of Freddie Roberts trying to rescue the guns at Colenso. The loss of an only son was a terrible blow to the close-knit Roberts family (National Army Museum).*

Buller sent two telegrams to London. His first began: 'I regret to report a serious reverse.'[198] At 11.15 p.m. he had absorbed the full effect of defeat. He wired:

> A serious question is raised by my failure to-day, I do not now consider that I am strong enough to relieve Ladysmith. Colenso is a fortress, which, if not captured by a rush could, I think, only be taken by a siege. Within the 8 miles from the point of attack there is no water and in this weather that exhausts Infantry. The place is fully entrenched. I do not think we saw either a gun or a Boer all day, but the fire brought to bear on us was very heavy. The Infantry were willing enough to fight but the intense heat absolutely exhausted them. I consider I ought to let Ladysmith go and to occupy good position for the defence of South Natal and so let time help us. But I feel I ought to consult you on such a step.

He said he had faced 20,000 Boers – there had been 6,000 – and added: 'I was beaten. I now feel that I cannot say that with my available force I can relieve Ladysmith, and I suggest that for me to occupy a defensive position and fight it out in a country better suited to our tactics is the best thing that I can do.'[199] Three years later to the Royal Commission he claimed that 'let Ladysmith go' did not mean 'let fall'. The Commission did not believe his testimony.[200] Lansdowne replied: 'The abandonment of White's force and its consequent surrender is regarded by the Government as a national disaster of the greatest magnitude. We would urge you to devise another attempt to carry out its relief, not necessarily *via* Colenso, making use of the additional men now arriving if you think fit.'[201] Buller wired that he was much obliged; the message was 'exactly what I required'. In his distrait uncertainty, he wanted guidance. To White he signalled:

> I tried Colenso yesterday but failed. The enemy is too strong for my force except with siege operations, which will take one full month to prepare. Can you last so long. If not, how many days can you give me to take up a defensive position, after which I suggest your firing away as much ammunition as you can and making the best terms you can. I can remain here if you have alternative suggestion, but unaided I cannot break in.

A second signal cautioned him to burn his codebooks if he surrendered.[202] White replied that they could easily hold out for another month.[203]

In London after dinner on the 15th, Lansdowne met Balfour at his London house with news of Colenso, and said he thought it was necessary to supersede Buller and appoint Roberts with Kitchener as his chief of staff. The Unionists had never had much confidence in Buller. The next day his telegram announcing that he wished to 'let Ladysmith go' was read. That afternoon a Cabinet meeting was held in Lord Salisbury's room at the

Foreign Office. Salisbury, aged nearly seventy, was prepared to leave the initiative to others, but determined from his Zulu War experience to act swiftly to change command.[204] The reply to Buller was sent, and it was agreed to summon Roberts from Ireland and appoint him. On the morning of the 17th he met Lansdowne and said he was prepared to take command. Balfour and Lansdowne met him later in the day to confirm this. Balfour said: 'he showed neither depression nor misgivings nor overconfidence: he indulged in no unnecessary criticisms on others and made no boasts about himself'.[205] He said Kitchener's assistance was essential, but Salisbury would have insisted on the younger man.[206] In Egypt, Kitchener's acceptance was enthusiastic 'and Roberts expresses the greatest satisfaction at having Kitchener to work with'.[207] On the 18th Buller was informed that Roberts was to take supreme command. His attitude appeared to be relief: 'If I may be allowed to say so, I entirely agree with the reasons that have guided the action of Her Majesty's government.'[208] On the 22nd Lansdowne further sweetened the pill with a letter: 'I notice with pleasure that what we did has in no case been interpreted as a reflection upon you.' 'I am glad you are going to have another try at Ladysmith.'[209]

News of Freddie's death arrived after Roberts's appointment. It fell to Lansdowne to break it to his father. This was not just the loss of an only son in a close-knit family, but an end to so many hopes and aspirations. The blow was almost more than he could bear, but he showed immense courage in pulling himself together. He refused to allow the loss to turn him from the task ahead.[210] In those days the VC was not given posthumously, but the Queen found a way. Buller's commendation had been dated before Freddie's death, and she secured Salisbury's agreement. Forgotten were her objections to Roberts and his wife, that 'terrible jobber'. 'He was his poor parents' only son, a very distinguished young man,' she wrote. She wanted to hand the medal to Lady Roberts herself, but instead despatched it at the end of January, with a personal message: 'I send you . . . the Victoria Cross, with which I should have been so proud and pleased to decorate your darling son with myself.' Lady Roberts replied with 'heartfelt gratitude, love and devotion, and that of my two dear girls, who feel most deeply the honour done to the memory of their dearly loved brother . . .'[211] Roberts himself declared 'how splendidly' his wife and girls behaved in the week before he sailed. 'Though broken-hearted themselves they did their best to conceal their grief in order to try and cheer me up.'[212] He told the Queen before his departure that he could speak of 'anything but that [loss]'. He looked 'hale and well, although very sad'.[213]

Two days before Christmas, he was bade farewell at Waterloo Station by the Prince of Wales, Connaught, Cambridge, Balfour, Lansdowne and a large crowd. Comrades of the Delhi Ridge were there: Donald Stewart, Henry Norman, James Hills-Johnes, Hugh Gough. In the person of the little field marshal, the now-defunct Bengal Army was leading the forces of Empire.[214] His wife and daughters, Lansdowne, Gough and Hills-Johnes accompanied him to Southampton where he boarded the *Dunottar Castle*. Passing through the boat shed, he saw an Afghan War medal on a harbour constable's jacket, and characteristically stopped to speak to the veteran. Against a grey, overcast winter sky he stood on deck in black coat and top hat, 'vigorous, resolute, sorrowful ... in deep mourning'. To his wife he wrote: 'the rent in my heart seems to stifle all feelings ... I could not help thinking how different it would have been if our dear boy had been with me.'[215]

CHAPTER TEN

Turning the tide of war in South Africa – and failing to finish it[1]

Although Lord Roberts had not, hitherto, commanded much more than a division [in war], yet the nation and the army discerned rightly in him a leader equal to the most difficult situations of the South African campaign.

GERMAN OFFICIAL HISTORY

When Roberts came on the scene, there was something about the little man that put fresh heart and hope into everybody.

SIR ALFRED MILNER TO J.L. GARVIN

We have greatly underestimated the military strength and spirit of the Boers – at any rate a fierce and bloody struggle is before us . . .

WINSTON CHURCHILL

'There could be no greater contrast between two men than between Lord Roberts and Lord Kitchener,' wrote George Younghusband. One grew into 'the highest type of English gentleman', the other 'acquired more Teutonic characteristics'.[2] If their personalities, methods and manners had been that different, would the two have worked together so successfully? The Austro-Hungarian consul-general at Cairo noted that, despite many good qualities, Kitchener 'counts indeed as one of the most unpopular generals in the British Army. He exploits everybody to the last degree and in the most ruthless fashion . . .' He thought that as he was to serve with 'the most popular general in the British Army these two opposing temperaments should balance each other out'. It was a bold stroke appointing him, as 'he had never faced civilised troops and is quite untried in modern warfare'.[3]

Their appointment underscores once again the pre-eminence of politics in military matters. Both men had developed political contacts, Roberts with Lansdowne, Kitchener with the Cecils. Sending them to South Africa reassured public opinion, as Salisbury's ministry intended.[4] Their backgrounds almost guaranteed reporters' approval. While Roberts had carefully cultivated his press contacts, Kitchener had enjoyed almost uncritical adulation from thirty-odd journalists covering his Sudan campaign. G.W. Steevens of the *Mail* created the image of the 'Sudan machine': 'You cannot imagine the Sirdar otherwise than as seeing the right thing to do and doing it. His precision is so unhumanly unerring, he is more like a machine than a man.'[5] This precision and Roberts's bold tactical flair were to be tested to the utmost by a mobile enemy. Ian Hamilton, who had already been in action, told Alfred Milner that 'on their own Boer ground' the burghers were 'the most formidable foe in the world'.[6] Few British generals were capable of beating them. Kitchener being forty-first in seniority among major-generals shows the likely unfitness of his seniors. Of field marshals and full generals, Roberts was probably the only choice.[7] He was longing for action, confident of his own abilities and Kitchener's support, prepared to risk his name and reputation. The prize would be to avenge his son and to take the top job of the British Army. As he had written of Wellington: 'the paths of duty and of personal advancement were identical'. Yet there was still much that was noble in his sailing to South Africa to retrieve the army's fortunes, especially when his grief was so deeply felt.[8] To Pole-Carew he wrote: 'The voyage was the most terrible trial, nothing to do for nearly three weeks but think, think, of my dear boy, and that I should never see him again in this world.'[9]

The partnership of two strong men was assured by Kitchener. He spoke of Roberts 'with the deepest and most affectionate admiration' and had decided very consciously to subordinate himself. 'Lord Kitchener, who had always been cock of his own walk and was received at home after his victorious campaigns as a conquering hero,' wrote the future Lady Milner, 'fell quite naturally into the second place, becoming as Staff Officer and leaving all the panache to Lord Roberts.'[10] This was a huge advantage. Of the four men whom Roberts would most naturally have gathered round him, his son was dead at Colenso and his nephew Jack Sherston at Talana, and Hamilton and Rawlinson were shut up in Ladysmith.[11] With him were Neville Chamberlain, William Nicholson, George Pretyman and commanding a division Lt-General Thomas Kelly-Kenny, another Irish soldier who had been in Abyssinia in 1867–8. Colonels George Henderson, outstanding staff college lecturer, and Eddie Stanley, son of the Earl of Derby, had written with sympathy on Freddie's death and asked for posts: 'to the best of my abilities, I would endeavor to serve you faithfully in any office, however low you could put me', wrote Stanley.[12] He became press censor, Henderson head of intelligence.

FIGURE 13 *Roberts and Kitchener arrive at Cape Town. The Empire's new commanders had been appointed to reverse a tide of defeat. Their mutual admiration and Kitchener's decision to efface himself and give the older man every assistance made their partnership a greater success than many expected (Mary Evans Picture Library).*

Roberts and Kitchener reached the Cape on 10 January. They quickly put purpose into things. Leo Amery of *The Times* thought that Kitchener with Roberts in overall charge was absolutely unafraid of responsibility, gave straight answers to all, despised red tape and mastered a mass of detail. 'General Nicholson told us tonight that all the same Roberts is by no means a mere figurehead,' Amery wrote on 23 January. 'All the important decisions are made by him.'[13] Could defects in staff work, maps, intelligence and mounted troops be made good? Roberts issued new tactical instructions, 'Notes for Guidance in South African Warfare', to counter the threat from magazine rifles and to adapt to local conditions. He urged careful reconnaissance, open order, delegating responsibility to company and battalion officers, precise and accurate messages and use of cover. He exhorted cavalrymen to care for their horses. To fill a shortage of mounted men he ordered the 6th and 7th divisions to provide one company of mounted infantry per battalion. Two new mounted regiments, Roberts's and Kitchener's Horse, were raised.[14] Henderson confiscated a parcel of maps as contraband, and had copies printed by the *Cape Argus* newspaper for almost every officer in the field force. An intelligence department was formed including local men.[15] Kitchener's lack of seniority was a problem. Roberts wired Lansdowne asking that Kitchener succeed him with rank of full general in the event of death or serious injury. Lansdowne agreed.[16]

In the great spaces of South Africa, mobility was key. Horses gave mobility. Yet Roberts and his horsemen would pay a price for a measure which was none of their doing. Shortly before fighting began, the War Office had swept away the 'Sick Horse Depot', the Veterinary Department, as an active service unit. In a desperate improvisation the director of transport and supply in South Africa was constituted head of Remount and Veterinary Services, the latter being subsumed under the former. A huge army with thousands of horses, oxen and mules had only forty or fifty military vets and 100 civilians. Of the War Office measure, the Royal Army Veterinary Corps historian wrote: 'Never in the history of any British War has there been such a deliberate sacrifice of animal life and of public money.'[17]

The most controversial change was to centralise transport. To spring a strategic surprise, Roberts had to break away from the railway line. *The Times* had already noted that: 'In every part of the theatre of war our troops are tethered to a line of railway.'[18] Transport companies were taken from regimental control, augmented by extra wagons purchased in Cape Colony, 300 in January and 400 later; supply columns were taken from brigades and divisions; and the whole reformed into companies of forty-nine wagons each.[19] A change was risky in the midst of war and unpopular in some quarters. Lt-General John French commanding the cavalry division kept his wagons apart, but his force was not better or worse supplied. Colonels Wodehouse Richardson of the Army Service Corps and William Nicholson testified to the necessity of centralised control for the army to reach Bloemfontein.[20] Many new transport officers were able men such as Major

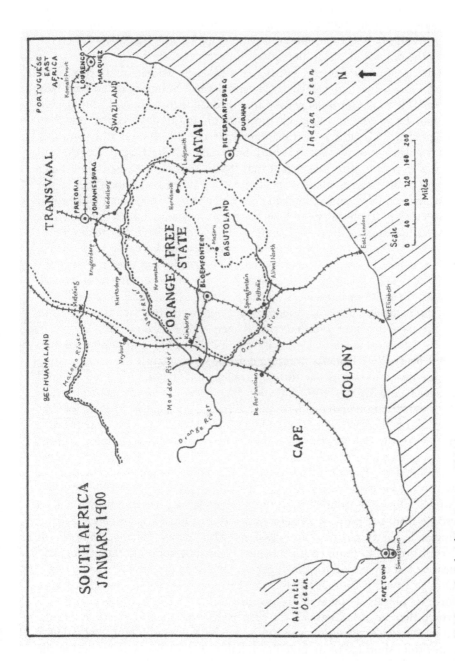

MAP 10 *South Africa, January 1900*

Ivor Maxse of the Coldstream Guards, his friend Seymour Vandeleur, praised by his divisional commander, and Captain Christopherson of the 9th division. Captain Ballard serving with Roberts's Horse wrote of the centralisation: 'Without doubt, this was the factor which enabled Roberts to leave the railway and plan operations on a wider scale.'[21]

On 22 January Roberts wrote to Lansdowne asking for twenty more good nurses. He had visited the hospitals; the failing was 'lack of lady nurses'. He took up the suggestion that medical men requested from Britain 'should be of the standing of surgeons or assistant surgeons' and had accepted an offer of ten Australian nurses.[22] The RAMC was still absorbing the amalgamation of the Medical Staff and Medical Staff Corps, and expectation of a short war meant that RAMC personnel were only 2.5 per cent of total strength whereas regulations laid down they should be 7.5 per cent. Even in the Crimea they had been 6 per cent. A report had highlighted that 'enteric' (typhoid) would be the greatest threat, but if fighting only lasted a few months the RAMC assumed it would not have time to develop.[23]

On his rounds of inspection, at a convalescent home at Cape Town, Roberts visited Captain Congreve, who with Freddie had tried to rescue the guns at Colenso. Congreve described his son's heroism and fatal wound. Roberts broke down and wept. '[Lord Roberts] sat on my bed & sobbed as tho' his heart was broken,' Congreve wrote in his diary.[24] 'What would I not give to have [my son] with me now,' Roberts told Lansdowne.[25]

To Roberts Lansdowne sent all the aid he could and supported him wholeheartedly.[26] Roberts in return defended him against the press, writing to Spenser Wilkinson that the government could not fully prepare until Kruger's ultimatum. 'From that moment I consider Lord Lansdowne has done everything which can be expected from a Sec[retar]y of State for War to push on the campaign.'[27] Following 'Black Week' a wave of patriotism had swept the Empire, and Lansdowne dispatched massive reinforcements, giving Roberts and Kitchener overwhelming numerical superiority. Against Boer mobility and defensive tactics, that did not guarantee success: as Winston Churchill wrote, the Mounted Boer was worth from three to five British soldiers on foot.[28] To spring a strategic surprise, the British had to escape from the railway. Roberts had sketched out his plan before leaving England, based partly on discussions with Henry Wilson, Major H.P. Northcott and Captain Hugh Dawnay.[29] Massing troops at Naauwport and near Colesburg would lead the Boers to believe he planned a crossing of the Orange River at Norval's Point and Bethulie; instead he would collect a force as rapidly as possible to advance round Piet Cronje's left flank. He would then be able to attack the rear of the Boer positions on the Orange river.[30] French's cavalry division supported by Mounted Infantry would play a key role: shortage of mounted men had been Colley's Achilles heel in the Transvaal War in 1880.[31] Henderson undertook elaborate measures of deception, including misleading, apparently confidential, news to a London newspaper correspondent. French appeared to threaten an Orange River crossing by the direct line over Norval's Point. The Highland Brigade marched westward as a decoy.[32]

Roberts's plan was kept secret until the last moment, disclosed only to Kitchener, Nicholson, Henderson and a few officers making railway arrangements. Kelly-Kenny leading the 6th Division and French commanding the cavalry were not told until 29 January. Roberts and Kitchener moved secretly to Methuen's camp on 8 February; he visited the troops and 'by his cheery smile and friendly recognition did much to revive the spirits of those who were feeling disheartened owing to previous failures and disappointments'.[33] On the 10th he told senior cavalry officers he was going to give them 'the greatest chance cavalry has ever had'. Major Edmund Allenby of the Inniskillings later wrote to his wife: 'Lord Roberts told us, before we started, that we should remember it all our lives.'[34] Ahead of the cavalry division would ride Rimington's Tigers, 200 colonial scouts led by Major M.F. Rimington. They were longing to avenge earlier defeats: one of them wrote: 'Bobs and Kitchener direct the advance; French heads it ... *At last!* is every one's feelings. The long waited for moment has come.'[35]

In the early hours of 11 February Roberts's offensive began: 37,000 men including nearly 8,000 cavalry and mounted infantry, more than 100 guns, and hundreds of supply wagons. French's cavalry, leaving their tents standing, headed south away from Kimberley. At daybreak a merciless sun rose into a clear blue sky. The heat was intense, the parched veld, suffering from an almost rainless summer, had turned its surface into powder, and the hot wind half smothered the troops in floury dust.[36] Cronje, expecting a frontal attack, drew in 8,000 men at Magersfontein. He had told his men: 'the English ... never leave the railway, because they cannot march'. Roberts's transport gave him the mobility to surprise the Boer commander. Cronje despatched Christiaan de Wet to keep pace with French. De Wet thought the cavalry were mounting a raid to Fauresmith; then Jacobsdal, just north of the Riet, seemed a likely objective. Uncertain where the blow would fall, de Wet fell back and remained inactive for a critical two days. By 13 February Roberts's main force had reached the Riet River, where a confused pile-up of supply wagons delayed the advance until Kitchener diverted to another ford approaching columns stretching for miles. French now led off his horsemen towards the Modder, twenty-five miles away. Roberts told Lansdowne: 'French's performance is brilliant considering the excessive heat and a blinding dust storm during latter part of day.'[37] On 15 February French neared the Modder's green banks, wheeled his whole force and galloped for the ford. A handful of Boers were scattered and the British crossed.

The advance was now at a crucial stage, at a cost already of 500 dead or unfit horses.[38] French watered his horses and men at the Modder, and then set out at 8.30 a.m. on the 15th for the final ride to Kimberley, while Kitchener supervised the rear and pressed forward the thirsty, dusty troops. Cronje posted 800 men with guns in two strong positions on adjoining

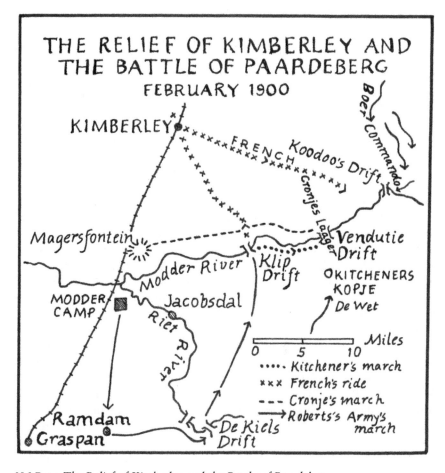

MAP 11 *The Relief of Kimberley and the Battle of Paardeberg*

ridges to the north of Klip Drift. French resolved to push through. The 9th and 16th Lancers led wave after wave of horsemen with five to eight yards between each rider. Covered by the artillery firing until the last moment, they cantered forward in clouds of dust at a steady fourteen miles per hour. The Boers fled, leaving a score captured or speared. At additional cost in horses, French had opened the way to Kimberley.[39]

After an hour's rest, he led the cavalry straight for Kimberley, pushing aside a feeble Boer counter-attack. An Australian patrol rode in just after 4 p.m. French followed with the main force at 6 p.m. The *Daily Mail* announced on 17 February: 'Kimberley is won, Mr Cecil Rhodes is free, the De Beers' shareholders are all full of themselves, and the beginning of the war is at an end. It is a great feat . . . there is no one like Bobs.'[40]

With the siege of Kimberley broken, Cronje left his rabbit warren of trenches, inspanned and made a bid to escape. On 16 February his huge convoy drove at top speed, wagons plunging into holes, others collapsing with wheels fallen to pieces. Despite losing seventy-eight wagons, Cronje kept together the other 450, several thousand horses, the families and over 4,000 fighting burghers. French set off in pursuit, but his horses were in a parlous state from exhaustion, and unwisely he went after a force under J.S. Ferreira now making north. He failed to run them down, and it appeared Cronje would escape too.[41] A serious setback for Roberts's campaign was de Wet's swooping down on the British supply park on the north bank of the Riet at Waterval Drift and scattering the 3,000 oxen drawing the wagons. Kitchener was busy 'hustling' the pursuit of Cronje and Major-General W.F. Kelly acting as Roberts's chief of staff had refused to increase the escort of 500 men with the convoy. To maintain the momentum of the advance, Roberts took the difficult decision to abandon the 176 wagons with their precious load of four days' supplies. The wagons were less than a sixth of Roberts's total of 1,200, so it was a reasonable gamble.[42] The troops had two full days' supplies with them, remaining companies of the supply park were moving up, and there were slaughter cattle available; putting the troops on half rations of breadstuffs and groceries and increasing the fresh meat allowance enabled him to continue the advance.[43] Milner was impressed: 'certainly the little man must have had an iron will, as well as a clear insight to push along as resolutely as he did'.[44] He also decided to separate supply and transport, giving the latter to Nicholson, a step that might have been better earlier.[45]

Kitchener, trying to catch Cronje, sent a message which reached French at 10 p.m. on the 16th asking for his intervention: 'unless you can come we are too slow'. At 3 a.m. on the 17th French mustered 1,200 sound horses and fifteen guns and sent off Brigadier Broadwood, following himself an hour later. French beat Cronje to the Modder. At about 10 a.m. on the 17th his artillery brought a salvo of shells down on Cronje's column as it prepared to cross the Modder to reach the Bloemfontein road. Boer artillery unlimbered and fired back, and riflemen skirmished forward. All day French's men fought, expecting the nearby forces of Ferreira, de Wet, burghers from Bethlehem and reinforcements from Bloemfontein. Then at 6 p.m. they saw the clouds of dust raised by divisions of British infantry, pressed on by Kitchener. Cronje, now trapped, dug into the banks of the winding Modder. Its banks, much broken up by ravines, provided excellent natural cover which the Boers rapidly improved.

Roberts had held the initiative since the opening of his offensive. To attack and capture Cronje's *laager* and then continue the advance was essential, and he told Kitchener by telegram: 'We must not let Cronje escape now or be able to hold out until reinforcements can reach him.'[46] He had ordered Kelly-Kenny to push on with all possible speed.[47] Kitchener's advance in the Sudan had been careful, deliberate and calculated. Now, at Paardeberg, he tried to carry out Roberts's wishes for a quick victory. Early on the morning of 18 February he issued orders for attack. In this he was overhasty, and his chief subordinates were not enthusiastic. French said his men and horses were 'too done up' to take part in any attack. Colville commanding the 9th Division and Brigadier Horace Smith-Dorrien, normally 'a glutton for fighting', were reluctant. Kelly-Kenny, the senior man present, resented instructions to regard Kitchener's orders as coming from the commander-in-chief.[48] Just after 7 a.m. the British opened 'a most terrific artillery fire'.[49] Kitchener attempted an assault from east and west on both river banks and a frontal attack from the south. None succeeded. Throughout the morning and afternoon, Boer marksmen stopped them well short of their objectives and inflicted significant losses: 1,262 dead and wounded, the most on any single day of the war.[50] Of the expected Boer reinforcements, the Bethlehem commando arrived first, seizing a ridge south of the Modder, but the Royal Artillery put their two guns out of action.[51] De Wet's 600-strong commando unit next appeared, having ridden through the night, attacked the outlying farm of Stinkfontein and tried to open a route by which Cronje might escape.[52]

On the 18th Roberts lay unwell at Jacobsdal. On the 19th the seriousness of the situation and his own improving health resolved him to go straight to Paardeberg. He arrived that morning, toured the regiments and praised all for their conduct. Still determined on a quick victory, he wished to renew the assault. 'Our being checked here is having a bad effect throughout the [Orange Free] State,' he telegraphed Lansdowne, 'and it seems to me necessary to assault the Boer position, which I propose to do to-morrow morning, shortly before daybreak.'[53] At a conference his senior commanders were divided. Their words doubtless had effect, but Roberts's statement that reconnaissance convinced him must be right. His attacks in Afghanistan had been preceded by detailed scouting for weakness, but here the strength of Cronje's *laager* was only too apparent.[54]

The siege that followed was active on both sides. On 20 February Roberts had directed Major-General Chermside with two battalions to extend the line of investment sealing in the Boers. From the 23rd to the 25th de Wet was under relentless assault from the British. He claimed to have opened a gap, 'but General Cronje would not move'. On the 25th de Wet ordered his men to retire from Stinkfontein, living up to its name from the smell of rotting carcasses in Cronje's *laager*. Reinforced from Bloemfontein, the Boers outside Roberts's trenches attacked, but were driven off. Torrents of rain fell, the river rose preventing escape while dead animals and the bodies of the Boers' black servants drifted down in the flood. On the 26th and 27th the British closed in. On 26 February Major John Headlam, RA, looked up from the entrance of his tent to see none other than 'the chief himself with a great scheme for crushing brother Boer',[55] but the decisive initiative was Colville's and Smith-Dorrien's. An observation balloon showed how the capture of an advanced trench would enable them to enfilade Boer defences. The Royal Canadians supported by sappers achieved this early on the morning of 27 February. They dug in, close to the *laager*. As day broke, white handkerchiefs began to appear from the nearest trench. Cronje had yielded to his men's demands for surrender, and at 8 a.m. preceded by his secretary he went out to yield formally to Roberts.[56]

It was Majuba Day. 'All in great excitement and joy over Cronje's surrender, especially today,' wrote Colonel James Grierson, just arrived.[57] Roberts met Cronje in a simple, but well-tailored uniform with his Kandahar sword and black armband for Freddie. He said: 'I am glad to see you. You have made a gallant defence, sir.'[58] The bitter Cronje did not reply. Wrote Grierson: 'The Boers were a fine stalwart lot, all in plain clothes of course and very dirty. They didn't look a bit cast down, but seemed rather glad to be done with it. Poor devils, they have been harried and bombarded for ten days.' Everywhere were dead horses killed by artillery fire, smashed carts, baggage strewn about. The stink was awful.[59]

The surrender of 4,105 Boers and the relief of Kimberley marked the war's turning point. Buller successfully crossed the Tugela and reached Ladysmith, a culmination of several attempts. A second had ended in the defeat of Spion Kop, with even heavier casualties than Paardeberg, 1,439 dead and wounded and 300 prisoners. The government would have liked Roberts to sack Buller: 'you must deal with him as you think proper and you may rely on support from us', Lansdowne telegraphed.[60]

Buller's third attempt at Vaal Krantz also failed. Buller telegraphed Roberts that he was not strong enough to relieve Ladysmith.[61] Further pessimism ended when Colonel Lawrence Parsons, RA, convinced him that artillery held the 'key' to a successful right-hand advance. Parsons's carefully orchestrated bombardments opened the way.[62] The 118-day siege of Ladysmith ended on 1 March.

At Paardeberg, Roberts moved his force away from the stinking Boer camp to rest a week before resuming the advance. The few days were welcome to weary men. Grierson noted that the horses of cavalry and artillery were very thin and 'suffering much from short commons', the men seemed 'extraordinarily healthy and in the best of spirits'.[63] The drinking of 'dead horse soup', however, as soldiers called the polluted water of the Modder, was to reap a bitter harvest.

The Boer Presidents Kruger and Steyn conferred at Bloemfontein, but the British rejected peace proposals of full independence for the republics. Despite desertions and defeats, they still expected to confront Roberts with 12,000 men. On 6 March, he summoned his generals and gave orders for the advance on Bloemfontein. At Poplar Grove, the advancing British met Christiaan de Wet's men entrenched in a strong position above the Modder, with a cleverly placed second line of trenches. Roberts gave orders for Colvile's 9th Division to engage the enemy's right while the cavalry and mounted infantry made a march of seventeen miles round their left flank, followed on a shorter axis by the 6th Division. Poor staff work failed to provide timings for the respective divisions, and the verbal briefing was not followed by written orders.[64] Nonetheless, Roberts's intentions were clear enough, and they required the cavalry to be well ahead of the 6th Division.[65] The cavalry did not move off until 3 a.m. while the 6th Division marched at 2 a.m. and had to wait. Even with his late start, French halted two hours for daylight and again at 7 a.m. to water his horses. This might have been reasonable if he had warned Roberts that his horses' condition made his wide march difficult; he did not. His slowness meant that he failed to cut off the Boers, but the threat to their flank and rear was decisive. Still demoralised by the defeat of Paardeberg, the burghers retreated in disorder. British gunners enjoyed 'the cheering spectacle of several hundred Boers running like hares'. They abandoned ammunition, cooking utensils, prepared food and tents.[66] They escaped, however, to fight again. Roberts's frustration doubled when he learnt that Steyn and Kruger had been present.[67] Their capture, coming quickly after Paardeberg, might have ended the war.

Whatever Roberts felt in private, in public he never complained.[68] French may have been resentful because of a mistaken dressing down from Roberts over the quantity of fodder consumed. Roberts had, however, given way when French wished to restore Haig as his chief of staff in place of Lord Erroll. Was there a clash of personalities between the ascetic Kitchener and the pleasure-loving French?[69] In fact, French had written admiringly of Kitchener's energy and purpose in the march to Kimberley.[70] If French's mercurial temperament meant he was now brooding, it was likely his chief of staff, on whom he depended, was to blame. Haig could have coordinated timings with the 6th Division. He made a stream of pointed criticisms of Roberts's leadership in letters home to his sister Henrietta. The Prince of Wales, who saw them, became rather sick of them and told Henrietta so.[71] Haig's letter after Poplar Grove is typical, giving no idea that the advance was not in accord with Roberts's orders, laying any fault of the cavalry at horses that were 'beat'.[72]

The action of one mounted infantry commander showed what could be done. Captain Henry Beauvoir de Lisle, a brilliant horseman, had trained his men rigorously on the voyage out. In South Africa he proved himself an outstanding mounted leader, soon a brevet lieutenant-colonel leading larger formations than his rank would normally have merited.[73] 'My Regiment marched wide on the left flank, carrying out orders given me personally by Lord Roberts two days before ...' He attacked burghers with three guns holding a strong position south of Boshof and drove them from it.[74]

Roberts did not linger moaning over missed opportunities, but kept up the momentum of advance. On the day after Poplar Grove, he hurried his chief of staff to De Aar to deal with a Boer commando trying to raise rebellion in Cape Colony. Kitchener rode forty miles, just missing his quarry, and sent out flying columns to frustrate their intentions.[75] Meanwhile, at Abraham's Kraal, thirty-five miles from Bloemfontein, Kruger, de Wet and Koos de la Rey stopped the rout and took up defences on a line of kopjes. The British advanced in three columns. Honours of the day belonged to Kelly-Kenny and the Essex Regiment in the centre, who led the charge of long lines of infantry up and over the shallow breastworks. Only thirty burghers were captured, but 102 of the enemy were buried on the battlefield.[76] On 12 March Roberts told French to make a dash for Brand Kop, a prominent cluster of hills overlooking Bloemfontein from the south-west, barely four miles away. French sent forward Allenby with the vanguard and Major Scobell with a Scots Greys squadron, both to seize important ridges. During the night Major Hunter-Weston with mounted sappers and colonial scouts rode round to the east of Bloemfontein, blowing up a culvert on the railway and cutting the telegraph wires, thus enabling the British to seize twenty-five railway engines and over 100 trucks. Other trains escaped earlier, including one with Steyn and his government on board.[77]

French sent ahead a prisoner with a proclamation of protection for the town; on 13 March he learnt that entry would be unopposed. On the 14th three enterprising newspapermen rode into Bloemfontein, and at their suggestion the mayor and executive council drove out and presented Roberts with the keys in a formal submission. When the commander-in-chief and cavalry rode in they found cheering crowds and the streets brightly decorated with British flags. At the Presidency they ran up the little silken Union Jack which Lady Roberts had sewed.[78] Capture of the Orange Free State capital was accompanied by other successes: Stormberg, Aliwal North and Prieska were taken and a column advanced through the south-west of the Free State. Burghers were handing in rifles.[79] Nine weeks after Roberts's arrival and four from his launching the offensive, the fortunes of war had been reversed.

At Bloemfontein Roberts launched a press offensive. The Boers much relied on their newspapers for accounts of the war that kept up morale and reassured them that British resolve was about to crack.[80] He closed down the anti-British *Express* and the *Friend of the Free State*, and with the help of Colonel Stanley, press censor, established the *Friend*. Aristocrats on his staff, Lord Dudley and the Duke of Westminster, contributed £400 to buy the *Friend*'s offices and equipment. Arthur Conan Doyle and Rudyard Kipling served on the editorial staff. In the year before the war, Kipling had nearly died in New York of pneumonia; his beloved daughter Josephine *had* died aged six; he could appreciate Roberts's grief and admired his coming out to South Africa.[81] At a Bloemfontein dinner for correspondents, Roberts spoke: 'There is one among you who has a special claim on the hearts of the soldiers, my friend Rudyard Kipling. I can assure him that of all those who watched anxiously for good news during his recent severe illness, none were more interested than the soldiers, amongst whom his name is a household word.'[82]

Roberts was extraordinarily modern in his press awareness. To South Africa he brought his experiences from Afghanistan, Burma and India, and appeared to treat correspondents with affability and liberality. The American James Barnes of the New York *Outlook* recorded him saying he was glad to have reporters with him, he would be much interested to read their criticisms, and all he asked was that they would try not to get shot. They could speak their minds and tell the truth. This was tongue-in-cheek, for he insisted that no telegrams about operations be sent to England until his own despatches had gone. These were regular and full enough to satisfy most readers.[83] Among the reporters, Winston Churchill had offended Kitchener by outspoken criticism in *The River War* and believed Roberts owed him favours because of Lord Randolph. He was fortunate in finding friends close to Roberts in Ian Hamilton and William Nicholson.[84] Of Roberts's press control he wrote: 'Alas! The days of newspaper enterprise in war are over. What can one do with a censor, a forty-eight hours' delay, and a fifty-word limit? Besides, who can compete with Lord Roberts as a special correspondent? None against the interest of his daily messages; very few against their style and simple grace.'[85]

Despite Roberts's apparent mastery of the papers, news reached home of an epidemic of enteric (typhoid). The outspoken MP William Burdett-Coutts visited Bloemfontein and wrote a series of reports published in *The Times*.[86]

The RAMC was understrength, had just undergone reorganisation and had to care for a huge army. The first cases of enteric occurred in late December. After Black Week, reinforcements brought army strength to 220,000, a number that remained relatively constant. Eight private hospitals were organised, and by March 1900 six extra general hospitals had been sent to South Africa.[87] Real problems began when Roberts launched his offensive. To maintain secrecy he did not tell his principal medical officer (PMO), Wilson, of his intentions, and Wilson was wrong-footed by the speed of the advance. One mistake of the transport reorganisation was cutting the number of ambulances; after Paardeberg Roberts restored these. At Paardeberg, dead bodies of men and horses were lying in the open, decomposing. Many of the defenders had typhoid.[88] The Modder was polluted, and when Roberts continued the advance he was obliged to use the river. The Royal Engineers tried to blast through layers of rock for wells; there were never enough. Soldiers and some officers drank water they had been expressly forbidden to touch.[89] Colonial mounted infantry suffered less because they boiled their water and carried it as strongly brewed tea in water-bottles.[90]

The medical crisis at Bloemfontein arose from the army's inability to provide clean drinking water. Poor hygiene and sanitation caused over 60 per cent of hospitalisations. The epidemic peaked in mid-May with nearly 4,000 men in hospital. There was insufficient cooperation between the RAMC and staff officers, particularly over siting of camps, and for this Roberts must take responsibility. He told Lansdowne that Grierson was 'almost the only officer in this force I can depend upon to lay out a camp and perform the legitimate duties of Q.M.G.'.[91] Latrines quickly filled as the rainy season was at its height, and the filth was flushed into the army's water supply. Three general and three private hospitals arrived, but all filled quickly. Leadership in the hospitals was mixed. Lt-Colonel Richard Beamish of No. 8 General Hospital, described by one of nurses serving there as 'too idiotic for anything', was dismissed with instructions never to serve again. Colonel F. Barrow of No.9 General Hospital, brought out of retirement, was dismissed by Wilson for incompetence. Roberts gave priority to military supplies until mid-April; Wilson was unable to get his medical necessities up to Bloemfontein quickly.[92] Roberts had a low opinion of Wilson,[93] but the military hospitals did well despite overcrowding. Their mortality rates were similar to those of lavishly equipped private hospitals which took only 7 per cent of total sick.[94] The Royal Commission appointed by the government to investigate reported:

> ... taking their work as a whole, and considering the difficulties they have had to contend with, we think that the Principal Medical Officer [Wilson] and his head staff have done excellent work. They have never spared themselves, and have shown a great devotion to their duty, and every desire to make due provision for the care of the sick and wounded, and when their conduct is fairly judged we think that they deserve great praise.[95]

The epidemic cost the British over 1,000 men and raised a storm in Parliament when Burdett-Coutts's letters were published. On 28 June 1900, MPs debated the hospitals, and Balfour answered the government's critics by reading Roberts's telegram beginning: 'I have no wish to shirk responsibility in the matter or to screen any shortcomings.' It produced an excellent effect, as did his details of improvements. Just as his victories had solved the government's first crisis, so his dispatches helped counter another.[96]

At Bloemfontein Roberts appealed to the burghers, his proclamations offering an amnesty and respect for property to all who took the oath of loyalty, except leaders.[97] Christiaan de Wet claimed his appeal had the effect of exploding lyddite bombs. 'It was enough to break the heart of the bravest man among us.' Burgher morale fell. Two parties had already returned home without permission, and others were hurrying back to their districts. On 16 March Roberts optimistically told Lansdowne: 'So far as the Orange Free State is concerned I do not think there will be much more opposition, the Burghers have evidently had enough of fighting and realise that they cannot stand against us.'[98] His hopes were to be dashed the next day. Boer leaders met at a war council at Kroonstad. They determined to continue the war, to abandon the clumsy wagon trains which had been Cronje's undoing, but allow commandos leave until the 25th. Young leaders replaced the old: De la Rey, de Wet, Smuts and others. Within ten days there was a complete reorganisation.[99] On 31 March de Wet ambushed a British brigade at Sannah's Post. His commando took seven guns and inflicted losses of nearly 600. A subaltern of Rimington's scouts saw hundreds of unarmed black drivers shot dead in cold blood.[100] He followed this success with a second, on 3–4 April at Mostertshoek, east of Reddersburg, where fire from his three Krupps guns forced the surrender of the garrison.[101] Roberts withdrew small garrisons and sent Kitchener down the railway line to ensure important stations were on the alert. De Wet unwisely turned his attention to the hated loyal colonials at Wepener. The siege, fiercely contested from 9 to 25 April, was raised by the arrival of mounted columns. *The Times History* thought the columns missed a golden opportunity to surround de Wet.[102] Repeatedly in South Africa, British sluggishness could not match Boer mobility. Major-General Leslie Rundle, chief of staff in the Sudan, was re-named 'Leisurely Trundle'.[103]

From Ladysmith, Hamilton and Rawlinson were delighted to rejoin their old chief. On 9 March Hamilton told his wife he had been in bed with 'a sharp go of Peshawar fever ... A man of 46 don't live on biscuit and horseflesh & drink muddy water for a month without some derangement to his constitution'. He had wired Roberts to accept the offer of a brigade. 'I am all for the fighting part of the business.'[104] Rawlinson reached Bloemfontein by train at 7 a.m. on 20 March and breakfasted with Roberts. 'I am to work on the H.Q. staff under Grierson as Q.M.G.,' he wrote, elated; 'this is the most interesting and responsible work and I am delighted to be with Johnny [Hamilton] ... Chief asked me to be a member of his mess so I have fairly fallen on my legs.' Shortage of HQ staff meant their work was in disorder.[105]

Hamilton later summarised Kitchener's relations with Roberts as 'not exactly those either of a Chief of the Staff or of a second in command'. Roberts acted as his own chief of staff, and with one exception all orders Hamilton received were signed by him. He used Kitchener 'as a sort of understudy, sending him off on independent stunts and delegating to him *ad hoc* the whole of his own authority'. Roberts had implicit confidence and gave him a free hand. The military machine worked because of this confidence and because Kitchener 'in word and deed was always loyal and true to Bobs'. He was a tower of strength, and other staff leaned on him.[106] Hamilton wrote of one black spot: relations between Kitchener and William

Nicholson. '[Kitchener] could not bear [Nicholson's] envious quality or his habit of detraction however amusingly he expressed himself. Latterly he never saw Sir William Nicholson, saying simply he was a man he could not and would not work with.' Perhaps this friction was a result of the breakneck pressure of the transport reorganisation.[107]

In London Lady Roberts and her daughters were preparing to travel to South Africa. Her husband had told Lansdowne that his family would join him.[108] She and the girls boarded the *Dunottar Castle* on St Patrick's Day, their cabin decorated with garlands of shamrocks. *The Times* reported: '[Lady Roberts] is going out with the intention of joining her husband as soon as the opportunity offers and of visiting the grave of her son, Lieutenant the Hon. F. Roberts V.C.' The newspaper did not say that her husband would, as in India, give her responsibility for nursing.[109] At Bloemfontein she accompanied him visiting hospitals, shaking hands with patients, wishing them well. A lady who complained about the doctors wrote of one hospital: 'The only time I have ever seen any organised attempt to clean the place was during the two or three days prior to the visit of Lady Roberts.' Major Headlam, critical of Lady Roberts 'driving the poor doctors wild', admitted, 'I daresay she does a great deal of good.'[110]

It was seven weeks before sufficient supplies, fresh horses and replacements had come up the single-track railway to Bloemfontein to enable Roberts to begin his next advance. Before the next phase of the offensive began, Hamilton's brigade became a division of 10,000 mounted infantry: 'no one has ever had such a command in the army before'. He was first busy with an obituary of Sir Donald Stewart, who had passed away quietly in Algiers. Hamilton thought Roberts did too much and looked 'rather thin and worn', perhaps partly the effect of losing one of his oldest friends.[111] He had been briefly unwell in late April, and Kitchener anxiously watched his chief's health: 'it was nothing serious and a few days' rest cured him', he reassured the Queen. Lady Roberts and their daughters had had a good effect on his morale. By the start of May he was ready to advance.[112]

Milner favoured no step forward until rear and flanks were absolutely safe from local risings or commando raids. Both Ian Hamilton and Captain Ballard of Roberts's Horse, later biographer of Kitchener, believed the chief of staff did too. Years later Hamilton told Spenser Wilkinson that it was against the advice 'of Kitchener and every one else' that Roberts undertook the march to Pretoria. It was, wrote Hamilton, the boldest gamble of Roberts's life. 'Had the [railway] line been seriously cut and held, our retreat would have been like that of Napoleon across the Beresina.'[113] Roberts's plan to aim at the capital came from military theory taught at the Staff College. G.F.R. Henderson had had to return to Britain in poor health. His biography *Stonewall Jackson* giving weight to the effect upon the Union armies of Jackson's advance up the Shenandoah Valley on Washington, continued to influence Roberts. He later wrote in the preface to Henderson's posthumous *Science of War*, 'I determined that marching on the capitals was the wisest thing to do, both from a military and political point of view.'[114] The War Office's secret intelligence memorandum (1896) supported this: once the Boer's home had been his saddle, but now the mining fields, railway junctions and population centres were the decisive strategic points 'and these must be the principal objectives'.[115] Seizing the capital and the railway line to Delagoa Bay would stop the flow of reinforcements, the railway workshops producing guns, the engineering works of Johannesburg manufacturing ammunition and the Witwatersrand gold financing war.[116]

He hoped to secure the cooperation of Buller, whose force had grown to 55,000. After Spion Kop, Lansdowne had given Roberts *carte blanche* to sack Buller. After the relief of Ladysmith, he felt it would be most unwise: 'I do not know who you would put in his place, nor have we yet been told that his troops have lost confidence in him . . .' His sacking would be received 'in many quarters, some of them very exalted, with indignation'. Roberts agreed that a storm would be best avoided 'for the credit of the Army'.[117] In April, he had asked Buller to remain on the defensive, but at the start of May he telegraphed asking him to leave a containing force opposite the Biggarsberg and swing round through Van Reenen's Pass to Harrismith, crossing the plains of the northern Free State. Were the two generals communicating at cross-purposes? One officer wrote: 'Buller is very jealous of Roberts and is inclined to ignore him instead of working with him.'[118] Buller wired his willingness, but then fell back on a usual formula: 'I am in rather a tight place at present . . .' When on 4 June he said he was ready to take Lang's Nek, the exasperated Roberts replied: 'Don't bother now as we are in possession of Pretoria.'[119]

Despite disagreements, the British were overwhelmingly superior: Roberts's 38,000 moving up the railway, Hunter and Methuen on the left with 10,000 each, Hamilton on the right with the mounted infantry. The outnumbered Boers were never more than 30,000. De Lisle had his command increased by two Australian regiments, 'all picked men and wonderful fighters'. His force became known as 'the galloping column' from its tactic of charging with horsemen fifty paces apart.[120] With the columns were 17,200 horses, 40,000 oxen and 22,000 mules, but only a tiny number of vets. For the horses the march was a trial, the Boers burning the grass from the River Vaal onward: 'not a blade of anything was left', wrote the chief vet. 'The whole country in all directions was blackened by fire.'[121]

Roberts's tactics on the march were simple but effective: his centre kept to the railway while the wings, composed largely of mounted troops, spread wide on each side and threatened to envelop the enemy if he made a stand. In early May, he was unable to bring on a battle, despite the best efforts of Major-General Edward Hutton leading Hamilton's division with mounted infantry. On 8 May French and the cavalry division rejoined: remounts had brought their strength up to 3,000. There followed a frustratingly indecisive fight at Zand River before Kroonstad: the Boers were hugely outnumbered, French's flanking movement was shorter and slower than hoped, and on the

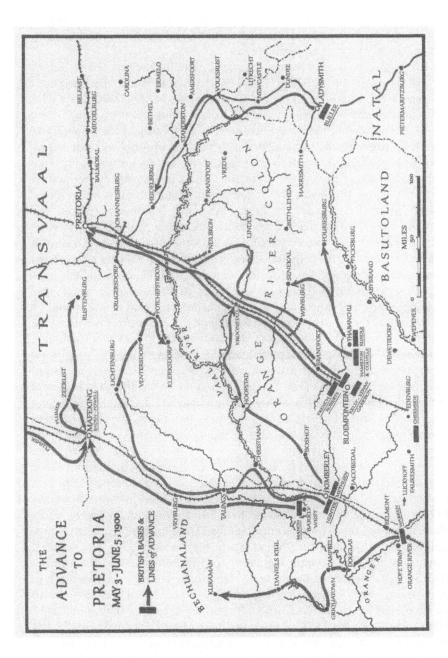

MAP 12 *The advance to Pretoria*

evening of 11 May the burghers escaped as fast as they could. 'We must make a supreme effort to run the Boer Army down between [here] and Kroonstad,' Roberts had telegraphed Hamilton, and in his disappointment he blamed French. 'The Field Marshal was in a bad temper yesterday,' Haig told his sister, 'and opened upon French . . .'[122]

Meanwhile, a detached column covered 230 miles and successfully raised the 217-day siege of Mafeking on 15 May. Colonel Robert Baden-Powell and the garrison had drawn off for several weeks 6,000–8,000 Boers who might have raided south, disrupting the British offensive.[123]

At Kroonstadt burghers were handing in weapons and the population, 'especially the natives', welcomed the British. Rawlinson was not happy when Roberts decided to halt for ten days.[124] Roberts's fear was for his line of communications. Lt-Col. Girouard, the Canadian who had masterminded the Sudan Military Railway, was 'full of resource' and able quickly to renew broken lines. The railway had been blown up in seventeen places, but Girouard's repair train made it good. Roberts thought the burghers were much disheartened by their inability to stop the British.[125] At Kroonstad men had fallen sick from the poor water supply, and Roberts telegraphed Wilson to come up and superintend a new hospital. He ordered Wilson at Cape Town to send 800 medical personnel to Buller's force which was suffering enteric and to arrange for another general hospital from England.[126]

On 22 May the advance began again, and on the 27th the army crossed the Vaal. Hamilton told his wife afterwards that his division 'had all the fighting', marching 401 miles on the map ('at least 450 in reality'), fighting ten general engagements and eighteen sharp skirmishes. The last big fight was before Johannesburg.[127] Roberts drew his lines round the city, with its tall chimneys and slag heaps. The Transvaal *Volksraad* had already decided not to defend either Johannesburg or Pretoria from the huge but useless forts built at great expense encircling the capital; their artillery was removed. Despite this decision, Louis Botha concentrated in a strong position extending eighteen miles on the Doornkop and other hills, his front protected by the Klip River, spreading into marshes and swamps. The Boers burnt the battlefield so that British khaki would stand out against blackened stubble. Just after 2 p.m. on 29 May, British field batteries and the great 5-inch 'cow' guns, pulled by teams of oxen, opened fire. The guns got the range, and the waiting infantry saw a hail of shrapnel dusting the ground where the Boers lay. The City Imperial Volunteers, the elite London regiment, and six companies of the Gordon Highlanders attacked the Boer centre. Hamilton extended their formation to allow thirty yards between each man. The burghers fled and the way to Johannesburg was open. The Gordons lost twenty dead to exploding bullets.[128] Johannesburg mayor Dr Krause agreed to surrender unconditionally, but to avoid street-fighting asked Roberts not to attack or enter the town until 10 a.m. on 31 May. Roberts agreed, not just to avoid damage to the mines, backbone of the economy, but also because of his vivid memories of the savage street fighting in Delhi in 1857. Krause prevented two German adventurers and their associates from blowing up the mines.[129] The Johannesburg commando helped themselves to government stores and fled. 'The roads to Pretoria were crowded with men, guns, and vehicles of every description,' wrote their leader, 'and despondency and despair were plainly visible on every human face.' Roberts marked the fall of Johannesburg by hoisting his wife's Union Jack with an Irish shamrock in the design. He told Lansdowne why he had negotiated: the British losses were tiny, considering the natural strength of surrounding hills. Why lose more men? Supply lines stretched a thousand miles, making provisioning difficult, and he expected Johannesburg to provide those supplies. Soon the mines were working again.[130]

Should Roberts have turned his forces loose to chase down and destroy the Boer army? Was an army mainly of infantry and of cavalry with spent horses capable of that? Did his officers show sufficient resource and initiative? He was about to advance on Pretoria, the capital to which British intelligence and his study of Henderson attached such importance.[131] He spent two days gathering supplies, and started north on 3 June. He was starved of intelligence, unaware that 20,000 burghers had defected, leaving only 7,000 with Botha. He ordered French on to Commando Nek to the west, rather than sending him round to the east to cut off escaping Boers. Smuts thought this decision 'one of the most momentous of the whole war'.[132] The Boer retreat might have been cut off.

On 4 June De Lisle's mounted infantry reached a height above the capital, and de Lisle sent forward Lt. Watson of the New South Wales Mounted Rifles with a white flag wrapped round his riding-crop. He returned with senior Boers, and De Lisle gave them the impression that the whole army lay close by. The bluff worked. The Boers were taken to Roberts's headquarters in his wagon tent, where he had been asleep, but he soon sat up to receive visitors. He insisted on unconditional surrender, and the town was accordingly given up. 'Well, De Lisle,' he said, 'you have managed to accomplish in half an hour what the whole army has been trying to do for six months.'[133] The following day, 5 June, the army made its formal entry. At the railway station, burghers in three trains with steam up were prevented from escaping by a company of the Grenadier Guards doubling forward. The 3,500 privates and 150 officers held captive at nearby Waterval were released. Others in the 'Bird-Cage' at Pretoria overpowered their guards in time to join the crowds watching the troops' entry. Private Arthur Haddock of the CIV never forgot the two commanders taking the salute:

[Roberts] looked the very picture of a General, alert and determined, while there was that about him that would command implicit trust and obedience under any circumstances. Beside him sat Lord Kitchener, stern and fixed, as immovable as marble. He appeared to be looking right through us, and it was gratifying to know afterwards that he was well satisfied with our appearance and with the work done.[134]

The march-past lasted two hours, a way for Roberts to salute his troops for their efforts.

Throughout the Empire there was rejoicing. Among telegrams received was one from Henry Norman: 'Your Delhi comrades heartily congratulate you on your glorious success and enthusiastically drink your health.'[135] A surge of confidence on the London Stock Exchange followed news that the mines of the Rand were secure.[136] The capture of a second Boer capital dismayed the burghers. Boer commanders, Ben Viljoen and Louis Botha included, proposed to Kruger that resistance cease. Kruger sent a despairing telegram to his fellow-president, Steyn. His reply was blunt: we shall never surrender. The Free Staters, Steyn and de Wet, were the rock of Boer resistance. Philip Pienaar of the Transvaal telegraph service wrote: 'it is chiefly owing to de Wet and Steyn that the war did not end with the fall of Pretoria. What is the secret of de Wet's success? Only one idea – if the English win, the heavens will fall.' At the ensuing *krijgsraad* on 2 June, Captain Danie Theron, 'the prince of scouts' rose 'and amid general cheers said that he who spoke of peace was a traitor and ought to be dealt with as such'.[137] Botha gathered a force. Kruger, who had led his people to war, travelled to Portuguese territory and thence to Holland, in vain hope of rallying European aid. Steyn, de Wet and others would battle on. The fall of Pretoria, claimed Ben Viljoen, was a sham victory, but he admitted that eminent citizens, members of the *Volksraad* and erstwhile fighting burghers surrendered and joined the British.[138]

These *hensoppers* (hands-uppers) were flocking to accept Roberts's neutrality-oath proclamation. From March to July, 5,940 Free State burghers surrendered arms; before the end of June, 7,960 Transvaalers did too; a quarter of those liable for military service.[139] Had this continued, Roberts's combination of overwhelming military might and offers of amnesty might have worked. To rally the burghers, the brothers Christiaan and Piet de Wet struck at overlong British lines of communication. Christiaan captured a convoy of fifty-six heavily laden wagons and then fell upon Roodewal Station; the garrison of 4th Derbyshires had camped below *kopjes* and failed to guard the tops.[140] Brother Piet with 2,000 burghers and guns captured a battalion of Imperial Yeomanry at Lindley.[141] Boer morale lifted.

At Pretoria the hospitals ran well. Lady Roberts deserves much credit. Roberts justified his wife's presence and tried to take her mind off grief for Freddie with this responsibility. Dashing from hospital to hospital, she made her daily rounds, issuing orders in her husband's name. 'Lady [Roberts] has appointed herself PMO and makes all the doctors and nurses hop around.' On 18 July Roberts wired Kelly-Kenny at Bloemfontein: 'please take every opportunity of sending to Johannesburg and Pretoria hospital comforts, warm under-clothing, in parcels for distribution to the troops. Those for Pretoria to be addressed to Lady Roberts'. The Robertses enlisted the local help of businessmen and doctors, formed a civilian medical committee and converted the Palace of Justice into a 500-bed hospital.

Improved care at Johannesburg and Pretoria meant that in South Africa the percentage of deaths from disease was the lowest in Victorian colonial wars. Soldiers of the CIV visiting Johannesburg hospitals were 'greatly surprised at the neatness and general arrangements . . . any one of these would do credit to any London hospital. [One] in particular . . . seemed . . . to leave nothing to be desired in the way of comfort or attention from the nurses and doctors'.[142] On 12 June, Roberts telegraphed London to reassure Lansdowne that the army in Pretoria was 'perfectly safe' despite de Wet's cutting the line. He knew how close Botha had come to negotiating, but not the Boer change of heart wrought by Steyn and de Wet.[143] This became clear, however, as Botha's burghers mustered on Diamond Hill to the east. Skilful dispositions compensated for the weakness of 6,000 Boers defending a position thirty miles long. On the battle's first day, 11 June, he countered Roberts's well-tried flanking movements; but on the 12th the centre of his position was taken. De Lisle's New South Wales mounted rifles swarmed up a kopje in open order, covered by the fire of pompoms. Botha rode forward only to meet his men in disordered retreat. A mere dozen followed him in a counter-attack. That night he ordered withdrawal. Once again the Boers escaped, their spirits lifted.[144]

Roberts, however, by driving them away from Pretoria, was able to turn and deal with commandos in the Free State. He planned to send columns to pen them into the mountains forming the boundary between Basutoland and Natal, where they had taken refuge. On 14 June a circular telegram to his generals ordered concerted action. Major-General Archibald Hunter, just arrived from the western Transvaal, took charge in the place of Hamilton, who broke his collarbone in a fall from his horse. Hunter's columns drove almost the whole fighting force of the Orange Free State into a huge horseshoe, the Brandwater Basin. De Wet and Steyn with 2,000 men escaped through Slabbert's Nek. Most of the rest were taken: 4,314 burghers and 5,000 good horses. It was the biggest capture of the war. Hunter had shown marked ability and judgement, Roberts approvingly told Lansdowne.[145]

De Wet's escape decided Roberts to send Kitchener and several columns after the 'Boer Pimpernel'. Twice his actions had rescued the Boer cause at its lowest ebb. Capturing de Wet, thought Roberts, might end the war. The 'first de Wet Hunt' narrowly ended in failure. Kitchener and Methuen doggedly pursued across the Vaal and towards the Magaliesberg. An exchange of telegrams on 14 August told headquarters that he was heading for Olifant's Nek, the last escape route. Roberts had sent Hamilton orders to block it, but according to Smith-Dorrien the mistake had already been made in not keeping Hamilton to the north. He was too distant from the Nek to cut it off. Frustrated, Kitchener wired on 15 August: 'De Wet has gone through Olifant's Nek. I thought it was held by us.' Privately the next day he telegraphed Rawlinson: 'We ran him hard into a corner and fully relied on your closing the door at Olifant's Nek how was this missed.'[146]

Kitchener went straight from 'the hunt' to relieve a garrison of Australians and Rhodesians at Elands River besieged by de la Rey.[147] The mobility of de la Rey and de Wet pointed to the guerrilla war. Even in the optimism of taking Pretoria, Roberts warned Lansdowne that 'a kind of guerrilla warfare has been commenced, which will give us trouble for a short time'.[148] The short time lasted until May 1902. Could it have been shorter? The experience of twentieth-century insurgencies suggests not. Without detracting from the skill and courage of commando leaders, they operated in ideal circumstances: known territory, wide sweeping expanses suited to their mobility, better fieldcraft and shooting, every farm a base for horses and supplies. The British Army had superior numbers, but was handicapped by immobility from poor horsemastership[149] and men guarding lines of communication and bases. It has been claimed that 'the citizen soldiers and improvised generals of the veld would not have withstood a few well-disciplined seasoned regiments, vigorously led'. In pitched battle they did not always withstand them, but ran away to fight again; in others they used surprise on chosen ground. Roberts's indirect approach wrong-footed them strategically; his securing a communications network laid the basis for Kitchener's counter-insurgency.[150] He can be better criticised for his optimistic predictions and misjudgement over farm-burning. This measure followed the Boers firing upon or dynamiting trains and raising white flags apparently as a decoy. By September the British were regularly burning farms: 'Unless the people generally are made to suffer for misdeeds of those in arms against us the war will never end,' he wrote in frustration.[151] Some British soldiers hated the burning.[152] Others thought it richly deserved: Private Tucker of the Rifle Brigade noted Canadian cavalrymen being lured towards a farmhouse by a white flag, two men coming out apparently to surrender, and then a volley fired by 'some more Boers, killing one and wounding two others'. The first internment camps arose as a consequence of farm burning.[153]

Burning did not intimidate the Boers. Boer women were at the heart of continuing resistance when they saw their homes go up in flames.[154] Cape South Africans fighting for the British were ready with the torch, for they found the burghers 'cleared the houses of British sympathisers and made a huge bonfire of their contents'.[155] As the burning spread, Roberts pursued a conventional victory. In late August his forces move east from Pretoria to meet Buller from Natal. Colonel Parsons' artillery cleared the way over the Biggarsberg, into the Orange Free State and through Alleman's Nek. *The Times History* approved: 'Then it was that Buller completed the perfect co-operation between artillery and infantry . . .'[156]

Ian Hamilton had written to his wife that Buller was 'a man of straw' and to Spenser Wilkinson that he '*is no use*'. Doubtless he told Roberts, but the commander-in-chief could not ignore Buller's victories.[157] He met Buller at Pretoria. There could easily have been a row, especially over the exchange of telegrams. Instead, as Parsons wrote in his diary: 'I think the interview with

Lord Roberts was an excellent thing & that the little man made many things all right.' Buller's ADC agreed: 'From what I gather they had a most satisfactory interview, and everybody was most civil . . .'[158] Roberts took particular trouble to be tactful. At Bergendal he paid Buller's army 'the greatest complement' by putting it in 'the place of honour'; there was 'enthusiasm and gratification' in the ranks. He detached 4.7-inch naval guns to support Parsons' artillery.[159] The two generals were in a cooperative frame of mind, and when Roberts rode down to warn Buller and Parsons of the strength of the Boer position, it was with good intent. The Boer line extended fifty miles, but Bergendal was the key. In an isolated position on a natural platform were sixty-seven 'Zarps', Transvaal policemen with a Maxim, and behind them at Bergendal Farm a pompom. Parsons' barrage silenced Boer gunners, isolating the Zarps, and the post was stormed. This decided the battle. The *kopje* was a terrible sight: huge boulders smashed by howitzer fire, bodies mangled. 'Buller is working up very well,' Roberts told Lansdowne.[160]

The last step of conventional war was to send Buller, French, Hamilton and Pole-Carew eastwards towards Delagoa Bay through mountainous country. Buller in a despatch explained: 'For a great portion of its length [our track] was more like a staircase than a road.'[161] Ben Viljoen thought the relentless advance 'knocked the spirit out of some of our weaker brethren'. Hundreds of burghers rode into Pretoria with white flags suspended from their Mauser barrels.[162] The British advance reached its finale on 24 September when Pole-Carew and Hamilton found Komati Poort abandoned, stores destroyed, smouldering stacks of equipment, thirty railway engines and 1,500 trucks laden with stores and ammunition. French captured more trucks, locomotives and stores at Barberton, terminus of a branch line. Many Boers entered Portuguese territory, some returning to the Transvaal after taking the oath of loyalty. The *bittereinders*, however, headed north with carefully selected transport wagons loaded with the pick of the stores. They blew up and sank in the Komati River nearly all their remaining guns. Roberts told Lansdowne that a few months would suffice to end resistance, praised Kitchener for 'the remarkable manner in which he has effaced himself', but also warned his commanders that de Wet was urging the burghers to keep fighting.[163]

In August he had told the Queen that the war was dragging on in its guerrilla form, and that the burghers' knowledge of the country and 'of the whereabouts of all our troops, and with everyone ready to assist them . . . the advantage is all on their side'. By 17 September he warned that the country would not settle down quickly, but outbreaks would become fewer. A week later he asked Lansdowne and Milner for a proclamation to warn all who remained under arms that they were rebels.[164] British frustration was palpable: the Boers were beaten, but they would *not* stop fighting. A Gordon Highlanders captain wrote home: 'The government should declare the war over and shoot anyone found with arms – this is the way to treat them.'[165] The legal basis existed, for Roberts had annexed the Orange Free State on 24 May as the Orange River Colony and the Transvaal on 1 September. Colonial Secretary Joseph Chamberlain minuted: 'Surely the Commander of victorious forces can do what he likes practically with the property, the people, the country invaded.'[166]

Shooting 'rebels', however, did not become policy. Instead, the government tried to wind the war down. On the back of Roberts's victories, Salisbury's ministry called a 'khaki election' in September, which they won, polling over half the votes cast, the Liberals about 5 per cent less. In October and November, the Household Cavalry, the CIV, Canadians and other colonial volunteers went home. Soldiers could be replaced by the South African Constabulary organised by Colonel Baden-Powell, for guerrillas were banditti and could be dealt with accordingly.[167] The government 'had not sufficient confidence in Buller to have him finish up the war', but he was glad to return to Aldershot.[168] By contrast, they wanted Roberts back to take the top job he had long coveted.

On 19 September Salisbury wrote to the Queen that it was the general expectation that Roberts would succeed Wolseley. Roberts already had considerable claims, 'but the popularity he has obtained and the great services he has tendered during this war make it almost impossible that any other nomination should be made.' This was almost a necessity. Army reforms were being urged 'in a very democratic spirit', and a member of the royal family, namely Arthur of Connaught, whose claim the Queen was pressing, would be a focus for discontent against the War Office. The Queen accepted reluctantly, and hoped the commander-in-chief's powers would be increased.[169]

At the same time both Roberts and the viceroy, Curzon, were pressing Kitchener's claim for the Indian command. Roberts reassured Lansdowne: 'Kitchener would I feel sure follow my advice in dealing with the native army ... He gets on well with everyone in this force and inspires confidence.'[170] For Kitchener there was to be other work for eighteen months. Was Roberts's departure premature? Many officers thought it was time he handed over to Kitchener who would bring the Boers to heel.[171] On 15 September Kitchener urged him to announce his intention of leaving the moment Komati Poort was occupied. When Buller wired home about his own departure, Roberts's staff persuaded him to tell Lansdowne that it seemed hardly necessary to keep a field marshal in the field for a guerrilla war.[172]

Lansdowne confirmed Roberts as Wolseley's successor and that Kitchener was not prejudicing chances for Indian command by taking over in South Africa. The delighted Roberts agreed. Rawlinson thought the sooner he went the better, as Kitchener could initiate harsher measures.[173] In October an intercepted letter from Louis Botha saying that he would surrender unless Kruger secured European assistance gave Kitchener hope.[174]

Boer intentions were otherwise. At Syferfontein in the Ventersdorp District, Botha, de la Rey, Smuts and Steyn held a council of war. Steyn urged action to show the British they had not won. The burghers planned ambitiously: attack and destroy the goldmines, disrupt the Delagoa Bay Railway, invade Cape Colony. Destruction of the mines was abandoned, but the commandos soon attempted the other measures.[175] De Wet was not at Syferfontein, and early in October De Lisle and Colonel Le Gallais nearly got him in the 'second De Wet Hunt'. His commando was caught by surprise at Bothaville, and he and Steyn narrowly escaped in their Cape cart. Unsubdued, he sprang back into action, and captured the Dewetsdorp garrison dispersed in poorly sited narrow trenches.[176]

'The ubiquitous De Wet is still at large,' Roberts warned the Queen. In late October, Roberts was laid up in bed with a temperature, and the Boers launched a series of attacks on the railways. On the 24th he was still in bed: 'Not a very cheerful day,' Rawlinson recorded. 'The Boers seem to be bucking up all round. Railway and telegraph cut . . .' No sooner did Roberts rise from his bed than their daughter Aileen was stricken. One of his ADCs, Prince Christian Victor, the Queen's grandson, died of enteric, and a fearful anticipation passed through the Robertses. 'Aileen was so seriously ill, I did not feel capable of settling down to my desk,' he told Lansdowne. 'Greatly shocked to hear that Lord Roberts's eldest daughter, his great favourite and help, is ill with enteric at Johannesburg,' wrote the Queen.[177] Lady Roberts was concerned about her husband: 'The strain is telling on his health, which, I need scarcely say, it is most important should be kept in as vigorous condition as possible.' 'We have had an awful week,' Roberts told Lansdowne on 9 November, 'and are still in great anxiety.'[178] 'At present,' wrote Haig on 14 November, 'all is at a standstill waiting for Lord Roberts's daughter to get well and his departure!!'[179] Suspense continued until the day when she was much better, but on the 18th Roberts was thrown from his horse and broke an arm. 'Aileen is getting on capitally,' wrote Rawlinson, 'but the Chief is in a good deal of pain.' The British were inactive, and the *bittereinders* recouping their strength. They soon showed their teeth against Kitchener, to whom Roberts handed command on 29 November, and began his journey via the Tugela battlefields to see his son's grave. His younger daughter Edwina, Hamilton, Rawlinson and ADCs accompanied him. His wife and elder daughter went to Durban by train.

On Buller's departure, he had dined with Roberts who had published a short general order praising him.[180] Good feelings changed when Roberts visited Colenso on 1 December. Rawlinson noted: 'The Chief also seemed much annoyed at Buller having sent forward a few ADCs to try and extricate the guns. Had he sent out Barton's Brigade which was doing nothing at the time there might have been some chance of getting the guns out.' Roberts stared in silence over the battlefield. On 4 December they went to Freddie's grave. 'It was a sad visit just as day was dawning,' wrote Rawlinson, 'and the chief and Edwina were both of them much affected.'[181] Roberts's friendlier feelings to Buller dissolved. To Kitchener he wrote later: 'I confess after visiting the scenes of his operations before the relief of Ladysmith, I don't think he deserves much consideration.'[182] They went on to Durban and thence to Cape Town. Everywhere he was greeted by crowds cheering the man who had turned the tide of war. Others thought it was time he went. Milner wrote: 'Lord Bobs ought to go at once . . . my admiration of him is unaltered . . . He is head and shoulders above every Englishman in S.A. today. But when it comes to a most complicated problem, half military, *half political*, & wholly unprecedented, he is out of his depth. And he is 60 & very *fatigued*.'[183] On 11 December he and his family and staff embarked on HM hospital ship *Canada*. Did Kitchener have a last-minute premonition? He sent a farewell telegram: 'Good bye to you all and best of wishes. Don't forget those you leave behind.'[184]

CHAPTER ELEVEN

Good work for army and Empire

*I feel sure I may look forward to your doing great & good work
for the efficiency & welfare of my army & for the general
benefit of the empire.*

QUEEN VICTORIA TO LORD ROBERTS, 5 OCTOBER 1900

*Mr Punch [to Lord Roberts]: 'Well done, indeed, Sir! You have
had a tough job in South Africa; but Heaven help you when
you get into the War Office!'*

PUNCH, 2 JANUARY 1901

*You well know the insurmountable obstacle which
Lord Roberts' retention of the Command of the Army would
place in the way of War Office Reform. His retirement
unfortunately is the condition precedent upon which our
scheme hinges.*

VISCOUNT ESHER TO J.S. SANDARS, ARTHUR BALFOUR'S SECRETARY

Embarking for England, Roberts did not leave the war behind. The burghers
were still fighting, radical and Irish MPs attacked the government, and as
Lady Briggs who had nursed in South Africa wrote: 'Since my return . . .
what to my mind has been the most remarkable result of the war is the
readiness of everybody to find fault, and that on the merest rumour, with
those charged with its conduct.'[1] The Liberals resented how Joseph
Chamberlain coined the phrase that a vote for them was one for the Boers,
and how Salisbury used Roberts's success to win votes.[2] The election was
just in time. Milner told Chamberlain that widespread guerrilla warfare
starting earlier would have changed electors' views.[3]

On his voyage home, Roberts received from the new Secretary of State for War, Brodrick,[4] a letter telling him of an outspoken Buller and Colville and the shortcomings of the War Office.[5] He reached England on 2 January 1901 and visited the Queen at Osborne, receiving the Garter and an earldom. The next day in the royal carriage on a special train he steamed into Paddington Station to be greeted with flowers, bunting and a band playing 'See the Conquering Hero Comes'. The Prince and Princess of Wales welcomed him in person. The procession to Buckingham Palace passed along a route lined by 14,000 troops and spectators six deep, placards bearing the slogan, 'Bravo Bobs'. Parliament voted him a grant of £100,000. The Kaiser, who believed he had inspired Roberts's campaign, awarded him Prussian chivalry's highest order, the Black Eagle.[6] Roberts however soon wrote to the Lord Mayor of London asking him for no more. There was news of Boer resurgence. Roberts's optimistic predictions, based on information that they were running out of ammunition and horses, proved wrong.[7] The enemy had routed Major-General Clements's force at Noitgedacht, capturing 500 men, and crossed into the Cape in two invading columns. Kitchener assembled 4,000 horsemen to meet the threat. Brodrick warned of a struggle with the Chancellor of the Exchequer, who expected troop reductions and savings. 'The public are getting restive about the cost, but at all hazards we must raise men & horses to whatever standard is necessary.'[8]

Roberts's luck had not entirely deserted him. Public attention had partly been diverted by the Boxer Rebellion at Peking in August 1900. Reporters left South Africa when it appeared the war was nearly over. *The Times* commented on 5 November: 'The operations in South Africa no longer involve military problems of special interest.' One soldier still serving was angry when he read of the CIV's enthusiastic reception in London: 'I see they are going to give Roberts an Earldom and a hundred thousand. This seems to me remarkably like putting a premium on lying. He was reported to us to have said "the war is practically over" . . . this is past a joke . . .'[9] Roberts had gone home because of his over-sanguine prediction, but also because his loyal staff wanted him to. An anonymous writer defended him in a letter to *The Review of the Week* printed in May 1900. Had he left South Africa too soon? The answer:

No sane person learning that during the month of September last Mr. Kruger and his Government had fled, that Botha had resigned the command, that Lydenburg and Komati Poort were occupied, that from all parts of the country hundreds of prisoners, cattle, wagons, and tons of ammunition were being brought in, could do otherwise than believe with the Chief that "the organised resistance of the two Republics" was at an end. He was always careful to point out plainly that there were many marauding bands who gave considerable trouble. No more schemes for a continued advance were necessary, no need for the c-in-c of the whole Army to be in the field; and so Lord Roberts, having seen Lord Kitchener's capabilities to sweep away the guerrillas, came home to take up the important position which he ought to have taken up in November last, when Lord Wolseley's term expired. He was badly wanted at home; he was no longer necessary in South Africa.[10]

On 2 January at a private interview Roberts told the Queen of her grandson Christian Victor's death, and presented members of his staff and his six Indian orderlies; 'such fine-looking men', she thought. The decline in her health was visible.[11] He met her again on 14 January, and told Kitchener she was greatly changed, but talked for nearly an hour about the war.[12] A week later her last words were: 'What news is there from Lord Kitchener? What has been happening in S. Africa?' Her death came on 22 January. Kitchener wrote to Roberts on the 25th describing how a mine planted for his train nearly killed him, adding: 'The death of the Queen seems terribly sudden . . . She took such an intense interest in all that went on out here that I greatly fear the strain of this war may have shortened her life.'[13]

Great hopes rested on the new commander-in-chief, striding up the steps of the War Office in a cartoon with Britannia urging, 'Clean it up, My Lord.' The belief that army reform was badly needed and Roberts and his men were the ones to bring it about inspired the first big history of the war. Leo Amery of *The Times*, the only correspondent to visit the Boer forces in the build-up, was assigned to organise the paper's newsmen. He was the ideal man to plan, edit and coordinate *The Times History of the War in South Africa*. He described the British Army as a 'Dotheboys Hall', failing in almost every respect. He viewed Roberts as reformer and Buller, who had spent sixteen years at the War Office as QMG and then adjutant-general, as the image of this incorrigible army.[14] *The Times History*'s third volume described Roberts's campaign to the capture of Bloemfontein most favourably. Amery liked and admired Roberts – 'His light blue eyes shone, as a rule, with good humour, but could, on rare occasions blaze with terrifying anger. He was the kindliest and most considerate of hosts' – but thought his optimism made him 'too ready to believe that the enemy was crushed when he was only dispersed'.[15] Volume two was outspoken in its criticism of Buller. In volume four, Basil Williams criticised Roberts for not reading signs of continuing Boer resistance.[16] Despite its didactic purpose, *The Times History* was a remarkable work with a wealth of detail and eye-witness battle accounts from both sides. It dominated South African war writing until Thomas Pakenham's *The Boer War* in 1979.[17]

Roberts and his staff helped Amery's team, not only to show their roles in the best light, but to further reform. Roberts invited Amery to use his papers and made official documents available.[18] The War Office's own history could not match Amery's. Colonel Henderson began it, but his health gave way, and he died in March 1903. Roberts praised him posthumously: 'what a high opinion I had formed of Henderson's abilities. I was convinced that he was well fitted for employ[ment] in the field . . .' His work in charge of intelligence, 'this most important department', had much aided Roberts's campaign.[19] The work passed to Major-General Frederick Maurice, but much had to be omitted that would offend the Boers, who had become subjects of the crown, and it became 'a colourless statement of facts rather than one which might guide and form the opinions of a soldier'.[20] Fiercer criticism than Amery's was found in E.H. Cairns's *An Absent-Minded War: Being some Reflections on our Reverses and the Causes which have led to Them*. The writer chose Methuen and Buller as chief targets: Methuen for sticking to the railway line and for alerting the Boers with a two-hour bombardment, Buller for the failures in officers' education, for claiming at Spion Kop he was in 'unknown country' when there were maps available. Had Roberts not relieved Bloemfontein, wrote Cairns, Buller might still have been knocking his head against rocky barriers on the Tugela.[21]

Political will for reform was uncertain. Salisbury's government had established Lord Elgin's Royal Commission after an uncharacteristically bad-tempered debate between Lansdowne and Wolseley in the Lords over war readiness, because the Unionist government was in a 'rather awkward corner'. The Prime Minister wrote: 'Every effort will be made to render the enquiry innocuous.' The King objected on the grounds that it might 'do the Army ... harm in the eyes of the civilised world'. Politicians, press and public could not be fobbed off. Away from the public's gaze, the courtier Viscount Esher plotted reform of the War Office pursuing the Hartington Commission's recommendation.[22]

Brackenbury had warned Roberts that he would find the position of commander-in-chief very unsatisfactory. Wolseley found his powers severely restricted – the 'fifth wheel' he had called himself. The War Office was 'a slough of despond' (Brodrick's words). The position of commander-in-chief at Whitehall was the summit of Roberts's career, but he saw that it might be a disappointment. He wrote to Brodrick while at sea near Gibraltar, on 27 December 1900, that he would be overwhelmed by minor detail in the present situation; he should be responsible to the secretary of state for discipline, education and efficiency of the army, collection of intelligence, strategic schemes and appointments. The letter set out roles of the adjutant-general, the QMG, and a director-general of supply and transport.[23] In May the Dawkins Committee reported that the War Office suffered from confusion of roles and a lack of clearly defined responsibility. An Order in Council of 4 November 1901 followed, giving Roberts responsibility for discipline, training, mobilisation and staff planning and placed the adjutant general under him. This only partly met Roberts's requests. It failed to create subordination and a chain of command. Roberts, keen for War Office personnel to have a soldierly purpose, ordered officers on duty to wear uniform, and hoped in due time that military would replace civilian personnel.[24] One War Office historian wrote that Roberts was 'more of a real Commander-in-Chief, perhaps, than Lord Wolseley had ever been', partly from his South African prestige, partly by avoiding Wolseley's clashes with Lansdowne, wisely refraining from public complaints of the limitations of his post.[25]

Wolseley and his followers were not pleased at 'the scheming little Hindoo' introducing his band of 'Indians' to key offices, but the Ashanti ring was long broken. Of its later leaders, Evelyn Wood was working with Roberts, and Buller hanging on at Aldershot. Roberts wanted to assemble a familiar team. Kitchener was still in South Africa, and he hated the thought of the War Office. 'I know he does not care for staff duties,' Roberts had warned Lansdowne, 'and he has told me over and over again that he would infinitely prefer India to the WO.' Roberts thought he would be more use in India.[26] Nicholson returned there, but soon had an offer from his chief. 'It is rather a wrench giving up India after having served there for nearly thirty years,' he replied, 'but as your Lordship thinks it best for me to come to the War Office, I shall be glad to heed your wishes.'[27] He became director of mobilisation and military intelligence. Hamilton returned with Roberts, with whom he had had a mild disagreement over the award of a KCB, which he did not want. 'I have told the Chief this and he won't agree with me. In fact he is such a masterful little man that it is no use arguing with him.' It wasn't, and his wife was pleased to become Lady Hamilton. Military Secretary was an important post with a say in promotions.[28] Roberts and Brodrick had two of the best soldier administrators, Adjutant General Wood, despite deafness a first rate advisor, and Brackenbury. Roberts involved his adjutant-general 'in decisions more than Wolseley had ever done, and Wood responded by offering support and advice . . . both were able to relax and exchange ideas.'[29] John Ardagh moved from intelligence to personnel, but left the War Office in March. Kelly-Kenny succeeded Wood in October 1901. Sir Edward Ward, an outstanding quartermaster in South Africa, was under-secretary of state. Hamilton went to war again, but on his return became QMG. 'Wully' Robertson took over the foreign section of the intelligence department. Henry Rawlinson and Henry Wilson both joined the military training branch. Pole-Carew refused the Egyptian command and took the 8th Division at Cork.[30]

Parallel with reform at home had to be support for the continuing guerrilla war. Early in 1901 Kitchener restored the situation in Cape Colony and put new life into garrisons. He began to use a system of 'drives' by columns, adapted from Roberts's advance to Pretoria. Later he built lines of blockhouses, notably along the railways. Talks at Middelburg in the eastern Transvaal beginning on 28 February 1901 proved abortive. Kitchener continued his drives, farm-burning and camps, the last two started by Roberts. Ian Hamilton recalled that the decision to begin farm-burning had been agreed by Roberts and Kitchener 'in the Chief's railway carriage after the battle of Belfast', i.e. Bergendal, on 27 August 1900. With systematic farmhouse burning, somewhere had to be found for the families. Refugee camps followed. Kitchener extended the policy, putting ruthless measures into effect: 30,000 farms burnt and 160,000 Boers placed in fifty camps.[31] Chaotic disorganisation and poor staff work led to a human tragedy in badly-run camps. Inmates fell prey to measles, typhoid, jaundice, malaria, bronchitis and pneumonia, and over 20,000 died.

It was a courageous spinster, the daughter of an archdeacon in Cornwall, Emily Hobhouse, who brought news of the camps she visited. Campbell-Bannerman, Lloyd George, C.P. Scott and other Liberals forced Brodrick to admit in the Commons on 17 June 1901 that numbers in the camps were still growing. The ministry sent a commission headed by Mrs Millicent Fawcett, a feminist Liberal Unionist, but composed mainly of ladies from high Tory families. A blunt and honest report brought improvement just at the time that the measles epidemic was burning itself out. By the end of the war, the death rate had fallen below pre-war levels. The 'concentration camps' as they were called by two radical MPs became a *cause célèbre*. There were also camps for Africans, which historians long neglected, but numbers interned and losses were possibly as great; improvement was slower.[32]

In his advance to Bloemfontein, Roberts employed 5,000 Africans as transport drivers and leaders. There is not one mention in his despatches of their presence. Kitchener employed them increasingly as combatants, and he and his men recorded frequent Boer atrocities against them.[33] Probably in all the British employed about 100,000, the Boers one-tenth that number.[34] Kitchener had proposed using Bengal Lancers because of a shortage of mounted troops. Roberts put the plan to Brodrick and the Duke of Devonshire, president of the Defence Committee, but they refused: 'sending Indian troops would have a very bad effect', wrote Roberts. 'It would look as if we had no more white troops left.' He added, 'Not far wrong perhaps, but it is as well this should not be generally known.'[35] Nonetheless, over 10,000 Indian troops served as *syces* (grooms), orderlies, *bhisties* (water-carriers) and in auxiliary roles.[36] At Tweebosch, when de la Rey's commando defeated Methuen's column, the whole Indian and African establishment of the field veterinary hospital were ruthlessly shot dead by the burghers after surrender.[37]

Brodrick justified farm-burning to the Commons: 'Every farmhouse became a fresh recruiting agency for the enemy, and after the men had gone back on commando the farmhouses occupied by the women became depots from which they got supplies and stores and from which they obtained information of the movements of our troops.' Of the camps he claimed the Boers 'persistently threw on us the charge of looking after their women and children; they traded on our humanity in the matter.'[38] Meanwhile, against the ministers who doubted Kitchener's ability to finish the war, Roberts defended his successor. Then on 30 October 1901, the Ermelo and Carolina commandos attacked and overwhelmed the column of Lt-Colonel Benson, one of Kitchener's best commandos. Benson died of his wounds. On 1 November Kitchener despaired to Roberts: 'I see the papers say I am not much good as a strategist . . . Can you get anyone to do it better, if so please do not hesitate – A new man at the head might evolve some new ideas for finishing the war – I try my best. I am afraid it is not much.'[39] Roberts wrote urgently to Brodrick:

It seems clear to me from reading the enclosed letter that Kitchener is overworked and I blame myself for not having proposed long ere this to give him the assistance of a General Chief of Staff ... Ian Hamilton is quite the best man I can think of for such a position, and if you approve, I will ascertain from Kitchener whether Hamilton's appointment would be agreeable to him. Hamilton would be a great loss to me, but I daresay I could find someone to take his place temporarily.[40]

Kitchener quickly accepted: 'I am extremely grateful; there is nothing I should like better. Hamilton will be a great help to me.'[41] In a kind letter to Lady Hamilton Roberts softened the blow of further separation.[42] Roberts instructed Hamilton 'to tell me exactly how you think Kitchener is, whether he is able to carry on in the event of the war continuing for another six months or so.' Honourably, however, he added, 'I don't think I can ask you to communicate with me publicly again without shewing [sic] your messages to Kitchener, it would look as if you were working behind his back and that would never do.'[43] Hamilton tried to show Kitchener the reports. Kitchener thanked him and refused to look at them.[44] Hamilton enabled Kitchener to relax and to leave headquarters on tours of inspection to the garrisons and columns. He was unable to prevent the highly-strung Kitchener having a nervous collapse when Methuen's column was routed by de la Rey and the wounded Methuen fell into Boer hands. He retired to his bed and would not eat. Hamilton recorded: 'at the end of the forty-eight hours he said to me, "My god, I believe I'm losing my nerve!" I said, "Yes, certainly you are losing your nerve in proportion as you starve yourself to death!" He then had some breakfast and became quite right again'.[45] Hamilton travelled next to the western Transvaal to control a number of columns hunting de la Rey. British columns had adopted Boer tactics, carrying only a greatcoat, rifle and three bandoliers of ammunition, moving fast and being led to Boer camps by black scouts employed by Colonel Aubrey Woolls-Sampson.[46]

At Roodewal, Hamilton, Rawlinson (who had returned after six weeks), Bruce Hamilton and Kekewich inflicted a heavy defeat on Potgieter's commando, Potgieter himself being killed.[47] This and a Zulu victory at Holkrans over another commando brought the Boers to negotiation at Vereeniging. By now the veldt was swept bare and divided by blockhouse lines, the farms which had sustained the commandos burnt, the livestock driven off. One-quarter of Boers under arms were National Scouts, fighting for the British. Kitchener offered a limited compromise. At Vereeniging on 31 May 1902, the burghers agreed to end the war. The *bittereinders* promised to live under the crown, but in return self-government was soon restored and the blacks and 'coloureds' lost the franchise they had enjoyed in the Cape. 'In the longer view,' as John Darwin writes, however, 'the unification of South Africa as a self-governing, British dominion ... created a vital adjunct of British world power in the century of global wars.'[48] The route via the Cape and the naval base at Simonstown was preserved.[49] Botha and

Smuts, former commando leaders, led the *Volk* into two world wars as Britain's ally. Milner, whose attempt to introduce numbers of English settlers failed, nonetheless built the infrastructure of a modern South Africa.[50]

One legacy of Milner and Roberts was the South African Constabulary, initially under Colonel Baden-Powell, which at its peak comprised over 10,000 officers and men, with 2,000–3,000 Africans as teamsters, servants, cooks, scouts and, crucially, as second-class constables. Roberts drew on his police experience in India and Burma, Milner from the Cape and Natal Police as well as the Egyptian force reformed by Kitchener. After the war, the SAC undertook its policing duties until its disbanding after the Transvaal and the Orange River Colony became self-governing in 1907, the men mostly joining the constabularies of those respective colonies and in 1913 the South African Police.[51]

Kitchener's triumphant return from South Africa was a moment of celebration for Roberts and his men. Hamilton, who was in the second coach in the victory parade, later regarded this as the zenith of his career.[52] The contrast with Kitchener's homecoming from the Sudan when many of the Wolseyite War Office shunned a dinner for him was striking. Roberts received almost as many cheers from the crowds as Kitchener. It was a belated triumph for the 'Indians', but in the conqueror of the Boers there was a new power in the army, a younger man to whom 'Johnny' and 'Rawly', William Birdwood and 'Conk' Marker of the Coldstreams would attach themselves.[53]

Kitchener gave evidence to the Royal Commission convened under Lord Elgin to investigate preparations for the South African War. He then departed to take up the Indian command. Brodrick pressed ahead with reform. In March, 1901, he introduced his scheme for three regular army corps and three reserve. In an advance on the Stanhope memorandum, which had placed home and imperial defence at the head of priorities, he included the possibility of European war. He faced opposition within his own party: Hicks-Beach, the Chancellor of the Exchequer, fought for economies; malcontents led by the young Winston Churchill argued that excessive expenditure on the army limited that on the navy.[54] Roberts wished to support his colleague's reforms, but the two increasingly seemed to be pulling against one another. Roberts's force of personality and persuasiveness had enabled him to get his own way in India. At Whitehall, by contrast, he felt he should have a freer hand. He sought higher pay and better barracks. Brodrick opposed further increased expenditure, and accused Roberts of being bogged down in paperwork.[55] Roberts wished to restore a system whereby the QMG took charge of operations and intelligence, as in India, and passed supply to an administrator-general. He became so disillusioned over what he thought was Brodrick's interference in his distribution of honours and handling of disciplinary cases that in September 1901 he offered his resignation. 'I have made it clear,' he told Hamilton, 'that things cannot go on as they are now. I have in fact placed my resignation in

FIGURE 14 *Roberts as commander-in-chief and Brodrick as Secretary of State for War steering a bumping road to reform, traversing the rocky ground of 'scandals', 'rumours', 'muddles' and 'enquiries'. Despite this, achievements included the new rifle and new guns which the army took to war in 1914 (National Army Museum).*

Brodrick's hands, and he and the Cabinet must now decide whether they will have me as their Commander-in-Chief.'[56] Brodrick drew back, replying that pressure from Parliament and the absurdities of the War Office were at fault. The army corps scheme was not realised, and Brodrick suffered from criticisms implicit in the publication of the Elgin Commission findings.[57]

Spenser Wilkinson had called at the Roberts's home on Portland Place to advise him. He gives a last instance of Lady Roberts's influence, despite worsening health. Wilkinson relates that he told Roberts if he did not have Brodrick in his pocket, he would be in Brodrick's, and if he supported Brodrick's military estimates in Parliament, Brodrick would prevail. 'Lady Roberts was present and I feared that she might be offended at my presuming to press my advice upon the Field Marshal,' wrote Wilkinson. 'At the end of my argument Lady Roberts turned to me and said that she was delighted that I had said what I said.'[58]

Brodrick's failure was only partial, for there were successful reforms. Credit was shared by Roberts and his men, by Brodrick and by Balfour, who was interested in defence. A new rifle, the magazine-fed Lee-Enfield, cheap, light, easy to carry, an improved version of the Lee-Metfords and Lee-Enfields of South Africa, was introduced for all units including the cavalry. South African experience vindicated the teaching of Hamilton and Roberts on the value of shooting; the British soldier became adept, a good marksman capable of fifteen rounds a minute. Between 1910 and 1912 the rifle gained better ammunition and new sights, and the emphasis changed to volume of fire, 'winning the fire-fight'.[59] As a gunner, Roberts took a keen interest in artillery reform. The Ehrhardt guns which Brackenbury bought from Germany had, Roberts said, 'advanced us by five if not ten years in our knowledge of what field guns might do'. Brackenbury drew up conditions for the new quick-firing gun. In 1903 orders were placed for the Mark 1 18-pounder. Ian Hamilton's reports from the Russo-Japanese War supported this over any lighter gun.[60] A new quick-firing 13-pounder was introduced for the Royal Horse Artillery. There were improved vehicles – ambulances and store wagons – and khaki service dress. By the Army Order of 1 February, 1902, the army abandoned its red coat except ceremonially and would train at home in the uniform it would wear abroad. The unpopular peakless cap introduced by Brodrick was replaced by a peaked version. Officers' uniforms were simplified. A single-pattern greatcoat was introduced.[61] Salisbury Plain, which had been acquired by Wolseley, became Britain's second military station, with new barracks at Tidworth. In September 1903, Roberts held manoeuvres by four infantry divisions with supporting arms across more than 1,000 square miles. This repeated experience in India. The Times called the exercises 'a decided success', which proved 'of an interest comparable to that of real operations' and Roberts and Hildyard, in charge of training and education, were 'to be heartily congratulated'. Roberts sent his 'high appreciation' to commanders and troops of the manner in which manoeuvres were carried out. Weaknesses remained: an inability to conceal guns and to gather intelligence. Perhaps remembering how he was starved of information in South Africa, he urged 'sparing no pains and shrinking from no risk to ensure efficient scouting'.[62]

Two departments badly found wanting in the South African War were Remount and Medical. Both were the subject of reports, the former by a committee of the House of Commons urging drastic alterations; the latter by a Royal Commission on 27 January 1901. The Veterinary Corps, which had been grossly understaffed, received improvements in pay, promotions and pensions.[63] Brodrick announced his intention to reorganize the RAMC. The chief problem was one of money, pay being insufficient to attract suitable doctors. The estimates for 1901–2 provided about £125,000 as a permanent addition to RAMC funding. There were improved rates of pay, six months' study leave after three years' service, and lectures at the Millbank Military Hospital.[64] Queen Alexandra's Imperial Military Nursing Service,[65] which absorbed army nurses at home and Lady Roberts's in India, was established. The newly unified service counted Queen Alexandra as president of a nursing board, and under her a matron-in-chief to run the service; in India there was a principal matron.[66] This was established by Royal Warrant on 27 March 1902. The first Nursing Board meeting was held in the Roberts's levee room at Horse Guards. Lady Roberts attended as vice-president. Queen Alexandra's Military Nursing Service for India was an offshoot.[67]

Most important were changes made by a newly created Department of Military Education and Training under General Hildyard. Hildyard had been commandant of the Staff College and had sought with G.F.R. Henderson to broaden its teaching.[68] The Akers-Douglas Committee to examine the education and training of officers reported with damning emphasis in 1902 on 'the widespread dissatisfaction – a feeling expressed by practically all the witnesses – with the present state of education, both military and general, among the officers of the Army as a class'. One witness told the committee: 'I am sorry to say that the officer wanted in the Army is only one who can command from £150 to £1500 a year.' Roberts instigated sweeping changes. Hildyard's men, besides performing duties hitherto carried out under the previous director of military education, dealt comprehensively with peacetime manoeuvres, staff tours and all matters connected with practical training for active service. Rawlinson and Wilson, appointed to this department, produced a *Manual of Combined Training*, which became Part II of *Field Service Regulations*, under Roberts's personal direction. After that a staff manual was drafted, which became the nucleus of Part I of the *Field Regulations*. A committee looked at Sandhurst and Woolwich courses. Roberts even obtained a Treasury grant to restore the Camberley Staff College drag, whose hounds had been dispersed during the South African War. Riding to hounds, it was widely believed, 'braces the nerves, quickens decision and teaches the art of getting over a country with a minimum of exertion'.[69]

The full effect of Roberts's tenure at the War Office on army education was seen at the Staff College at Camberley. Staff work in South Africa had been chaotic, Roberts telling the Elgin commission: 'the absence of a definite system of Staff duties, leading sometimes to an overlapping of responsibilities, sometimes to waste of time, and sometimes to a neglect of indispensable precautions, was undoubtedly prejudicial to the smooth running of the military machine . . . Staff Officers cannot be improvised'. Grierson thought controlling a division was the limit of staff capabilities.[70] More staff officers were badly needed. The Staff College acquired a new sense of purpose. Remaining traces of the old curriculum were swept away in favour of practical training in staff duties in the field. The war game was introduced. Two of Roberts's protégés, Rawlinson and Wilson, drove change. In late 1903 Rawlinson, now a brigadier, became commandant, a post which he held with distinction for three years: '. . . he was one to inspire his students unconsciously to follow in his footsteps'. He reduced the number of exams and introduced continuous assessment, resumed staff rides to inspect Franco-Prussian War battlefields and annual staff tours at the Navy's War College at Portsmouth to study combined operations.[71]

In 1906 Roberts's influence helped secure Wilson's appointment to succeed Rawlinson. Wilson's promotion was much opposed at first, Neville Lyttelton, the CIGS (Chief of Imperial General Staff) maintaining that he had too many enemies. Esher and Roberts, however, pressed his case, Esher writing that he was 'qualified perfectly to hold that post, by intellectual attainments and general capacity'. Roberts wrote to Haldane at the War Office:

> I should say that Wilson is perhaps the best known and the most popular man in the Army. He is looked up to as a very promising officer, chiefly I believe on account of the excellent manner in which he performed his Staff duties in South Africa, and I know that the Officers now at the Staff College are looking forward with great hopefulness to his being Rawlinson's successor.[72]

Wilson became one of the remarkable commandants in Staff College history. His sharp intelligence, caustic tongue, oddities of dress, quirky humour and irregular features impressed everyone, not always favourably, but his teaching was inspirational. He created a school of thought among the ablest younger officers who looked to him for guidance just as he had looked to Roberts. In these years British military planning swung powerfully towards intervention in a continental war.[73] Wilson preached the gospel of a 'continental commitment' at France's side and became a friend of Foch, head of the *Ecole Superieur*. As director of military operations from 1910, he perfected the plans for mobilising and deploying the Expeditionary Force to France.[74]

Wilson's successor was a third member of 'the Roberts kindergarten'.[75] 'Wully' Robertson, the only British soldier to advance from private to field marshal, had worked with Brackenbury, Henderson and Nicholson.

Nicholson selected him as Staff College commandant in November 1910. He followed Wilson in urging staff and students to focus on training for war against the strongest likely enemy, Germany. He lacked Wilson's flair, but his prepared lectures were noteworthy for their clarity.[76]

Roberts's dealings with cavalry reform were far less fruitful. He and Hamilton believed the day of shock action was past, the sword or lance 'a medieval toy'[77] and that cavalry should become mounted riflemen on South African lines. French and Haig especially interpreted the fight at Zand River and charges at Elandslaagte and Klip Drift as showing 'cold steel' still effective. The *Cavalry Training* manual of early 1904, with a foreword by Roberts encapsulating his memorandum on the abolition of the lance, failed to note how modern cavalry were moving toward reform and how his approach would antagonise them. This was unfortunate: in India Roberts was keenly interested in cavalry, and had appointed an inspector-general to raise standards. His methods against the cavalry may reflect his having got his way earlier, through charm and persuasion, the prestige of his reputation or by tirelessly writing to everyone involved. After Roberts's departure as commander-in-chief, new *Cavalry Training* manuals of 1907 and 1912 combined fire and shock action. Cavalry did not altogether adapt: on manoeuvres they waved their swords in the air, and they spent 80 per cent of their time on shock tactics, 10 per cent each on shooting and reconnaissance. De Lisle, who had proved himself in South Africa, thought training should be devoted 40 per cent on reconnaissance and 30 per cent each on shock and fire tactics. One achievement of the Roberts–Brodrick era was the establishment of the Cavalry School at Netheravon.[78]

Would Boer War lessons apply in a European war? In 1904–5, the Russo-Japanese War in the Far East dwarfed the South African War. Both Hamilton and Nicholson went as British observers.[79] The lesson drawn from Japanese attacks was that offensive spirit, cold steel and high morale could overcome trench-works. The Staff College entrance examination from 1903 to 1913 included a specific paper on 'small wars', but the South African War was not one of these. The Russo-Japanese War was examined yearly from 1910 to 1913.[80]

Absorbing war's lessons was essential; so too was encouraging the right leaders. An example of Roberts's dealings with those he respected was related by Horace Smith-Dorrien, an up-and-coming brigadier. He committed a serious breach of regulations by an injudicious speech before reporters at a dinner. Roberts summoned him, and demanded why he had so forgotten his position as to advocate publicly compulsory military service. He showed the culprit an angry letter of eight sides from Brodrick, questioning whether his appointment as adjutant-general in India should not be cancelled. Smith-Dorrien made a dutifully humble apology. 'Seeing me taking matters so seriously the little Chief got up,' he wrote, 'and putting his hand on my shoulder calmed me down, saying he would explain matters to the secretary of state. Instantly my wrath vanished, and I was ashamed of my vehemence. Who could resist the magic persuasion of that wonderful personality – so gentle and so considerate and yet so firm and determined when occasion demanded?'[81]

Herbert Plumer, who had fought well in South Africa, was advanced by Roberts, first to command an army district, and then to a post on the Army Council. Plumer's chief of staff and future biographer approvingly quoted Roberts's charming letters.[82] After Roberts had stepped down as commander-in-chief, Plumer wrote to him on the advice of his wife, in August 1911. He had been offered the northern command, but was tempted to refuse and leave the army, bitter at being superseded by officers junior to him, and take lucrative civilian employment. Roberts admitted the northern command was not a very exciting one for an active soldier, but it would keep him on the active list for seven years. There was 'trouble in the air', war might break out and 'you would bitterly regret having left the Army'. 'It is, as I have said, difficult to advise,' wrote Roberts, 'but I feel that were I in the same quandary I would accept the Command and trust to its leading to something better.' Plumer took the advice, and was still there in 1914 at the outbreak of war in which he gave distinguished service.[83]

Roberts opposed the harsh punishments which Brodrick and his Cabinet colleagues wanted for officers who had surrendered in South Africa. There were many. Roberts wrote on 2 September 1901 that he was not keen on severe measures or courts-martial unless the case was a sure one. 'I am very averse to a young officer's whole life being ruined, unless he has committed some disgraceful act unworthy of a gentleman. Under ordinary circumstances I would make him leave a service for which he has shown himself unfitted, but I would not do so in a way that would debar him from gaining a livelihood in some other profession.' He also feared attacks would be directed 'less against the individual than against the honour and reputation of the British Army'.[84] Roberts and Kitchener combined against Brodrick in the case of Clements, defeated at Noitgedacht, but who extricated most of his force. Kitchener had been harshly inclined, but Roberts wrote to him to delay the court-martial and consider further, and he was won round. Roberts was equally determined to defend officers involved in the disgrace of Nicholson's Nek on 30 October 1899. In this prolonged case he continued to press for them to be spared the ignominy of a court-martial.[85]

Roberts failed in the battle for Captain Duncan, who surrendered there. At the end of 1902, however, he prevailed in the case of Major Stapleton Cotton of the Liverpool Regiment, cashiered for the surrender of the garrison at Helvetia. His detachment had been overwhelmed. He held out until the enemy surrounded and overlooked his position. Surgeons testified on his behalf. He had been twice wounded, once severely in the head. He was too ill to defend himself at his court-martial, according to the *Daily Express* of 31 December 1902, and was led to believe the proceedings were informal. 'By all the rules of warfare he had acted well and surrendered only when hopelessly outnumbered . . .' Roberts was convinced of the injustice of the case and placed it before Brodrick. When Brodrick would not overturn the court-martial's findings, Roberts petitioned the King. Cotton received a royal pardon and was reinstated.[86]

In South Africa, he had not always taken a detached view. He reminded Brodrick that in eleven months in South Africa, 'I got rid of 5 Generals of divisions for incompetency, 6 Brigadiers of Cavalry, and 11 out of the 17 commanding officers of Cavalry regiments, besides some half a dozen Infantry Colonels.'[87] Earlier experiences led him to believe quick action against incompetents was necessary in war. He had told Lockhart in India: 'I remember the dreadful old women who were in responsible positions when the Mutiny broke out, and I am not likely to forget the inexperienced officers Sir F. Haines and [Peter] Lumsden weighted me with when I took command of the Kuram Field Force, and went to Kabul a year later.'[88] Good leadership counted most in cavalry: to grasp a situation and act decisively was of the utmost importance. In India he had written: 'We want to get the best fitted for command, and unless I am mistaken, very few men possess all the qualities required in a cavalry leader.'[89] His ruthlessness with cavalry COs was shared with Sir John French.[90]

Among generals sacked was Sir Henry Colvile, sent home for successive blunders at Sannah's Post and Lindley. Ordered to give up the governorship of Gibraltar, he (in Brodrick's words) 'made a statement to the press attacking his superior officers in such terms that in any army in the world he could not keep his commission'. He was called upon to resign in February 1901. Colvile's case was championed by *The Review of the Week* which put a series of articles together in a pamphlet. He wrote his own defence in a book on the Ninth Division. He had, however, twice failed in moments of decision, and had defied army discipline. He was, as Methuen said, 'an impossible man . . . clever, very secretive, neither seniors nor juniors could get on with him'.[91]

Buller's case was a temporary sensation. After a disastrous start in South Africa, he had done better once Colonel Parsons took over his guns. When the war ended, Roberts assumed he would be given a peerage: 'He is a General, a G.C.B., and a G.C.M.G., and I presume will be made a Peer.' Brodrick mentioned it to the Prime Minister, but Salisbury was no admirer.[92] Buller received a rapturous welcome at Aldershot on his return in November 1900. He told his wife in early February 1901 that he was 'very busy here [Aldershot] writing letters abusing the War Office'.[93] Lansdowne had already written to Roberts: 'it will be interesting to see what his public utterances are'.[94] His return to command at Aldershot was a red rag to politicians, press and public who held that Brodrick's three regular army corps for service abroad should be commanded by the officers who would lead them to war. Kipling wrote angrily to the *Spectator* that the English people had paid a heavy price to acquire an army led by proven leaders. Leo Maxse's *National Review* published Buller's notorious Ladysmith telegrams (some heliograms) in abbreviated form to broadcast his pusillanimity. Buller asked for a full version, but the government would not agree. Ministers hardly wished to defend a general whose defeats had nearly caused their political demise. Buller's discontent at press attacks came to a head in his speech at a dinner for the Queen's Westminster Volunteers on 10 October 1901. He intended to defend an officer who had been ambushed, but he was in a 'combative and quarrelsome' mood (his own words), not made better by spotting his chief tormentor, Leo Amery of *The Times*. He spun a fantastic tale about a visit paid to him at Aldershot by 'an international spy' who warned him of enemies who meant to get him out of the way and 'you had better get out of it quietly'.[95] The speech was unwise, as Buller later acknowledged, and contravened Article 423 of King's Regulations by referring to a secret despatch and threatening to publish it; Buller admitted as much in a private letter.[96] 'In his recent speech he disregarded the King's Regulations,' Roberts told Brodrick, 'but that is not the only or indeed the principal point at issue. He displayed in his speech a want of temper and judgement which throws the gravest doubt on his capacity for command.'[97] In an angry interview with Brodrick and then Roberts, and in equally heated letters, Buller refused to admit wrongdoing. Eventually, with bad grace, he retired from command on 22 October 1901.[98] Opinion was strongly in favour of this, except among friends in Devon and some Liberal politicians. Methuen wrote from South Africa: 'Is not R.B. making himself rather too cheap? In olden days we used to come home and hold our tongues unless we spoke at a missionary meeting in a village school when called upon.' Sir Edward Grey took up the case in the Commons. Brodrick checkmated him by reading his despairing messages. Grey claimed Roberts had ordered Buller to remain on the defensive. Brodrick read Roberts's telegram: 'Ladysmith must be relieved . . . Let the troops know that in their hands is the honour of the Empire, and of their success I have no possible doubt.'[99]

Brodrick called the removal of Buller 'one of the most painful episodes in my official life'. Roberts did not agree. He told Hamilton that the publication of Buller's telegrams and despatches would show 'how utterly Buller's character has been mistaken, and how absolutely unfitted he is even to be placed in any position of responsibility'.[100] From South Africa Birdwood told his wife that they were all agog 'about this rumpus over poor old Genl Buller'. 'When he went home he must have realised that it would be quite impossible for him to work smoothly with Lord Roberts, so it was *very* foolish of him not to have quietly resigned . . . I am ever so sorry that he didn't . . .'[101] Buller continued to enjoy support from fellow Devonians and an anonymous pamphlet, *The Burden of Proof: England's Debt to Sir Redvers Buller*.

Newspapers mostly agreed with Buller's departure, just as in South Africa they had largely given Roberts wholehearted support. At Whitehall he kept his contacts, especially with *The Times*,[102] but relations were mixed. In July 1902 letters from Winston Churchill to that newspaper revealed blanket punishments inflicted on cadets at Sandhurst after five fires at the college. When the twenty-nine cadets of 'C' Company were rusticated as punishment, cadets broke bounds and smashed three lamps in Camberley. Further punishments – the reduction of four cadet corporals to the ranks and restriction drill for another thirty – followed. As Churchill showed, one of the cadet corporals was innocent, having been away when the Camberley disorder happened, and was a 'King's India Cadet', thus a poor man's son. Churchill commended the case to Roberts 'to bring before him clearly the consequences which have followed from the callous, careless, and utterly unjust action taken under his name and authority'. The Sandhurst authorities had made a nonsense of a routine matter. It ended in a debate in the Lords. Roberts, by a tactful speech heard with respect, defused things, promising to go into individual cases; if cadets were not guilty, they should forfeit no seniority. The *Times* applauded this, but it was surely not a busy commander-in-chief's job to 'go carefully into each individual case' when other matters pressed.[103]

Equally unimportant should have been the subalterns' courts-martial in the 1st Battalion Grenadier Guards, reported to him by two peers. Ensigns (i.e. second lieutenants) had to undergo trials by unofficial kangaroo courts formed of young officers and receive vicious physical punishments if found 'guilty'. The commanding officer, Lt-Colonel David Kinloch, was condemned by his own mouth, knowing nothing of this in his own battalion. Roberts heard his appeal personally, and retired him, he being lucky not to have undergone his own court-martial. He had powerful friends, however, three of them writing to *The Times* to complain. The admission that Kinloch was ignorant of events led *The Times* to declare: 'The public have learned with a feeling of stupefaction that a commanding officer in the British Army can allow discipline to pass out of his own hands altogether and into those of an illegal and irregular tribunal of subalterns . . .' Unfortunately the powerful friends had gone to the King; Edward VII was not pleased when the commander-in-chief after a review of the evidence refused to bow to the royal will and change his judgement. Roberts was aghast at the burst of publicity – scandal among the wealthy and privileged sold newspapers – which might divert him from army reform. The Liberal opposition was delighted: 'The Bobs bubble is about to burst,' Chief Whip Herbert Gladstone wrote to Campbell-Bannerman. He was wrong. Supported by his military and civilian colleagues and defended by Brodrick in the Commons, Roberts replied in the Lords to the charges, asserting that he had the right to place any unsatisfactory officer on half-pay. His highly principled if emotional counter-attack carried the day. Historian T.C. Kennedy regards his victory as one for army reformers, opposed to posh regiments being the domain of the rich, privileged and inefficient.[104]

Press criticism of Roberts as commander-in-chief appeared in the *Saturday Review*, 12 April 1902 and the *Naval and Military Gazette*, 10 May 1902. He replied in a letter signed 'Miles' ('Soldier') in the *Spectator*. This reply from a master writer of despatches showed the achievement of reform, listing increased soldiers' pay and improved recruiting, more comfortable barracks, abolition of irksome roll calls, the status of NCOs raised, Sandhurst training and organisation transformed, officers' expenses much reduced; an increase in mounted infantry, an improved rifle, the canteen system overhauled and temperance recreation rooms provided where space permitted. The *Spectator*'s editor agreed that this was an impressive record, but wondered whether the War Office itself was soundly organised.[105]

Unease over War Office organisation was strengthened by the Elgin Commission's report. The Commission, constituted 'to Inquire into the Military Preparations and other Matters connected with the War in South Africa', sat for fifty-five days, heard 114 witnesses, and collected evidence including written statements to 22,200 questions. The printed evidence has proved invaluable to historians of the war, but must be used with caution. Men were fighting their corners after the event, and some were wiser then than in the war.[106] Roberts commented on a lack of plans, praised regimental officers rather than COs and generals and thought better staff work was essential. 'Brains are more important than numbers,' he said. He considered the regular soldier of his time, 'in no single respect inferior to his predecessor', and in some 'greatly superior'. There were differing views on centralised transport, but agreement that soldiers were better fed than in previous wars. The Commission recorded the terrible loss of animals: of 518,794 horses and 150,781 donkeys and mules, some 347,007 horses and 53,339 donkeys and mules 'expended during the campaign' and 13,144 horses and 2,816 mules and donkeys 'lost on voyage'.[107]

The commission censured Wolseley as commander-in-chief for failing to inform Lansdowne of the intelligence received, the War Office for failing to draw up war plans, and both soldiers and politicians for lack of consultation. Esher told the King after hearing Roberts's evidence: 'the Commander-in-Chief of Your Majesty's force, although nominally in a position of great responsibility, is so hampered by the organisation of the War Office, and by the Parliamentary customs which hem that officer within an impassable fence, that his responsibility is an illusion'.[108] He and two others presented a minority view advocating firstly reconstitution of the War Office and secondly a system of national military education as the practical alternative to conscription. Esher called on Roberts at the War Office and found him interested in the proposals, inclined to give them careful consideration.[109] Five days after the report's publication, Roberts wrote to Brodrick to express agreement with Esher that his position as commander-in-chief had become anomalous.[110]

The report was published in July 1903. Esher advised Brodrick in August to resign; he did not, but in the ministerial reshuffle in October Balfour removed him from the War Office to the India Office. His scheme for six army corps was dropped. One of his reforms did take root however; in 1902 he and Lord Selborne, First Lord of the Admiralty, recommended a Committee of Imperial Defence (CID) to provide a central body for planning imperial strategy. Brodrick told the Commons that the CID's duty was to survey as a whole 'the strategical military needs of the Empire'. Roberts sat on the CID with the Prime Minister and Cabinet ministers, the First Sea Lord and the heads of naval and military intelligence.[111] This was the belated fruit of writing by Dilke, Wilkinson, Brackenbury and Roberts.

Brodrick's successor, H.O. Arnold-Forster, was equally keen for reform, and had a long-standing interest in the army, but lacked the character and tact to draw conflicting personalities together.[112] His plan to create two forces, one for imperial defence, one for home, met opposition from *The Times* and others. The question was confused by the report of the Norfolk Commission into auxiliary forces in May 1904, favouring some form of national service. Roberts supported this and was soon to champion it. Arnold-Forster was undermined, however, by the establishment of a committee under Esher for War Office reform.

Esher, Admiral Sir John Fisher and Sir George Clarke made up 'the War Office Reconstitution Committee' – 'to advise as to the creation of a Board for the administrative business of the War Office, and as to consequential changes thereby involved'. Colonel Gerald Ellison was secretary. He and Esher wrote most of the report, calling no witnesses and taking no evidence. To achieve a general staff on German lines, Ellison drafted a plan for an army council to include three civilian and four military members (chief of the general staff, adjutant-general, QMG and major-general of the ordnance). Roberts warned Kitchener that Esher's committee would bring change on Admiralty lines and he would be 'the last Commander-in-Chief'. Esher's letters suggest Roberts's mixed feelings: 'Lord Roberts alone among the older men is full of congratulations. He says that we have carried out everything he has for years wished for, and he is most anxious to be the first in assisting to carry out the scheme.' He was not, however, enthusiastic to give up his command, the summit of his long career. Esher feared he might make the new inspector-general's post a centre of influence; Edward VII had to persuade him to decline.[113] Then all was ready for Esher's 'torpedo' to sink the existing system.

The reform's headlong implementation abolished Roberts's post in February 1904 without his being warned beforehand. He left the War Office in high dudgeon – 'the little C.-in-C. has left the W.O. for good in a devil of a temper'. After two-and-a-half centuries, the commander-in-chiefship vanished into history without note, save a special army order of Roberts's retirement.[114] A completely new team of officers replaced those who served him, including William Nicholson, whom Esher thought the 'cleverest soldier I have yet seen'.[115] Roberts told Arnold-Forster that the soldiers were treated disgracefully, 'when all could have been carried out in order and with decorum' if a date had been agreed.[116]

Years later, Sir Charles Harris, the Financial Secretary at the War Office, told Ellison that he felt sure if Esher 'hadn't ridden roughshod over everybody (including Bobs!) to put Bobs's best idea through with a heavy fist, it would have been wrecked by a "compromise" devised by some second-rater ...' Harris thought that Roberts hoped for a commander-in-chief on Indian lines. He added, 'He was such a sterling chap that when the soreness over the rough handling of that point had worn off, he bore no grudge against Esher at all and they were good friends very soon after.' This is only part of the truth. Roberts, with his widespread reform connections, was a power in the army. If the Machiavellian Esher could remove him and ensure he did not take the inspector-general's post, he would have a clearer field for his own measures. In February 1904 Roberts was in Henry Wilson's words 'more hurt & angry than I ever saw him, & no wonder'.[117]

Later, Ellison, in an article in *The Nineteenth Century* and a letter to *The Times* in 1932 on the centenary of Roberts's birth, told how Roberts had already decreed that the QMG's branch was to be expanded into an operations staff. Ellison was to prepare a suitable staff manual. When Esher's committee was formed, Ellison brought this to their notice, and they made the work already started the basis of the new War Office. At the last moment Esher substituted 'General Staff' as the operations branch's name, leaving the QMG as controller of supply services, removing obvious traces of Roberts's work. In his article Ellison belatedly conceded that 'to Lord Roberts is due the initiative which gave us a staff system in 1914 so widely at variance with what had obtained in the Boer War'. Writing to *The Times* he went further: 'The staff system which saw us successfully through the Great War was due to Lord Roberts, and Lord Roberts alone. He was the inheritor of a great tradition which he handed on intact to the present generation, and of all the distinguished services he rendered his country none surpasses in importance this . . .'[118] 'Alone' gives Roberts too much credit: these ideas came from Spenser Wilkinson, with whom he was of one mind. Nonetheless, Ellison's story shows that this, with the Lee-Enfield, the 18-pounder and army education reform, makes a worthy legacy of Roberts's time as commander-in-chief.[119]

CHAPTER TWELVE

Trying to arouse his countrymen

My Lords, during the last two years I have endeavoured from time to time to induce your Lordships to take into your serious consideration the vitally important question of home defence, but for some reason unaccountable to me, my efforts have hitherto been in vain.

ROBERTS TO THE HOUSE OF LORDS, 23 NOVEMBER 1908

Lord Roberts is like one of the old Jewish Prophets trying to awaken us out of our apathetic sleep. But we have ears & hear not.

CHARLES CROSTHWAITE TO IAN HAMILTON

Had a most harassing day on account of General Gough & most of the officers of the Cavalry Brigade resigning at the Curragh . . . Lord Roberts came to see me & was in despair about it all & said it would ruin the Army.

DIARY OF KING GEORGE V, 21 MARCH 1914

The most famous soldier in the Empire could not just be put out to pasture. The post of inspector-general had been specially created for him, but as he wanted control of appointments, the King persuaded him not to take it. Instead, Balfour offered Roberts a continued seat on the Committee of Imperial Defence, which he took.[1] Esher's reform supplemented by the creation of a general staff two years later laid the foundations of the system that endured in essentials throughout the two world wars. In 1908 Arnold-Forster and Esher's hopes were fulfilled when Nicholson became CIGS (Chief of the Imperial General Staff). Roberts too had sought this post for him, knowing of his staff talents from India and South Africa.[2] Reform of the army's fighting organisation, at which Brodrick and Arnold-Forster stumbled, was achieved by R.B. Haldane of the new Liberal government which came to power in 1906. Haldane profited from the trials of Brodrick and Arnold-Forster. His proposals were more modest – divisions instead of corps. Ellison became his private secretary and Esher continued behind the scenes. Roberts was soon to be involved in a different campaign.[3]

As commander-in-chief and afterwards, Roberts continued his keen interest in the Indian Army, especially after Kitchener landed at Bombay on 28 November 1902. He told Kitchener that he proposed to write regularly and keep him informed of events at Whitehall, hoping 'you will let me hear from you occasionally'. Roberts imagined the scene of turmoil in Delhi before Curzon's great durbar to proclaim George V king-emperor: 'I can picture to myself the Railway Station, trains arriving hours late, the platform crowded with luggage, and the *tikha Gharis* with their half starved ponies waiting to take travellers at exorbitant rates to the camps. I must say I should like to see it all . . .'[4]

Curzon as viceroy was a man of exceptional industry, breadth of vision and 'a surpassing knowledge of Indian affairs'. He was, however, unaware of Kitchener's capacity for intrigue or that Brodrick (now Secretary of State for India) thought his judgement was unsound.[5] He had welcomed Kitchener warmly as the man to bring new life to the Indian Army. They were to fall out profoundly over the role of the military member as the viceroy's personal staff officer. Kitchener's strong views on the Indian Army, received from Birdwood and from Smith-Dorrien, were reinforced after his arrival. The Indian Army was curiously unwarlike, HQ was 'paper-logged' and in March 1903 he told a friend that he had done nothing but write minutes.[6] He was intent on abolishing the military member's powers.[7] Roberts had found the duplication frustrating, but with Chesney and Brackenbury, the system worked. General Sir Edmond Elles was a forceful military member, who had strengthened his position when commanders-in-chief were weak or unwell. Roberts hoped to restrain Kitchener from this change.[8] The two continued on good terms: Kitchener wrote in May with news for Lady Roberts that he had rebuilt the dining room and would send a photo. He told her that he would 'set up as a House Decorator when I leave here'.[9] The Indian government had purchased Snowdon as the commander-in-chief's official residence shortly after the Robertses' departure. Kitchener entertained lavishly on gold and silver plate. He gathered about him a 'ring': Frank Maxwell, Raymond Marker, Victor Brooke, Hubert Hamilton, William Birdwood.[10] His measures, like Roberts's, were intended to make the Indian Army an effective fighting instrument. He organised it in divisions for war. He doubled the size of the field army. He continued recruiting the 'martial races', while southern regiments were disbanded. In four years, Kitchener recruited 6,000 Gurkhas.[11] He obtained approval for an Indian Staff College, whose teaching would dovetail with Camberley's.[12] He called for an Indian

General Staff. He even proposed to open the higher ranks of the army to Indians.[13] When Roberts was ousted as commander-in-chief, Kitchener wrote sympathetically: 'I am distressed to learn that you are no longer at the War Office. I cannot imagine what will be the results of the violent changes that have been recently introduced with apparently very little consideration.'[14]

Roberts was in the unhappy position of wishing to help him, but also to defend a system which he had made a success. On 18 June 1903, while admitting friction with dual control, he wrote: 'I accepted the fact that all the spending departments must be under the Government of India, and that the Commander-in-Chief's duties were limited to the Executive charge of the Army. I found this system worked well . . .'[15] Initially there was a compromise: the removal of supply and transport from the military member. This did not satisfy Kitchener, who wanted control of all sides of military administration. Roberts fought against this. In March 1905, George White told him: 'I agree generally with the principles circulated by Lord Kitchener.' Roberts used his formidable powers of persuasion in his counter-minute. In May, White changed his mind. 'Brodrick tried to shake me on my views but I would not tone them down,' he told his old mentor. 'He opposes our views as they will leave things as they are.'[16] Roberts wrote to Spenser Wilkinson at the *Morning Post* that if Kitchener had only found fault with the working of the system, he would gladly have helped, but 'it would be infinitely better to allow Kitchener to resign than to let him have his own way in this matter'. He doubted that any future Indian commander-in-chief, lacking Kitchener's drive, could do two men's work. 'I most sincerely hope that the existing system will be maintained . . .'[17]

Matters came to a head in 1905. The viceroy's council rejected Kitchener's memorandum for abolition of the military member and his department. A weak Unionist ministry at a time of international instability could not allow Kitchener to carry out his threat to resign.[18] On 8 May a committee in London including Balfour, Brodrick, Roberts and Lansdowne considered and proposed to replace the military member with a military supply member who would not sit on the Viceroy's Council. Roberts alone dissented. To Lansdowne he wrote: 'I personally think it would be better for India that Kitchener should resign rather than that the Military Member should be abolished.'[19] His fellow committee members did not agree. He had to write to both protagonists to inform them before the official dispatch. He told Kitchener: 'all your wishes have been met, as far as is possible, without placing the Gvt [*sic*] of India in a very difficult position. The Military Member is to be retained, but he will be powerless to interfere with the C-in-C in any matter which directly comes within that official's control'. He added, sadly: 'every one of those consulted, who was personally acquainted with the working of the Government of India, agreed that it would be most unwise to deprive the Members of a Colleague to whom they could look for advice on the many delicate and difficult questions which often arise in regard to the Native Army'. As noted, he believed no successor to Kitchener could do the work of two men.[20] A discourteous dispatch to Curzon and the rejection of his nominee for the new post added insult to injury. Curzon resigned and left India, an embittered man, on 18 November 1905.[21]

Curzon's defenders have pointed to Kitchener's aptitude for intrigue.[22] Was Curzon right to defend the system? Esher thought that two senior soldiers on the Council were 'a source of inconvenience and confusion'. The historian Gopal wrote of 'the illogical system of military administration in India' which broke under the stress of rivalry between two masterly personalities. Curzon's claim that Kitchener's proposal would overthrow civilian control of the army and establish a military dictatorship exaggerated wildly.[23]

Roberts's worry that the Indian commander-in-chief would not cope with the work was more substantial. In 1907 the entente with Russia over central Asia led Morley, then Indian Secretary, to cut the Indian defence budget. Preparations to defend India against Russian invasion to which Roberts had devoted much effort were no longer necessary. 'The Great Game' was over with Russian recognition of Afghanistan as a British sphere of influence. The military supply member was abolished, thrusting the whole burden of staff work onto the commander-in-chief and his staff. A plan to create an Indian General Staff was shelved. Kitchener's successors were, as Roberts guessed, less capable. In the First World War the Expeditionary Force sent from India to Mesopotamia performed poorly. A Royal Commission reported in July 1917: 'The combination of the duties of C-in-C in India and the military member of Council cannot adequately be performed by any one in time of war.'[24] The Indian Army in Mesopotamia also suffered from Morley's economies and the over-sanguine ambitions of politicians and commanders.[25]

Curzon's viceroyalty marked a turning point in British rule, for as he left so did some of the British confidence. Henceforward, the Raj was on the defensive. Political dissent spread from Bengal to the Punjab, Oudh and Agra. Curzon's successor, Roberts's former Afghan war ADC Lord Minto, faced strong nationalist feeling on the fiftieth anniversary of the Mutiny. Roberts wanted the anniversary celebrated with a special medal for surviving veterans of 1857. He told Minto, the King approved, 'but Morley is a little nervous as to whether any reference to the Mutiny is advisable, considering the disloyal feeling in Bengal and other parts of India'.[26] There was to be no medal, and the veterans' dinner at the Royal Albert Hall on 23 December given by the proprietors of *The Daily Telegraph* was for the old field marshal a consolation. At the Albert Memorial the event began with a review of veterans by Roberts. In the Hall Roberts presided at a long table with many distinguished guests, including Curzon, Rudyard Kipling, recent Nobel Laureate, and General Sir Hugh Gough. The old soldiers were cheered as they took their places.

Curzon spoke first and finished with a toast to the veterans. Roberts replied. Modestly he pointed out that those present were mere boys at the time and must all feel that this celebration was an honour paid to the memory of those by whose skill and courage 'that great epoch' in our Indian history was brought to a successful close. He specially remembered Sir Henry Lawrence and John Nicholson. The occasion closed with the playing of 'The Last Post', the singing of Kipling's 'Recessional' and 'Auld Lang Syne'. At Roberts's request Kipling had specially written a poem for the occasion, 'The Veterans':

> Today, across our fathers' graves
> The astonished years reveal
> The remnant of that desperate host
> That cleansed our east with steel.
>
> Hail and farewell. We greet you here
> With tears that none will scorn
> Oh keepers of the house of old
> Or ever we were born.

By speaking to every veteran Roberts discovered that many were living in the workhouse in bitter poverty. Within a fortnight he obtained the King's patronage for an appeal, which raised £38,000. Over 800 men were taken from poorhouses and ended their lives in modest comfort. *Punch* ran a cartoon in support; the 'Fair Stranger' whom the aged veteran takes for 'Charity' replies: 'No, I am gratitude, come to pay my debt.'[27]

If anything could show Roberts how India was changing, it was news from the sub-continent. During the first quarter of 1907, reports reached Indian Army headquarters of agitation in the Punjab. An informer claimed that two Punjabi junior officers had approached the Congress leader Gokhale and promised him that the army would rise against the *Feringhis* if necessary. Gokhale, who led the moderate wing of Congress, spurned the offer.[28] B.G. Tilak headed the radicals advocating non-cooperation with the British. There were outbreaks of communal violence and a number of terrorist murders almost unknown in late-nineteenth-century British India. Nationalist pamphlets were discovered in army lines. Roberts was alarmed. He told Kitchener in a letter of September 1907 that he was glad he was there for two more years: 'the Natives should clearly understand that any one who tries to upset our rule will be treated with the utmost rigour of the law . . .'[29] He wrote to Minto in June advocating that repressive measures 'if they are to succeed, must be swift and summary. The long-protracted enquiry, the cross-examination of the defence, and the daily spectacle of the accused coming to, and leaving, the Court are a huge attraction for the crazy youth of India. The procedure should be swift, summary, and secret'. He told Minto's secretary, Colonel James Dunlop Smith, that he read the newspapers every morning in the hope that he had been able to bring in some law 'by which assassinations, bomb outrages, etc., may be summarily dealt with . . .' In May 1908 terrorists were discovered in Calcutta plotting to kill Minto and Kitchener. In July, there were a series of disorders in Bombay, coinciding with economic distress, and the governor moved in troops. Tilak was arrested, and the trouble died down after his conviction and six-year-gaol sentence.

Although the Raj had a strong army and 200,000 civilian police, ruling a population of over 300 million depended upon cooperation and acquiescence. John Morley, an old-fashioned radical, was in the Ripon tradition. The British established a growing number of municipal authorities in the 1890s with places for educated Indians. In November 1908 another step was taken with the Indian Councils Act (the Minto–Morley reforms): sixty Indian representatives to be elected to the viceroy's executive council, and between thirty and fifty to provincial legislative councils, helping to frame laws. At George V's coronation durbar in December 1911 a proclamation reunited the Bengal which Curzon had divided in an unpopular act. Roberts changed his mind on Indians receiving commissions. In July 1908 Dunlop Smith, on leave in England, dined at Roberts's home, and wrote to Lord and Lady Minto: '[Roberts] quite agrees as to the proposed regiment in which Imperial cadets will receive combatant commissions and will give it his hearty support.' Roberts also offered help in obtaining a stricter press law.[30] In February 1909, he wrote again, from Khartoum, where he and Lady Roberts had gone for her health – 'She had several attacks of influenza last year, and suffered much from sciatica' – and to see progress under British rule. Hardly a day had passed in the last year or two, Roberts said, that Kitchener, the viceroy and the Indian Army had been absent from his thoughts. He rejoiced at the Indian soldiers' loyalty.[31]

In Britain, following the creation of the BEF of six regular divisions, Haldane turned to the reserves, 'the Territorial Force', to replace the old militia and volunteers. A committee he chaired, with Roberts, Haig and Ellison as members, failed to agree. There was opposition from vested and county interests, but fortunately Haldane enjoyed royal backing through Esher. In October 1907 Edward VII personally asked a meeting of lords-lieutenant to support the new Territorials, which he justified as a reserve for overseas service. Roberts, following private discussions with Esher, supported the measure. On 1 April 1908 the force came officially into being. The first annual fortnight's training camp was held. By the beginning of 1910 the Territorials numbered 276,618 officers and men – 88.5 per cent of intended establishment. This was an important achievement, for invasion of England seemed to have become a threat. The Royal Navy felt a landing by 70,000 men was *just* possible; others thought more.[32] The *Observer* criticised Haldane in a strong article on 5 April 1908 claiming he had not created the ideal British Army, but rather one of 'German dreams', i.e. not strong enough.[33] An attempt to amend Haldane's plan by adding compulsory service to the Territorials was defeated on its first reading.[34]

Roberts still sat on the Committee of Imperial Defence and enjoyed an enormous reputation. Victorian certainties had gone. Germany across the

North Sea was building battleships. The United States, inspired by the writings of Admiral Mahan, launched a powerful fleet, in 1898 defeated Spain and acquired Puerto Rico, Guam and the Philippines. The Japanese became formidable in the Far East. The Russo-Japanese War was the first defeat of a European by an 'Asiatic' power. The young Jawaharlal Nehru dreamt of similar triumph. Could a small country like Britain with just over 40 million people match the larger continental powers? She fell behind in the new electrical and chemical industries. She was wedded still to free trade; other nations' protection hit her commerce.[35]

The early twentieth century was marked by fears for British security, only partly reassured by a naval alliance with Japan in 1902, an entente or understanding with France in 1904 and a similar agreement with Russia in 1907 defining the two powers' position in central Asia. In 1904 Admiral Sir John Fisher became First Sea Lord, and set out to modernise the Royal Navy.[36] The building of the *Dreadnought* gave Britain a lead in battleships, but there was continued anxiety about national security. 'The Blue Water School' put its faith in the fleet. The ironically named 'Bolt from the Blue School' believed invasion could catch England by surprise. A series of invasion stories beginning with Erskine Childers' *The Riddle of the Sands* alarmed many. All Europe knew of the dangerous inconsistency of Kaiser Wilhelm II; of the expanding German navy; of the *arriviste* German Empire's mixture of admiration and envy towards its older British relation; of the restless German *Weltpolitik*.

Roberts's answer was to rouse his countrymen to service. As early as December, 1901 he asked Kipling: 'If you are in favour of compulsory service for home defence would it be possible to write some stirring lines to bring home to the public the danger of allowing ourselves to be a second time in the same risky position without any properly trained troops in the country.' Carrie Kipling recorded that Roberts's letter arrived on 3 December, and on the 4th Rudyard was composing 'conscription verses'. 'The Islanders' appeared on 3 January 1902 in *The Times*.[37]

> Then were the judgements loosened; then was your shame revealed,
> At the hands of a little people, few but apt in the field . . .
> Then ye returned to your trinkets; then ye contented your souls
> With the flannelled fools at the wicket or the muddied oafs at the goals.

Kipling asked editor Moberley Bell to back him with an editorial. On 4 January Bell wrote that he hoped the verses would prove a ringing call to action. 'There is much that touches the consciences of us all in the stern and stinging rebuke addressed to his "Islanders" by one who has given the noblest expression to the pride and to the duty of Empire.' Readers' letters were mainly favourable: 'An Islander' wrote, 'All honour is due to Mr Kipling for sounding loud the trumpet of warning, and I hope the notes will ring from end to end of the Empire.'[38] Roberts's advocacy of national service did not follow until he had given up his seat on the Committee of Imperial Defence. Haldane's Expeditionary Force was good but small. The army was the poor relation of the navy: in 1914 its budget was £28.84 million, the Royal Navy's £51.55 million.[39] The National Service League had been formed in 1902 by George Shee to demand compulsory national service for home defence, but not service abroad. One of several Edwardian patriotic organisations born out of the South African War, fears of foreign threats, internal weakness and the physical decline shown in the poor quality of Boer War recruits, it was modelled on the Navy League of 1895 and inspired by Shee's book *The Briton's First Duty: The Case for Conscription* published in March 1901. Warning of the possible fall of Britain and her Empire, Shee claimed that the Royal Navy alone was insufficient. A home defence army was needed. Compulsory service would counter degeneration and make better citizens. The League was founded at a meeting on 26 February 1902 at Apsley House, by the invitation of the 4th Duke of Wellington, who became its president. As its secretary, Shee organised the movement and edited its journal. Compulsory service was unpopular; the League advocated a citizen army to defend Britain: its members would undergo two months' initial training followed by annual camps for three years. It did not advocate attack or pre-emptive war. It counted famous names such as Garnet Wolseley, Kipling and Moberly Bell of *The Times*, but by 1905 still had only 2,000 members.

In that year, Balfour made public the findings of a Committee of Imperial Defence investigation to assure Parliament that there was no danger of invasion. Against this Roberts published an article in *The Nineteenth Century* in January calling for a defence force to protect the nation if the regular army were abroad. In August, in a Mansion House speech, he suggested that war on the North-West Frontier might require more men than South Africa. How would Britain raise them? How would the nation's safety be assured with every soldier at the front? He had returned from South Africa to find only 19,000 regulars to defend England. His speech gave an enormous boost to League standing. In November, after vainly attempting to convince the Committee of Imperial Defence of the danger, he resigned and accepted the presidency of the League. Milner and Amery had already invited him. His prestige and energy transformed its campaign. It became to press and public, 'Lord Roberts's crusade', and he became the idol of those who shared his fears and the object of hatred of those who opposed compulsory service as anti-democratic, militaristic, un-English. He was assisted by Amery who became his first 'ideas man' and wrote some of his speeches; Leo Maxse of the *National Review*, Repington of *The Times*; Professor John A. Cramb; and Henry Wilson. Press support came notably from the *Morning Post* owned by Countess Bathurst, a League member. The shrewdest of his advisors was probably Charles a Court Repington, who had predicted a Japanese victory over Russia in 1904–5, and regarded that war between an island power and a continental one as instructive for Britain.

He respected Roberts's knowledge of Indian warfare, but saw him as a figurehead to be primed with clever ideas. As German power grew, Roberts hoped national service would create a large army for continental deployment. This aim was not made public. As the League's Unionist members were far more numerous than Liberals, it was a realistic aim to convert their party leaders, but was never achieved.[40] Haldane's Territorials might become an adjunct to Roberts's proposed national service; in May, 1909, he and Lord Newton placed before the Lords a bill for four months' compulsory training in the Territorials for men reaching the age of eighteen. It was defeated on its second reading.[41]

The League's campaign was aided by William Le Queux's *The Invasion of 1910*, written to order for Lord Northbrook and serialised in the *Weekly News*. Readers were fascinated by Le Queux's account of England alive with German spies: 50,000 German waiters crouched under railway bridges, asked questions about water supplies, gathered intelligence on early morning walks. Roberts advised him and in a foreword urged readers to take up the cause of military preparedness. In the winter of 1908 and 1909 serials with titles like 'The Great Raid', 'The Invaders' and 'While England Slept' were published.[42] More important, Roberts and Repington marshalled evidence before a Committee of Imperial Defence panel to overturn the view that the Royal Navy could prevent invasion. Asquith as chairman, Esher and an array of powerful admirals and generals held sixteen meetings from 27 November 1907 to 28 July 1908 to consider evidence. Roberts made an eloquent presentation. Repington ably described a possible German landing, and asked effective supplementary questions. How many troops were assigned to home defence? How long to muster them? What about transportation and supply? Esher had thought the idea of invasion absurd; now he was not so sure. Admiral Fisher fumed and was rude to everyone, and Baron Tweedmouth, First Lord of Admiralty, attacked Roberts in a gratuitously offensive cross examination, against which the field marshal stood his ground. Tweedmouth was removed from the Admiralty after the publication of letters to him from the Kaiser.[43]

In the 1908 summer invasion exercise, a small force had eluded the defending fleet and scrambled ashore at Wick in the north of Scotland. This seemed proof of a 'Bolt from the Blue'. Repington and Roberts pressed unsuccessfully for the publication of the CID panel's report. The story spread that 70,000 men could have landed. Roberts scored a further triumph by a speech in the Lords demanding that the government state the results of the CID's investigation and appealing for a citizen defence force. When he withdrew the second part of his proposed motion, the first passed 74 votes to 32: 'That in the opinion of this House the defence of these Islands necessitates the immediate attention of His Majesty's Government to the provision (in addition to a powerful Navy) of an Army so strong in numbers and so efficient in quality that the most formidable foreign nation would hesitate to attempt a landing on these shores . . .' Next day the newspapers were full of his speech. Further success followed as he was denounced in the Reichstag, the newsmen resenting German threats.[44]

Roberts did not win over either political party. The long Liberal tradition against compulsory service was strong. Unionist leaders thought supporting Roberts's National Service Bill introduced in the Lords in July 1909 would cost votes. Roberts's campaign made ground in other quarters. By July 1908 most senior soldiers accepted that an invasion of 33,000 men would 'probably be successful'. League membership grew to a peak in 1912 of 98,931 members and 218,513 'supporters' who paid just a penny. Roberts won an influential friend and supporter in J.L. Garvin, the Tory editor of the *Observer* and *Pall Mall Gazette*, the latter being more formidable than Maxse's *National Review*. He was delighted with Garvin's support, and read his frequent articles with great satisfaction. Garvin was impressed by both Roberts's demeanour and ideas, and became a sturdy public advocate, drafting detailed notes for many of Roberts's speeches and writing letters that appeared over his name in the press.[45]

Esher had said in a Lords' debate of July 1910 that the Territorials had reached their limit under the voluntary system. The inference was that compulsion would be necessary. To answer this Haldane asked General Sir Ian Hamilton, then inspector general of overseas forces, to write an opposing pamphlet, Haldane adding a long introduction. This attack on the League was a sensation, for everyone knew Roberts's friendship for Hamilton. On the eve of publication Lady Hamilton was staying at Englemere and wrote in her diary: 'Unhappy thought that the dear Bobs are nourishing vipers in their bosom.'[46] Hamilton and Haldane's pamphlet 'Compulsory Service: a study of the question in the light of experience' appeared in November 1910. The second edition included a memorandum by the First Sea Lord Wilson ridiculing the idea of an invasion. Complimentary copies were showered on everyone. Hamilton deeply hurt his old mentor.[47] Within months Roberts with Amery and Professor J.A. Cramb replied. 'Fallacies and facts: an answer to "Compulsory Service" ' charged Hamilton and Haldane with shortsightedness and abused the latter for using a serving officer to argue political questions in public. Newspapers found it the more convincing. The *Daily Mail* of 4 April 1911 stated that Roberts 'has no party axe to grind in his fight for military efficiency . . . The War Office will drift and live in a world of make-believe till disaster overtakes British arms. It is to avert such a calamity that Lord Roberts has made his impressive appeal to his countrymen'.[48]

For a time the controversy drove an unhappy wedge between Roberts and Hamilton. The gap was filled by Henry Wilson, who left the Staff College in 1910 to become director of military operations at the War Office, a key job in which he prepared for the BEF's successful mobilisation in 1914. He supplied Roberts with advice and information in support of the National Service campaign, and was impressed by his indomitable optimism. Wilson and his wife Cecil ('Cessie') became close friends of the Robertses, spending Christmases with them. In his diary of 8 June 1911, Wilson wrote:

Went to see the little Chief ... I developed my ideas, already written to him on Sunday and Monday last, about our talking of peace, and every other nation talking of war, and how this would be the ruin of us. And at the end he chimed in with, 'Very well, my dear boy, what we have to do is to change the whole mind of the nation. Now we must see about that at once.' And he is 79![49]

At this time Roberts was also fighting as a *Bittereinder* in the Lords. The constitutional battle between Liberals and Unionists over reducing the power of the House of Lords began with the peers' rejection of Lloyd George's budget of 1909, and became a full-scale crisis after the two elections of 1910 in which the Lords' role was a major issue. After the second of these elections, Liberals and Unionists had almost the same number of seats. Irish and Labour MPs held the balance and supported the Liberals.[50] Roberts had been out of England after the death of Edward VII, when the new king, George V, chose him to announce his accession formally to the courts of Europe. On his return he became one of the die-hards opposing a reduction of the Lords' powers. With Lord Lansdowne he preferred a smaller body made up of members nominated by the Commons, the peers and the crown, to reduction of Lords' power. Instead, the Liberals' Parliament Bill was brought in and passed. Curzon took the lead in persuading twenty-nine Unionist peers and eleven bishops to accept it. Many assumed this to be a preliminary to a third Irish Home Rule bill. Roberts, taking his stand with the opponents, wrote in a letter to *The Times* that Lansdowne's amendments were 'essential to the maintenance of the Constitution', believing that Lords' powers were a safeguard against 'single chamber domination and dangerous constitutional innovations'.[51] In the House he declared: 'We are links in a living chain pledged to transmit to posterity the glorious heritage we have received by those who have gone before us.'[52]

At the beginning of 1912 the fears of those urging compulsory military service became more serious. The Agadir Crisis of July 1911 had brought threat of imminent war, although the effect of German sabre-rattling was to drive the entente closer. Lloyd George and Winston Churchill among Liberal ministers joined those taking a stronger line in foreign policy.[53] In early 1912, writing to Churchill, Roberts declared: 'those summer months showed us that our Regular Army – small as it is – was unprepared for war, whilst our Territorial Force was wholly unfitted to take the field'. He praised Churchill's firm stand in the crisis and went on 'to hope that you will come to the decision that the continued existence of our Empire cannot rest on the voluntary efforts of a few of the best of our citizens, and that, if we are to continue amongst the Great Powers of the world, we must adopt compulsion as the bedrock of our military system'.[54] Churchill's reply was careful: 'I am disposed somewhat differently toward [compulsory service] now. As to the right of the State and the duty of the citizen there can be no doubt. But I am far less certain that it is necessary or that it would be convenient.'[55] Roberts followed with another letter. He had effect; in September 1914, when Kitchener put forward his argument for mass armies, Churchill alone in the Cabinet pleaded for conscription.[56]

In 1912, the old field marshal promised his friends that he would work harder than ever. His speech to an overflowing audience at the Free Trade Hall in Manchester on 22 October caused a sensation for his comments on Germany:

> *Germany strikes when Germany's hour has struck.* That is the time-honoured policy relentlessly pursued by Bismarck and Moltke in 1866 and 1870. It has been her policy decade by decade since that date. It is her policy at the present hour. It is an excellent policy. It is or should be the policy of every nation prepared to play a great part in history.

The first Balkan War being then fought added weight to his words, emphasising the danger of unpreparedness.[57] The radical press rounded on him, claiming that his real wish for an attack on Germany was unmasked. The *Nation* claimed: 'Lord Roberts is a mere jingo in opinion and character, and he interprets the life and interests of this nation and this Empire by the crude lusts and fears which haunt the unimaginative soldier's brain.'[58]

In his support, the *Daily Mail* insisted:

> Our politicians must give a clear lead in a matter which is vital to the nation. Not one of them but feels in his heart that Lord Roberts speaks the truth. Not one of them but is aware of the grave weakness of the Territorial Force ... Is there no man in the Ministry with courage to stand out, tell the nation the truth, and call upon it to give its answer before reform is too late?

Henry Beauvoir de Lisle, former leader of mounted infantry, approved Roberts's words, and was convinced they came from his observations on a tour of Germany.[59] That year even the reluctant *Times* came to his support. By early spring 1913 the case for compulsion enjoyed its greatest success. Roberts spoke to huge, wildly enthusiastic public meetings: 5,000 listeners at Bristol, over 7,000 at Wolverhampton, more than 10,000 at Leeds. In Glasgow there were 30,000 applications for tickets. The League used new technology: at Leeds, open-air spectators watched his speech flashed paragraph by paragraph on a 45-foot-square screen. A gramophone record presented his case.[60] At a new invasion enquiry which began meeting in 1913, the navy admitted that serious invasion was not impossible, faced by evidence from Roberts and his supporters. The naval manoeuvres of 1913 resulted in the successful landing of an invasion force.[61]

Roberts enjoyed the backing of nearly every important soldier. In December 1910, Ian Hamilton wrote to Lady Roberts that the entire General Staff favoured conscription. Whereas serving soldiers could not speak openly, retired heroes like Evelyn Wood could. In March 1910, the *Daily Express* reported Wood's striking arguments for universal military training in a speech at a City of London Yeomanry dinner. At the Royal Academy banquet earlier that year, he spoke of training soldiers as artists must be trained. Roberts wrote to thank him. In February 1914 although not a League member, Wood accompanied a deputation led by Roberts to urge the Prime Minister to agree to an immediate strengthening of the army.[62]

Roberts's admirers claimed he had aroused public opinion, that the declaration of war in 1914 vindicated his warnings, that Territorial Force deficiencies in numbers, discipline, training and equipment made it incapable of home defence alone and thus regulars must be kept back at a war's outset.[63] Was there any substance to his invasion claims? Colonel Frederic Trench, British military attaché in Berlin 1906–10, warned of a possible German invasion and reported that 'a systematic and thorough study is being made of the possible terrain of operations in Great Britain'.[64] Trench's reports arrived just as the Committee of Imperial Defence was investigating the possibility of invasion under the probing of Roberts and Repington. Not until 23 August 1911, following Agadir, did a small group of ministers, Asquith, Grey, Haldane, Lloyd George, McKenna and Churchill, agree a 'continental commitment' to make arrangements to transport the BEF to France.[65] Fear of invasion before 1914 was real, although Germany's war plan was to throw three-quarters of her military strength through Belgium and into France to gain victory in a rapid campaign. In the East against Russia there would be a holding operation. German planning assumed Britain's army would play a minor role at most. The wartime stationing of Britain's Grand Fleet far to the north in the Orkneys and at Rosyth left the east coast exposed, as German battlecruiser raids showed, but no invasion was attempted. What Roberts's scheme might have done was to provide the BEF with a large reserve of trained men who, mobilised and thrown into battle in 1914, could have inflicted a severe defeat on the German invaders.[66]

Roberts remained an inspiration to reformers. On New Year's Day 1910, Esher drove to Ascot 'to see little Bobs . . . Wonderfully open-minded and virile for so old a man. He is full of modern ultra radical ideas about the army and tactical fighting . . .' Esher was pleased Roberts shared his interest in 'bicycles and motors in war' and believed cavalry charges obsolete. As yet, in the absence of a faster cross-country vehicle for reconnaissance and pursuit, this was not so, although Roberts was worried that 'no steps had been taken to supply aeroplanes and trained aviators'. He had read R.P. Hearne's *Aerial Warfare*. Hearne's widely known book highlighted British vulnerability to German airships in a future conflict. When William Nicholson pooh-poohed the aerial threat, Roberts wrote an open letter to the *Army & Navy Gazette* in 1911 pointing out that Britain had only four military aircraft and it was time something was done.[67]

Roberts's 'Indians' underwent the same transformation as Wolseley's 'Africans'. As his 'young men' became older and senior, they fell out and attracted their own followers. Most successful in this was Henry Wilson through his Staff College teaching. He became close to the Robertses in the years after the South African War.[68] Wilson and Ian Hamilton disagreed on conscription. Years later, after Wilson was shot dead by two IRA men on the steps of his Eaton Square home, Hamilton told Sir Frederick Maurice: 'I have known him better and more intimately and worked more closely together with him than with any other soldier but I had a bad quarrel with him on the conscription question and over what I considered to be his bad influence on Lord Bobs.' He was glad they had made it up and been again on friendly terms.[69] Hamilton had had his ups and downs with the Robertses. Perhaps his marrying the beautiful Jean Muir at Simla had surprised Lady Roberts, who may have had her eyes on the dashing Highlander for one of her daughters.[70] They remained close, however, until the National Service controversy. In November 1905, Roberts congratulated him on *A Staff Officer's Scrapbook* about the Russo-Japanese War. Aileen told 'My dear General Johnnie' how he would have enjoyed seeing her father 'sitting reading to Mother the first chapter of your book – enjoying it so thoroughly – saying "its splendid" to its sentiments – & being interrupted by Mother's "*dear* Johnnie" at intervals; he is quite enthusiastic about it.'[71] They were very unhappy over 'Compulsory Service'. Lady Roberts told him: 'I think Mr Haldane should be made aware of what your devotion to his scheme has cost you in the estimation of your friends & many of the public. I can assure you we *all* have had a hard time of it lately, since that book of yours come [out].'[72] Rawlinson sided with the Robertses. In April 1911 he told his old chief that he was greatly enjoying *Facts and Fallacies*: parts were 'unanswerable'.[73] Nicholson became his own man as his career advanced. In December 1905 he was appointed QMG, and in April 1908, CIGS. He lived up to his sobriquet 'Old Nick'. Repington wrote in January 1906: 'The truth is that he has made so many enemies among our big generals that he is put in as Q.M.G. on trial to see if they will get used to him. He promises to be good and at present butter will not melt in his mouth.'[74]

The saddest rift for the Robertses was with Pole-Carew, the handsome Coldstream Guardsman. Pole-Carew thought Roberts's view of events in South Africa was altogether too optimistic, and he wrote to his Devonshire neighbour Buller: 'I think you know that I having had the temerity to tell Bobs what I considered to be the truth more than once in South Africa have been in his black books ever since. He has done a good deal to make me feel small . . .'[75] He felt his division had been neglected in rewards at the war's end, and hoped Buller, who knew the War Office, might help. Buller replied: 'Between you & me and the doorpost Roberts is a dirty little snob, and it is difficult to say how we could corner a snob.'[76] He gave suggestions, but it was unlikely the lumbering Buller would corner any snob as nimble as Roberts. Eventually Pole-Carew had an answer from Roberts himself: 'It is of course very annoying to you to see people go over your head especially after a career of meritorious service like yours, but it is a matter of common occurrence. I do not agree in your estimate of Nicholson & Ian Hamilton, but everybody has a right to his own opinion.'[77] Roberts had highly commended Pole-Carew in South Africa, but not as highly as Hamilton and Nicholson.[78] To the Rev. J.W. Adams, who had won the VC outside Kabul in 1879, he wrote:

> I need hardly tell you that the breach which has arisen between Pole-Carew and myself has grieved me almost more than anything that has happened to me of late years, and I have found it hard to believe that a man who was my friend from the day he joined me in 1879, should have allowed his judgement and better feelings to be so warped as to render such a breach possible.

Roberts would still have been glad to welcome him to his home 'and forget it all'.[79] It was not to be.[80] Hills-Johnes attempted to mediate and wrote to Pole-Carew: 'I cannot but believe that the action of Lord Roberts which has vexed you must be a passing shadow, and that all will be put right between you two.'[81] Sadly, he was wrong: there was to be no renewal of the friendship.

Letters between Pole-Carew and Buller reinforce the inference that the 'rings' were not exclusive. The historian Tim Travers argued that the Edwardian army's promotions depended on personal favouritism and the patronage of a senior figure.[82] Unfortunately, one of Travers' examples, Henry Wilson, won his advance to Staff College commandant through the support of several men and against the attempt to impose a less well-qualified candidate.[83] Roberts's patronage had aided his protégés, but did they rise beyond their capacity? Neville Chamberlain and George Pretyman got no further than their deserts, which is perhaps why only Roberts experts and snooker historians know their names. Pole-Carew may have been an example of a man who was an able divisional commander, but no better. Henry Wilson was primarily a staff officer. Nicholson's strength too was in administration, his abilities were widely recognised; he reached the rank of British field marshal without commanding troops in battle. Hamilton did well in South Africa, as a fighting general and as Kitchener's chief of staff. At the Dardanelles he failed a stern test, having been dealt a difficult hand by Kitchener. Rawlinson's First World War career was similar to that in South Africa; a shaky time, especially on the Somme, followed by brilliant success, beginning the victorious 'hundred days' on 8 August 1918. Both men enjoyed a leg-up from Kitchener after Roberts's retirement from Whitehall.[84] Travers argues that the personalised nature of the Edwardian army owed much to the Victorian 'rings' and led to career and intellectual rivalries.[85] Keith Jeffery, while admitting strength in Travers's argument points out that it seems 'wholly fanciful' to find a promotion system which did not involve favouritism, regimental loyalties or other intangible personal factors.[86] Roberts's support for reform encompassed a wide range of men.[87]

The two generals who advanced furthest in the Edwardian army were French and Haig. French's forward-looking *Cavalry Drill* manual was partly influenced by the work of General Luck whom Roberts had appointed cavalry inspector in India.[88] Despite Poplar Grove, Roberts looked on French with favour. A gunner colonel told Lawrence Parsons in August 1900: 'Lord Roberts did not seem to like French at first but had gradually come round to have great confidence & dependence in him.'[89] In May 1901 French thanked him for 'a most kind wire' asking about his health and for 'gracious [?] kindness in the expression you have made in your dispatches.'[90] In October, Roberts told Brodrick: 'French has proved himself to be possessed of more than ordinary nerve, more than any other commander in South Africa except Ian Hamilton.' Roberts's criticism was that he was a bad horsemaster and poor staff officer.[91]

French overcame staff work difficulty by relying on Haig.[92] Roberts's alleged antipathy to cavalry is better proven in Haig's case than French's. Roberts praised Haig as a promising officer, but in September 1903 told Kitchener: 'Haig I am surprised to find clings to the old *arme blanche* system, and in the chapter for the Revised Edition of the Drill Book, which was entrusted to him to write, on Collective Training, there is not one word about Artillery or dismounted fire.'[93] His rise was the product of staff professionalism, but also the approval of diverse supporters: Evelyn Wood, French, Kitchener, whom he served as inspector-general of cavalry in India, Haldane and George V.[94] The advance of these future BEF commanders points to a variety of patrons, but also their own merits.

In summer 1903 the Robertses acquired Englemere and settled there. Jean Hamilton, visiting in June 1906, recorded: 'The house is almost a new house and delightful to live in. Lady Bobs delighted with their additions. I am so glad, and it is nice to be with them again.'[95] Roberts wrote from Englemere to Kitchener to renew their friendship, congratulating him on his promotion to field marshal and concluding:

> Now my dear Kitchener, good-bye. Knowing, as I well do, all that you have done for the good of the Indian Army, and remembering how closely we were associated during the war in South Africa, it has caused me real pain to disagree with you on the most important point . . . It will be a great pleasure to all of us at Englemere, to welcome you here when you come home.[96]

Roberts did welcome him, and Edmund Barrow, also a guest, remembered how as a junior officer he was put at ease by the two 'big men'. On another occasion Barrow visited to take tea, and was shown the gun which Freddie had tried to save at Colenso. The guests were late catching their return train and had to run. 'Bobs ran too and the last we saw of him was waving his hat like a boy to us as the train moved off.'[97] In contrast to his undiminished vitality, Lady Roberts's health was poor. To an old friend of Indian days she wrote: 'the horrible depressing climate is such a drawback. I hardly ever go out in the winter. I get such bad attacks of bronchitis and influenza'.[98] Her husband gave her a motor car on their forty-sixth wedding anniversary. He was president of the Berkshire Automobile Club, and told members that he hoped soon to drive himself, but employed a chauffeur. His wife and elder daughter were witnesses of an early fatal road accident in October 1913. A young gentleman cycling with his fiancée swung out to pass their car and ran head-on into another vehicle driven by a young officer of the King's Royal Rifle Corps at the outrageous speed of twenty-five miles per hour. The cyclist was killed instantly. Aileen took the shocked fiancée home.[99]

Roberts confided to Henry Wilson his worries about his name being carried on and whether his daughters would marry.[100] He may have sought a surrogate son in Euan Miller, his godson, whom he took in his carriage to Sandhurst to start there as a cadet. Miller's father, a doctor, had served under Roberts in South Africa. Miller had a distinguished career, joining the King's Royal Rifle Corps, Freddie's old regiment, serving in both world wars, commanding his regiment's 2nd battalion in the defence of Calais in 1940.[101]

As Lady Roberts's health declined, Aileen accompanied her father on public engagements, particularly the opening of rifle-ranges where she would fire the opening shot and almost invariably score a bull. She did not marry, remaining close friends with 'Johnny', 'Rawly', Birdwood and others. Her younger sister Edwina was more fortunate in love. On 9 January 1913, her engagement was announced to Major Henry Lewin, an old friend of her brother's commanding the Royal Field Artillery's 142nd Battery at Bordon. Two days later, she wrote to thank Colonel Dunlop Smith for his congratulations: 'The only sadness is leaving such a beloved home; but I am very wonderfully happy & such a lucky person.'[102] The marriage was at Ascot on 26 February 1913. A dense crowd waited outside the church 'testifying at once to the popular interest in the wedding and the esteem in which Lord Roberts is held'. A carriage driven by officers of the groom's battery took the couple back to Englemere for the reception, cheering spectators lining the route. The Lewins' only child, a son, Frederick, was born after his grandfather's death.[103]

In contrast to family domestic happiness, Roberts was closely involved in Irish events, which appeared in the early months of 1914 to be leading to civil war. Roberts shared his Irish origins with many officers. From Ireland, the British Army drew famous generals and numerous rank and file. While 30,000 Irishmen fought for Britain in South Africa, the war itself and the presence of the much smaller Macbride's Legion with the Boers was a catalyst for Irish nationalism.[104] The Liberals were committed to Irish Home Rule. Irish Unionists mostly in Ulster were opposed. Sir Edward Carson and James Craig mustered Ulster resistance. Huge demonstrations culminated in the signing of the Solemn League and Covenant by close to half a million men and women pledged to refuse the authority of an Irish Parliament. Among Covenant supporters were Roberts, Milner, Lord Halifax, F.E. Smith, Kipling and the composer Edward Elgar.[105] The third Home Rule Bill introduced in April 1912 was a moderate document, but John Redmond and Irish Nationalist MPs regarded it as a step on the road to independence.[106]

It passed the Commons in January 1913; the Lords remained an obstacle. Tension mounted as the Ulster Volunteers under Carson began to arm, matched in the south by the formation of the Irish Volunteers, infiltrated by the fanatical Irish Republican Brotherhood. King George V worked for a compromise without success. In March 1913, Ulster's leaders asked Roberts to command their volunteer 'Army of Ulster'. He declined, and sought someone suitable. 'I have been a long time finding a senior officer to help in the Ulster business,' he said.[107] In April he discreetly approached Lt-General Sir George Richardson who had served on the Bengal staff and in Afghanistan and retired to Ireland. The two were not close, but Richardson accepted after conditions were agreed.[108] In July the Ulster Unionist leadership appointed him GOC the Ulster Volunteer Force (UVF), and in September he told Roberts that soon the UVF 'would be able to hold its own any-where'.[109]

Colonel Jack Seely, War Secretary, and Winston Churchill, First Lord of the Admiralty, took the lead in applying pressure on Ulster. Churchill ordered the Third Battle Squadron to hold its manoeuvres in Irish waters and told Sir John French, then CIGS, 'that if Belfast showed fight his fleet would have the town in ruins in twenty-four hours'.[110] Seely summoned Lt-General Sir Arthur Paget GOC Ireland to the War Office to receive his instructions. Roberts had made his position clear, saying in the Lords that it was unthinkable that the army should be used against the Ulster Volunteers.[111] Paget so hugely misinterpreted and exceeded his instructions that historians have sought explanation in some form of conspiracy. He told senior officers on 20 March 1914 that operations were intended against Ulster to support the government, he expected Ireland 'to be in a blaze by Saturday', and gave them an ultimatum: follow orders or face dismissal, although those domiciled in Ulster could temporarily 'disappear'. He told Brigadier Hubert Gough commanding the 3rd Cavalry Brigade: 'You need expect no mercy from your old friend [Sir John French] in the war office'. Gough decided to offer his resignation, the great majority of officers agreeing. Paget failed to win them over on 21 March, and had to telegraph: 'Regret to report brigadier and fifty-seven officers 3rd Cavalry Brigade prefer to accept dismissal if ordered North'.

How responsible was Roberts for the Curragh Crisis? Wilfrid Blunt and Asquith both saw him behind the army troubles.[112] Gough knew the Robertses well. After leaving Eton he had spent a summer at Versailles learning French with Aileen and Edwina. His father, Charles Gough, had fought in Afghanistan; his uncle was Hugh Gough. He made no contact with Roberts, however, until Seeley's precipitancy and Paget's blundering had created the crisis. Roberts can be indicted more substantially for assisting the creation of an illegal Ulster army. Had Asquith grasped the Ulster nettle early, however, he could have acted effectively against the separate Volunteers.[113]

Word of Paget's bungling and Gough's resistance speedily reached soldiers in England. Henry Wilson and Roberts together drafted a letter on 20 March warning the Prime Minister of the dangers of splitting the army.[114] Gough and two of his three colonels were summoned to the War Office. French as

CIGS tried to arrange measures to prevent further resignations and to extract a Liberal promise not to use the army to coerce Ulster. The Cabinet would not agree the latter. Roberts telephoned French that morning of 21 March, asking him to come to Englemere to discuss matters. French said he was too busy. There were strong words. French recalled a part of their fraught exchange as follows:

> *Roberts:* I am speaking from Ascot. What do you think of this terrible state of affairs?
> *French:* It is very difficult to talk about such matters on the telephone.
> *Roberts:* I hope you are not going to associate yourself with this band of (certain epithets were used which I could hardly catch). If you do you will cover yourself with infamy.
> *French:* I must do my duty as a soldier like everyone else and put up with whatever consequences may ensue.
> *Roberts:* Good-bye.

Roberts admitted he had 'felt strongly and spoke strongly' and warned French that he would have to bear his share of 'obloquy or calumny (I forget which word I used)', if he helped the cabinet to 'carry out their dastardly attempt to bring Civil War'.[115] Both field marshals sought to prevent the army being used for coercion and a split. French, determined to remain loyal to the government, believed resistance to its measures was unconstitutional. Shortly afterward, Roberts received a telegram from Hubert Gough, telling him of events at the Curragh and seeking advice. It was too late for that. Roberts, however, stirred into further action, telephoned the King's private secretary, Lord Stamfordham, and requested an audience. Stamfordham asked him to come at once. When he arrived the King told him that Seely maintained he was 'at the bottom of all the trouble with the army', had incited Gough and called the politicians 'swine and robbers' in his telephone conversation with French. Roberts indignantly denied these charges, assured the King he had not been in contact with Gough for years, and had always advised officers not to resign over the Ulster question. He admitted he was opposed to coercion of Ulster, and told the King that at least half the officers in the army would resign rather than participate in such an operation.[116] The King saw that he was in despair, convinced the crisis would ruin the army. Roberts's depression was deepened by a most unprofitable interview with Seeley at the War Office. He departed in even lower spirits, feeling that the secretary of state was 'drunk with power'. He had discovered that Paget had acted without authority in offering the alternatives to his officers, and left a note telling Gough this. Meanwhile, Asquith insisted Gough be persuaded to return to the Curragh and order restored. He told Seely that there were no grounds for punishing or dismissing the officers, who had only taken a choice forced on them by Paget. Gough arrived at the War Office with his brother Johnny from Aldershot. They found Roberts's note which strengthened their case. French assured them there had been a misunderstanding. He gave his word that the army would not be used to enforce Home Rule on Ulster, but felt unable to put his assurance in writing. French took Gough to see Seely, with Paget and Adjutant-General Spencer Ewart also present. Seely vainly attempted to browbeat Gough, who stubbornly demanded written assurance. Adjutant-General Ewart finally asked Gough whether an officer had any right to question orders to support the Civil Power. Gough replied, 'None whatever, sir. If the GOC-in-C had ordered my brigade to go to Belfast, I should have gone without question.' The mutiny, such as it was, had been sparked by Paget's muddled grasp and inflammatory language.

Gough now sought assurance that the troops under his command 'will not be called upon to enforce the present Home Rule Bill on Ulster, and that we can so assure our officers'. Asquith's Cabinet repudiated such assurances, and Seely resigned. Gough seemed to have triumphed, and was welcomed by cheering troops at the Curragh. Many officers sympathised with him. The Unionist press was jubilant. By contrast, the Liberal *Daily Chronicle* claimed 'the sinister attempt by a military cabal to intimidate the government has signally failed'. In fact, there was a last-ditch effort to produce a Home Rule amendment: the exclusion of Ulster by plebiscite. Redmond, committed to unity, would not accept it.

While Asquith defended his government in the Commons and Wilson strode jubilantly about the War Office boasting that the army had succeeded where the Unionists had failed, French and Roberts sought reconciliation. The former was deeply hurt that he should be accused of betraying the army. Roberts had written him a pained letter on 22 March, denying the 'swine and robbers' comment, and regretting their inability to work together in the crisis. French replied: 'I am bound to say it caused me great pain to hear you conceived it possible that I could adopt any course of action which might "cover me with infamy in the eyes of the army."' On 27 March a general army order tried to prevent a recurrence of Paget's blunder, and reminded officers and men of their duty to obey lawful commands. On 28 March, French and Ewart resigned.[117]

Roberts had supported unconstitutional resistance to an elected government. Yet in the last instance majority rule depends upon respect for minorities, and only belatedly did the Liberals show that. In 1922, the intrinsic strength of the forces for partition was too great: six Ulster counties did split away from Ireland. Roberts and his family were never ashamed that he had acted as he did in a national crisis in which 'the army he loved was in danger of being pulled apart by the alternate forces of duty and conscience'. His speeches and letters were privately printed in a pamphlet entitled 'Ulster and the Army'.[118] His daughter Aileen defended him:

His attitude with regard to the Ulster crisis had been misconstrued by Mr Asquith's Government & he had been accused of having instigated Hubert Gough's action at the Curragh earlier in the year. This accusation

was quite false, & the true account of Father's part in the whole matter
& his opinion of the effect the Government policy would have on the
Army is to be read in the little pamphlet he drew up at the time.[119]

The Liberals' show of strength had failed. Repington wrote in *The Times*
on 23 March 1914, that 'the whole affair had been grossly mismanaged by
Colonel Seely, Mr Churchill and Sir John French, and these three men are
mainly responsible for an episode without parallel in the history of the
army'. The Curragh Incident was the most serious in modern British civil-
military relations; nonetheless, while Gough and sixty officers were prepared
to choose dismissal, 280 others at the Curragh resolved to do their duty. No
direct orders were disobeyed. The army was not torn apart, and those in the
'Mutiny' served valiantly in 1914. The worst military effect was to deepen
suspicion between soldiers and politicians, 'the frocks and the brass-hats'.
The government's defeat did nothing to restore Irish trust. The lesson to
Irishmen was that force, or its threat, brought results. Both sides continued
to arm, the Ulster Volunteers bringing in weapons at Larne, the Irish
Volunteers in broad daylight at Howth. Troops were called out, too late, and
at Dublin as they returned to barracks were stoned by a crowd. They opened
fire, killing three and wounding thirty-eight. To Germans it seemed that
Britain would be paralysed by mutiny and dispute.

The Home Rule Bill passed onto the statue books, but, on the outbreak
of war in August, its coming into effect was postponed. On 3 August,
Redmond pledged Ireland's support against Germany.[120] On both sides of
the border, Ireland temporarily united behind the war effort: 140,460 men
volunteered and 29,779 gave their lives, plus another estimated 5,000 in the
Dominion and American armies. Irishmen fought for the rights of small
nations, to defend Belgium against military despotism.[121]

EPILOGUE

Armageddon

The German Military Power has been a curse to the world . . .
SIR FRANCIS BERTIE, 7 AUGUST 1914

The sad news came in that the gallant and high-minded
bulwark of the Empire, Lord Roberts, had passed away . . .
in a house close by. It had been very sudden.
GENERAL SIR HORACE SMITH-DORRIEN

The assassination of the Austrian Archduke Franz Ferdinand on 28 June at Sarajevo passed almost unnoticed in England because of the Ulster Crisis. The Austrian ultimatum to Serbia, published on 24 July, suddenly made plain the possibility of war to a nation enjoying exceptional summer weather. That day, Henry Wilson and his wife arrived at Englemere for the weekend with the Robertses, Wilson saying the news was more serious than he had ever known it before. On 2 August Germany declared war on Russia, which was mobilising in Serbia's defence, and presented an ultimatum to Belgium for its armies to advance through a country whose neutrality had been guaranteed by treaty. Britain's counter-ultimatum to Germany expired at midnight, Berlin time, on 4 August, when it was clear the Germans would not withdraw.

On the afternoon of 5 August, with Britain formally at war, Roberts with leading soldiers, Cabinet ministers and the First Sea Lord attended a council of war convened at 10 Downing Street by Prime Minister Asquith to decide the deployment of the six divisions of the BEF. Roberts was heard with respect when he questioned whether the BEF could be based at Antwerp to strike in conjunction with the Belgians against the flank and rear of the invading Germans. Unfortunately, the navy could not guarantee sea communications. The proposal was dropped. Roberts returned home to write to the Prime Minister urging decisive action, to send all six divisions of the BEF.[1]

He had already shown strategic insight, in a paper probably written about 1907–8, anticipating the need for no less than 300,000 men to repel a German attack 'that would undoubtedly be made thro' Belgium in order to turn the French left'. Britain had to be able to land 200,000 men on the French coast before the Germans got there. 'All our arrangements, naval and military, must be made with this object in view . . . Every regular soldier we can place in the field must be in readiness for what will be a life and death struggle for the maintenance of the British Empire.' German possession of Holland and Belgium would give her mastery of the northernmost coast of France. He urged the Committee of Imperial Defence to consider a possible invasion, command of home waters, of distant seas, the destination of the BEF, assistance from the Dominions and expansion if war should be prolonged.[2]

On the evening of 5 August, in a bold stroke, Asquith made Kitchener Secretary of State for War. His famous moustache was instantly recognisable, a symbol of military success. He predicted a war of at least three years and sought to raise a huge volunteer army. The task of transforming Britain into a military superpower was immense, and Kitchener knew nothing of the War Office. He lacked good staff officers.[3] On the morning after his appointment, Roberts went to the War Office to congratulate him and seek employment. He suggested that Kitchener appoint an officer as equivalent to a home commander-in-chief, and added that he would be proud to serve. This was too much for a man in his eighty-second year, even an imperial hero. Instead, he was appointed 'Colonel-in-Chief of the various expeditionary forces from the Dominions & also of the Indian Expeditionary force'. His elder daughter wrote: 'He was thrilled by the knowledge that these forces were over to help the Mother Country & pictured the great convoys on their way, from India, Australasia & Canada.' Kitchener may have missed a trick: alone of British generals Roberts had taken note of the writings of Jan Bloch, the Polish banker, and his sage advice might have been invaluable to British strategy. Bloch predicted that conditions of modern warfare gave the defence pre-eminence. Esher wrote: 'Although [Bloch's] book received much attention at the time of its issue, and his theories were given wide publicity, military opinion, except that of Lord Roberts, was hermetically closed against his arguments. But Lord Roberts, in spite of his seventy years, had preserved a mind which, though eager in convictions, was singularly open to novel ideas and new impressions.'[4]

Roberts busied himself assisting batteries of artillery to acquire field telephones and twisting the arm of the War Office to pay for them.[5] He wished 'Godspeed' to departing regiments, notably the Irish Guards and Freddie's 60th Rifles. Major Hugh Dawnay asked him to speak to the 2nd Life Guards and he told them a cavalryman should never be separated from his rifle.[6] This made sense as in the Lee-Enfield the British cavalry had the best firearm of any army. Kitchener kept him informed as master gunner of the BEF's artillery, writing on 15 September 1914: 'We have already taken steps to provide a large number of 6-inch howitzers carrying

FIGURE 15 *The 81-year-old Roberts called on Kitchener the day following his appointment as Secretary of State for War to offer his services in gratitude for Kitchener's help in South Africa, 'but (in his wife's words) above all from his ardent longing to the service to his country'(National Army Museum).*

a hundred-pound shell, both lyddite and shrapnel. We have also made arrangements for 6-inch guns on mobile carriages . . .'[7] His two daughters were on the staff of the Ascot military hospital, and the whole family was instrumental in raising funds to provide comforts for Indian troops deployed to the Western Front. His National Service League collected saddles and bridles, field glasses and telescopes. The 'Lady Roberts Field Glass Fund', mainly driven by Aileen, carried on to the end of the war.[8]

Roberts was desperate to do more. After his death his widow told Kitchener how wholehearted was his desire to give any help because of 'what *you* did for him in South Africa, because of his great anxiety that as the first *soldier* Minister of War you should have a grand success, but above all from his ardent longing to the service to his country . . .'[9] In January 1917 Rawlinson commanding the 4th Army wrote to Aileen: 'So often it crosses my mind when difficult decisions have to be made, "now what would the little man have done" . . .'[10] We know what 'the little man' would have done, from a memorandum of October 1914: the immense British losses could be sustained only if they could turn the German left flank to obtain a decisive victory. If not, it was better to strengthen our existing line 'and let the Germans knock their heads against it'. 'In other words, to set on the defensive not the offensive . . .' This would have been wise until the BEF had the men, heavy guns and ammunition it lacked.[11] Kitchener wished to wait and train his new divisions; but French demands and threatened Russian collapse on the Eastern Front made this impossible.

The help which Roberts gave to one friend had sad consequences. Rudyard and Carrie Kipling's son John longed to enlist, prevented by poor eyesight. In August 1914, he twice failed the eye test for a commission. He seemed set next on enlisting as a private soldier. Then the field marshal became involved. A friend of the Kiplings, Julia Depew, wrote: 'Lord Roberts was an intimate friend of Rud's, and John insisted so much that I believe Lord Roberts rather overlooked the calendar.' Roberts told Kipling: 'I write to say I will gladly nominate John for the Irish Guards if that Regiment will suit him . . . If you would rather not no doubt I could get him nominated for some other Regiment. Kindly let me know.' The offer was accepted and the commission granted. After a year's training John Kipling landed in France on 17 August 1915, his eighteenth birthday. He went into action on the afternoon of 27 September at Loos. Within forty minutes he was fatally wounded. His death left a gap in his parents' lives as great as Freddie Roberts's had left in his.[12]

Roberts intended to visit Indian troops from the time of their landing in France. Sir John French was only too agreeable. He had a good opinion of Roberts's possible influence on Indian morale. He and Aileen set off in November, dining with the Hamiltons the night before the Channel crossing, a reconciliation following the differences over compulsory service. 'I have never seen him more happy or full of go,' thought Hamilton.[13] He was in great spirits, like a boy going on his holidays, shaking off the sadness of the last few weeks when news of the deaths of old friends had come all too often. Leo Amery wrote: 'I doubt if he ever enjoyed two days more . . . Meeting the Indians was a special delight to him and he insisted on stopping his car and talking to every turbaned soldier he met, and visited them in their hospitals . . .' Colonel Percival Marling shook hands with him on the 12th: 'He is wonderful, nearly eighty-three years of age . . .'

On 12 November at 4th Division HQ he called on Rawlinson: 'Lord Bobs and Aileen turned up to tea, both in the best of health and spirit. They went round the Indians and the 6th Division, and I took him to see some of the wounded Indians who are in hospital here.' On 13 November they climbed to the top of the Scherpenberg near Messines for a distant view of the trenches; the day was cold and wet and windy, and Roberts caught a chill. It quickly turned to fatal pneumonia, and after a brief rally he died at 8 p.m. the next day.

Rawlinson recorded 15 November as: 'one of the saddest days of my life. I went in to pay my last respects to my dear chief. I could not believe that he was dead'.[14] Sir John French published a moving tribute on general orders and wrote to Lady Roberts.[15] Kipling, who had known Roberts since the writer was a seventeen-year-old in Lahore, felt his death as a personal loss. Indian soldiers on the Western Front remembered him with affection.[16] At a short funeral service at St Omer on 17 November, Pertab Singh was foremost among mourners; Hindus, Muslims, Protestants and Catholics stood together to sing 'O God our help in ages past'.[17] Marling thought Roberts 'would himself have wished for no happier end . . . in harness to the very last, and with the sound of the shells and the cheers of the Army, British and Native, which he had served so well and commanded so ably, still ringing in his ears'.[18] The view, that his was a good end, was broadly accepted and passed to his family. His younger daughter wrote six days after his death to Dunlop-Smith, who had offered to answer the many telegrams from India: 'You are so kind & I know you loved Father; there was no one like him and it is impossible to believe he is not there to tell all one's troubles & joys to. But he was so happy in France and his leaving was very perfect. No pain & so near the Army he loved.'[19]

The private soldiers too felt his loss. Captain M.D. Kennedy of the Scottish Rifles (the Cameronians) was leading his company with the battalion along rough, muddy roads when a motor-cycle despatch rider approached, dismounted, saluted and told the colonel of Roberts's death. The colonel's face 'assumed a look of incredulity mixed with an expression as though some catastrophic disaster had occurred'.

'What's the trouble?' someone called out.

'Lord Roberts died yesterday,' came the reply.

'Lord Roberts died yesterday? Bobs, the idol of the Army, dead? Why, it couldn't be true!' was the thought that came to everyone's mind as the news was passed from man to man. 'Bobs, dead?' The battalion which had been swinging along to snatches of popular song lapsed into gloomy silence.[20]

The Sunday night edition of *The Times* headed its front page 'Sudden Death of Lord Roberts'. 'One of the most famous and best beloved of British soldiers passes away in an hour of national trial, to prepare for which he had exerted himself with unsparing devotion.'[21] At Oxford, undergraduate Vera Brittain wrote: 'Very sad news greeted us this morning in the death of our dear old Lord Roberts . . . It seems so tragic that he has not lived to see how England, to which his whole life was devoted, will emerge from the struggle in which she is now engaged.'[22]

In death as in life, Roberts's luck did not desert him. On 17 November, the Prime Minister moved in the Commons 'that a monument be erected at the public charge to the memory of the late Field-Marshal Earl Roberts'. In the Irish Crisis Asquith had spoken privately of Roberts 'in senile frenzy'. Now there was a great war; they needed volunteers and an imperial hero would bring them. 'The British Empire experienced a sense of personal loss for which it was wholly unprepared,' said Asquith, 'when it realised that death had suddenly taken from us the oldest and most illustrious of our soldiers.' He recalled not Roberts's devious plotting, but 'the last talk which I had with him only two or three weeks ago, when he pressed upon me his desire to be of use in whatever capacity in this the latest and the greatest of our wars'. Bonar Law, Unionist leader, was less out of place praising Roberts for dying as he had lived 'in the path of duty'. John Redmond, Irish leader, had found Roberts and the Ulster soldiers blocking his great desire, Home Rule: nonetheless, he eulogised Roberts 'as a Waterford man' from a family 'of good old Irish stock'.[23] Soon a recruiting poster would appear beside Kitchener's enormous moustache and pointing finger: one of a white-haired, red-faced little field marshal with the slogan: 'He did his duty, now you do yours.'[24]

Two days after Asquith's speech, Roberts was laid to rest at St Paul's in the presence of the King-Emperor. His widow and daughters at first hoped there would be a small service in the Ascot church where they had worshipped, but there were many who wished to pay tribute, and the government desired to show how the path of duty beckoned. Roberts belonged to the nation. His tomb was to be in St Paul's, near Nelson and Wellington. He was taken to Ascot station on the gun carriage from Colenso which had been a memorial of his son. The procession from Charing Cross Station to St Paul's, of khaki-clad men on both horse and foot escorting the coffin, was watched by vast crowds of men and women of all classes, for at the end of his life Roberts came to epitomise what many believed were intrinsically British qualities: patriotism, courage, duty, family. The war justified him as Cassandra. His pall-bearers were five field marshals, five generals and two admirals. After the service hundreds of mourners waited three hours in driving sleet to file by his open grave in the great cathedral.[25] Nearly all present found the service 'solemn and affecting', the exception being Kitchener who said afterwards to a friend: 'I lay a solemn charge on you; if anything should happen to me in

FIGURE 16 *Field Marshals and Indian Mountain Guns escort Roberts's coffin to his last resting-place at St Paul's Cathedral. His death visiting Indian soldiers on the Western Front was taken as proof of his devotion to duty and the Empire (National Army Museum).*

this war, take care they do not give me a military funeral.'[26] The hymns included 'For all the Saints':

> O may Thy soldiers, faithful, true and bold,
> Fight as the saints who nobly fought of old,
> And win with them the victor's crown of gold.
>
> And when the strife is fierce, the warfare long,
> steals on the ear the distant triumph-song,
> and hearts are brave again, and arms are strong.

Roberts was no saint, but his heart was always brave, and his arm remarkably strong for a small man. The Empire which he championed, however, has long vanished, the causes which he espoused are politically unacceptable, and his whole life was entirely different to ours. Few modern families, even churchgoing ones, start the day with Christian prayers: Roberts told Curzon in a last letter: 'We have had family prayers for fifty-five years. Our chief reason is that they bring the household together in a way that nothing else can.'[27]

So why should we remember today this great Anglo-Irishman's remarkable life? Unlike Marlborough and Wellington, Haig and Montgomery, he was not tested in European war, although both Afghans and Boers proved formidable on their ground. In fact, he has strong claims to be admired, especially by soldiers. His defeat of Ayub Khan on 1 September 1880 finished the Second Afghan War on a high note and ushered in forty years of peace between that country and British India. He turned the tide of war in South Africa by a brilliant strategic offensive, reversing humiliating defeats. He campaigned for better soldiers' pay and conditions of service.[28] He built up a comradeship-in-arms with 'the martial races' of northern India; among these Gurkhas continue to serve with the British army. He and his wife pioneered Army Nursing in India. Inspired by the ideas of Spenser Wilkinson, he initiated reforms which gave the British Army the staff system that saw it through two world wars. He warned of the coming threat from Germany and urged readiness for a conflict which he predicted. After his October 1912 speech in Manchester the *Evening Standard* declared angrily: 'Do not talk to us as if the Kaiser could play the part of a Genghis Khan or an Attila, ravening round the world at the head of armed hordes to devour empires and kingdoms.' The fires of Louvain and the massacre of Dinant, Bethmann-Hollweg's 'September Programme' of annexations in Belgium and France, the treaty of Brest-Litovsk by which Germany took Russian Poland, Lithuania, Courland and Finland, and installed a puppet regime in the Ukraine – all these justify Roberts in his warning.[29]

Posterity will judge, but the men of his time knew a man of flesh and blood. For all his contradictions and the divisions he raised, Roberts drew friends and admirers. One of these, Lord Curzon, told his fellow peers:

> We see his alert figure . . . kindly in manner, exquisite in courtesy, modest in bearing. In the later years of his life he seemed to combine the ripe wisdom of years with the eternal fresh-heartedness of youth, and that was perhaps the explanation why he found himself so easily in touch with men of every age and period of life, and became the friend, and even the confidant, of those who very likely had only entered the world when Lord Roberts's name had already been made.

Kitchener, his comrade-in-arms, told the Lords of

> the affectionate veneration and high esteem with which the Army regarded the late Field-Marshal . . . I, more than most men, had occasion to learn and admire his qualities of head and heart; his ripe experience and sage counsel were fully and freely offered to me to the end. To us soldiers, the record of his life will ever be a cherished possession.[30]

NOTES

Chapter 1: A visit to Lord Roberts

1   Staff at the house told me there had been a private halt serving Englemere, but A. Jowett, *Jowett's Railway Atlas of Great Britain and Ireland* (London, 1989) shows no such stop.

2   Chartered Institute of Building, *The History of Englemere* (Woking, 1997). Personal visit.

3   J. Viscount Morley, *Recollections* (2 vols, London, 1917), II, p. 188; D. Hamer, 'John Viscount Morley', ODNB.

4   Leo Amery, *My Political Life* (3 vols. London, 1953), I, p. 216; letter from the late Major Douglas Goddard, former Deputy Chief Executive, Chartered Institute of Building; D. Goddard, *Master of None: the Life Enriched: Reminiscences of a 20th Century Survivor* (privately printed, 2009), pp. 216–18.

5   Dolaucothi-L9188, Edwina to Lady Hills-Johnes, 7 March 1895; L13401, Roberts to Lady H-J, 5 January 1910.

6   J.F.C. Fuller, *The Last of the Gentleman's Wars* (London, 1937), p. 48.

7   W.S.Churchill, *Ian Hamilton's March* (London, 1900), pp. 281–2; G. Seaver, *Francis Younghusband* (London, 1952), p. 95.

8   IOL, Mss Eur F206/312, Dorothy MacNabb's account of a dinner party at Englemere, Ascot with Lord and Lady Roberts, 6 December 1906. The Peiwar Kotal painting now hangs in the National Army Museum.

9   M.V. Brett, ed., *Journals and Letters of Reginald, Viscount Esher* (4 vols, London, 1934–8), I, p. 78; II, pp. 265, 270, 432.

10 Bodleian Library, Violet Milner papers, C557/2, 11 January 1900.

11 Letter to the author from Major Douglas Goddard. The camp was dispersed long before the gates of Englemere and the guns went for scrap metal in the Second World War.

12 IOL, Eur Mss F206/312, Dorothy Macnabb's account.

13 Bobs, 228–11.

14 Maj-Gen Sir G. Younghusband, *A Soldier's Memories in Peace and War* (London, 1917), pp. 228–30.

15 NAM, 2008-11-55, Charles Hume papers, Chamberlain to 'Dear Ursula', 21 December 1930.

16 E.T. Raymond, 'Roberts and Kitchener', in *Portraits of the New Century* (London, 1928), p. 165.

17 Speech at the Albert Hall, 23 December 1907, reported in *The Times*,
    24 December 1907.

18 W.S. Churchill, *Life of Lord Randolph Churchill* (2 vols, London, 1906), I,
    p. 490.

19 IOL/L/MIL/17/5/1613. *Short Report on the Important Questions dealt
    with during the tenure of Command of the Army by General Lord Roberts
    1885–1893* (Simla, 1893), *passim*, pp. 122–4 for nursing.

20 P. Mason, *A Matter of Honour: an Account of the Indian Army, its Officers
    and Men* (London, 1974), p. 341.

21 A start on the 'rings' could be made in I.F.W. Beckett, 'Wolseley and the ring',
    SOTQ, no. 69 (January 1992), pp. 14–25 and I. Hamilton, *Listening for the
    Drums* (London, 1944), pp. 212ff.

22 By now he was a field marshal, and field marshals never retired.

23 Bobs 83/1, 19 December 1899.

24 L. Scholtz, *Why the Boers Lost the War* (Basingstoke, 2005), p. 59.

25 N. d'Ombrain, *War Machinery and High Policy: Defence Administration in
    Peacetime Britain 1902–1914* (Oxford, 1975), p. 141 *et seq.*

26 NAM, Ellison papers 8704-35-621, Harris to Ellison, 31 December 1934.

27 A.J.A. Morris, *The Scare-mongers: the Advocacy of War and Rearmament*
    (London, 1984), pp. 320–1.

28 M. Gilbert, *Servant of India: a Study of Imperial Rule from 1905 to 1910 as
    told through the correspondence and diaries of Sir James Dunlop Smith*
    (London, 1966), pp. 6, 13, 164.

29 J.M. Brown, *Modern India: the Origins of an Asian Democracy* (Oxford,
    1994), pp. 189, 193.

30 Morley, *Recollections*, II, 20 July 1909.

31 K26, Curzon to Kitchener, 26 August 1900.

32 Col. H.B. Hanna, *Lord Roberts in War* (London, 1895), pp. 5, 57–60.

33 *Inter alia*, Bobs 148, Neville Chamberlain's comments on Hanna's history and
    King's College, Liddell Hart archives, Maurice papers, Roberts to Maurice,
    28 August 1904.

34 Gen. J.L. Vaughan, *My Service in the Indian Army – and after* (London, 1904),
    p. 216.

35 C.R. Low, *Major-General Sir Frederick Roberts: a Memoir* (London, 1883), pp. 386–7.

36 Low, preface, p. iiin.

37 Note 33 above.

38 Bobs 139, vol. 10, 4 January 1897.

39 As 1972 when W.H. Hannah's *Bobs: Kipling's General: the Life of Earl
    Roberts of Kandahar* appeared.

40 G.W. Forrest, *Life of Lord Roberts* (London, 1914), preface, p. v.

41 *The Times*, 16 November 1914, p. 9, editorial and 'Nestor of the Army'. The
    year following, 1915, a number of biographies appeared, usually like Harold

Wheeler's, quoting Roberts's words: 'this great Empire can only be maintained by the exercise of self-denial, by training, by discipline, by courage'.

42 Bobs 203–5, Aileen Roberts to Churchill, 15 March 1930 and 7101-23-181, Sandars to Aileen Roberts, 7 May 1921.

43 *Letters written during the Indian Mutiny by Fred. Roberts. Afterwards Field-Marshall Earl Roberts*, With a preface by his daughter Countess Roberts (London, 1924).

44 S.H.F. Johnston, *British Soldiers* (London, 1944), p. 36.

45 Hamilton, *Listening for the Drums*, p. 159.

46 G. Powell, *Buller: a Scapegoat: a Life of General Sir Redvers Buller 1839–1908* (London, 1994), pp. 199–200 states this, but I can find no mention in J. Hussey, 'John Fortescue, James Edmonds and the History of the Great War: a Case of "Ritual Murder"?', *JSAHR*, 70 (1992), pp. 101–13.

47 Sir J. Fortescue, 'Lord Roberts', in W.R. Inge, ed., *The Post Victorians* (London, 1933). Cf. L. Strachey, *Eminent Victorians* (1918). Roger Stearn kindly brought Fortescue to my attention.

48 See Hamilton 13/91, Aileen Countess Roberts to Ian Hamilton 11/9/1933 and Hamilton to Aileen, 13/9/1933 on Fortescue's inaccuracies.

49 James, pp. 122–3.

50 James, preface, p. xiv. He also destroyed Ian Hamilton's letters, but these are preserved elsewhere.

51 R. Kruger, *Good-bye Dolly Gray* (London, 1959 and 1964), p. 369.

52 T. Pakenham, *The Boer War*, pp. 242–3.

53 Pakenham, *The Boer War*, p. 458. Pages 456–8 summarise Pakenham's defence of Buller and indictment of Roberts.

54 See comments in preface: Lady MacGregor, ed., *The Life and Opinions of Major-General Sir Charles Metcalfe MacGregor* (2 vols, Edinburgh, 1888), I, p. x.

55 W. Trousdale, ed., *War in Afghanistan 1879-1880: the Personal Diary of Major General Sir Charles Metcalfe MacGregor* (Detroit, 1985), pp. 63, 70, 117, 236.

56 E. Spiers, *The Late Victorian Army 1868–1902* (Manchester, 1992).

57 Spiers, *Late Victorian Army*, pp. 310, 314.

58 B. Robson, *The Road to Kabul: the 2nd Afghan War,* pp. 273–4. Robson also wrote the biography of Roberts in the new ODNB and edited an Army Records Society volume.

59 D. Judd and K. Surridge, *The Boer War* (London, 2002).

60 Judd and Surridge, *The Boer War*, pp. 161, 167.

61 *Why the Boers Lost,* pp. 59, 70. Essential reading: K. Surridge, *Managing the South African War: Politicians v. Generals, 1899–1902* (Woodbridge, 1998), A. Wessels, *Lord Roberts and the War in South Africa 1899–1902* (Stroud, 1900) and R.J.Q. Adams, 'Field Marshal Earl Roberts: Army and Empire,' in J.A. Thompson and A. Meija, *Edwardian Conservatism: Five Studies in Adaptation* (London, 1988). Modern critics are H. Strachan, *The Politics of the British Army* (Oxford and New York, 1997), pp. 93–5, 109–115 and H. Streets,

'Military Influence in Late Victorian and Edwardian Popular Media: the Case of Frederick Roberts', *Journal of Victorian Culture*, vol. VIII, pt. II, pp. 231–56, and, *Martial Races: the Military, Race and Masculinity in British Imperial Culture 1857–1914* (Manchester and New York, 2004).

62   D. French, *British Strategy and War Aims 1914–1916* (London, 1986), p. 33.

63   Imperial War Museum, *The 1912–1922 Memoirs of Captain M.D. Kennedy, OBE*.

64   P. Marling, *Rifleman and Hussar* (London, 1931), p. 349.

65   F.S. Oliver, *Ordeal by Battle* (London, 1915), preface, pp. xxiv–v.

Chapter 2: Irish and Indian beginnings

1   W.J. Bayley, 'The Roberts Family of Waterford', *Journal of the Waterford and South-East of Ireland Archaeological Society*, vol. 2 (1895), pp. 98–103.

2   T. Hennessey, *Dividing Ireland: World War I and Partition* (London, 1998), pp. 8–124.

3   Lecture by Nicholas Perry at Army Records Society AGM, 2007: analysis of 1,100 landed families between 1828 and 1927 showed 53 per cent of sons were commissioned, ten times the number entering the law or the Church.

4   K. Jeffery, *An Irish Empire: Aspects of Ireland and the British Empire* (Manchester, 1996), pp. 8, 9, 17, 77.

5   NAM 1955-04-66, 'Statement of the Services'; Low, pp. 2–3; Lt-Col Ivor Edwards-Stuart, *A John Company General* (Bognor Regis, 1983), *passim; The Times*, 30 September 1932, p. 13.

6   Jeffery, *An Irish Empire*, p. 78. The author points out that the two greatest 'Indian' field marshalls, Roberts and Auchinleck, fit this pattern exactly.

7   Maj. G.F. MacMunn, *The Armies of India* (London, 1911), pp. 1–81.

8   NAM 1955-04-66, 'Statement of the Services', extract of letter dated 11 January 1815; Low, p. 3 footnote cites the letter as if referring to Abraham.

9   NAM, 1955-04-66, nos 15 and 16. This collection (1801–34) comprises mostly testimonials.

10   NAM, 1955-04-66, f. 21, 10 January 1833.

11   He did attend the wedding of Frederick Roberts's younger daughter; see below.

12   B. Robson, 'Abraham Roberts', in ODNB; R.B. Saksena, *European & Indo-European Poets of Urdu & Persian* (Lucknow, 1941), pp. 128–31; G. Moorhouse, *India Britannica* (London, 1983), p. 184. Family information based on researches of Lt-Col R. Ayers.

13   Edwards-Stuart, *John Company General*, p. 38.

14   Bristol Street Directories list him at 1, The Mall in 1835 and No. 8 from 1836–44, an impossibility as he was in Afghanistan. He was on leave to 1851, but no longer listed. Information from Mrs Jane Bradley of Clifton Library Service.

15 D. Jones, *A History of Clifton* (Clifton, 1992); information from Mrs Angela Brown, Blue Badge Guide.

16 N. Pevsner, *The Buildings of England: North Somerset and Bristol* (Harmondsworth, 1958), pp. 444–5, 449.

17 Information from Mrs Jane Burgess, Evercreech Historical Society.

18 Edwards-Stuart, *John Company General*, p. 150.

19 Letters, preface.

20 Written on the 100th anniversary of the Field Marshal's death: *The Times*, 30 September 1932, p. 13: 'Lord Roberts – Some personal memories – Field Marshal and Reformer' by Brig. H.F.E. Lewin (son-in-law).

21 The loss was revealed to the public by the *Daily Express* of 28 October 1930. See NAM, Ellison papers 8704-35-711.

22 P. Macrory, *Signal Catastrophe* (London, 1966), p. 127; M. Yapp, *Strategies of British India* (Oxford, 1980), p. 312; Sir J. Fortescue, *A History of the British Army* (13 vols, 1899–1935), XII, pp. 144–5.

23 Letters, preface, p. xii.

24 Information from Mr John Sheaf of Hampton. The filter beds have now been replaced by a modern version of the green which was in front of Hill House when Roberts was at Hampton. Roberts inspected Indian troops at Hampton Court for the 1902 and 1911 coronations.

25 G. Orwell, *The Lion and the Unicorn* (London, 1941). Orwell's view is not supported by Roberts's career.

26 According to B. Robson in the ODNB, he was on leave 1844–51, presumably using influence to try to obtain this regiment; Edwards-Stuart, *John Company General*, p. 176.

27 Letters, preface, p. xviii.

28 H.C. Maxwell Lyte, *A History of Eton College* (4th edn, London, 1911), pp. 436, 452, 459. Information from Mrs Penny Hatfield, college archivist.

29 Low, p. 12; *Eton Chronicle*, no. 1505, 19 November 1914.

30 Lyte, *History of Eton*, p. 569.

31 *Eton Chronicle,* no. 1382, 20 December 1911.

32 *Eton Chronicle,* no. 1505, 19 November 1914.

33 Information from Sebastian Puncher, assistant archivist at Sandhurst.

34 H. Thomas, *The Story of Sandhurst* (London, 1961), pp. 80–103.

35 *The Times*, 5 December 1923, p. 18, Godwin-Austen obit.

36 Roberts's *Sandhurst Record*, downloaded from their website; information from Sebastian Puncher, to whom I am grateful; James, p. 8. Paucity of Sandhurst cadet records is a handicap to biographers. They were thrown out during the Second World War.

37 *The Times*, 30 September 1832, p. 13, 'Field Marshal Lord Roberts' by Brig-Gen. Lewin.

38 Letters, preface, p. xviii.

39 Bobs, 5504–64, item 3.

40 'Seminary' became 'College' in 1856. J.M. Bourne, 'The East India Company's Military Seminary, Addiscombe, 1809–1858', *JSAHR*, 57 (1979), p. 206, n. 1.

41 It closed in 1892, its buildings now used by the Catholic school, Wimbledon College. Information from Mr Charles Toase, Museum of Wimbledon.

42 Caulfield's details in Major V.C.P. Hodson, *List of the Officers of the Bengal Army* (London, 1927), p. 327.

43 Roberts's details are in IOL/L/MIL/221, ff. 248ff. and IOR/L/MIL/9/335.

44 Col. J.M. Vibart, *Addiscombe: Its Heroes and Men of Note. With an Introduction by Lord Roberts of Kandahar* (Westminster, 1894).

45 Vibart, *Addiscombe*, p. 315 lists 3,466 cadets.

46 P. Stanley, *The White Mutiny: British Military Culture in India 1825–1875* (1998), p. 30, n. 93.

47 J. M. Bourne, 'The East India Company's Military Seminary, Addiscombe, 1809–1858', *JSAHR*, 57 (winter, 1979), pp. 206–22.

48 Bobs, 5504–64, item no 9; also Low, p. 13 and James, p. 11.

49 Low, p. 13; F.S. Price, *History of Caio* [Carmarthenshire] (Swansea, 1904), p. 67.

50 Vibart, *Addiscombe*, intro, p. v.

51 Bourne, 'East India Company's Military Seminary', p. 222.

52 Bobs, 5504–64, item 12. Addiscombe closed in 1861 with the abolition of the EICo. Army and was sold to developers in 1863 for £33,600.

53 Letters, preface.

54 Low, pp. 13–14.

55 P. Sykes, *Sir Mortimer Durand* (London, 1926), pp. 25, 39; cf. *Forty-One Years*, pp. 3–6.

56 *Forty-One Years*, pp. 5–6.

57 R. Hyam, *Empire and Sexuality: the British Experience* (Manchester, 1991), pp. 117–18; L. James, *Raj: the Making and Unmaking of British India* (London, 1997), pp. 207–30.

58 *Forty-One Years*, p. 9; Elsmie-Stewart, *Field-Marshal Sir Donald Stewart*, p. 15.

59 W.W. Hunter, *The Imperial Gazetteer of India*, vol. VII, (Calcutta, 1881), p. 356; *Forty-One Years*, pp. 11–12.

60 *Forty-One Years*, p. 10. Major-generals normally retired at sixty-two.

61 *Forty-One Years*.

62 Low, pp. 15, 45, quoting letter from Brind; James, p. 16.

63 *Times*, 5 December 1823, p. 18, Godwin-Austen obit.

64 Deputy Assistant Quartermaster-General.

65 Bobs, 225, 'Some turning points . . .' Some disparity in detail between this account written in 1910 and *Forty-One Years*, pp. 25–6.

66 Edwards-Stuart, *John Company General*, p. 206.

67 *Forty-One Years*, p. 15.

68 P.E. Roberts, *History of British India* (3rd edition, Delhi, 1977), pp. 359–60; D. Gillard, *The Struggle for Asia 1828–1914* (London, 1977), p. 97.

69 *Forty-One Years*, p. 30.

70 *Memorials of the Life and Letters of Major-General Sir Herbert Edwardes . . . by his wife* (2 vols. London, 1886), pp. 261–2.

71 *Forty-One Years*, p. 10.

72 *Forty-One Years*, p. 31.

73 Yapp, *Strategies of British India*, pp. 578–9.

74 H. Kakar, *A Political and Diplomatic History of Afghanistan* (Leiden, 2006), p. 161. For a favourable account of Britain's Afghan policy, see C. Tripodi, 'Grand Strategy and the Graveyard of Assumptions: Britain and Afghanistan, 1839–1919', *Journal of Strategic Studies*, vol. XXXIII, pt V, pp. 701–25.

75 *Forty-One Years*, p. 33.

76 C. Allen, *Soldier Sahibs* (London, 2001), pp. 243, 248.

Chapter 3: 1857

1 Quoted in R. Kipling, *Something of Myself* (London, 1937), pp. 193–4.

2 Letters, p. 4, n. 2.

3 Bobs, 225, 'Some of the Turning Points in my Career'.

4 *Forty-One Years*, p. 241.

5 C. Hibbert, *The Great Mutiny: India 1857* (London, 1988), p. 217. Lt-Gen S.L.Menezes, *Fidelity & Honour: the Indian Army from the Seventeenth to the Twenty-First Century* (New Delhi, 1993), p. 189 gives a higher sepoy number, 313,500. For Oudh, R. Mukherjee, *Awadh in Revolt 1857–1858* (Delhi, 1984).

6 *Forty-One Years*, pp. 236–43.

7 Quoted in H.F.B. Wheeler, *The Story of Lord Roberts* (London, 1915), p. 33. C.A. Bayley, *Empire and Communication* (Cambridge, 1996), pp. 331–2 questions the chupattis story as a mistake by the Lt-Governor of the North-West Provinces. See R. Johnson, *Spying for Empire* (London, 2006), p. 77 for the ambiguity.

8 Bobs, 97, Vol. I, p. 43, to R. Bosworth Smith, 15 April 1884. Bayley, *Empire and Communication*, p. 318.

9 Bobs, 8310–155.

10 See note abbreviations.

11 Bobs, 97–1, to R. Bosworth Smith, 15 April 1884; *The Times*, 10 July 1890, p. 8, 'The Flag on the Lucknow Mess-House'; letters to Lee Warner and Colvin quoted in James, pp. 258–9.

12 Sir G. Forrest, *A History of the Indian Mutiny, 1857–58* (3 vols, Edinburgh, 1904).

13 Sir G. Forrest, *Life of Lord Roberts,* preface, p. v.

14 Good arguments in Menezes, *Fidelity & Honour*, pp. 157ff., 182–3; an exception is S. David, The *Indian Mutiny 1857* (London, 2002); see his appendices. Also Hibbert, *The Great Mutiny*, p. 408, n. 27.

15 Bobs, 8310-155-3, 22 May 1857; Letters, p. 6.

16 *Forty-One Years*, pp. 231–40.

17 Bobs, 8310-155-13, to mother, 30 September 1857, his twenty-fifth birthday; Letters, p. 72.

18 Two Bombay regiments mutinied, none in the Madras Army. Menezes, *Fidelity & Honour*, pp. 179–82.

19 Edwardes, *Memorials of the Life and Letters of Edwardes*, I, p. 261.

20 *Forty-One Years*, p. 35; Sir G. Forrest, *Life of Field Marshal Sir Neville Chamberlain* (London, 1909), pp. 331–2 has the conference on 13 May.

21 Low, p. 18.

22 *Forty-One Years*, pp. 37–8; Forrest, *Field Marshal Neville Chamberlain*, p. 332.

23 Bobs, 8310-155-1, 14 May 1857; Letters, p. 2.

24 *Forty-One Years*, p. 35; Gen. Sir E. Hamley, 'Low's Life of Sir Frederick Roberts,' *Blackwood*, CXXIV (1883), p. 779.

25 Bobs, 8310-155-3, 22 May 1857; Letters, p. 7.

26 *Forty-One Years*, pp. 60–2. His Mutiny experience made Roberts a believer in swift action, but Menezes, *Fidelity & Honour*, p. 170 points out that clumsy disarming could tip regiments into mutiny.

27 Bobs, 8310-155-2, 21 May 1857: Letters, p. 4.

28 Col. G.J. Younghusband, *The Story of the Guides* (London, 1908), pp. 1–3; A.J. Guy and P.B. Boyden, *Soldiers of the Raj: the Indian Army 1600–1947* (London, 1993), p. 133.

29 *Forty-One Years*, p. 40.

30 Bobs, 8310-155-2 & 3, 21 and 22 May 1857. He was wrong. Afghans killed women and children in the retreat from Kabul of 1842. Sikhs were among the mutineers. See Menezes, *Fidelity & Honour*, pp. 173, 185.

31 Bobs, 8310-155-2, 21 May 1857; Letters, p. 4; *Forty-One Years*, p. 5, n. 1.

32 Bobs, 8310-155-4, 11 June 1857; Letters, p. 12. On blowing mutineers from guns, see Neville Chamberlain's justification, Forrest, *Field Marshal Neville Chamberlain*, p. 333 and G. MacMunn, *Turmoil in 1914 and After* (1925), p. 35.

33 *Forty-One Years*, pp. 67–9; see also David, *Indian Mutiny*, p. 146.

34 *Forty-One Years*, p. 57.

35 MacMunn, *Armies of India*, pp. 102–3; T.A. Heathcote, *The Military in British India* (Manchester and New York, 1995), pp. 90–5.

36 Allen, *Soldier Sahibs*, p. 284.

37 Bobs, 8310-155-4, 11 June 1857; Letters, p. 12.

38 Low, p. 21.

39 Low, pp. 22–3; Bobs, 8310-155-5, 29 June 1857; Letters, p. 18; *Forty-One Years*, pp. 78–82.

40 Quoted in Hibbert, *Great Mutiny*, p. 122.

41 *Forty-One Years*, p. 89 and footnote.

42 Heathcote, *The Military in British India*, p. 109.

43 Major H.W. Norman, *A Narrative of the Campaign of the Delhi Army* (London, 1858), p. 20.

44 Hibbert, *Great Mutiny*, p. 275.

45 Hibbert, *Great Mutiny*, pp. 275–6.

46 Menezes, *Fidelity & Honour*, pp. 176–7.

47 Hibbert, *Great Mutiny*, p. 283.

48 *Forty-One Years*, p. 96; Letters, p. 29.

49 Elsmie-Stewart, *Stewart*, p. 121.

50 Elsmie-Stewart, *Stewart*, pp. 47–64. Part of the account Stewart wrote in 1894 for his friends. Roberts inserted it as Appendix I to *Forty-One Years*, pp. 544–6.

51 W. Lee-Warner, *The Life of Field Marshal Sir Henry Wyllie Norman* (London, 1908). See Roberts's admiring comments, ibid., pp. 309–10.

52 Elsmie, *Stewart*, p. 69.

53 Bobs, 225, 'Turning points'; *Forty-One Years*, p. 97 and Appendix I, pp. 544–6.

54 Low, pp. 26–7.

55 Low, pp. 28–9; NAM 6208-94, 'Extract from a letter home written by Lt J Hills . . . 19 July, 1857'; *Forty-One Years*, p. 103. Cf. David, *Indian Mutiny*, p. 273.

56 Bobs, 8310-155-6, 23 July 1857; Letters, pp. 24–5; 41, *Forty-One Years*, p. 106.

57 A. Ward, *Our Bones are Scattered: the Cawnpore Massacres and the Indian Mutiny of 1857* (London, 2004) and R. Mukherjee, 'Satan Let Loose upon the Earth: the Kanpur Massacres of India in the Revolt of 1857', *Past & Present*, vol. 128 (1990), pp. 92–116.

58 Bobs, 8310-155-8, 25 August 1857.

59 *Forty-One Years*, pp. 114–16; Low, p. 343; Allen, *Soldier Sahibs*, pp. 308–11; David, *Indian Mutiny*, p. 291, n.

60 Bobs, 8310-155-9, August 1857; Letters, pp. 50–1.

61 *Forty-One Years* p. 118.

62 *Forty-One Years*, p. 121.

63 Allen, *Soldier Sahibs*, pp. 167, 173–5, 286–8.

64 Bobs, 8310-155-10, 7 September 1857; Letters, p. 55.

65 Bobs, 8310-155-12, 26 September 1857; Letters, p. 61ff.

66 Letters, p. 61ff.; *Forty-One Years*, pp. 128–30.

67 Bobs, 8310-155-11, 16 September 1857; Letters, p. 60.

68 Bobs, 8310-155-12; Letters, p. 68; *Forty-One Years*, pp. 135, 142.

69   NAM, 8310-155-11, 16 September 1857; Letters, pp. 58–61.

70   David, *Indian Mutiny*, p. 301 n.

71   Bobs, 8310-155-11; Letters, p. 61.

72   Elsmie-Stewart, *Stewart*, p. 69, Henry Norman's account.

73   David, *Indian Mutiny*, p. 306; Allen, *Soldier Sahibs*, pp. 326–7.

74   Forrest, *Field Marshal Neville Chamberlain*, p. 374. This was generous of
     Lawrence as he and Nicholson were no friends. See Nicholson's letters to Herbert
     Edwardes in IOL, Eur Mss E211/3. Allen's *Soldier Sahibs* conveys the power of
     Nicholson's presence; other modern writers deplore his intolerance and brutality.

75   Elsmie-Stewart, *Stewart*.

76   Bobs, 8310-155-12, 26 September 1857; Letters, p. 70.

77   Norman, *Narrative of the Delhi Army*, pp. 23, 26.

78   *Forty-One Years*, p. 139; the 4th was the 60th Rifles; H. Streets, *Martial
     Races: the Military, Race and Masculinity in British Imperial Culture
     1857–1914* (Manchester and New York, 2004), p. 80. The Sirmur battalion
     became the 2nd King Edward VII's Own Gurkha Rifles.

79   Menezes, *Fidelity & Honour*, pp. 173–4, 185. I am grateful to Dr Peter
     Boyden for pointing this out.

80   Bobs, 8310-155-12, 26 September 1857; Letters, p. 69; Low, p. 48.

81   Low, p. 52, quoting battery commander's letter.

82   Bobs, 8310-155-13, 30 September 1857; Letters, pp. 72–3.

83   Bobs, 8310-155-14, camp near Agra, 15/10/1857; Letters, pp. 79–80.

84   Quoted in Low, p. 58.

85   Low, p. 323.

86   Bobs, 8310-155-15, 27 September 1857; Letters, pp. 87–8; Low, pp. 60–1.

87   Hibbert, *Great Mutiny*, p. 330.

88   Bobs, 8310-155-16, 1 November1857; Letters, p. 94; Low, p. 64.

89   Bobs, 8310-155-18, 25 and 30 November 1857; Letters, pp. 103–4.

90   Bobs, 8310-155-18; Letters, pp. 109–10; Low, p. 65.

91   Bobs, 8310-155-18; *Forty-One Years*, pp. 179–83.

92   Low, pp. 60–7; *Forty-One Years*, p. 187; J. Lehmann, *All Sir Garnet: A Life of
     Field-Marshal Lord Wolseley* (London, 1964), p. 65: Campbell ordered Robert
     'to go and place a regimental colour at top of the newly won Mess House . . .'
     Wolseley was brevet (acting) major.

93   Bobs, 8310-155-18; Letters, pp. 104–6.

94   Bobs, 8310-155-18; Letters, p. 109. He was mentioned seven times.

95   Bobs, 8310-155-19 & 20, 12 and 20 December 1857; Letters, p. 116.

96   Bobs, 8310-155-21, 31 December 1857; Letters, p. 119.

97   Bobs, 8310-155-21, 31 December 1857 and 8310-155-22, 21 January 1858;
     Letters, p. 122. Maxwell (1828–89) attended Addiscombe, commissioned
     June 1848, retired as Hon. Col., 25 December 1878.

98 Bobs, 8310-155-22, 12 January 1858. He also understated it in *Forty-One Years*, p. 215, but by then he was famous.

99 *Forty-One Years*, p. 215.

100 Stanley, *The White Mutiny*, pp. 94–5.

101 NAM, 6301-70, 'Copy of a letter by Lt Hills . . .'.

102 Bobs, 8310-155-28, 11 February 1858; Letters, p. 135. For the citation Bobs, 5504-64, no. 15, Hope Grant's letter, 8 February 1858; 'Lieutenant Roberts's gallantry has on every occasion been most marked.'

103 David, *Indian Mutiny*, pp. 335–6; *Forty-One Years*, p. 216.

104 Bobs, 8310-155-25, 25 February 1858; Letters, pp. 139–40.

105 *Forty-One Years*, p. 218; Captain O. Jones, *Recollections of a Winter Campaign in India, 1857–1858* (London, 1859), p. 145.

106 *Forty-One Years*, pp. 226–7; David, *Indian Mutiny*, pp. 342–3.

107 Bobs, 8310-155-28, 27 March 1858; Letters, p. 155.

108 Hamley, 'Low's Life of Sir Frederick Roberts,' pp. 779–82.

109 Bobs, 8310-26, 12 March 1858; Letters, pp. 148–9.

Chapter 4: Marriage and staff service

1   Bobs, 8310-155-21, 31 December 1857; Indian Mutiny Letters, p. 119.

2   *Forty-One Years*, p. 252.

3   *The Times*, 22 December 1920, p. 13.

4   His military record is in WO25/465. Bews's wife Mary Elizabeth may have died soon after, for she does not appear in *Forty-One Years* whereas Roberts's parents do frequently. Lt-Col. R. Ayers kindly traced family details.

5   Local information from J. Walton, historian in residence, Dunhill Education Centre, Waterford.

6   *The Mail and Waterford Express*, 18 May 1859, 'Marriage in High Life' on the front page. J. Walton supplied details on Rev Ryland.

7   Reproduced in James, facing p. 97 and Major-General Sir Owen Tudor Burne, *Memories* (London, 1907), facing p. 50.

8   Burne, *Memories*, pp. 48 and 50.

9   *The Times*, 9 June 1859, p. 12.

10 *Forty-One Years*, p. 252.

11 *Forty-One Years*, p. 253. Roberts's harrowing accounts of journeys of earlier years are partly to show how the British improved communications. The account of this voyage must have owed something to his wife's vivid memories of the ordeal, her first such journey.

12 A. Lycett, ed., *Kipling Abroad: Traffics and Discoveries from Burma to Brazil* (London, 2010), p. 35.

13 *Forty-One Years*, pp. 253–4.

14 Judith M. Brown, *Modern India: The Origins of an Asian Democracy* (Oxford, 1994), p. 105.

15 *Forty-One Years*, pp. 260–2.

16 Account of changes mainly from Spear, *Oxford History of Modern India*, pp. 229–36; Roberts, *History of British India*, pp. 380–95; J. Keay, *A History of India* (London, 2000), pp. 445–7.

17 Stanley, *White Mutiny*, p. 139. This was not the first; see S.L. Menezes, 'Race, Caste, Mutiny and Discipline in the Indian Army . . .' in Boyden and Guy, *Soldiers of the Raj.*

18 Heathcote, *Military in British India*, Ch. 7, pp. 160ff. explains its evolution. *Forty-One Years*, pp. 270–1 simplifies.

19 B. Robson in ODNB.

20 Stanley, *White Mutiny, passim*, esp. Ch. 10, pp. 205ff. for the changes; quote from p. 271.

21 Heathcote, *The Military in British India*, pp. 80–5; D. Omissi, *The Sepoy and the Raj: the Indian Army 1860–1947* (London, 1994), pp. 76–112.

22 Bobs, 8310-155-27, 15 March 1858; Letters, p. 151.

23 Roberts, *History of British India*, pp. 383–4; Heathcote, *Military in British India*, pp. 109–10.

24 R.B. Saksena, *European & Indo-European Poets of Urdu & Persian* (Lahore, 1941), pp. 128–31; cf. W. Dalrymple, *The Last Mughal: the Fall of a Dynasty: Delhi, 1857* (London, 2006), pp. 291–2. I am grateful to Tony Heathcote for clarification. It is unclear whether he fought against the British or was merely caught up in the terrible events of 1857.

25 Bobs, 49, 'Turning points'; *Forty-One Years*, p. 254.

26 Low, p. 92.

27 *Forty-One Years*, pp. 254–6.

28 *Forty-One Years*, pp. 255–9.

29 T.R. Metcalfe, 'Charles John, Earl Canning', ODNB.

30 *Forty-One Years*, pp. 268–9.

31 Hamley, 'Low's Life', p. 782.

32 *Forty-One Years*, pp. 264–5, early 1860. The only Roberts story in Max Hastings's book of military anecdotes.

33 Burne, *Memories*, p. 48.

34 *Forty-One Years*, p. 273.

35 Bobs, 51, see also Bobs, 51, 25 March 1862 when he was still hoping she had recovered her strength.

36 *Forty-One Years*, p. 277.

37 L/MIL/7/10631, extract of letter from QMG, 2 July 1861. The Umbeyla Expedition papers are in IOL: L/MIL/7/10631-10634. In Forrest, *Field Marshal Neville Chamberlain*, Ch. XIV.

38 C. Allen, *God's Terrorists: the Wahhabi Cult and the Roots of Modern Jihad* (2006); S. Haroon, *Frontier of Faith: Islam in the Indo-Afghan Borderland*

(New York, 2007), pp. 42–3; also Q. Ahmed, *The Wahhabi Movement in India* (London, 1994). I owe this point to Keith Surridge.

39 L/MIL/7/10631, Durand letter, 24 September 1863.

40 Allen, *God's Terrorists*, pp. 169–70.

41 L/MIL/7/10632, Col. Heythorne memos, 19 and 22 November 1863; E.M. Lloyd and J. Lunt, 'John Adye' in ODNB.

42 Adye's sketches enclosed in IOL, L/MIL/7/10634, his (and Roberts's) reports so combined 'purely private matter . . . with military information, that they are unfit for submission to the Government'.

43 *Forty-One Years*, p. 289.

44 *Forty-One Years*, p. 286 and n. See also R. Johnson, *The Afghan Way of War: Culture and Pragmatism: a Critical History* (London, 2011).

45 L/MIL/7/10632, secret telegraph no 379, 25 December 1863. In *Forty-One Years*, p. 292, Roberts attributes the words to one chief, a man with one eye and one arm.

46 Quoted in Forrest, *Field Marshal Neville Chamberlain*, p. 445.

47 L/MIL/7/10633, *Gazette of India Extraordinary*, 30 January 1864, also giving Chamberlain's closing dispatch.

48 E.M. Lloyd and J. Lunt, 'Neville Chamberlain', ODNB; Low, pp. 95–7.

49 H.L. Nevill, *Campaigns on the North-West Frontier* (London, 2005 reprint), pp. 50–62; T.R. Moreman, *The Army in India and the Development of Frontier War, 1849–1947* (London, 1998), pp. 24–5.

50 *Forty-One Years*, p. 286 n.

51 IOL, Mss Eur, D951/3, Owen Tudor Burne papers, 3 March 1864.

52 *Forty-One Years*, p. 293.

53 *Forty-One Years*, pp. 293–4; Low, pp. 97–8.

54 *Forty-One Years*, p. 295. Cholera is caused primarily by drinking infected water or eating infected food. The Allahabad outbreak was probably part of the Fourth Pandemic in 1863–75. For British policy see M. Harrison, *Public Health in British India: Anglo-Indian Preventive Medicine 1859–1914* (Cambridge, 1994), pp. 99ff.

55 P. Curtin, *Disease and Empire: the Health of European Troops in the Conquest of Africa* (Cambridge, 1998), pp. xi, 40; T.J. Holland and H.M. Hozier, *Record of the Expedition to Abyssinia* (London, 1870), the official account; D. Bates, *The Abyssinian Difficulty: the Emperor Theodorus and the Magdala Campaign 1867–68* (Oxford, 1979).

56 Bobs, 5504-04, 'Highlights of career', letter dated 30 September 1867.

57 *Forty-One Years*, p. 296.

58 *Forty-One Years*, p. 297.

59 Bobs, 140, 'Abyssinia Notebook'.

60 J.K. Laughton and A. Lambert, 'George Tryon', ODNB.

61 *Forty-One Years*, p. 301, and for Roberts's praise of Tryon.

62 D.G. Chandler, 'Magdala', in B. Bond, ed., *Victorian Military Campaigns* (London, 1967), p. 135.

63 Chandler, 'Magdala', pp. 107–59.

64 Low, pp. 103–4. See also Maj-Gen Russell's comments in Low.

65 Bobs, 5504-04, no. 25, 'Services of Lt-Col Roberts . . .'; F. Myatt, *The March to Magdala: the Abyssinia War of 1868* (London, 1870), p. 175: it was unusual to choose an officer from the base; '[Napier] did this to indicate his satisfaction at the way the various administrative arrangements had been carried out . . .'

66 *Forty-One Years*, p. 302.

67 Curtin, *Disease and Empire*, p. 46. Those from the followers, the Bombay Coolie Corps, were more numerous.

68 Low, p. 107; *Forty-One Years*, p. 302.

69 And a watery grave when *HMS Camperdown* rammed his flagship *Victoria* during manoeuvres.

70 James, p. 59.

71 *Forty-One Years*, p. 303.

72 James, p. 67.

73 *Forty-One Years*, p. 309.

74 Elsmie-Stewart, *Stewart*, pp. 186–7, letter, 6 September 1871 to his wife. Their house was 'Ellerslie' so presumably lent to the Robertses for certain periods.

75 Bobs, 49, 'General Orders . . . 10 April 1876', Napier's parting shot.

76 T.R. Moreman, 'Robert Napier', ODNB.

77 *Forty-One Years*, p. 328.

78 Elsmie-Stewart, *Stewart*, p. 186, letter of 17 August 1871.

79 Low, pp. 109–12.

80 Low, p. 114; the original was published in the *United Services Institute of India Journal*, vol. 2.

81 *Forty-One Years*, p. 315.

82 Bobs, 140, 'Narrative of the Cachar Column, Lushai Expeditionary Force by Major-General Fred Roberts . . .'

83 Low, p. 125.

84 *Forty-One Years*, p. 319.

85 Low, p. 126.

86 Low, p. 126.

87 Bobs, 140, 'Narrative of the Cachar Column . . .' published in the *Gazette of India*, 4 May 1872. The expedition lasted from November 1871 to February 1872.

88 *Forty-One Years*, p. 319.

89 *Forty-One Years*, p. 320.

90 T. A. Heathcote, *The Indian Army: the Garrison of British Imperial India* (Newton Abbot, 1974), p. 161.

91 Elsmie-Stewart, *Stewart*, pp. 191–5; Allen, *God's Terrorists*, pp. 198–9.

92 The Indian Army and Civil List for July 1873, p. 75 and January 1874, p. 75.

93 Vibart, *Addiscombe*, p. 598; James, p. 71.

94 Robson-India, p. 7, letter dated 21 May 1874.

95 Edwards-Stuart, *John Company General*; NAM, Hodson Card Index; *Forty-One Years*, p. 325 gives date of death incorrectly. On his house there is a plaque: 'Sir Abraham Roberts, GCB. A distinguished Indian General lived in this house for many years and died here on December, 28th, 1873. His son Field Marshal Earl Roberts also lived here in his early life.'

96 Elsmie-Stewart, *Stewart*, p. 136.

97 Low, p. 128.

98 P. Magnus, *Edward VII* (New York, 1964), pp. 132–43.

99 Wheeler, *The Story of Lord Roberts*, p. 109; A.P. Macdonnell, *Report on the Food-Grain Supply . . . during the Famine of 1873–4* (Calcutta, 1876); R. Temple, *The Story of My Life* (2 vols, London, 1896), I, pp. 226–48 does not name Roberts, only 'the assistance of many excellent military officers'. *Forty-One Years*, pp. 325–6 underplays this; presumably Roberts did not want specially to draw attention to famines.

100 Magnus, *Edward VII*, p. 139; Hibbert, *Great Mutiny*, p. 391.

101 Bobs 49 for both items, the letter, 11 June 1874.

102 Bobs, 139, vol. 1; *The Times of India,* 9 November 1878.

Chapter 5: War in Afghanistan

1 Bobs 225, 'Some of the Turning Points in my Career'; also Low, p. 131.

2 RA, VIC/ADDE/1/8225, Napier to Cambridge, 25 May 1878.

3 IOL, Eur Mss E218/18, 8 April 1876, pp. 70–3.

4 O.T. Burne, 'The Empress of India', *Asiatic Quarterly Review*, III (1978), p. 22; B.S. Cohn, 'Representing Authority in Victorian India', in E. Hobsbawm and T. Ranger, *The Invention of Tradition* (Cambridge, 1983); *Forty-One Years*, pp. 332–5; Low, p. 130.

5 Roberts, *History of British India*, pp. 452–3; Cf. defence of Lytton in B. Balfour, *The History of Lord Lytton's Indian Administration 1876–1880* (London, 1899), pp. 189–239 and attack in M. Davis, *Late Victorian Holocausts* (London, 2001).

6 A. Preston, 'Frustrated Great Gamesmanship: Sir Garnet Wolseley's Plans for War against Russia 1873–1880', *International History Review*, II (1980), pp. 239–67.

7 IOL, Eur Mss E218, Lytton papers, Lytton to Salisbury, 30 July and 28 September 1876, to Disraeli, 3 October 1876.

8 Low, p. 130.

9   Robson-India, p. 3.

10   Preston, 'Frustrated Great Gamesmanship', p. 242.

11   S. Gopal, *British Policy in India 1858–1905* (Cambridge, 1965), p. 66.

12   Robson-Kabul, pp. 42–6.

13   *Forty-One Years*, pp. 304–8.

14   The classic account of Central Asian rivalry is P. Hopkirk, *The Great Game* (London, 1990); supplemented by D. Gillard, *The Struggle for Asia 1828–1914* (London 1977); W.C. Fuller, *Strategy and Power in Russia 1600–1914* (New York, 1992); D. Lieven, *Empire: the Russian Empire and its Rivals from the Sixteenth Century to the Present* (2003); A. Marshall, *The Russian General Staff and Asia 1800–1917* (Abingdon, 2006).

15   Published 1883. Analysis in Lieven, *Empire*, pp. 108–9, extended to decline of British Empire pp. 108–127.

16   Hopkirk, *Great Game*, p. 363; A. Preston, 'Sir Charles MacGregor and the Defence of India, 1857–1887', *The Historical Journal*, XII, I (1969), pp. 58–77.

17   H. Lee, *Brothers in the Raj: The lives of John and Henry Lawrence* (Oxford, 2002), pp. 413–6; Hopkirk, *Great Game*, p. 386.

18   Marshall, *The Russian General Staff and Asia*, p. 135.

19   *The Times*, 23 August 1878, p. 10 'Abdullah Jan'. He had imprisoned Yakub for four years.

20   RA, VIC/ADDE/1/8397, Haines to D. of Cambridge, 26 September 1878.

21   Forrest, *Neville Chamberlain*, p. 471 quoting letter 2 September 1878.

22   Robson-Kabul, pp. 46–52. In *Forty-One Years*, pp. 335, 341–8, Roberts outlines the events clearly while throwing the entire blame on the Russians and the Amir.

23   Forrest, *Neville Chamberlain*, p. 485; M. Lutyens, *The Lyttons in India* (London, 1979), p. 153; W.S. Blunt, *Secret History of the English Occupation of Egypt* (London, 1907), p. 64.

24   RA, VIC/ADDE/1/8397, 26 September 1878.

25   Hanna, *Lord Roberts in War*, esp. pp. 5, 7–8, 60, 62–3.

26   Col. H.B. Hanna, *The Second Afghan War 1878–79–80* (3 vols, London, 1899–1910), I, pp. 280–2; Lady B. Balfour, *Personal and Literary Letters of Robert Lord Lytton* (2 vols, London, 1906), ii, p. 131.

27   Elsmie, *Stewart*, p. 214.

28   RA, VIC/ADDE/1/8408, Hardinge to Cambridge.

29   R. Goldsborough, 'Passed over for "Strong Political Reasons": Sir Frederick Maude and the Politics of Appointment in the Second Afghan War', *JSAHR*, 90 (autumn 2012), p. 158.

30   Quoted T. Barfield, *Afghanistan: a Cultural and Political History* (Princeton and Oxford, 2010), p. 139.

31   Background analysis, Barfield, *Afghanistan, passim* and Johnson, *The Afghan Way of War*.

32   Marshall, *Russian General Staff and Asia*, p. 138.

33 For a full account of the war the reader is referred to Hanna, *The Second Afghan War* and Robson-Kabul. Atwood's *March to Kandahar: Roberts in Afghanistan* (Barnsley, 2008) focuses on Roberts.

34 Description in Major J.A.S. Colquhoun, *With the Kurram Field Force* (London, 1881).

35 Hanna, *Second Afghan War*, I, pp. 326–32.

36 Dolaucothi L13355, R to Hills, 20 December, 1878. Tytler played a part in capturing Ft Ali Masjid in the Khyber Pass for Sam Browne's column.

37 RA, VIC/ADDE/1/840, 8448 & 8712. Later Villiers was ordered to Africa.

38 RA, VIC/ADDE/1/840, 8448 & 8712 and *Forty-One Years*, p. 355.

39 Dolaucothi L13355, R to Hills, 20 December, 1878 and *Forty-One Years*, pp. 355–64; IOL, L/MIL/5/678, no. 2538 incl. R's despatch 5 December 1878; description and illustration in T.A. Heathcote, *The Afghan Wars 1838–1919* (London, 1980), pp. 106–10.

40 Maude letterbook in posession of his descendant Mrs Alexandra Gray, p. 137; Napier's speech in Lords, *Hansard*, vol. 249, column 18, 4 August 1879.

41 H. Hanna, *Lord Roberts in War*, pp. 16–19. Cf. Hanna, *Second Afghan War*, II, pp. 85–92.

42 Dolaucothi L13355, R to Hills, 20 December 1878.

43 Dolaucothi L13355, R to Hills, 20 December 1878; IOL, L/MIL/5/678, No.2697 sentences on sepoys confirmed, 26 December 1878.

44 C.G. Robertson, *Kurum, Kabul & Kandahar: Being a Brief Record of Impressions in Three Campaigns under General Roberts* (Edinburgh, 1881), p. 41

45 Lytton, *Personal and Literary Letters*, II, p. 131.

46 RA, VIC/ADDE/1/8550, 20 February 1879. Cf. Hanna, *Lord Roberts at War*, p. 11.

47 Dolaucothi L13355, R to Hills, continuation of letter, 22 December 1878. For Cory see C. Allen, *Kipling Sahib* (London, 2009), pp. 115–16. Cory left the paper before the young Rudyard Kipling joined it in 1882. The story is supported by the future Lord Minto: see IOL, Mss Eur D1227, f. 177, letter to mother, 2 March 1879.

48 RA, VIC/ADDE/1/8434, Baker to Cambridge, 7 November 1878.

49 Robson-Kabul, pp. 92–3; IOL, L/MIL/5/678, nos 2707–2710.

50 IOL, L/MIL/5/678, nos 2710 & 2712; L/MIL/5/680 no. 5949, telegram 30 January 1879. Robson-Kabul, pp. 93–4.

51 Quoted, apparently with approval, by H. Streets, 'Military Influence in Late Victorian and Edwardian Popular Media: the Case of Frederick Roberts,' *Journal of Victorian Culture*, Vol. VIII, pt II (2003), p. 236.

52 Streets, 'Military Influence', pp. 236, 153, n. 37; Robson-India, p. 85.

53 IOL, L/MIL/17/14/35, 'Return to . . . the House of Commons, dated 16 June, 1879 – 'A Copy of papers relating to the Proceedings of Maj-Gen Roberts in the Khost Valley on the 7th & 8th days of January 1879'; *Hansard*, 3rd ser., CCXLIII, cols 1312–13.

54 *Hansard*, 3rd ser., CCXLIII, cols 1312–13, see enclosures.

55 Robson-Kabul, p. 94.

56 Robson-India, pp. 61–8, 81–3, 85–7.

57 *Times of India*, 10 April 1879, p. 2, 'General Roberts and the "Standard" Special'; *Hansard*, Commons Debates, 18 March 1879, vol. 244, c1159.

58 Robson-Kabul, p. 111.

59 OH, II, p. 194; Lt-Col C.G. Gardyne, *The Life of a Regiment: the History of the Gordon Highlanders from 1816 to 1898* (London, 1929), p. 101; T. Gould, *Imperial Warriors, Britain and the Gurkhas* (London, 1999).

60 Hanna, *Second Afghan War*, II, p. 345. C.B. Mitford, *To Caubul with the Cavalry Brigade* (London, 1881), p. xv states Cavagnari was in low spirits.

61 Lee, *Brothers in the Raj*, p. 416.

62 Lutyens, *The Lyttons in India*, p. 158.

63 Quoted in Robson-Kabul, p. 121; stand of the Guides: C.M. MacGregor, *The Second Afghan War* (6 vols, Calcutta and Simla, 1885–6), II, pp. 281–6, account of Rissaldar-Major Kakshband Khan; Younghusband, *The Story of the Guides*, pp. 97–116.

64 IOL/P&S20/Memo5/6, 'Attack on the British Embassy at Kabul, Sept, 1879'; Hanna, *Second Afghan War*, III, p. 37; Elsmie-Stewart, *Stewart*, p. 296.

65 Lytton, *Personal and Literary Letters*, II, p. 196.

66 Lytton, *Personal and Literary Letters*, II, p. 131.

67 Bobs, diary.

68 Hanna, *Second Afghan War*, III, p. 61.

69 RA, VIC/ADDE/1/8908 & 8917, 9 and 16 October 1879, to E. Johnson and Haines respectively; for Baker as an 'African' see H. Brackenbury, *Some Memories of My Spare Time* (London, 1909), p. 228 and T.R. Moreman in the ODNB.

70 Trousdale, *War in Afghanistan*, p. 101.

71 *The Times*, 19 October 1878 and 18 August 1879. He just missed being with Cavagnari.

72 Price, *History of Caio*, p. 69; Dolaucothi, L11092 and L11094, Chamberlain to Hills-Johnes, 11 and 14 December 1900.

73 IOL, L/MIL/5/680, nos 7733 and 7922, telegrams 10 September and 3 October 1879; Robson-India, p. 113; Gen. Sir J.L. Vaughan, *My Service in the Indian Army – and After* (1904), p. 212.

74 Hanna, *Second Afghan War*, III, pp. 45–6.

75 Ibid, III, pp. 47, 63; Trousdale, *War in Afghanistan*, p. 92.

76 R. Johnson, 'General Roberts, the Occupation of Kabul, and the Problems of Transition', *War in History*, 20(3) (2013), p. 306 citing *Forty-One Years*, p. 244. Johnson's is a very full and balanced account of Roberts at Kabul; Robson-Kabul, p. 125.

77 Trousdale, *War in Afghanistan*, pp. 104–5.

78 Low, p. 240.

79 MacGregor, *Life and Opinions*, II, p. 125; Hanna, *Second Afghan War*, III, p. 79; Bobs diary, 1879, entry 6 October; account of battle IOL L/MIL/5/681, nos 7924, 7925 and 7959 encl. R's despatch 20 October 1879.

80 Mitford, *To Caubul with the Cavalry Brigade*, pp. 36–7.

81 Bobs diary, 1879, entries 10 and 11 October; Low, p. 248 n.; IOL, L/MIL/5/681, nos 7926 and 7927.

82 SOAS, Durand papers, Item PP Ms55/21 (Diary 1875–80), entry 15 October 1879; Trousdale, *War in Afghanistan*, p. 104; H. Hensman, *The Afghan War* (London, 1881), p. 54.

83 Mitford, *To Caubul with the Cavalry Brigade*, p. 84.

84 SOAS, Durand papers, Item PP Ms55/21 (Diary 1875–80), entry 16 Ocober 1879; Trousdale, *War in Afghanistan*, pp. 104, 106.

85 Johnson, 'General Roberts, the Occupation of Kabul and the Problems of Transition', p. 307; Eur Mss. E218, vol 21, pp. 93–5, Lytton to Roberts, 21 October 1879.

86 Low, p. 250.

87 Hanna, *Second Afghan War*, II, p. 99.

88 Eur Mss 108/101(a), P6/36a, 15 October 1879.

Chapter 6: 'One equal temper of heroic hearts'

1 Lutyens, *The Lyttons in India*, p. 164. The Liberals had scant respect for the veracity of these letters, but Lytton was greatly disappointed when Disraeli would not allow them to be published, thinking this would vindicate his policy. Ibid., p. 165. Roberts published them as Appendix VII of *Forty-One Years*, pp. 556–60.

2 SOAS, Durand diary item PP/MS/55/31, personal letters, no.19, 25 October 1879.

3 RA, VIC/ADDE/1/8995, Baker to Cambridge, 20 November 1879.

4 IOL, L/MIL/5/681, no. 7959, enclosures.

5 Low, p. 250.

6 Price, *History of Caio*, p. 69; *The Times*, 9 October 1878, p. 11.

7 Dolaucothi L13649, Stewart to Hills, 2/12/1879. Stewart repeated the view of Sher Ali, governor he appointed at Kandahar, but Sher Ali's troops deserted to the enemy in July 1880.

8 Hanna, *Second Afghan War*, III, p. 139 and footnote.

9 Dolaucothi L11099, Chapman to Hills, 17 October 1879.

10 NAM, Baker papers 7804–76–14, Lady Edith Lytton to Baker, 24 October 1879.

11 IOL, Mss Eur LP518/4, pp. 732–5.

12 RA, VIC/ADDE/1/8882, Cranbrook to Cambridge, 11 November 1879.

13 IOL, Eur Mss 108/101(a), p6/38, 12 November 1879 and 108/98(a), P3/57, 15 November; Trousdale, *War in Afghanistan*, pp. 101, 108, 111–12, 114.

14 Hanna, *Second Afghan War*, III, p. 140.

15 Trousdale, *War in Afghanistan*, p. 108, 113–14. He claimed to have saved five, but eighty-seven were hanged.

16 Hanna, *Second Afghan War*, III, p. 140; IOL, L/MIL/5/682, nos 9661–7.

17 Hensman, *The Afghan War*, pp. 54, 111–12, 132–7, 177.

18 Vaughan, *My Service*, p. 216.

19 Robson, *Roberts in India*, pp. 131–3.

20 *The Times*, 15 November 1879, p. 5.

21 Robson-Kabul, p. 141; Robson-India, p. 163 giving the printed despatch of 18 February 1880; Appendix A to vol. III of MacGregor's official history states in contrast to his journal that trials were properly carried out and all evidence heard.

22 Quoted Robson-Kabul, p. 179, n. 14.

23 Sir M. Gerard, *Leaves from the Diary of a Soldier and Sportsman during Twenty Years Service . . .* (London, 1903), p. 283; Mitford, *To Caubul with the Cavalry Brigade*, p. 85; Dolaucothi, L14195, Hills to Roberts, 25 January 1880.

24 Hanna, *Second Afghan War*, III, pp. 149–50; Robson-Kabul, p. 144.

25 Hanna, *Second Afghan War*, III, pp. 158–9 shows *Forty-One Years*, p. 427 is not entirely truthful.

26 For Massy, see Atwood's *The March to Kandahar: Roberts in Afghanistan*, pp. 79, 106–9, 118–19, based on IOL, L/MIL/5/683, NO12513 nr.

27 IOL, L/MIL5/683, nos 10049–53; SOAS, Durand papers, PP MS 55/21, diary 1875–80, entry 19 December 1979.

28 See Chapter 1, p. 4; for the fighting Hanna, *Second Afghan War*, III, pp. 185–94.

29 IOL/L/MIL/5/683, no. 10625 ops at Kabul, December, 1879.

30 IOL, Eur Mss 108/101(a), letter to wife begun 18 December 1879.

31 Hanna, *Second Afghan War*, III, pp. 226–7; SOAS, Durand Papers, PP MS 55/21, diary 1875–1880; RA, VIC/ADDE/1/9028, 13 January 1880.

32 J. Duke, *Recollections of the Cabul Campaign of 1879 and 1880* (London, 1883), pp. 300–1; E. Yorke, *Playing the Great Game* (London, 2012), p. 277.

33 Hanna, *Second Afghan War*, III, pp. 243–51; Robson-Kabul, pp. 170–3. SOAS, Durand Papers, item PP MS 55/21, diary 1875–80, 23 December; IOL, L/ MIL/5/683, no. 10625; Maj-Gen. L.N. Soboleff, *The Anglo-Afghan Struggle* (trans. Major Gowan, Calcutta, 1885), p. 86. Tony Heathcote introduced me to this source.

34 Hove Public Library, Wolseley papers, SA2 South Africa 1879–1880 Military: Private Letterbook, p. 217.

35 Hanna, *Second Afghan War*, III, pp. 292–3.

36 Soboleff, *Anglo-Afghan Struggle*, pp. 84–5.

37 Hensman, *Afghan War*, pp. 298, 302.

38 Dolaucothi, L14194, Hills to Roberts, 17 January 1880.

39 Mitford, *To Cabul with the Cavalry Brigade*, pp. 197–8.

40 IOL, Eur Mss F108/101(a), P6/36, Geo White letter 15 to 17 October 1879; SOAS Library PP MS 55/212, Durand to sister, no. 19, 26 October 1879; Soboleff, *The Anglo-Afghan Struggle*, pp. 60–1.

41 IOL/L/MIL5/681, mp 1959, R's report 20 November 1880; L/MIL/5/683, no.12513, letters between R and Adjutant-General Greaves.

42 NAM 8304–32–220, Charles Gough papers, 29 January 1880.

43 RA, VIC/ADDE/1/9067, Haines to Cambridge, 4 February 1880; Bobs, 147–3, removal of Massy.

44 NAM, 8108/9–46–10, 13, 18, Haines papers, Cambridge to Haines, 5 and 26 March and 30 April 1880. Under pressure, Haines eventually revised his judgement. NAM Haines papers, 9148, to Cambridge, 5 April 1880. Hanna, *Second Afghan War*, III, p. 193, always a critic, blames Roberts and claims this was Cambridge's fair-mindedness.

45 RA, VIC/ADDE/1/9173, Baker to Cambridge, 21 April 1880, written to support Roberts.

46 The newspaper extract is in Bobs, 160, letters to Martin Dillon. There is no evidence for this in Cambridge's correspondence.

47 F. Harrison, letter to *The Times*, 17 February 1880, p. 10, 'The Executions in Cabul'.

48 SOAS, Durand Papers, item PP MS 55/21, diary 1875–80, 10 January 1880.

49 F. Harrison, 'Martial Law in Kabul', reprinted from the *Fortnightly Review*, with additions (London, 1880).

50 For example, *Hansard*, Commons Debates, 15 February 1880, vol. 251, cc. 1008–9.

51 *The Times*, 6 February 1880, p. 5, 'General Roberts at Cabul'.

52 *Hansard*, H of L debates, 13 February 1880, vol. 250, cc. 579–82; *The Times*, 14 February 1880, pp. 6, 9.

53 Hanna, *Second Afghan War*, III, pp. 272, 273–4: Hensman, *Afghan War*, p. 204.

54 Robson-India, intro, pp. xix–xi

55 Correspondence in Robson-India, p. 432, n. 9 and 10; Bobs 23 to Lytton, 29 January 1880.

56 *Hansard*, Lords Debates, vol. 249 c. 19, tribute by Napier in H. of Lords, 4 August 1879.

57 MacGregor, *Second Afghan War*, v, p. 258; Barfield, *Afghanistan*, p. 142.

58 Dolaucothi, L3651 & L3653, 7 and 26 March 1880.

59 Elsmie-Stewart, *Stewart*, pp. 315–16, Stewart to wife, 16 March 1880.

60 Elsmie-Stewart, *Stewart*, pp. 331–3, 333–5; Gen E.F. Chapman, 'Two Years under Field-Marshal Sir Donald Stewart in Afghanistan 1878–1880,' *Blackwoods Magazine* (Edinburgh, 1902), pp. 259–60.

61 J. Morley, *Life of Gladstone* (3 vols, London, 1903), II, p. 595.

62 Elsmie-Stewart, *Stewart*, p. 321.

63 IOL, Mss Eur 108/98(b), P3/64, 13 April 1880.

64 See A. Denholm, *Lord Ripon 1827–1909: a Political Biography* (London, 1982); R.C.K. Ensor, *England 1870–1914* (Oxford, 1936), p. 64.

65 Elsmie-Stewart, *Stewart*, p. 350.

66 Elsmie-Stewart, *Stewart*, p. 360.

67 Robson-India, pp. 157, 160–1; also Eur MssD951/3, f,161,R. to Burne, 1 February 1880.

68 James, pp. 146–7; also in Elsmie-Stewart, *Stewart*, p. 143.

69 Dolaucothi, L13663, 4 June 1880; L14205, Hills to V. Pugh, 14 August 1880.

70 IOL, Eur Mss. F132/31, letters of 8, 17, 28 April 1880.

71 James, pp. 146–7. In *Forty-One Years*, p. 465 Roberts hints at his chagrin: 'it was not in human nature to feel absolute satisfaction in yielding up the supreme command . . . into the hands of another . . .'

72 IOL, Eur Mss, F426/11, f. 22, 10 June 1880, Euan-Smith to Griffin.

73 IOL, Eur Mss. F132/31, 10 March 1880. The British still intended to separate Herat and Kandahar from Kabul.

74 H.K. Kakar, *Government and Society in Afghanistan: the Reign of Amir Abdul Rahman* (Austin, 1979); Barfield, *Afghanistan*, pp. 142–3; Johnson, *The Afghan Way of War*, intro.

75 Elsmie-Stewart, *Stewart*, pp. 365–6, letter to wife, 5 July 1880.

76 Dolaucothi, L14205, 21 August 1880. See also OH, IV, pp. 96–7; Griffin's key role is described with tactful reference to Roberts in his obit., *The Times*, 11 March 1908, p. 11 and less tactfully by K. Prior in ODNB.

77 RA, VIC/ADDE/1/1880, 12 April 1880.

78 Heathcote, *Afghan Wars*, p. 148.

79 Add Mss 43,574, Ripon papers, ff. 141 et seq.; Soboleff, *Anglo-Afghan Struggle*, pp. 264–8.

80 Accounts of Maiwand are also *beshumar*. I have used L. Maxwell, *My God Maiwand* (London, 1979); B. Robson, 'Maiwand, 27 July 1880,' *JSAHR*, 51 (1973), pp. 194–221; Robson, 'The Kandahar Letters of the Rev. Alfred Cane', *JSAHR*, 69 (1991), pp. 146–60, 206–20; Heathcote, *Afghan Wars*, pp. 148–51.

81 Heathcote, *Afghan Wars*, pp. 151–3.

82 *The Times*, 29 July 1880, p. 5.

83 RA, VIC/ADDE/1/9268, 28 July 1880.

84 *The Times*, 30 July 1880, p. 10. Perhaps from Lytton.

85 IOL, Kandahar Correspondence (2 vols, Simla, 1880–1), i, p. 45; NAM, Haines papers, 8108/9–29, no. 23.

86 Elsmie-Stewart, *Stewart*, p. 375; Kandahar correspondence, pp. 56–7, 61, 68, 66B, 74–4a.

87 Robson-Kabul, pp. 251–3.

88 NAM, Haines papers, 8108/9–29 and 35, 31 July 1880.

89 NAM Haines papers, 8108/9–30; also nos 9–30, no. 3. 'Now Genl Phayre . . . is headstrong, impulsive, and in a word dangerous, besides this he does not possess the faculty of organisation.'

90 NAM Haines papers, 9–30, no. 1; the honour of selecting Roberts is shared by Ripon and Stewart. The Haines, Ripon and White papers point to Ripon. On distrust of Phayre see RA, VIC/ADDE/1/9411, Stewart to Cambridge, 24 November 1880.

91 Lieutenant-Colonel E.F. Chapman, 'The March from Kabul to Kandahar in August, and the Battle of the 1st September, 1880', *Journal of the R.U.S.I.*, vol. xxv (1882), pp. 282–315; Low, p. 345 n.

92 Elsmie-Stewart, *Stewart*, p. 376.

93 Kandahar Correspondence, I, pp. 99 and 110.

94 Low, p. 348 n. and p. 349.

95 Vaughan, *My Service*, p. 229.

96 Soboleff, *Anglo-Afghan Struggle*, pp. 137, 143, 144.

97 Certainly MacGregor's speaking of 'a disorganised rabble' refers to the camp followers. Trousdale, *War in Afghanistan*, p. 236.

98 Hensman, *Afghan War*, p. 490.

99 Vaughan, *My Service*, pp. 230–5; *Kandahar Correspondence*, appendix, Geo White's letter, no. 5, pp. 7–11, 3 September 1880.

100 Vaughan, *My Service*, p. 132; WO106/167, *Report by Major A.R. Badcock, Deputy Commissary General, on Arrangements for Supplies made during the March from Kabul to Kandahar, 1880* (Simla, 1880); RA, VIC/ADDE/1/9332, Baker to Cambridge, 9 September 1880.

101 *Kandahar correspondence*, I, p. 228a.

102 Chapman, 'The March from Kabul to Kandahar', pp. 282–3, 286, 288–9, 297.

103 RA, VIC/ADDE/1/9332, 9 September 1880; also Heathcote, *Afghan Wars*, pp. 155, 158.

104 NAM, Bobs, 5504, item no 38, results of a medical board, . . . 8 September 1880; diary quoted, James, p. 159.

105 According to a diarist, the besieged crowded onto the walls to see the signal. *Times of India*, 6 October 1880.

106 OH, VI, p. 29 n.

107 Low, p. 346 n.

108 IOL, L/MIL/5/684, no 13117; *Kandahar correspondence*, I, p. 183.

109 RA, VIC/ADDE/1/9347, 5 October 1880.

110 *Kandahar Correspondence*, I, pp. 200–2.

111 Hensman, *Afghan War*, p. 506.

112 Eur Mss D625/14, Merewether papers, translation of Russian abstract, 28 August 1880.

113 MacGregor, *Second Afghan War*, VI, p. 36.

114 *Kandahar correspondence*, II, p. 8.

115 Royal Artillery archives, Woolwich, Headlam papers, H.L. Gardner letter, 1 December 1935; Maj-Gen. Sir J. Headlam, *History of the Royal Artillery from the Indian Mutiny to the Great War* (Woolwich, 1940), III, pp. 55–6; MacGregor, *Second Afghan War*, VI, pp. 35–41; IOL, Eur Mss F108/101(b) and (c), P6/73, White's letter to wife, 6 September 1880.

116 MacGregor, *Second Afghan War*, VI, pp. 432–3; Hensman, *Afghan War*, p. 521; Travers, 'Kabul to Kandahar 1880,' *JSAHR*, vol. 60 (1982), p. 36. The victors buried 800 enemy on the battlefield; Gough reported his cavalry killing 300, the Bombay horsemen 100, giving the 1,200 total.

117 *Kandahar correspondence*, I, p. 232, no. 637.

118 *Kandahar correspondence*, I, p. 232; IOL, Mss Eur 108/101 (b) and (c), P6/73, 6 September 1880.

119 Vaughan, *My Service*, p. 230.

120 Lt-Col. C.G. Gardyne, *The Life of a Regiment*, pp. 157, 315; *History of the 5th Royal Gurkha Rifles (Frontier Force) 1858 to 1928* (Aldershot, 1928) is dedicated to Countess [Aileen] Roberts in memory of her father 'under whom the regiment gained many of its early and great distinctions'.

Chapter 7: In command at Madras

1   *The Times*, 13 September 1880, p. 5.

2   S. Gopal, *The Viceroyalty of Lord Ripon* (Oxford, 1953), p. 23.

3   Hopkirk, *The Great Game*, pp. 406–7.

4   H.C.G. Matthew, ed., *The Gladstone Diaries with the Cabinet Minutes and Prime Ministerial Correspondence* (Vol. IX, January 1875–December 1880. Oxford, 1996), p. 577, Cabinet meeting 7 September 1880.

5   Fuller, *Strategy and Power in Russia*, pp. 332–5.

6   NAM, Haines papers, 8108/9–32, no. 12, to Dillon 5 October 1880.

7   Marshall, *Russian General Staff and Asia*, p. 139.

8   K. Surridge, 'The Ambiguous Amir: Britain, Afghanistan and the 1897 Frontier Uprising', *Journal of Imperial and Commonwealth History*, vol. 36, no. 3 (September 2008), pp. 417–34. Gillard, *Struggles for Asia*, p. 141.

9   Dolaucothi, L14205, 21 August 1880; Kandahar correspondence, pp. 228a–30, 'Account of march . . .'

10 NAM, Gough papers 8304–32–204 & 249, 20 November 1879 and 5 September 1880; cf. Elsmie, *Stewart*, p. 388.

11 Robson-Kabul, appendix, p. 297.

12 Bobs, 5504, items no. 38, 39, 40.

13 National Library of Scotland, Melgund-Minto papers, 19 September 1880.

14 RA, VIC/ADDE/1/9324, 7 September 1880. This followed the Cabinet meeting of that day. See n. 4 above.

15 Low, pp. 388–9. He and Stewart received a baronetcy, the GCB and £12,500. Wolseley got double that for Ashanti, Napier a peerage for Abyssinia.

16 Bobs, 97, I, pp. 81, 226–8, to Lytton 22 May 1883 and to Chapman, 9 February 1885. On 19 April 1885, defending Wolseley's annuity, Hartington deprecated Roberts's march. *Hansard*, Commons Debates, vol. 278, cc.705–9.

17 Also, Bobs, 225, 'Some turning points . . .' excluding Childers and Hartington from Liberal antipathy.

18 RA, VIC/ADDE/1/8832, Cranbrook to Cambridge, 11 September 1879, 9200, Johnson to Haines, 18 May 1880.

19 RA, VIC/ADDE/1/9078, Cambridge to Johnson, 18 February 1880; also NAM, Haines paper 8109/9–41–11, 4 May 1880.

20 Stewart was appointed to the viceroy's council 18 October 1880; to succeed Haines 7 April 1881.

21 RA, VIC, ADDE/1/9414, 26 November 1880; 9431, 15 December 1880; 9433, 17 December 1880.

22 Lyte, *History of Eton*, p. 555 incorrectly giving '1880'; *Eton College Chronicle*, no. 326.

23 *Hansard*, Commons Debates, 5 May 1881, vol. 260, cc. 1842–70.

24 Bobs, 108, scrapbook. Hamlet: 'Thou art a fishmonger.' *Moonshine* appeared weekly from 1879 to 1902. Dr Alastair Massie kindly identified this periodical.

25 IOL, Eur Mss C336, p. 15.

26 J. Laband, *The Transvaal Rebellion: the First Boer War 1880–1* (London, 2005); Sir W. Butler, *The Life of Sir George Pomeroy-Colley* (London, 1899); I.F.W. Beckett, 'George Colley' in I.F.W. Becket and S. Corvi, *Victoria's Generals* (Barnsley, 2009). Correspondence with Colley and Wood in S. Childers, *Life and Correspondence of the Right Hon. Hugh C.E. Childers* (2 vols, London, 1901), II, pp. 1–26.

27 Bobs, 225, 'Some turning points'.

28 RA, VIC/ADDE/1/9546, 4 March 1881; also 9547, to Curzon, 4/3/1881.

29 Robson-India, p. 230. Wolseley later described this as 'the greatest blow I had ever received'. Surridge, *Managing the South African War*, p. 9.

30 Laband, *Transvaal Rebellion*, p. 215.

31 R. Robinson and J. Gallagher, *Africa and the Victorians: the Official Mind of Imperialism* (London, 1965), pp. 66–72.

32 Robinson and Gallagher, *Africa and the Victorians*; IOL, Eur Mss C212, f. 73.

33 A. Preston, *In Relief of Gordon: Lord Wolseley's Campaign Journal of the Gordon Relief Expedition* (London, 1967), p. 179. This finished Wood's fighting service, although he was to do excellent work training the Egyptian Army.

34 Bobs, 108; Spiers, *The Victorian Soldier in Africa* (Manchester and New York, 2004), p. 73; P. Marling, *Rifleman and Hussar* (London, 1931), pp. 55–6, 63.

35 *Forty-One Years*, p. 497. Written in 1897 after the Jameson Raid.

36 Feuchtwanger, *Democracy and Empire*, p. 153; Gallagher and Robinson, *Africa and the Victorians*, pp. 72–3, 205–6.

37 *Forty-One Years*, p. 497; Robson-India, pp. 238–9.

38 E.M. Spiers, *The Late Victorian Army 1868–1902* (Manchester, 1992).

39 Bobs, 17/3, 23 December 1881. Robson-India, p. 230, regards this offer as part of royal opposition to the rise of Sir Garnet Wolseley.

40 *Forty-One Years*, p. 497.

41 Bobs, 46–12, 26 October 1881.

42 IOL, Eur Mss F234/3, III, 26 December 1882 (an enclosure to Madras Governor Grant Duff).

43 M.E. Grant-Duff, *The Afghan Policy of the Beaconsfield Government and its Results* (London, 1880).

44 IOL, Mss Eur F234/54, f.55, 3 February 1885.

45 IOL, Mss Eur F234/88, 'Amalgamation of the Three Indian Armies'.

46 India List, January 1882, January 1884. There were also an AG and QMG with their staff.

47 G.F. MacMunn, *Martial Races of India* (n.d.) and MacMunn, *Armies of India*, the latter with a foreword by Roberts, classic statements of the theory; modern treatment in H. Streets, *Martial Races: the Military, Race and Masculinity in British Imperial Culture 1857–1914* (Manchester and New York, 2004); summary in Heathcote, *Indian Army*.

48 RA, VIC/ADDE/1/8550, Lytton to Cambridge, 20 February 1879.

49 Ibid. 9330, Stewart to Cambridge, 15 December 1880.

50 Gerard, *Leaves from the Diary*, p. 302; cf. *Forty-One Years*, pp. 484–5. Sir Patrick Cadell, *The Bombay Army* (London 1938), p. 244 defends.

51 Menezes, *Fidelity and Honour*, pp. 295–6.

52 RA/VIC/ADDE/1/8896, Chamberlain to Cambridge, 26 September 1879.

53 Menezes, *Fidelity and Honour*, p. 203.

54 Bobs, 97, vol. I, p. 28, R. to Cambridge, 23 June 1882.

55 *Forty-One Years*, p. 500.

56 Robson-India, pp. 309–14, Roberts to Napier, 10 October 1884.

57 Bobs, 97, vol I, pp. 27, 30, 1882, 23 and 30 June 1882.

58 IOL, Eur Mss F234/3, Vol. III, Roberts to G-Duff, 11 August 1883.

59 Elsmie, *Stewart*, p. 411. The dates do not correspond.

60 Eur Mss F234/4, III, 24 February and 9 March 1882.

61 Eur Mss F234/4, III, Roberts to G-Duff, 28 July 1882.

62 RA, VIC/ADDE/1/9602, 27/4/1881; Bobs, 97, Vol. I, p. 197, 9 July 1884.

63 *Imperial Gazetteer of India*, ix (London, 1881), pp. 220–2; for the HQ move and for 'Snowdon', Sir F. Price, *Ootacamund: a History* (Madras, 1908), pp. 98, 158–9. Roberts was a tenant.

64 IOL, L/MIL/5/1697; B. Robson, 'The Eden Commission and the Reform of the Indian Army – 1879–1895', *JSAHR*, 60 (1982), pp. 4–13.

65 Robson-Kabul, p. 11.

66 Quoted T.A. Heathcote, *The Military in British India*; B. Robson, 'The Eden Commission and the Reform of the Indian Army'; IOR, L/MIL17/5/1687 and L/MIL/7/54345.

67 Bobs, R37/16, Lytton to R., 11 June 1879 gives the former's viewpoint on 'prejudice opposed to Army reform'; also Heathcote, *Military in British India*, p. 138.

68 Opposition can be followed through the Cambridge correspondence.

69 RA, VIC/ADDE/1/9136, 'Most private' 24 March 1880.

70 Robson-India, p. 7, Napier to Cambridge, 21 May 1874; RA, VIC/ADDE/1/8882, 11/9/1879.

71 IOL, Eur Mss F234/3, III, 30 June and 5 August 1882. The correspondence was about which Indian regiments would be sent to Egypt with Wolseley.

72 Henry Norman doubted the savings could be made: see IOL, L/MIL/5/17/1709.

73 L. Wolf, *The Life of the First Marquess of Ripon* (2 vols, London, 1921), II, p. 57; RA, VIC/ADDE/1/9502, 4/2/1881: 'We decided in Council today, Haines alone dissenting, to recommend abolition of Commander in Chief of Madras and Bombay – but please keep secret at present.'

74 *Forty-One Years*, pp. 13–14.

75 Stanley, *White Mutiny*, p. 70.

76 James, pp. 183–4.

77 NAM, Haines papers 8108/9–47–7, 18 February 1881.

78 H. Kochanski, *Sir Garnet Wolseley: Victorian Hero* (London, 1999) pp. 115–7.

79 Bobs, 97, vol. I, p. 6, 20 February 1882.

80 Bobs, 97, vol. I, p. 176, R. to Churchill, 28 April 1884; James, p. 187.

81 WO33/52 incl 'Free Trade in the Army', pp. 1–14.

82 N. Ferguson, *Empire: How Britain made the Modern World* (London, 2003), p. 245. Self-supporting India paid for her army and British soldiers stationed there.

83 Hanna, *Lord Roberts at War*, p. 59.

84 Bobs, 97, vol. I, p. 16, 6 March 1882.

85 R. Johnson, 'Russians at the Gates of India? Planning the Defence of India,' *The Journal of Military History*, 67 (July 2003), p. 711.

86 Preston, 'Wolseley, Khartoum Relief Expedition and the Defence of India', p. 277, n. 16; Streets, 'Military Influence in Late Victorian and Edwardian Popular Media', *passim*; Wolseley papers, Hove W/Mem/2, section 17.

87 S. Gwynn and G.M. Tuckwell, *The Life of the Rt. Hon. Sir Charles W. Dilke* (2 vols, 1918), pp. 88, 122.

88 A. Preston, 'Sir Charles MacGregor and the Defence of India, 1857–1887', *The Historical Journal*, XII, I (1969), p. 68.

89 Preston, 'Sir Charles MacGregor', pp. 74–7.

90 Eur Mss F234/99, 'Confidential Memorandum by M.E. Grant Duff . . .'

91 Bobs, 97, Vol I, p. 129, 5 December 1883.

92 Roberts, *History of British India*, pp. 463–70.

93 Eur Mss F234/4, III, G-Duff to Roberts, 1 June 1883.

94 Quoted, James, p. 193, letter 27 March 1883.

95 Bobs, 97, vol. II, pp. 82–3, 8 March 1883.

96 Quoted by R. Davenport-Hines in ODNB.

97 The ICS (Imperial Civil Service, also known as Indian Civil Service) administered British India from the abolition of the East India Company until Independence.

98 Brown, *Modern India*, p. 146.

99 A. Seal, *The Emergence of Indian Nationalism: Competition and Collaboration in the Later Nineteenth Century* (Cambridge, 1968), p. 147.

100 Bobs, 100, VIII, p. 161, 4 November 1888.

101 Price, *History of Caio*, p. 62.

102 In *Much Ado About Nothing*, hardened bachelor Benedick falls in love with and marries Beatrice. Hills was nearly fifty when he married.

103 Dolaucothi, L13357 & L9206, 21 and 22 July 1882.

104 Price, *History of Caio*, pp. 67–9.

105 Dolaucothi, L14205, 21 August 1880.

106 Dolaucothi, L13439, 12 March 1882.

107 Bobs, 97, vol. I, p. 135.

108 Bobs 97, vol. I, pp. 262–3, 3 July 1885. Freddie entered Everard's that September.

109 Liddell Hart Archives, Hamilton papers, 5/1/16, Aileen to 'Dearest Janet', 28 November 1942.

110 Childers, *Life and Correspondence*, II, pp. 77–80.

111 Preston, *In Relief of Gordon*, intro, p. xliii. Preston claims it 'broke Wolseley physically, morally and professionally'.

112 IOL, Eur Mss F234/3, vol III, 8 February 1885. Wolseley divided his force into Herbert Stewart's Desert Column and Earle's on the Nile.

113 Bobs, 97, vol. II, pp. 168–9, 8 February 1885.

114 J. Lunt on Graham in ODNB; B. Robson, *Fuzzy-Wuzzy: the campaigns in the eastern Sudan 1884–85* (London, 1993), p. 185.

115 Hamilton, *Listening for the Drums*, p. 177. Roberts himself years later told Charles Dilke that he could have marched from Suakim to Khartoum 'with an exclusively Indian force'. Gwynn and Tuckwell, *Life of Charles Dilke*, II, p. 44.

116 Hamilton, *Listening for the Drums*, p. 177. Wolseley admired Gordon and afterwards blamed and despised Gladstone.

117 Hamilton, *Listening for the Drums*, pp. 124–5; Bobs 97, vol. I, p. 191, R to Cambridge, 11 June 1884.

118 Hamilton, 5/1/16, letter dated 28 November 1942.

119 Hamilton, 1/2/10, 22 January 1884. There is some difficulty with the dating; the Eton Register lists Freddie 1885–7.

120 I. Hamilton, *The Happy Warrior* (London, 1966), pp. 46–9.

121 S. Badsey, *Doctrine and Reform in the British Cavalry 1880–1918* (Aldershot, 2008), p. 26.

122 Hamilton, *Listening for the Drums*, pp. 150–1; Hamilton, *Happy Warrior*, pp. 49–51.

123 Hamilton, 1/2/9, 28 October 1884.

124 Also Sykes, *Durand*, pp. 153–6.

125 Hopkirk, *Great Game*, pp. 412–15.

126 James, *Raj*, p. 380.

127 Hopkirk, *Great Game*, pp. 425–8.

128 Gillard, *Struggle for Asia*, pp. 144–7; Fuller, *Strategy and Power in Russia*, pp. 332–5.

129 Marshall, *Russian General Staff and Asia*, pp. 142–3.

130 Quoted Hopkirk, *Great Game*, p. 431.

131 The Cabinet would have considered an advance on Herat as a *casus belli*. A. Hawkins and J. Powell, eds, *The Journal of John Wodehouse, First Earl of Kimberley for 1862–1902* (London, 1997), p. 353, n. 1044.

132 R. Johnson, 'Russians at the Gates of India', pp. 717–18. The paper is in IOL, L/MIL/A/1714/80.

133 Robson-India, pp. 309–14, letter of 10 October 1884.

134 Childers, *Life and Correspondence*, II, pp. 79–80, 27 April 1882. Roberts noted that in the China expedition of 1857 the troops wore a khaki blouse over their scarlet coats. At Ashanti Wolseley gave his men a more serviceable uniform.

135 Bobs, 139, vol. V, *Madras Mail*, 3 August 1885.

136 *Hansard*, H. of Commons deb., 4 November 1880, vol. 256, cc. 1282–3.

137 Bobs, 21 for letters.

138 R. Foster, *Lord Randolph Churchill: a Political Life* (Oxford, 1981).

139 Ibid., pp. 171–2, 184, 213.

140 M. Barthorp, 'The Battle of Tofrek, 1885', *JSAHR*, 63 (spring, 1985), pp. 1–10.

141 Robson-India, p. 232.

142 Bobs, 12/2, 9 July 1885. 'Your best friend' was ironic. Arthur Edward Hardinge was the son of Henry Hardinge, Viscount, Field Marshal, governor-general of India. Christopher Brice kindly pointed out the connection.

143 Cambridge, RA, VIC/ADDE/1/11214, 13 June 1885.

144 Robson-India, pp. 324–5.

145 Robson-India, p. 422, n. 17.

146 Robson-India, p. 184, n. 23.

147 W.S. Churchill, *Life of Lord Randolph Churchill* (2 vols, London, 1906), I, pp. 490–1.

148 IOR/L/MIL/715507, appointment of Lt-Gen Sir F S Roberts as commander-in-chief in India.; Bobs, 225, 'Turning points . . .'

149 Eur. Mss. F234/3, III, 13 August 1885.

Chapter 8: Commander-in-chief, India

1   Foster, *Lord Randolph Churchill*, p. 184.

2   RA, VIC/ADDE/1/11239, Stewart to Cambridge, 10 July 1885 and 11356, Wilson to Cambridge, 15 December 1885.

3   Bobs, 46–23, Nightingale to R., 4 November recommending a deputy surgeon general. She took a keen interest in India; see P. Sen, ed., *Florence Nightingale's Indian Letters 1878–1882* (Calcutta, 1937).

4   C. Woodham-Smith, *Florence Nightingale* (London, 1952), p. 372.

5   IOL, Eur Mss. D951/3, f.173, 18 October 1885; ODNB.

6   RA/VIC/ADDE/1/11252 and 11221, 31 July 1885 and 2 August 1885.

7   RA/VIC/ADDE/1/11261, 7 August 1885; 11292, 8 September 1885; 11320, 29 October 1885.

8   RA, VIC/ADDE/1/11284, Dillon to Cambridge, 3 August 1885 and 11347, Hardinge to Cambridge, 31 November 1885.

9   Ibid., 11349, Roberts to Cambridge, 2 December 1885.

10 RA, VIC/ADDE/1/11349 and 11357, 3 and 19 December 1885. In *Forty-One Years*, p. 509 n., Roberts lists more battles.

11 RA, VIC/ADDE/1/11361, 26 December 1885 encl. 11362, diary of movements, 11374, 12 January 1886 with attachments, 11386, 22 January 1886 with encl. 11387–11391.

12 RA, VIC/ADDE/1/11386, 22 January 1886. *The Times of India*, 18 January 1886, p. 4 reported live firing using Lt. Mayne's pamphlet 'Fire Tactics'.

13 Spiers, *The Late Victorian Army*, pp. 22, 143, 263. Manoeuvres were held in 1871, 1872 and 1873 but phased out for economy, and resumed in 1898 when the government acquired Salisbury Plain.

14 RA, VIC/ADDE/1/12841, W. to Cambridge, 18 August 1892. He drew consolation from better manoeuvres in Cork, but COs still 'lack a good deal of tactical instruction'. RA, VIC/ADDE/1/12842, 21 August 1892.

15 A.T.Q. Stewart, *The Pagoda War: Lord Dufferin and the fall of the Kingdom of Ava 1885–6* (London, 1972); T. Myint-U, *The River of Lost Footsteps: Histories of Burma* (London, 2007).

16 RA, VIC/ADDE/1/11372, 10 January 1886.

17 M. Jones, 'The War of Lost Footsteps: a Re-assessment of the Third Burmese War', *Bulletin of the Military Historical Society*, vol. XXXX, no. 157 (August 1989), pp. 36–40.

18 Marchioness of Dufferin and Ava, *Our Viceregal Life in India* (2 vols, London, 1890), I, p. 294.

19 M. Durand, *The Life of Field Marshal Sir George White* (2 vols, Edinburgh and London, 1915), I, p. 320.

20 IOL, Eus Mss 108/101 (b) and (c), P6/77 and 78, 12 and 19 October 1880.

21 RA, VIC/ADDE/1/11425, 20 February 1886.

22 IOL, Eur Mss F108/98 (b), P3/93, 19 February 1885.

23 Stewart, *Pagoda War*, pp. 120–7; *The Times*, 5 December 1885, pp. 5, 16 December 1885, p. 8 'The Sword is Mightier than the Pen' reprinted from *Punch*.

24 Stewart, *Pagoda War*, pp. 154–7; Col. H.M. Vibart, *The Life of Sir Harry N.D. Prendergast* (London, 1914). In 1902 the army belatedly awarded a GCB. He died in 1913.

25 J. Falconer, 'Willoughby Wallace Hooper: a craze about photography,' *The Photographic Collector*, vol. 4, no. 3 (winter 1983), pp. 258–86; Stewart, *Pagoda War*, p. 154; RA, VIC/ADDE/1/11425, R. to Cambridge, 20 February 1886.

26 RA, VIC/ADDE/1/11483, Dufferin to Cambridge, 9 May 1886.

27 RA, VIC/ADDE/1/11396, Cambridge to Roberts, 28 January 1886.

28 RA, VIC/ADDE/1/11529, 2 July 1886.

29 Stewart, *Pagoda War*, pp. 176–8; *The Times*, 21 January 1886.

30 IOL, Eur Mss. F108/98 (b), 10 January 1886; Durand, *Field Marshal Sir George White*, I, p. 344.

31 IOL, Eur Mss. F108/98 (b), 18 December 1886.

32 Appendix XI in *Forty-One Years*.

33 RA, VIC/ADDE/1/11634, R. to Cambridge, 14 November 1886.

34 RA, VIC/ADDE/1/11660, R. to Cambridge, 10 December 1886 and 11673, Baker to Cambridge, 25 December 1886.

35 IOL, Eur Mss.E290/52, 3 December 1887. Sladen's family were connected by marriage to Roberts. D. Sladen, *Twenty Years of My Life* (London, 1915), p. 120.

36 RA, VIC/ADDE/1/11591, 26 September 1886.

37 Eur Mss. P3/101, White to brother, 21 November 1887.

38 Durand, *Field Marshal Sir George White*, I, pp. 362, 368.

39 Sir C. Crosthwaite, *The Pacification of Burma* (London, 1912); T. Myint-U, *The Making of Modern Burma* (Cambridge, 2001).

40 *The Times of India*, 9 September 1887, p. 3.

41 Durand, *Field Marshal Sir George White*, I, pp. 375–6.

42 *Hart's Army List* (London, 1887), p. 787.

43 RA, VIC/ADDE/1/11512, R. to Cambridge, 11 June 1886.

44 RA, VIC/ADDE/1/11523, Cambridge to R., 25 June 1886 and 11569, R. to Cambridge, 20/8/1886.

45 R. Stearn on Chesney in ODNB; *Forty-One Years*, p. 514.

46   RA, VIC/ADDE/1/11601, 16 October 1886.

47   Bobs, 100, VIII, pp. 318, 376; IOL, L/MIL/17/5/1613, 'Short Report on . . .
     tenure of command of the army in India by General Lord Roberts' (Simla,
     1893), p. 44. Henceforth 'Short Report'.

48   Forty-One Years, p. 521.

49   S. Gopal, British Policy in India 1858–1905 (Cambridge, 1965), pp. 215–16.

50   Streets, Martial Races, pp. 93–100.

51   Menezes, Fidelity and Honour, pp. 289–91.

52   RA, VIC/ADDE/1/11464a, 13 April 1886.

53   RA, VIC/ADDE/1/11517, Macpherson to Cambridge, 17 June 1886.

54   Forty-One Years, pp. 484–5; Gerard, Leaves from the Diary, p. 302; Kandahar
     Correspondence, II, p. 10, White to Ripon, 10 August 1880;. Against this too,
     Menezes, Fidelity and Honour, p. 298 has good arguments.

55   'Short Report', pp. 147–51.

56   RA, VIC/ADDE/1/11218, Stewart to Cambridge, 19 June 1885.

57   RA, VIC/ADDE/1/11466, R. to Cambridge, 14 April 1886. The Gahrwali
     came from country 'which hangs under the buttress of the Himalaya in the
     hills west of Nepal' and previously enlisted in Gurkha regiments. MacMunn,
     Armies of India, pp. 164–5.

58   RA, VIC/ADDE/1/12719, 12812, R. to Cambridge, 4 May 1891 and 8 April
     1892; 'Short Report', pp. 152–3, 157.

59   IOL, L/MIL/17/5/1617, Record of Lord Kitchener's Administration of the
     Army (Simla, 1909), pp. 301–3.

60   Sir J. Keegan, 'Better at fighting: how the "martial races" of the Raj still
     monopolize service in the Indian Army,' Times Literary Supplement,
     24 September 1995.

61   E. Candler, The Sepoy (London, 1919).

62   RA, VIC/ADDE/1/11466, 14 April 1886.

63   'Short Report', pp. 76–8, 87–9, 93–106; Hamilton, Listening for the Drums,
     pp. 150–1; RA, VIC/ADDE/1/ 12705, 12829, R. to Cambridge, 14 March
     1891, 14 June 1892; Bobs, 10, R. to Buller, 30 March 1891; Hamilton, The
     Happy Warrior, pp. 80–1.

64   'Short Report' p. 8. Robson-India, pp. 314–15, 329. Robson states that Roberts
     failed to foresee its full potential, but he seems to have been ahead of others.

65   RA, VIC/ADDE/1/12784, 29 December 1891; WO106/16, Chapman to
     Roberts, 25/8/1892; IOL,L/MIL/5/1613, p. 8.

66   Robson-India, pp. 305–7; Bobs, 100, X, p. 281, 7 October 1887 and XIII,
     p. 819, 17 August 1889.

67   S. Badsey, Doctrine and Reform in the British Cavalry 1880–1918 (Aldershot,
     2008), p. 62.

68   'Short Report', p. 27; Marling, Rifleman and Hussar, pp. 116, 187.

69   IOL, L/MIL/17/5/1617, Record of Lord Kitchener's Administration, pp. 303–4.

70 'Short Report', pp. 85–7, and L/MIL/17/5/1617, *Record of Lord Kitchener's Administration*, pp. 336, 339–43.

71 Mason, *A Matter of Honour*, p. 401.

72 IOL, L/MIL/5/1613, p. 167; MacMunn, *Armies of India*, pp. 191–207.

73 R.A. Johnson, ' "Russians at the Gates of India?" Planning the Defence of India, 1885–1900', *The Journal of Military History*, LXVII (July 2003), pp. 697–744, a thorough account of his defence views; D. Omissi, *The Sepoy and the Raj: The Indian Army 1860–1940* (1994), pp. 192–231 outlines the threat.

74 Omissi, *Sepoy and Raj*, p. 192; Roberts, *History of British India*, pp. 483–6. The rupee fell until 1895.

75 Menezes, *Fidelity and Honour*, p. 209; B. Robson, 'Changes in the Indian Army,' *JSAHR*, vol. 70 (1992), pp. 126–7.

76 Quoted Omissi, *Sepoy and Raj*, p. 204.

77 Quoted, Omissi, citing R's note of 22 May 1885 on 'General Kuropatkin's Scheme for a Russian Advance upon India', CID 7-D, CAB 6/1.

78 B. Parrott, *The Intelligencers: British Military Intelligence from the Middle Ages to 1929* (Barnsley, 2011), p. 96.

79 Preston, 'Sir Charles MacGregor and the Defence of India', pp. 72–3.

80 Preston, 'Sir Charles MacGregor and the Defence of India', pp. 105–7; Younghusband, *History of the Guides*, pp. 138–42.

81 Preston, 'Sir Charles MacGregor and the Defence of India', pp. 76–7.

82 Dufferin, *Our Viceregal Life in India*, I, p. 50.

83 Dufferin, *Our Viceregal Life in India*, I, pp. 284, 286, II, pp. 35, 117, 176.

84 Eur Mss F108/101 (g), P6/259, White to wife, 13 July 1889. Some muddle in document order; possibly P6/262.

85 E.J. Buck, *Simla, Past and Present* (Bombay, 1925), pp. 79–80.

86 IOL, Eur Mss F108/101 (f), P6,/229, 12 July 1888.

87 IOL, Eur Mss F108/101 (f) P6/230, 17 July 1888.

88 I.F.W. Beckett, 'Women and Patronage in the Late Victorian Army,' *History*, vol 85 (2000), pp. 463–480, the best starting point on the roles of Victorian generals' wives.

89 National Library of Scotland, Melgund-Minto papers, 24 March, 19 May and 24 August 1880; Trousdale, *War in Afghanistan*, p. 204. See also Atwood, *March to Kandahar*, pp. 127 and 190, n. 15.

90 E.g. C. Allen, *Plain Tales from the Raj* (London, 1976), p. 191.

91 IOL, Eur Mss C262, *Diary of Hugh Bixby Luard, Indian Medical Service 1862–1944*, pp. 7–8.

92 Rawly, 7212–6, 26 April, 3 and 11 May 1886.

93 Rawly, 7212–6, 30 August and 7 September 1888.

94 Marling, *Rifleman and Hussar*, p. 198.

95 P. Barr, *The Memsahibs: the Women of Victorian India* (1976); review by Jan Morris, *The Times*, 30 August 1976, p. 5.

96 Maud Diver, *The Englishwoman in India* (London, 1909).

97 Diver, *Englishwoman in India*, pp. 92–7, 103ff.; Dufferin, *Our Viceregal Life*, I, p. 190; S. Lang, 'Saving India', *History Today*, 55(9) (September 2005), pp. 46–51.

98 Bobs, 100, vol XI, p. 805, Lady R. to Brigade Surgeon Hamilton, 1 August 1889.

99 RA, VIC/ADDE/1/11631, 11 November 1886.

100 'Short Report', p. 122.

101 'Short Report', p. 123; Bobs, 139, vol. V, pp. 144–50, newspaper cuttings of scheme for nurses.

102 Bobs, 139, vol. VI, pp. 50, 53, 96, 159, *The Pioneer*, 25 August 1890.

103 Bobs, vol. VII, p. 39.

104 'Short Report', pp. 121–4; see also IOR/L/2/1813 and 1814, both dated 17 October 1923, Lady Roberts's deed granting home estate at Murree to Indian government as a hospital.

105 Heathcote, *The Indian Army*, p. 65.

106 Allen, *Plain Tales from the Raj*, p. 191; D. Gilmour, *The Long Recessional: the Imperial Life of Rudyard Kipling* (2002), p. 46.

107 Hyam, *Empire and Sexuality* and K. Ballhatchet, *Race, Sex and Class under the Raj: Imperial Attitudes and Policies and their Critics, 1793–1905* (London, 1980).

108 The campaign against Contagious Diseases Acts is often depicted as a feminist battle: see A. Burton, *Burdens of Empire: British Feminists, Indian Women and Imperial Culture 1865–1915* (Chapel Hill and London, 1994), pp. 133–6, 167.

109 'Short Report' p. 36.

110 *Hansard*, House of Commons Debates, 5 June 1888, vol. 326, cc. 1187–216.

111 Bobs, 100, VIII, pp. 77–8, 84, Dufferin to Josephine Butler and to Roberts, 1 June and 30 May 1888; Roberts to Cambridge, 15 June 1888; Ballhatchet, *Race, Sex and Class*, pp. 11–12, 38–9, 51–72.

112 RA, VIC/ADDE/1/12963, White to Cambridge, 13 June, 1893.

113 Lt-Gen Sir N. Cantlie, *A History of the Army Medical Department*, (vol. II, London and Edinburgh, 1974), p. 380.

114 Bobs, 49, General Orders by the Rt Hon the CinC, 10 April 1876.

115 RA, VIC/ADDE/1/11588, 20 September 1886.

116 Bobs, 100, vol. X, pp. 201, 207, 209; James, p. 217.

117 Quoted in James, p. 217; *Forty-One Years*, p. 519.

118 Childers, *Life and Correspondence*, II, p. 285. The presence of the commander-in-chief and a distinguished guest may well have increased the rooms' popularity on this occasion.

119 RA, VIC/ADDE/1/12796, R. to Cambridge, 12 March 1892

120 *Kipling Journal*, no. 110 (July 1954), pp. 14–16; Allen, *Kipling Sahib*, pp. 152–5.

121 'Short Report', p. 90.

122 RA, VIC/ADDE/1/11631, R. to Cambridge, 11 November 1886. J. Buchan, *The History of the Royal Scots Fusiliers 1678–1918* (London, 1925), pp. 250–1 suggests the second in command gave the leadership. Buchan and *Hart's Army List* agree that Winsloe was replaced in 1887. Interestingly, Roberts also arranged the abolition of infantry paymasters in India, adding an extra subaltern per battalion.

123 *Civil & Military Gazette*, Lahore, 20 September 1889.

124 *The Times*, 3 April 1893, p. 6; Bobs, 100, vol. X, p. 207; *Forty-One Years*, p. 519. Kipling's poems give some idea of the feeling among rank and file; most accounts were written by officers.

125 Badsey, *Doctrine and Reform in the British Cavalry*, p. 70.

126 RA, VIC/ADDE/1/11467, 16 April 1886.

127 Robson-India, p. 379, to Major-General Martin Dillon.

128 RA, VIC/ADDE/1/11200, 4 June 1885.

129 RA, VIC/ADDE/1/11361, 26 December 1885.

130 RA, VIC/ADDE/1/11372, 10 January 1886.

131 RA, VIC/ADDE/1/11634, 14 November 1886.

132 Bobs, 100, IX, pp. 99–100; VIII, p. 353; IX, p. 163.

133 Captain Fitzgeorge became Colonel Sir August Fitzgeorge and died in 1933.

134 Rawly 7216–16, letters from India, 7 September 1888 and 7 May 1889, the latter from Burma.

135 R. Kipling, *Something of Myself* (London, 1937), p. 55.

136 A. Lycett, *Rudyard Kipling* (London, 1999), p. 126, quoting R. Mitford, *Orient and Occident*.

137 Kipling, *Something of Myself*, pp. 56–7.

138 Sussex University Library kindly sent me a copy of this poem, which is not in Kipling's published works.

139 Bobs, 100, vol. XI, p. 533, R. to Elles, 9 September 1888; for George Allen, see Allen, *Kipling Sahib*, pp. x–xi, 50–1.

140 Bobs, 139, vol. VI, scrapbook.

141 Becket, 'Women and Patronage in the Late Victorian Army', p. 478. Edinburgh Military Museums, Egerton MSS M1994/112/92 'Reminiscences of the 72nd Highlanders, 16 February 1931, p. 4.

142 *Rudyard Kipling's Verse: Definitive Edition* (London, 1954), pp. 69–73. One line runs 'The North safeguarded – nearly (Roberts knows the rest)'.

Chapter 9: From Bengal to Southampton via *Forty-One Years in India*

1 Bobs, 100, VIII, p. 189, 29 December 1888.

2 *Eton School Register*, V, p. 66. Father corresponded with HM Warre on imperial matters.

3 Everard's house book (actually the debating society record), Eton Archives.

4 Dolaucothi, L13443, 28 February (?) 1886. At Eton terms are called halves.

5 Dolaucothi, L13450, 19 June 1887 and L13451, 14 August 1887.

6 Dolaucothi, L13456, 30 December 1887. For relations with the Hills-Johneses see also Dolaucothi, L9207, Lady R. to Lady H-J, 11 February 1885. 'It is so good of dear Sir James & you to take such an interest in our boy, and it is an intense happiness to us to know he has such kind friends.'

7 Dolaucothi, L9209, 16 February 1890.

8 His Sandhurst record downloaded from the website.

9 Dolaucothi, L9209, 20 May 1890.

10 Bobs, 100, IX, pp. 12, 88,

11 James, p. 219; he selected a hammerless twelve-bore. Dolaucothi, L13464, Freddie to H-J, 17 November 1890.

12 Bobs, 100, IX, p. 117, 5 February 1891.

13 Kipling, *Something of Myself*, pp. 4ff.; Kipling, 'Baa Baa Black Sheep' in *Wee Willie Winkie and Other Stories* (London, 1907).

14 Dolaucothi, L13466, from Rawalpindi.

15 Field-Marshal Lord Birdwood, *Khaki and Gown* (London, 1941), pp. 35–6; *The Times*, 1 September 1890, p. 3 and 30 May 1892, p. 5; also T. Mason and E. Riedi, *Sport and the Military: the British Armed Forces 1880–1960* (Cambridge, 2010), pp. 57–78. Page 73, n. 66 suggests that the figure of deaths is greater than thirty-seven.

16 Marquis of Anglesey, *History of the British Cavalry* (vol. III, London, 1982), pp. 143–4; Birdwood, *Khaki and Gown*, p. 60.

17 NAM 901142–14, R. to Wilkinson, 11 September and 31 December 1891.

18 Gwynn and Tuckwell, *Life of Sir Charles Dilke*, II, pp. 294–5.

19 On Maurice, J. Luvaas, *Education of an Army: British Military Thought 1815–1940* (London, 1965), p. 174. The NWF chapter was the only one not mainly written by Wilkinson.

20 S. Wilkinson, *Thirty-Five Years 1874–1909* (London, 1933), pp. 120–7, 135–6. Also Luvaas, *Education of an Army*, Chapter 8: 'The Volunteer Advocate: Spenser Wilkinson', unfortunately giving insufficient weight to his range of ideas; P. Ramsey, 'Analysing Defence and thinking Strategically: the Writings and Career of Spenser Wilkinson 1890–1900' (unpubl. MA thesis, King's College London, 2008). I am grateful to Paul Ramsey for sending me his paper. He is presently working on policy, strategy and statecraft in Wilkinson's work and career.

21 Bobs, 87, 28 July 1891.

22 Wilkinson, *Thirty-Five Years*, pp. 141–3.

23 Bobs, 87, 31 December 1892.

24 Wilkinson, *Thirty-Five Years*, pp. 163, 169–70. Dilke formed the same impression earlier: Gwynn and Tuckwell, *Life of Sir Charles Dilke*, II, pp. 294–6.

25   He established himself as chief leader writer on military and imperial affairs. In 1909 he was elected to All Souls and became the first Chichele Professor of Military History.

26   Wilkinson, *Thirty-Five Years*, p. 153.

27   Wilkinson, *Thirty-Five Years*, p. 153.

28   Bobs, 100, VIII, 939, R. to Nicholson, 17 December 1889.

29   Bobs, 100, IX, pp. 86, 87, 89–93, 103–4, 106, 110–4. Some letters in Hamilton 1/2/17 and 1/2/18; *Hart's Army List* of 1892 for dates of promotion. Hamilton, *Listening for the Drums*, pp. 213–15 says this exchange began 'the battle of the rings', but Roberts's opponents were Cambridge and his clique.

30   Bobs, 97, I, p. 85: they were Napier of Magdala and Stewart as commander-in-chief, Sir Patrick Grant, Sir Neville Chamberlain and Roberts at Madras and Napier alone at Bombay.

31   Eur Mss F132/31, Griffin to Lyall, 5 August 1880.

32   The phrase is in 'Gunga Din', Kipling's hymn to the regimental *bhistie* or water carrier.

33   Quoted Spiers, *The Victorian Soldier in Africa*, p. 93.

34   Wolseley papers, Hove Library, LW/P7/7/2, 15 January 1881.

35   Another dissenter was Buller, who thought they should be given more to eat, not illogical as soldiers testified that they had to supplement rations from their own pocket.

36   Bobs, 100, vol. IX, pp. 227–9, 29 November 1891. Spratt's evidence also in *The Times of India*, 31 May 1892, p. 5.

37   WO33/52 incl. Four Papers recently prepared or referred to by General Lord Roberts . . .(1892) questions 2054–2060 in Minutes of Evidence.

38   *The Times*, 26 February 1892, p. 6 prints the Committee's conclusions. Spiers, *Late Victorian Army*, pp. 137–8 and A.R. Skelly, *The Late Victorian Army at Home* (London and Montreal, 1977), discuss. Roberts claimed that 'Indian' views were not sufficiently appreciated. RA, VIC/ADDE/1/12750, R. to Cambridge, 16 August 1891.

39   WO33/52, letter to *The Times*, 25 February 1892, p. 3. In Roberts's time Indian cavalrymen's pay was increased, that of infantrymen after his departure.

40   WO33/52, pp. 1147, 1149, a shocking indictment of industrial society and army recruiting.

41   Preston, ed., *In Relief of Gordon*, intro; quote from H. Kochanski, [The] Wolseley Ring, ODNB.

42   Captain O. Wheeler, *The War Office Past & Present* (London, 1914), p. 250. Wood's protégés included Kitchener, Haig, Smith-Dorrien; Buller's Dundonald, French and Stopford.

43   S. Badsey, 'Fire and the Sword: the British Army and the Arme blanche Controversy 1871–1921' (unpubl. PhD thesis, Cambridge, 1982), pp. 82–3; Strachan, *Politics of the British Army*, p. 103. See Chapter 10.

44   Hamilton, *Listening for the Drums*, p. 149. Pakenham, *The Boer War*, p. 73 took this one step further.

45   Preston, 'Wolseley, the Khartoum Relief Expedition and the Defence of India',
     p. 270. The martinets he mentions were Lysons, Macdonnell, Parke,
     Beauchamp Walker and Lord Alexander Russell.

46   Strachan, *Politics of the British Army*, p. 103.

47   Hamilton, *The Happy Warrior*, p. 173.

48   S. Manning, *Evelyn Wood: Pillar of Empire* (Barnsley, 2007), p. 12. Manning
     notes the men had met in 1881, on campaign in Egypt and on training
     exercises.

49   The episode is in Robson-India, pp. xxi–ii; James, pp. 223–5; G.E. Buckle,
     The Letters of Queen Victoria . . . Third Series 1886–1901 (1930–2), I,
     pp. 567–623. Politicians also overrode soldiers by preventing Cambridge
     securing the adjutant-generalship for his military secretary Lt-Gen Sir George
     Harman, 'a good rider, a perfect gentleman, an excellent soldier, and I do hope
     he may be the man'.

50   Buckle, *Letters of Queen Victoria*, I, p. 623, 5 July 1890.

51   Bobs, 100, IX, pp. 158, 379; and Bobs 10, 14 letters esp. 30 April 1891 on
     musketry.

52   Lord Newton, *Lord Lansdowne* (London, 1929).

53   Bobs, 100, vol. IX, p. 661, to Sir D. Wallace, 13 November 1888.

54   Newton, *Lord Lansdowne*, pp. 69–70.

55   There was one minor Riponist reform, the India Councils Act (1892) by which
     Congress advanced to this hitherto aristocratic preserve.

56   Hawkins and Powell, eds, *Kimberley Diaries*, p. 457.

57   Gopal, *British Policy in India*, pp. 215–16.

58   Lord E. Gleichen, *A Guardsman's Memories in Peace and War* (London,
     1932), p. 176.

59   C.M. Brice, 'The Military Career of General Sir Henry Brackenbury
     1856–1904: the Thinking Man's Soldier' (unpubl. PhD thesis, De Montfort
     University, 2009), pp. 174–9. This and Dr Brice's published biography have
     rescued Brackenbury from ill-deserved obscurity. I am grateful to Christopher
     Brice's help and clarification. Evidence of Russian plans in WO33/46 'General
     sketch of the situation abroad and at home . . .' 3 August 1886 and WO32/6349
     'Capability of existing garrisons in India to meet a Russian invasion'.

60   Bobs, 59/15, Pole-Carew to R., 22 January 1891.

61   Bobs, 100, IX, p. 163, 20 June 1891; Preston, 'Wolseley, the Khartoum Relief
     Expedition and the Defence of India, 1885–1900', p. 274 draws attention to
     the significance.

62   Brice, 'The Military Career of Sir Henry Brackenbury', pp. 215–20, 235.

63   Brice, 'Military Career of Sir Henry Brackenbury', pp. 225–32.

64   WO33/46, 'General sketch of the situation abroad and at home from a Military
     Standpoint by Maj-Gen Brackenbury', 3 August 1886; also B. to Roberts, 22 July
     1886. Brice, 'Thinking Man's Soldier', pp. 178–9 points out how Brackenbury
     drew attention to British military weakness compared to continental powers.

65 R. Johnson, *Spying for Empire: the Great Game in Central and South Asia, 1757–1947* (London, 2006), pp. 161, 172–3.

66 Johnson, *Spying for Empire*, pp. 186–94; Hopkirk, *Great Game*, pp. 447–71. His fear of Afridi hostility came true in the 1897 Rising.

67 Quoted Seaver, *Francis Younghusband*, p. 95.

68 See above, Chapter 7, pp. 124–5.

69 Johnson, *Spying for Empire*, pp. 198–201.

70 Roberts, *History of British India*, pp. 490–3; Sykes, *Mortimer Durand*, pp. 206–25 present a favourable view. On Abdur's view of Roberts, Robson-Kabul, p. 178; on the Amir being mistaken as to Roberts's intentions, see Newton, *Lord Lansdowne*, p. 107. On the Mohmands information received from Keith Surridge, it may have contributed to the Great Frontier Rising of 1897.

71 The phrase is A. Preston's from whom I draw this paragraph: Preston, 'Wolseley, Khartoum Relief Expedition and India', pp. 274–5 and notes 81, 82 and 83 on p. 280.

72 Bobs 100, IX, p. 288, 18 May 1892. In fact, the Stanhope memorandum of 1888 had already done this.

73 WO106/16, Chapman letter book, 24 August 1893.

74 Preston, 'Wolseley, Khartoum Relief Expedition and India', p. 275.

75 Tables in P. Kennedy, *The Rise and Fall of the Great Powers* (London, 1988), pp. 255, 257.

76 E. Ingram, *The British Empire as a World Power* (London, 2001), p. 21 citing *The Economist* of 20 December 1997: US 100, China, 98, Britain 60, Russia 58, India 57, France 37, Germany 35.

77 Lord Curzon, *The Place of India in the Empire: being an address delivered . . . 19 October 1909* (London, 1909), pp. 9–14.

78 Newton, *Lansdowne*, p. 103.

79 Dolaucothi, L9209, Lady R. to Lady Hills-Johnes, 16 February 1890.

80 Powell, *Buller: a Scapegoat?*, p. 106

81 J.A. Spender, *Life of Sir Henry Campbell-Bannerman* (2 vols, London, 1923), I, p. 130.

82 RA, VIC/ADDE/1/12845, 30/8/1892.

83 Spender, *Life of Campbell-Bannerman*, I, p. 135.

84 RA, VIC/ADDE/1/12868, 12869, 12873, 12874.

85 RA, VIC/ADDE/1/12874, 11 November 1892.

86 Brice, 'Brackenbury: the Thinking Man's Soldier', pp. 21, 237, n. 28. See also Eur Mss F108/101(h), P6/290, White to wife, 17 October 1894, that Brackenbury had written to say he would support him.

87 Durand, *Sir George White*, I, p. 407, letter 20 August 1892. His letters are in Eur Mss F108, but Durand usefully prints them pp. 407–9.

88 Durand, *Sir George White*, I, p. 408.

89 RA, VIC/ADDE/1/, 12877, 12879.

90 Durand, *Sir George White*, I, pp. 415ff.

91 Robson, 'The Eden Commission and the Reform of the Indian Army', p. 13. White strictly was not an 'Indian' but a Gordon Highlander.

92 Bobs, 100, IX, pp. 160–3, to Lyall, 16 June 1891.

93 Marling, *Rifleman and Hussar*, p. 198.

94 Forrest, *Life of Lord Roberts*, preface: 'Lord Roberts kindly described to me on the theatre of their enactment the principal operations of the siege of Delhi.'

95 For details of farewells, see James, pp. 227–33 and Bobs, 139, scrapbooks, vols VII, VIII.

96 *The Times*, 3 April 1893, p. 6.

97 Durand, *Sir George White*, p. 405. This was before he knew he was to succeed.

98 IOL Eur Mss F108/98(b), P3/110, 25 April 1893. To Cambridge he was more circumstantial: 'The great name & influence which Lord Roberts brought to bear on the Council of the Viceroy has gained the Army great concessions; but the finances of India are now in a depressed Condition.' RA, VIC/ADDE/1/12948, 3 May 1893.

99 IOL Eur Mss, F108/98(b), P3/108, 6 December 1891.

100 K17, S9, 8 November 1900. Lepel Griffin charged him with extravagance in Afghanistan. Eur Mss F132/31, to Lyall, 11 July 1880. In the First Afghan War cutting subsidies to tribes like the Gilzais had had a disastrous effect on British lines of communication, so Roberts's extravagance may have been wisdom.

101 *The Times*, 8 May 1893, p. 8.

102 T. E. Buckle, *Letters of Queen Victoria*, 3rd series, 3 vols (London, 1930–2), p. 255.

103 Bobs, 100, IX, R. to Harman, 14 December 1891.

104 Bobs, 139, scrapbooks, VII, VIII.

105 Hamilton 1/2/9, 22 June 1893.

106 CAB41/22/47, 28 August 1893.

107 Bobs, 49, R51/27, Norman to R., 6 April 1894; Newton, *Lord Lansdowne*, pp. 113–14.

108 RA, VIC/ADDE/1/12964, 21 June 1893.

109 RA, VIC/ADDE/1/12964, Wolseley to Cambridge, 23 June 1893; 12968, C-Bannerman to Cambridge, 25 June 1893.

110 B. Robson on Roberts in ODNB; Buckle, *Queen Victoria's Letters*, II, pp. 255, 30S; Spender, *Life of Campbell-Bannerman*, I, pp. 135–6.

111 RA, VIC/ADDE/1/12981, 25 August 1893 and 12982, C-B to Cambridge, 2 September 1893.

112 James, pp. 243–5.

113 Bobs, 52, letters nos 7 and 13, 10 December 1893 and 6 June 1894. For 'golden pen' Birdwood, *Khaki and Gown*, p. 83.

114 Hamilton, 1/2/9, 12 and 18 May 1893.

115 Quoted Lord Birkenhead, *Rudyard Kipling* (New York, 1978), p. 176.

116 Spender, *Life of Campbell-Bannerman*, pp. 146–54; Buckle, *Victoria's Letters*, II, pp. 500–33.

117 Strengthened by the addition of Liberals against Irish Home Rule.

118 Quoted Beckett, 'Women and Patronage in the late Victorian Army', p. 478.

119 Newton, *Lord Lansdowne*, pp. 131–17; Buckle, *Victoria's Letters*, II, pp. 548–71.

120 Lehmann, *All Sir Garnet*, p. 384; Spiers, *Late Victorian Army*, pp. 50–3.

121 British Library, unclassified Lansdowne correspondence, no. 96, 1 and 17 July 1895.

122 British Library, unclas. Lansdowne corresp., no.305, 21 August 1895; James, pp. 247–8.

123 James, p. 247; he inherited that of Sir Patrick Grant, a former commander-in-chief of the Madras Army.

124 W. Lanceley, *From Hall-Boy to House-Steward* (London, 1925), p. 64. Roger Stearn kindly brought this book to my notice.

125 *Forty-One Years*, preface, p. vii.

126 Dolaucothi, L9197, 17 October 1896.

127 Neville, *Campaigns on the North-West Frontier*, pp. 150ff.

128 Hanna, *Lord Roberts in War*.

129 Hanna, *Lord Roberts in War*, pp. 14–19, 26–7, 40–1, 46–51.

130 NAM, Gough papers, 8304–32–220, 29 February 1880.

131 Hanna, *Lord Roberts in War*, pp. 60–2.

132 Bobs, 148, H-J to Chamberlain, 19 December 1911 on Hanna's three-volume Afghan War history.

133 Hanna's publication noted in *The Times* on 20 June 1895; letters from Gen Adye and J.B. Lyall on 30 March; Curzon on 4 April and Roberts on 12 April; Younghusband's speech 26 March 1895, p. 11.

134 Add. Mss. 55252, esp ff. 3, 53–4.

135 James, *Raj*, p. 494.

136 Bobs, 139, vol. X, for reviews; W. Churchill's mother: R. Churchill, *Winston Churchill: Companion Volume I, part 2, 1896–1900* (London, 1967), p. 744.

137 Sussex University Library, Kipling Papers, KP22/1, 10 January 1897.

138 Birkenhead, *Rudyard Kipling*, p. 153.

139 N.K. Moran, *Kipling and Afghanistan* (London, 2005).

140 Birkenhead, *Rudyard Kipling*, p. 176.

141 Reviews in Bobs, 139, vol. X.

142 All in Bobs, 110, letter books, vol. I.

143 Bobs, 110, letter books, vol. I., 10 May 1898. The saying was 'an old chestnut' long before Basil Liddell Hart told Alan Clark author of *The Donkeys* of an alleged exchange between Ludendorff and Hoffman. See J. Baynes, *Far from a Donkey: the life of General Sir Ivor Maxse* (1995), p. xi.

144 Bobs, 110, letter books, vol. I. In working on artillery Roberts may have been following Evelyn Wood at Aldershot Field Days: WO106/16, Chapman to Roberts, 24 May 1893.

145 *The Times*, 5 August 1899, p. 6, 31 August 1899, p. 6, 23 September 1899, p. 6; on limitations of training, R.H. Scales, 'Artillery in Small Wars: the Evolution of British Artillery Doctrine, 1860–1914' (Duke University PhD thesis, 1976), pp. 208–10.

146 Liddell Hart Archives, Hamilton papers 13/91, Aileen Countess Roberts to Hamilton, 6 April 1925; Lanceley, *Hall-Boy to House-Steward*, p. 81.

147 Robinson and Gallagher, *Africa and the Victorians*, pp. 348–9.

148 Lt-Col E.W.C. Sandes, *The Royal Engineers in Egypt and the Sudan* (Chatham, 1937), p. 222 and *passim*.

149 H. Keown-Boyd, *A Good Dusting: a Centenary Review of the Sudan Campaigns 1883–1899* (London, 1986); T. Royle, *The Kitchener Enigma* (London, 1985); K. Surridge, 'Herbert Kitchener' in S.J. Corvi and I.F.W. Beckett, *Victoria's Generals* (Barnsley, 2009).

150 Rawly 5201-33-4, Egypt and the Sudan, entries 2 January and 5 February 1898. The catalogue states 'copies of letters to Roberts, Col Kelly-Kenny, Captain [Henry] Wilson, and Sir George Clery . . . describing campaigning in the Sudan'.

151 Rawly 5201-33-4, 3 and 24 July 1898 to Roberts and 24 July 1898 to Clery.

152 Robinson and Gallagher, *Africa and the Victorians*, pp. 370–8; D. Bates, *The Fashoda Incident of 1898: Encounter on the Nile* (Oxford, 1984).

153 W.S. Blunt, *My Diaries 1888–1919* (London, 1932), pp. 313, 317, 324.

154 E.M. Spiers, ed., *Sudan: the Conquest Reappraised* (London, 1998), pp. 178ff., 188, 189. For the contrary view, Blunt, *Diaries*, pp. 313, 317, 323–4.

155 K10, 17 April 1898; Bobs, 33/1, 5 May 1898. These congratulations were for the victory at Atbara, before Omdurman.

156 *The Times*, 2 December 1898, p. 9; also 26 July 1899, p. 6.

157 Hamilton 13/6.

158 C. Headlam, ed., *The Milner Papers* (2 vols, London, 1931, 1935), I, p. 258.

159 For causes of war see I. Smith, *The Origins of the South African War 1899–1902* (London, 1996); Robinson and Gallagher, *Africa and the Victorians*, pp. 410ff.; G.H.L. Le May, *Afrikaners* (Oxford, 1995); P. Fraser, *Joseph Chamberlain: Radicalism and Empire 1868–1914* (London, 1934), pp. 168ff.

160 James, pp. 260–1; P. Magnus, *Kitchener: Portrait of an Imperialist* (London, 1958), pp. 150–1.

161 S.B. Spies, *Methods of Barbarism: Roberts and Kitchener and Civilians in the Boer Republics Jan 1900–May 1902* (Cape Town and Pretoria, 1977), p. 301.

162 Surridge, *Managing the South African War*, p. 65.

163 Bobs, 61/7, 24 April 1897.

164 Bods, 61/8, 26 April 1897. Roberts may have done so verbally, as there is no letter of the right date in the Lansdowne collection.

165 British Library, Lansdowne collection, no 1315, 27 March 1896.

166 British Library, Lansdowne collection, no. 1402, 20 June 1896.

167 British Library, Lansdowne collection, no. 4875, 20 June 1899.

168 D.M. Leeson, 'Playing at War: the British Military Manoeuvres of 1898', *War in History*, vol. 15, no. 4 (2008), pp. 432–61.

169 The Earl of Midleton, *Records & Reactions 1856–1939* (London, 1939), p. 133.

170 Viscountess Milner, *My Picture Gallery, 1886–1901* (London, 1951), p. 110. She was then married to the PM's son Lord Edward Cecil of the Grenadier Guards.

171 Hamilton, *Happy Warrior*, pp. 122–3.

172 Smith, *Origins of the South African War*, pp. 337–8.

173 TH, I, p. 281.

174 BL, Lansdowne correspondence, 7 September 1899.

175 TH, I, p. 372.

176 Review of T. Pakenham, *The Boer War*, by R. Oliver in *TLS*, no 4001, 23 November 1979, p. 33.

177 D. Reitz, *Commando: a Boer Journal of the Boer War* (1948), p. 29.

178 Sound accounts of the war: D. Judd and K. Surridge, *The Boer War* (London, 2002) and B. Nasson, *The Boer War: the Struggle for South Africa* (Stroud, 2011).

179 For Smuts's plans, W.K. Hancock and J. v.d. Poel, *Selections from the Smuts Papers* (vol. I, Cambridge, 1966), pp. 323–4.

180 Bobs, 110, 29 August 1899. Freddie had received another mention in the Sudan.

181 Bobs, 91/7 29 September 1899.

182 Bobs 91/8, 11 October 1899.

183 Bobs 98/8, 13 October 1898. Cf. Pakenham, *Boer War*, p. 214.

184 WO108/409, R. to B., 12 December 1899.

185 Gen. Sir N. Lyttelton, *Eighty Years: Soldiering, Politics, Games* (London, 1927), pp. 200–1; Col. C.H. Melville, *Life of General the Right Hon. Sir Redvers Buller* (2 vols, London, 1923), II, pp. 1–2.

186 WO132/6, 3 November 1899.

187 TH, II, pp. 126–30.

188 E. Spiers, 'Reforming the Infantry of the Line 1900–1914,' *JSAHR*, vol. 59 (1981), pp. 82–4.

189 [Cairns], *Absent Minded War. Being Some Reflections on Our Reverses and the Causes which Have Led to Them. By a British Officer* (London, 1900), esp. pp. 13, 136–7 and the comprehensive damnation of Methuen pp. 115–35.

190 NAM Birdwood papers 6709–19–254, 16 December 1899: 'the key of the position is hill on the right'; RA Institute, Woolwich, Parsons papers MD/1111/3, letter to wife, 21 December 1899: 'how that escaped Buller, I don't know'.

191 WO3232/7887, Buller's despatch after Colenso. I am grateful to Ken Gillings for pointing out that Buller had already damned Long for 'inconceivable stupidity' sending forward an armoured train. WO105/25, 'Confidential file, Colonel C.J. Long's case'.

192 Maj. D. Hall, *Halt! Action Front! With Colonel Long at Colenso* (Glenashley, SA, 1995), esp. pp. 52–6; J. Hussey's review in *JSAHR*, vol. 73 (1995), pp. 285–6; Captain C. Holmes Wilson, RA, *The Relief of Ladysmith: the Artillery in Natal* (London, 1901), pp. 28–9; Royal Artillery Institute, Woolwich, Headlam papers, MD183, extract from staff diary of Captain Herbert, R.A. defend Long.

193 Royal Greenjackets Museum, Winchester, Congreve Diary, 15 December 1899.

194 Royal Artillery Institute, Woolwich, Parsons papers MD/1111/1, diary of service in Natal, 15 December 1899.

195 Warre quoted in Lord Carver, *The National Army Museum Book of the Boer War* (London, 1999), p. 43; Treves in O. Coetzer, *The Anglo-Boer War: the Road to Infamy* (London, 1996), p. 98; NAM, Birdwood papers 6707–19–254, 16 December 1899. Gandhi later claimed to have removed Freddie's body from the battlefield, but his memory must have misled him, as the Indian 'body-snatchers' were not at Colenso: see counter-claims in *The Straits Times*, 23 June 1931, p. 15.

196 Pakenham, *Boer War*, p. 243 speaks of a 'four year siege of Lansdowne and the War Office'. This cannot be justified by correspondence in the Lansdowne papers or Bobs, 110.

197 Details in Bobs, 181, Lady Aileen Roberts's account of father's appointment.

198 WO108/399, p. 52, no. 53D, 15 December 1900.

199 WO108/399, p. 54, 15 December 1899, 11.15 p.m.

200 RCSAW, III, pp. 174–5; Churchill College Cambridge, Esher papers ESHR 15/1, pp. 66–8. 'He gave somewhat lame explanations of his telegrams to the Sec. of State . . . and his heliogram to Sir George White suggesting surrender.' Cf Pakenham, *Boer War*, p. 239.

201 WO108/399, p. 55, no. 57.

202 In various places including Packenham, *Boer War*, p. 239

203 Rawly 5201–33–7–1, *Boer War Diary*, vol. I, entries 15 to 17 December 1899.

204 D. Roberts, *Salisbury: Victorian Titan* (1999), pp. 226, 746–7, 750.

205 Add Mss 49835, ff. 16–17, Balfour to Lady Elcho, 23 December 1899.

206 Newton, *Lord Lansdowne*, pp. 165–7; Add Mss 49835, ff. 10–11, Balfour to Salisbury, 18 December 1899; Bobs, 181. Kitchener was sixteen years younger.

207 Add Mss 49835, f. 11, Balfour to Salisbury, 18/12/1899.

208 Melville, *Life of Buller*, II, pp. 128–9.

209 Newton, *Lansdowne*, p. 167.

210 Bobs, 181, Lansdowne to Countess (Aileen) Roberts, 11 May 1921; how the news was passed by Lady Aileen to her mother at the Curragh is in Lanceley, *Hall-Boy to House-Steward*, p. 84.

211 Buckle, *Victoria's Letters*, III, pp. 439, 447, 467–8, 471–2, 476–7, 489; WO32/8792, award of VC and other medals at Colenso. A mss sheet states: 'Lieut Roberts did not die till 17 Decr. He has therefore been recommended for the V.C. *before* his death.'

212 Bodleian Library, Oxford, Violet Milner papers, C557/2, 11 January 1900.

213 *Victoria's Letters*, III, pp. 445–6.

214 Stanley, *White Mutiny*, p. 283: 'the once despised Indian army in a sense eventually – if briefly – captured the queen's army's citadel'. This actually refers to Roberts's appointment later as commander-in-chief in London.

215 *The Times*, 25 February 1899, p. 8; Roberts to his wife, 11 January 1900 quoted in Pakenham, *Boer War*, p. 246.

Chapter 10: Turning the tide of war in South Africa – and failing to finish it

1   See R. Atwood, *Roberts and Kitchener in South Africa* (Barnsley, 2011).

2   Younghusband, *A Soldier's Memories*, pp. 228–9.

3   Quoted Spiers, *Sudan: the Conquest Reappraised*, p. 197.

4   *The Times*, 18 December 1899, p. 9, 'The command in South Africa'.

5   G.W. Steevens, *With Kitchener to Khartoum* (London, 1990; orig. published 1898), pp. 45–6. For the press, Spiers, *Sudan: The Conquest Reappraised*, Chapter 5, pp. 102–27.

6   Hamilton, *Happy Warrior*, p. 127.

7   B. Farwell, *The Great Boer War* (Harmondsworth, 1977), pp. 152–3.

8   J. L. Garvin, *The Life of Joseph Chamberlain*:Volume III: Empire and World Policy (London, 1934), p. 546.

9   Cornwall R.O., Pole-Carew papers, CO/F10/2, 12 January 1900.

10   Milner, *My Picture Gallery*, p. 161.

11   K. Jeffery, *Field-Marshal Sir Henry Wilson: A Political Soldier* (Oxford, 2006), p. 26.

12   Bobs, 83/1& 2, 19 December 1899 and 2 January 1900.

13   Churchill College Cambridge, AMEL1/1/2, Amery to Chirol, 23 January 1900.

14   WO108/399, no. 94, 9 January 1900.

15   WO32/7962, 'Situation on Arrival'.

16   WO108/409, 8 February 1900. K. was still junior to Buller and Methuen. See WO138/44, Lord Kitchener's personal file.

17   Maj-Gen. F. Smith, *A History of the Royal Army Veterinary Corps 1796–1919* (London, 1927), pp. 203–4; and *A Veterinary History of the War in South Africa 1899–1902* (London, 1919).

18   *The Times*, 25 December 1899, p. 6.

19   TH, III, p. 350 and VI, pp. 387–8. The best discussion is A.J. Page, 'The Supply Services of the British Army in the South African War 1899–1902' (unpubl.

DPhil thesis, Oxford, 1977), pp. 139ff., but Page does not note that Roberts acquired extra wagons.

20 RCSAW, Report, p. 113, Minutes of Evidence, I, p. 144 and II, pp. 342, 344 and Appendix no. 33A, 'Reports . . . on the field Transport in South Africa; Sir W. Richardson, *With the Army Service Corps in South Africa* (London, 1903), p. 105.

21 Baynes, *Far from a Donkey*, pp. 82–4 (Maxse); Col. F.I. Maxse, *Seymour Vandeleur: the Story of a British Officer* (London, 1905), pp. 258, 261–2; Gleichen, *Guardsman's Memories*, p. 202 (Christopherson); C.R. Ballard, *Kitchener* (London, 1930), p. 114. Cf. Melville, *Buller*, I, pp. 278–301 and Sir J. Fortescue, *The Royal Army Service Corps* (Cambridge, 1930), I, pp. 229–65.

22 WO108/409, R. to Lansdowne, 22 January 1900; WO108/238, I, pp. 9 and 11, to MacCormac and Wilson, 25 and 26 January 1900.

23 TH, VI, pp. 499–511 and M.S. Stone, 'The Victorian Army: Health, Hospitals and Social Conditions as Encountered by the British Army during the South African War, 1899–1902' (unpubl. PhD thesis, London, 1992), pp. 45–6, 81–3. Keith Surridge drew my attention to this thesis.

24 Royal Greenjackets Museum, Winchester, Hants, Congreve diary, 12 January 1900.

25 BL, unclassified Lansdowne correspondence, 5 February 1900.

26 K. Surridge, 'Lansdowne at the War Office,' in J. Gooch, ed., *The Boer War: Direction, Experience and Image* (2000), pp. 21–40.

27 NAM 9011–42–14, Spenser Wilkinson papers, R to SW, 23 January 1900.

28 Telegram to the *Morning Post* quoted in *My Early Life* (London, 1930), p. 316.

29 Keith Jeffery, *Field-Marshall Sir Henry Wilson: a Political Soldier* (Oxford, 2006), pp. 26–7.

30 WO108/409, R. to Lansdowne, 15 to 17 January 1900; B. Nasson, *The Boer War: the Struggle for South Africa* (Stroud, 2011), p. 167.

31 C.E. Callwell, *Small Wars: A Tactical Textbook for Imperial Soldiers* (London, 1990 repr., orig. published 1896, 1899, 1906), pp. 33, 402–3.

32 Field-Marshal Sir W. Robertson, *From Private to Field Marshal* (London, 1921), p. 106.

33 Robertson, *From Private to Field Marshal*, p. 107.

34 Major the Hon. G. French, *The Life of Field Marshal Sir John French* (London, 1931), pp. 69–71; B. Gardner, *Allenby* (London, 1985), p. 32.

35 M. Phillips, *With Rimington* (London, 1902), p. 59.

36 NAM 2006–07–29–1 and 1973–10–85, *Journals of Lt Le Poer Trench & Private Bly*; TH, III, pp. 379–86.

37 WO108/409, 14 February 1900.

38 TH, III, p. 388.

39 R. Holmes, *The Little Field Marshal: a Life of Sir John French* (2004, first publ. 1981), pp. 86–93; P. Trew, *The Boer War Generals* (Stroud, 1999), pp. 58–60; TH, III, pp. 379–93.

40 Quoted Judd and Surridge, *The Boer War*, p. 62.

41 For Cronje's convoy, W. Lane, ed., *The War Diary of Burgher Jack Lane 16 January 1899 to 27 February 1900* (Cape Town, 2001), pp. 93–5, 97; Trew, *Boer War Generals*, pp. 61–2.

42 Wagon numbers TH, III, p. 350.

43 TH, III, pp. 397–401. Nicholson's report in Bobs, 52/77, 10 April 1901.

44 Headlam, ed., *Milner Papers*, II, p. 51.

45 WO108/238, I, p. 34, R. to Col. Richardson, 18 February 1900.

46 WO108/238, I, p. 35.

47 Major-General Sir F. Maurice, ed., *History of the War in South Africa* (3 vols. London, 1906–8), II, p. 104–5.

48 Ibid., II, p. 117 notes his lack of staff.

49 *War Diary of Burgher Jack Lane*, p. 116.

50 TH, III, pp. 421–41; Gen. Sir H. Smith-Dorrien, *Memories of Forty-Eight Years Service* (London, 1925), pp. 150–62; NAM 1973–10–85, Pte Bly journal.

51 Maurice, *History of the War in South Africa*, II, p. 129.

52 C. de Wet, *Three Years' War* (1903), pp. 55–8.

53 WO108/409, 21 February 1900.

54 WO108/409, R. to Lansdowne, 22 February 1900.

55 Imperial War Museum, Headlam papers 05/18/1/file 2 Diary, p. 22, 26 February 1900. Headlam claimed the plan had produced the Boer surrender.

56 WO105/6, report of Gen Colville; Smith-Dorrien, *Forty-Eight Years Service*, pp. 157–61; TH, III, p. 482; Nasson, *Boer War*, p. 176.

57 D.S. Macdiarmid, *The Life of Lt-Gen Sir James Moncrieff Grierson* (London, 1923), p. 151.

58 James, p. 295.

59 Macdiarmid, *Grierson*, p. 151; WO32/7968, Narrative of the operations, Camp Paardeberg, 28 February 1900.

60 Surridge, 'Lansdowne at the War Office', p. 35.

61 WO105/31, no. 136, 10 February 1900.

62 This may be followed in Parsons' diary: RA Institute, Woolwich, MD/1111/1, diary of service in Natal, and MD/1111/3, letters to wife, and my article 'How the Royal Artillery Saved Sir Redvers Buller in South Africa' in R.J. Constantine, ed., *New Perspectives on the Anglo-Boer War, 1899–1902* (Bloemfontein, 2013).

63 Macdiarmid, *Grierson*, p. 153.

64 Smith-Dorrien, *Forty-Eight Years Service*, pp. 167–9; Robertson, *Private to Field Marshal*, p. 115.

65 Maurice, *History of the War in South Africa*, II, pp. 190–2; E.K.G. Sixsmith, *Douglas Haig* (London, 1976), pp. 39–40.

66 Imperial War Museum, Headlam papers 05/18/1/file 2, p. 31.

67 WO108/409, R. to Lansdowne and Milner, 8 March 1900.

68 RCSAW, Evidence, I, p. 465; H.F.P. Battersby, *In the Web of a War* (London, 1900), p. 81.

69 Holmes, *Little Field Marshal*, p. 51.

70 Imperial War Museum, French diary, 26 February and 2 and 7 March 1900.

71 G. Mead, *The Good Soldier: the Biography of Douglas Haig* (London, 2007), p. 117; J.P. Harris, *Douglas Haig and the First World War* (Cambridge, 2008), pp. 36–7.

72 Analysis in Sixsmith, *Douglas Haig*, p. 41. Cf. The Marquess of Angelsey, *History of the British Cavalry* (vol. IV, London, 1986), pp. 146–51 and Robertson, *Private to Field-Marshal*, pp. 115–16 emphasising muddled staffwork.

73 King's College London, Liddell Hart Archives, De Lisle, *My Narrative of the South African War, 1899–1902*, 2 vols, I, pp. 1–2 (henceforth 'De Lisle').

74 De Lisle, I, p. 42.

75 Sir G. Arthur, *Life of Lord Kitchener* (3 vols, London, 1920), I, pp. 299–300.

76 WO105/6, Kelly-Kenny's despatch; WO108/409, R. to Lansdowne, two successive despatches, 11 March 1900; TH, III, pp. 580–7.

77 Imperial War Museum, French diaries, 12 March 1900; TH, III.

78 TH, III, pp. 587–91.

79 TH, III, pp. 591–3.

80 F. Pretorius, 'Boer Propaganda during the South African War of 1899–1902', *Journal of Imperial and Commonwealth History*, vol. 37, no. 3 (2009), pp. 399–419.

81 See R. Atwood, '"Across our Father's Graves"; Kipling and Field Marshal Lord Roberts,' *Journal of the Kipling Society*, vol. 83 (March, 2009), pp. 9–28; and R. Atwood, 'Kipling and the South Africa War: "Dress Rehearsal for Armageddon"?', *Journal of the Kipling Society*, vol. 85 (December 2011), pp. 29–49.

82 A. Wessels, *Lord Roberts and the War in South Africa 1899–1902* (Stroud, 2000), p. 65.

83 J. Beaumont, 'The Press and Censorship during the South African War, 1899–1902, *South African Historical Journal*, vol. 41, no. 1 (1999), esp. p. 274; S. Badsey, 'War Correspondents in the Boer War,' in Gooch, ed., *Boer War*, pp. 198–200; Judd and Surridge, *The Boer War*, pp. 254–5.

84 R.S. Churchill, *Winston S. Churchill, Vol I, Companion Part 2 1896–1900* (London, 1967), pp. 1171–2.

85 W.S. Churchill, *Ian Hamilton's March* (London, 1900), p. 279.

86 These letters appeared in *The Times* on 24 March, 11, 13, 14 and 17 April, 14 May and 27 June 1900. Letters II, VIII and IX were published as an appendix to the *Report of the Royal Commission appointed to consider and report upon the care and treatment of the sick and wounded during the South African Campaign* (1901).

87 M.S. Stone, 'The Victorian Army', pp. 94–6.

88 Phillips, *With Rimington*, p. 79.

89 Report by Dr H.H. Tooth, a specialist physician attached to Roberts's forces, published in a paper read to the Clinical Society in London, 8 March 1901 and summarised in an article by 'Cuidich n' Ruih' in the *South African Military History Journal*, June 1976. Roberts foresaw water as a problem, as Buller's transport reform had not provided sufficient water carts. BL, Lansdowne papers, R. to Lansdowne, 6 February 1900.

90 WO108/411, R. to Lansdowne, 11 October 1900.

91 BL, Lansdowne papers, R. to Lansdowne, 5 March 1900.

92 Stone, 'The Victorian Army', p. 114ff.

93 He took a younger man Colonel Stevenson as PMO at headquarters. Stone, 'The Victorian Army', p. 109; WO105/25, letter of Mrs Chamberlain, 23 April 1900.

94 Stone, 'The Victorian Army', pp. 122–3.

95 Report of the Royal Commission, pp. 13, 37–8.

96 *Hansard*, Commons debates, 28 and 29 June 1900, vol. 84, cc. 1313–9 and vol. 85 cc. 89–184; Surridge, 'Lansdowne at the War Office', p. 37 in Gooch, ed., *Boer War*. Roughly one-sixteenth of British losses from disease occurred at Bloemfontein.

97 Spies, *Methods of Barbarism*, pp. 34–7; A. Grundlingh, 'Collaborators in Boer Society', in P. Warwick, ed., *The South African War: the Anglo-Boer War 1899–1902* (Harlow, 1980), p. 258.

98 WO108/409.

99 De Wet, *Three Years War*, pp. 77–9; Scholtz, *Why the Boers Lost*, p. 67.

100 De Wet, *Three Years War*, pp. 85–92; TH, IV, pp. 30–50; Lt-Col. Sir J. Rankin, *A Subaltern's Letters to his Wife in London* (London, 1930, orig. publ. 1901), p. 203; WO108/409, R. to Lansdowne, 31 March, 1 and 3 April 1900.

101 De Wet, *Three Years War*, pp. 95–100; TH, IV, pp. 51–5; WO108/409, R. to Lansdowne, 8 and 9 April 1900. British accounts sometimes confuse Moestertshoek and Dewetsdorp. I owe the distinction to Prof. Andre Wessels.

102 TH, IV, pp. 55–63.

103 Churchill, *My Early Life*, p. 352.

104 Hamilton 2/2/5, to wife, 9 March 1900. He was twice unlucky with the VC, too senior at Elandslaagte and too junior at Majuba. Letter from Col. Coleridge Grove in Hamilton 2/4/11, 7 July 1900.

105 Rawly 1–7–2, 7 March 1900.

106 Hamilton 13/6, typescript on relations between R and K.

107 Hamilton 13/6. See also Hamilton 13/21, 30 April 1918, letter to Col Sir Neville Chamberlain about the partnership. Hamilton and Nicholson fell out later, which may affect what the former writes. Hamilton, *The Happy Warrior*, pp. 79, 202; C. Lee, *Jean, Lady Hamilton 1861–1942* (privately printed, 2001), pp. 56–65, 159–60.

108 Unclas. Lansdowne correspondence, L. to Roberts, 17 March 1900. Lady R had been given the use of the London home of a friend, Sir James Mackay, until her departure: Lanceley, *Hall-Boy to House-Steward*, p. 85.

109 *The Times*, 19 March 1900, p. 9; K. Nagai, *Empire of Analogies* (Cork, 2006), pp. 82–4. Kipling composed for 'The Friend' a poem 'St Patrick's Day'. The United Irishmen were not impressed with an imperial display of Irishness: the shamrock was grossly outraged, 'our thanks for butcher service'.

110 NAM 2006–27–09–1, Lt. Trench diary, p. 231, 2 May 1900; p. 234 shows champagne used for medicinal purposes for officers; WO105/25, letter of 23 April 1900 from Mrs Chamberlain; IWM, Headlam papers 05/18/1/file 2, vol. 1, 1 May.

111 Hamilton 2/2/5, H. to Spenser Wilkinson, 31 March 1900; *The Times*, 27 March 1900, p. 9.

112 A. Wessels, ed., *Lord Kitchener and the War in South Africa* (Stroud, 2006), p. 31, 26 April 1900 (henceforth 'Wessels-Kitchener').

113 TH, IV, p. 8; Ballard, *Kitchener*, p. 139; NAM 9011–42–14, Spenser Wilkinson papers, 8 December 1931.

114 G.F.R. Henderson, *Science of War: a Collection of Essays and Lectures 1891–1903* (London, 1908), p. xxxv. For the breakdown of Henderson's health see Robertson, *Private to Field-Marshal*, p. 118. He died in 1903 in Egypt where he had gone to recoup his health.

115 The National Archives, Ardagh papers, PRO30/40/14, p. 112. Surridge, *Managing the South African War*, p. 88.

116 TH, IV, pp. 80–2.

117 Unclas. Lansdowne correspondence, L to R, 31 March 1900, R to L, 1 April 1900.

118 Liddell Hart Archives, Lyttelton papers, Major Stuart-Wortley to Mrs Talbot, 1 April 1900.

119 Telegraphic exchange WO105/13, bundle marked T/8/4 and Bobs, 118; also Rawly 33–7–3, 13/5. Cf. Pakenham, *Boer War*, p. 379.

120 De Lisle, *Reminiscences of Sport and War*, pp. 92–3, 111–14.

121 Smith, *Veterinary History of the War in South Africa*, p. 77.

122 TH, IV, pp. 102–4, 113–14 and 115–126; D. Scott, ed., *Douglas Haig: the Preparatory Prologue 1861–1914: Diaries and Letters* (Barnsley, 2006), p. 169. WO108/409, R. to Lansdowne, 29 April 1900 for his view of French; Badsey, *Cavalry Doctrine*, pp. 119–21 points to different conclusions about cavalry drawn from the battle.

123 TH, IV, pp. 229ff.; Lady Sarah Wilson, *South African Memories* (London, 1909) describes events in the town.

124 Rawly 11, 12 and 13 May 1900.

125 WO108/409, R. to Lansdowne, 17 May 1900.

126 WO108/409, R to Lansdowne, R. to Lansdowne 17 and 19 May 1900; WO108/139, II, pp. 437, 57, 60.

127 Hamilton 2/2/5, H. to wife, 9 June 1900.

128 Phillips, *With Rimington*, pp. 120–4; Churchill, *Ian Hamilton's March*, pp. 251–6; Smith-Dorrien, *Forty-Eight Years Service*, pp. 205–10; Headlam,

History of the Royal Artillery, III, pp. 418–19; for expanding bullets, Spiers, *The Victorian Soldier in Africa*, p. 169.

129 TH, IV, pp. 150–3; Meintjes, *Louis Botha*, pp. 63–4.

130 B. Viljoen, *My Reminiscences of the Anglo-Boer War* (London, 1900), p. 144; Lansdowne correspondence, R. to L., 30 May, 1900; H.W. Wilson, *With the Flag to Pretoria* (2 vols, London, 1901), II, p. 646.

131 Reitz, *Commando*, pp. 106–9 testifies to a staggering lack of initiative in a cavalry column moving parallel to the Boers without attempting to cut them off.

132 Smuts Papers, I, p. 549; Nasson, *The Boer War*, p. 203. This is a more substantial charge against Roberts than the claim that Dr Krause won vital breathing space. Roberts could hardly have renewed his advance from Johannesburg more quickly than he did – 'the necessities of supply imposed a two days' halt'. Churchill, *Ian Hamilton's March*, pp. 279–83, 297; TH, IV, pp. 154–5, 159. Cf. Pakenham, *Boer War*, p. 432.

133 De Lisle, I, pp. 63–71; De Lisle, *Reminiscences of Sport and War*, p. 94; TH, IV, pp. 157–9.

134 Churchill, *Ian Hamilton's March*, pp. 289–95; WO108/410, R. to the Queen, 6 June 1900; Haddock letter 18, 7 June 1900, Irene Camp.

135 Bobs, R35/21, 23 June 1900. Two Delhi comrades, Hugh Gough and Hills-Johnes, had by now joined him.

136 Bobs, R19/9.

137 P. Pienaar, *With Steyn and de Wet* (London, 1903), p. 96; Reitz, *Commando*, pp. 109–15; Viljoen, *Reminiscences*, pp. 145–9.

138 Viljoen, *Reminiscences*, p. 149.

139 Grundlingh, 'Collaborators in Boer Society', pp. 258–62.

140 De Wet, *Three Years War*, pp. 131–9; Wessels-Kitchener, p. 37, K. to the Queen, 30 June 1900.

141 TH, IV, pp. 245–59; S. Miller, *Lord Methuen and the British Army* (London and Portland, 1999), pp. 198, n. 124.

142 Stone, 'The Victorian Army', pp. 133–4; WO104/240, R to K-K, 18 July 1900; Wilson, *With the Flag to Pretoria*, II, p. 634; for total deaths Curtin, *Empire and Disease*, p. 240; hospitals quote, Haddock letters, no. 21, 15 July 1900; Lady Briggs, *The Staff Work of the Anglo-Boer War 1899–1901* (London, 1901), pp. 220–4, 236, 291.

143 WO105/31, no. 690, 12 June 1900.

144 TH, IV, pp. 276–94; KCL, De Lisle, I, pp. 73–84; Wilson, *With the Flag to Pretoria*, II, pp. 161–4; Hancock and Poel, *Smuts Papers*, I, p. 557; Nasson, *Boer War*, pp. 204–5.

145 TH, IV, pp. 297–343; A. Hunter, *Kitchener's Sword-Arm: the Life and Campaigns of General Sir Archibald Hunter* (Staplehurst, 1986), pp. 149–67; WO105/10, c-in-c/126/144, Hunter's despatch 4 August 1900 with R's covering letter. He had exercised independence from Roberts in his negotiations.

146 De Wet, *Three Years War*, p. 189 describes his escape; TH, IV, pp. 414–33; Rawly 33–7–3, 2 August 1900; WO105/16 telegrams in South Africa and

WO108/241, pp. 11–37; I follow Miller, *Methuen and the British Army*, pp. 206–7 in attributing the main fault for not blocking Olifants Nek to HQ rather than Hamilton.

147 TH, IV, pp. 358–9, 428–9.

148 WO108/409, 7 June 1900.

149 'Horsemastership': the care of horses, a constant theme of Roberts's letters and cavalry historians' writing.

150 Quote from *Warnotes, The Diary of Colonel de Villebois-Mareuil* (trans. F. Rees, London, 1902); H. Bailes, 'Military Aspects of the War', p. 95 in Warwick, ed., *The South African War*; and Scholtz, *Why the Boers Lost*, pp. xi, 58–9.

151 Quoted by S.B. Spies, 'Women and the War', p. 165 in Warwick, ed., *The South African War*.

152 Col. H.C.B. Cook, OBE, ed., 'Letters from South Africa', *JSAHR*, vol. 69 (1991), p. 77.

153 Spies, *Methods of Barbarism*, pp. 147–9.

154 Captain. J.P. Fletcher-Vane, *The War and One Year After* (London, 1903); H. Bradford, 'Gentlemen and Boers: Afrikaner Nationalism, Gender and Colonial Warfare in the South African War,' in Cuthbertson *et al.*, *Writing a Wider War* (Athens, Ohio and Cape Town, 2000).

155 P. Todd and D. Fordham, ed., *Private Tucker's Boer War Diary. The Transvaal War of 1899, 1900, 1901 & 1902 with the Natal Field Forces* (London, 1980), p. 106.

156 TH, IV, p. 192 for quote, pp. 170–97 for the campaign.

157 NAM, Spencer Wilkinson, 9011–41–14, 8 March 1900; Hamilton 2/2/5, to wife, 9 and 21 March 1900. Hamilton blamed Buller for hating him 'even worse than I thought', later 'a touch of Peshawar fever' caused the vitriol.

158 RAI, Woolwich, Parsons papers, 13 July 1900; NAM 8508–22 Trotter papers (etc.), 11 July 1900.

159 E. Blake Knox, *Buller's Campaign with the Natal Field Force of 1900* (London, 1902), pp. 285–6; Maurice, *History of the War in South Africa*, III, p. 398.

160 RA Institute, Woolwich, Parsons papers, MD/1111/1 diary of service in Natal, k 26 and 27 July 1900; WO108/410, 27 and 29 August 1900; Blake Knox, *Buller's Campaign*, pp. 287–91: 'Lord Roberts arrived on the field . . . and congratulated General Buller on the day's operations'.

161 WO105/10, 17 September 1900.

162 Viljoen, *Reminiscences*, p. 161.

163 TH, IV, pp. 480–5; WO108/411, 13, 16 and 17 September 1900 [one letter].

164 WO108/410 and 411, 7 June, 21 August, 17 and 24 September 1900; WO108/241, 18 August 1900.

165 D. Miller, *A Captain of the Gordons: Service Experiences 1900–1909* (London, n.d.), pp. 58–9.

166 Spies, *Methods of Barbarism*, pp. 57–62.

167 Surridge, *Managing the South African War*, pp. 104–10.

168 Rawly, 5201–33–7–3, 19 September 1900.

169 Buckle, *Victoria's Letters*, III, pp. 592–7; CAB37/53/53, Lansdowne's minute to the Cabinet, 20 June 1900.

170 Uncat. Lansdowne papers, R. to L., 18 July 1900. Also 28/8, 4 and 12/10, 8/11/1900; J. Pollock, *Kitchener: Comprising the Road to Omdurman & Saviour of the Nation* (London, 1998, 2001), pp. 184–5; D. Gilmour, *Curzon* (London, 1994), pp. 154–5, 192–4, 250.

171 NAM 6803–4, Marker papers; Surridge, *Managing the South African War*, pp. 111–12.

172 Rawly, 1–7–3, 15 to 19 July 1900.

173 Rawly, 1–7–3, 29 September 1900.

174 KCL, Liddell Hart Archives, Lyttelton papers, Lyttelton to wife, 25 October 1900.

175 Scholtz, *Why the Boers Lost*, pp. 85–92.

176 De Lisle, II, pp. 27–35; de Wet, *Three Years War*, pp. 215–16; Wilson, *After Pretoria*, I, pp. 174–9.

177 Buckle, Queen Victoria's Letters, III, pp. 613–18.

178 Uncat. Landsdowne correspondence, R to L, 11/10, 2 and 9 June 1900.

179 Anglesey, *British Cavalry*, IV, p. 210.

180 Rawly 1–7–3, 10 October 1900; unclas. Lansdowne correspondence, R. to L., 11 October 1900.

181 Rawly 1–7–3, dates as text.

182 Bobs, 13/12, 20 December 1900.

183 Bodleian Library, Violet Milner Mss. Add. 2, ff. 12–17.

184 Rawly 1–7–3, 11 December 1900.

Chapter 11: Good work for army and Empire

1 Briggs, *Staff Work of the Anglo-Boer War*, p. 453.

2 Kimberley Diaries, pp. 479–80, 18 October 1900.

3 Garvin, *Joseph Chamberlain*, III, p. 621.

4 In a Cabinet reshuffle Salisbury gave up the Foreign Office to Lansdowne. Lansdowne's under-secretary at the War Office succeeded him.

5 Bobs, 13/12, 20 December 1900.

6 Magnus, *King Edward VII*, pp. 270–1, 380, 404.

7 Wessels, *Lord Roberts and the War in South Africa*, p. 156.

8 Bobs, 13/12, 20 December 1900.

9 NAM 2006–08–4, Thurston letters, 27 January 1901.

10 Letter by 'S' [Eddie Stanley?] in *The Scapegoat: Being a Selection from a Series of Articles . . . on the case of Sir Henry Colvile* (London, 1901), pp. 21–2.

11 Buckle, *Queen Victoria's Letters*, III, pp. 598, n. 1, 628–9, 636–42.

12 K20/07, R. to K., 25 January 1901.

13 Bobs, 33/12, 25 January 1901.

14 Beckett, *The Victorians at War*, chapter 9; Spiers, *Late Victorian Army*, p. 314.

15 L. Amery, *My Political Life* (3 vols. 1953), I, p. 123.

16 TH, IV, pp. 8 and 493–4 (Roberts), pp. 177 and 189–194 (Buller).

17 For Amery's imperialism, see remarks of H.A.L. Fisher quoted by Dr P. Donaldson, 'Writing the Anglo-Boer War' in Constantine, ed., *New Perspectives on the Anglo-Boer War*, p. 262.

18 Amery papers, Churchill College, AMEL/1/1/11, letters from R to Amery, and 23 January, 6, 7 and 29 November 1903 and Amery's letters to R in Bobs 1.

19 Roberts's introduction to Henderson's *The Science of War*, p. xxxv.

20 Luvaas, *Education of an Army*, pp. 174 and 208; Donaldson, 'Writing the Anglo-Boer War', pp. 265–71; Becket, *Victorians at War*, pp. 88–91.

21 'By a British Officer', actually E.H Cairns, the title from Kipling's famous verse 'An Absent-Minded Beggar', pp. 13, 115–35, 140–1, 143, 155.

22 Hamer, *The British Army*, p. 201, n. 3; Page, 'Supply Services', p. 356; P. Fraser, *Lord Esher: a Political Biography* (London, 1973), pp. 18–19, 84–107.

23 Letter in James, pp. 372–3. QMG was traditionally head of ops under the commander-in-chief.

24 Briggs, *Staff Work*, p. 462; W.S. Hamer, *British Army: Civil-Military Relations 1885–1905* (Oxford, 1970), pp. 187–92; K20, 12 April and 18 June 1901; Bobs, 166/11, 17 December 1900; CAB 37/53 and 56; Midleton, *Records and Reaction*, pp. 372–5; L.J. Sartre, 'St John Brodrick and Army Reform, 1901–3', *Journal of British Studies*, vol. 15, pt 2 (1975–6), p. 119; Bobs, 124/1, p. 31, to Sec of State, 21 June 1901.

25 Wheeler, *War Office Past and Present*, p. 263. He complained in private.

26 Unclas. Lansdowne papers, R. to L., 4 October 1900.

27 Bobs, 52/72, 16 January 1901.

28 Hamilton, *The Happy Warrior*, p. 177.

29 Manning, *Evelyn Wood*, p. 224.

30 Midleton, *Records and Reactions*, p. 122.

31 Spies, *Methods of Barbarism*, pp. 147–52; E. Lee, *To the Bitter End* (London, 1985) pp. 162–90 for a heart-rending photographic record. Recent analysis shows a high proportion of young able-bodied men in these camps. E. von Heyningen, ' "Lies, damned lies and statistics": statistics and the British Concentration Camps Database', in Constantine, *New Perspectives on the Anglo-Boer War*, p. 129.

32 Warwick, 'Black People in the War', in P. Warwick, *The South African War*, p. 204; Wessels, *Lord Kitchener and the War in South Africa*, p. 103; Nasson, *Boer War*, pp. 245, 290.

33 *Correspondence relative to the Treatment of Natives by the Boers* (Cd. 821, 1901).

34 P. Warwick, 'Black People and the War', in P. Warwick, *The South African War*, pp. 195ff; Nasson, *The Boer War*, pp. 247–9.

35 K20, letter 08, R. to K., 31 January 1901.

36 Seamus O.D. Wade in the *Kipling Journal*, no. 273 (March), p. 55: 1,677 Indian soldiers and 9,065 followers received the South African War medal; another 1,600 including Mohandas Gandhi, resident in South Africa, served in ambulance units.

37 Smith, *Veterinary History*, p. 213; TH, V, p. 507 n.

38 *Hansard*, Commons Debates, 17 June 1901, vol. 95, c. 591. For whole debate cc. 573–629. These arguments have not cut much ice in South Africa.

39 Bobs, 33/55, 1 November 1901.

40 Wessels, *Lord Roberts and the War in South Africa*, p. 201; also K19, 045, 046 and 047, 25 October, 2 and 8 November 1901.

41 Bobs, 33/56, 5 November 1901.

42 Hamilton, *Happy Warrior*, p. 181.

43 Bobs, 122/2, no 175, R. to Hamilton, 22 November 1901.

44 Hamilton 2/3/2, 3, 4 and 6 to Roberts, November and December 1901; Arthur, *Life of Lord Kitchener*, II, p. 77, n. 1.

45 Battle of Tweebosch, 7 March 1902. Hamilton, *Happy Warrior*, p. 187.

46 Bobs, 61/24, 25 and 32, 25 November and 15 December 1901, 27 March 1902; Badsey, *War and the Arme Blanche*, pp. 169–70 from which I take the above. On black scouts, I. Hamilton and V. Sampson, *Anti-Commando* (London, 1931).

47 Hamilton 2/3/243, H. to Roberts, 18 April 1902; Hamilton, 2/3/25, typescript account of defeat of Potgieter, 18 April 1902.

48 J. Darwin, *The Empire Project: the Rise and Fall of the British World System* (Cambridge, 2009), pp. 246–7, 254.

49 Robinson and Gallagher, *Africa and the Victorians*, p. 461.

50 S. Marks and S. Trapedo, 'Lord Milner and the South African State,' *History Workshop*, IX (1979), pp. 50–80; Headlam, *Milner Papers*, II, pp. 457–71, 486–7.

51 S.C. Spencer, 'The British/Imperial Model of Administration: Assembling the South African Constabulary 1900 to 1902', *Scienta Militaria*, vol. 41, no. 2 (2013), pp. 92–115.

52 Hamilton, *Happy Warrior*, p. 191.

53 Strachan, *Politics of the British Army*, p. 103.

54 Midleton, *Records and Reactions*, pp. 123–4; Sartre, 'St John Brodrick and Army Reform', pp. 122–3.

55 Midleton, *Records and Reactions*, pp. 150–2, 201.

56 James, pp. 379–82 quoting letters to Brodrick and Hamilton, both 2 September 1901.

57 Sartre, 'St John Brodrick and Army Reform', p. 136.

58 Wilkinson, *Thirty-Five Years*, pp. 255–6.

59 S. Bidwell and D. Graham, *Firepower: British Army Weapons and Theories of War 1904–1945* (London, 1982), p. 29.

60 Brice, 'Brackenbury: Thinking Man's Soldier', p. 286; E. Spiers, Re-Arming the
    Edwardian Army', *JSAHR*, 57 (1979), p. 168; Bidwell and Graham,
    Firepower, p. 13.

61 A committee under Lt-Gen. Archie Hunter sat and made recommendations.
    Bobs, 124/1, pp. 150–2, 21 August 1901, memo on uniform.

62 *The Times*, 21 September 1903, p. 6 and 22 September 1903, p. 10.

63 Smith, *History of the Veterinary Corps*, pp. 207–13 and Maj-Gen. Sir J.
    Moore, *Army Veterinary Service in War* (London, 1921). Major improvements
    under Lt-Gen Smith 1907–1910 followed Roberts's command: Graham
    Winton, 'Horsing the British Army 1878–1923' (Unpubl. PhD thesis,
    Birmingham University, 1997), pp. 131ff. Horses were much better cared for
    in the First World War. Prof Stephen Badsey referred me to Dr Winton's work.

64 Col. J.K. Dunlop, *The Development of the British Army 1899–1914* (London,
    1938), p. 145; Midleton, *Records and Reactions*, pp. 163–6.

65 Today Queen Alexandra's Royal Army Nursing Corps.

66 *The Times*, 30 September 1901, p. 10 'Report of the Committee . . .'

67 J. Pigott, *Queen Alexandra's Royal Army Nursing Corps* (London, 1975),
    pp. 39–40.

68 Luvaas, *Education of an Army*, p. 224.

69 Robson, 'Roberts' ODNB; Dunlop, *Development of the British Army*, pp. 145,
    153–7; James, pp. 382–4; *Report of the Royal Commission . . . upon . . . the
    sick and wounded during the South African campaign*; Callwell, *Henry
    Wilson*, I, pp. 50–1; Barnett, *Britain and her Army* (London, 1970), pp. 343–4;
    Wood, *Winnowed Memories*, p. 125.

70 Godwin-Austen, *The Staff and the Staff College*, p. 235; WO108/184, 'Notes
    by Col J M Grierson . . .'.

71 Godwin-Austen, *The Staff and the Staff College*, pp. 242–7; M. Jacobson,
    Rawlinson in India (Army Records Society, Stroud, 2002), intro., p. viii.

72 B. Bond, *The Victorian Army and the Staff College 1854–1914* (1972),
    pp. 247–8; Esher, *Journals*, II, pp. 192–3; Jeffery, *Henry Wilson*, pp. 64–7
    citing an article by J. Hussey showing that Wilson's appointment was carefully
    considered by senior officers and successive Cabinet ministers.

73 Reginald, Viscount Esher, *The Tragedy of Lord Kitchener* (London, 1921),
    pp. 84–5; Jeffery, *Henry Wilson*, pp. 67–74.

74 K. Jeffery, 'The Impact of the South African War on Imperial Defence', in
    Lowry, *South African War Reappraised*, pp. 188–202, and H. de Watteville on
    Wilson in DNB.

75 N. d'Ombrain, *War Machinery and High Policy: Defence Administration in
    Peacetime Britain 1902–1914* (Oxford, 1975), pp. 141ff.

76 D. Woodward in the ODNB; Godwin-Austen, *The Staff and Staff College*,
    pp. 255–6; Robertson, *From Private to Field-Marshal*, pp. 169–85.

77 Hamilton's evidence to the RCSAW.

78 Badsey, *Doctrine and Reform in the British Cavalry*, Chapter 4, 'The Roberts
    era'; T. Bowman and M. Connelly, *The Edwardian Army: Recruiting, Training*

and Deploying the British Army (Oxford, 2012), p. 103; for the cavalry
school, Smith, *Veterinary History*, pp. 226–7 and Bobs, 124/4, to secretary of
state, forwarding report by Col. Rimington on German cavalry and field firing.

79 I. Hamilton, *A Staff Officer's Scrap Book* (London, 1912), pp. 8, 10.

80 K. Jeffery, 'The Impact of the South African War on Imperial Defence,' p. 196.
Bidwell and Graham, *Firepower*, p. 2, state that had Hamilton's 'perceptive
report been acted upon, the British Army might have been better prepared for
positional warfare'.

81 Smith-Dorrien, *Forty-Eight Years*, pp. 294–6; see also Bobs, 13/112, Brodrick
to Roberts, 11 October 1901 and 122, no.160, Roberts to Brodrick, 24
October 1901: 'He is greatly grieved and can be trusted not to blunder again.'

82 Gen. Sir C. Harrington, *Plumer of Messines* (London, 1935), pp. 55–6.

83 Harrington, *Plumer of Messines*, pp. 66–7.

84 K. Surridge, 'The Honour and Reputation of the Army: Lord Roberts, the
Government and the Fight at Nicholson's Nek', *SOTQ*, vol. 93 (June 1998),
pp. 12–14. Much of the following relies on Surridge's article.

85 Surridge, 'Honour and Reputation'; James, pp. 377–82; Wessels-Kitchener,
pp. 63–4, 67, 93–4.

86 Bobs, 127–1, cutting from *Daily Express*, 31 December 1902, 'Honour'
Restored and 'Cashiered Officer to be Reinstated'; details in WO32/8005,
surrender of a portion of the garrison of Helvetia on 29 December 1900 and
WO32/8006, Major Cotton, Liverpool Regiment. Cotton had fought in
Afghanistan and Burma and was to serve in the First World War; copies in
Kings Regiment papers, Liverpool Museum.

87 Quoted James, p. 380. See Atwood, *Roberts and Kitchener in South Africa*,
pp. 201–4 and 'Sackings in the South African War', *SOTQ*, 150 (September
2012), pp. 24–32.

88 Bobs, 100, vol. VIII, p. 359, 9 August 1889. Lumsden was adjutant-general.

89 Bobs, 100, X, p. 281, to Luck, 17 October 1887.

90 On French see Liddell Hart Archives, Lyttelton, 1–24/20, Porter to Talbot,
17/2/1901: '[French] was the cause of a very great number of men being
broken . . .'

91 BL, uncat. Lansdowne mss, Lansdowne to Bobs, 27 July 1900; Midleton,
Records and Reactions, pp. 130–1; *The Scapegoat, passim*; Sir H. Colvile, *The
Work of the Ninth Division* (London, 1901); Wilts and Swindon Archives,
Methuen Papers, 1742–12, 1903–4, mss note by Methuen on envelope.

92 WO108/411, R. to Brodrick, 15 November 1900; Roberts, *Salisbury: Victorian
Titan*, pp. 791, 822.

93 WO108/399, R. to Brodrick, 15 November 1900; uncat. Lansdowne mss,
Roberts to L., 4 October 1900; Bobs, 23–13/14, 20 December 1900; Rawly,
33–7–3, 1 and 4 December 1900; K20, 19 April 1900; Powell, *Buller*, pp. 194–5.

94 British Library, uncat. Lansdowne letters, 8 November 1900.

95 His speech in *The Times*, 11 November 1901, p. 10; see also J. Walters,
Aldershot Review (London, 1970), p. 160.

96 Brodrick's typescript account of interview 17 October 1901 in Bobs 183–6.

97 Bobs, 122, no. 2, letter no. 156, 20 October 1901.

98 Bobs, 183–6 and 13/112–25.

99 Midleton, *Records and Reactions*, pp. 131–7; *Hansard*, H. of Commons Debates, 17/71902, cc. 527–65 does not permit confirmation of Midleton's claim that cheering on the government benches drowned out Grey's words; Wilts and Swindon Archives, Methuen 1742/38, 1 January and 4 December 1901; Add Mss 49720, Brodrick–Balfour correspondence.

100 Midleton, *Records and Reactions*, p. 131; K20, 27 March 1902. The press overwhelmingly saw his retirement as essential, the *Westminster Gazette*, 23 October 1901 heading its account 'Inevitable'.

101 NAM, Birdwood 6707–19–239, 25 October 1901.

102 Streets, 'Military Influence in late Victorian and Edwardian Popular Media,' pp. 245–6.

103 *Hansard*, Lords debates, vol. 110, cc. 1339–41, 10 July 1902. The documents are printed in R. Churchill, *Sir Winston Churchill: Companion Volume 2*, part 1 (London, 1969), pp. 151–61.

104 T.C. Kennedy, 'Airing the Dirty Linen of an Unreformed Army: the Kinloch Affair, 1902–1903', *Military Affairs*, XLIII, no. 2 (April 1979), pp. 69–76, setting the affair in the context of post-Boer War reform; newspaper accounts in Bobs, 139, vol. 13. Similar bullying in the 2nd Life Guards led to similar results. Anglesey, *History of the British Cavalry*, IV, pp. 456–7.

105 Newspaper articles in Bobs, 139, vols 12 and 13, and James, pp. 386–7.

106 RCSAW, *passim*; Churchill College Archives, ESHR15/1, typescript copy of Esher's reports to Edward VII. His letters are an invaluable source for commissioners' views of witnesses.

107 Esher, II, pp. 355–6; RCSAW, *Evidence*, I, p. 7.

108 Churchill College, ESHR/1, 4 April 1902.

109 Churchill College, ESHR/1, Esher to the King, 21 May 1903.

110 Hamer, *British Army*, pp. 201–11; James, pp. 392–3.

111 C. Barnett, *Britain and Her Army*, pp. 355–7.

112 Hamer, *British Army*, pp. 229–30.

113 K28. Roberts to Kitchener, 8 and 20 November 1903; Midleton, *Records and Reactions*, pp. 151–2; Esher, *Journals* II, pp. 35, 42, 43.

114 Esher, 1, *Journals,* II, p. 44; Bobs, 196, Printed Army Order 18 February 1904. Wilkinson, *Thirty-Five Years*, p. 267 records indignantly that the Army Council did not have the courtesy to send Roberts a copy.

115 Esher Journals, p. 321, 28 November 1901.

116 Hamer, *British Army*, pp. 242–4.

117 NAM, 8704–35–620 and 621, Harris to Ellison, 17 and 31 December 1934; Jeffery, *Henry Wilson*, p. 57.

118 G. Ellison, 'Lord Roberts and the General Staff,' *The Nineteenth Century and After* (December 1932), pp. 722–32; *The Times*, 13 October 1932, p. 10; also Dunlop, *Development of the British Army*, pp. 204–12.

119 Repington later told Geoffrey Robinson of *The Times* that Roberts 'was omnipotent for three years and did nothing.' Both statements are false. A.J.A. Morris, *The Letters of Lieutenant-Colonel Charles a Court Repington, Military Correspondent of the Times 1903–1918* (Stroud, 1999), p. 194.

Chapter 12: Trying to arouse his countrymen

1 Bobs, 122, R to Balfour, 12 February 1904; d'Ombrain, *War Machinery and High Policy*, pp. 8, 18; Esher, *Journals*, II, pp. 42–3.

2 Bobs, 122, R. to Kitchener, 4 February 1904.

3 Fraser, *Esher*, pp. 179–80; ESHR 2/10, 10 December 1905. Fraser credits Esher rather than Haldane with creating the BEF of 1914. The classic account is E.M. Spiers, *Haldane: Army Reformer* (Edinburgh, 1984).

4 K28, 26 December 1902.

5 W. Lawrence, *The India We Served* (London, 1928), p. 244; Gilmour, *Curzon*, pp. 285ff.; Spear, *Oxford History of Modern India*, pp. 306–17.

6 Arthur, *Life of Land Kitchener* II, pp. 122, 124.

7 Smith-Dorrien, *Forty-Eight Years*, p. 348.

8 K28, 9 June 1903, 20 December 1902, 9 January, 19 March and 17 April 1903.

9 K29, 26 May 1904.

10 Buck, *Simla Past and Present*, pp. 80–2; Royle, *Kitchener Enigma*, p. 201.

11 IOL L/MIL/17/5/1617. *Record of Lord Kitchener's Administration of the Army in India*, pp. 296, 301–2.

12 Godwin-Austen, *The Staff and the Staff College*, p. 250.

13 IOL, L/MIL/17/5/1617. Record of Lord Kitchener's Administration, pp. 204–9, 210–12, 336–53; Menezes, *Fidelity and Honour*, pp. 227–8.

14 K29, 29 February 1904.

15 K28, 18 June 1903; K29, 7 July 1907.

16 Bobs, 90, R147 & R148, 5 March and 19 May 1905.

17 NAM, Spenser Wilkinson papers 9011–42–14, 22 April 1905. Wilkinson, *Thirty-Five Years*, p. 269 writes: 'Lord Glenesk was a great admirer of Kitchener, and an article appeared in the *Morning Post* supporting Kitchener's proposals. Lord Roberts attributing that article to me, wrote . . .' Paul Ramsey, who is studying Wilkinson, feels certain he would have supported Curzon and Roberts.

18 Gilmour, *Curzon*, pp. 312–15.

19 P. Boyden, 'Lord Roberts and the Kitchener-Curzon Debate,' *Annual Report of the National Army Museum* (1974–5), pp. 17–21.

20 K28, 1 June 1905. Gilmour states on p. 316 that only Roberts believed a true compromise had been reached in the military supply member; his correspondence to Kitchener suggests he knew the truth.

21 Gilmour, *Curzon*, pp. 324–46; Harold Nicolson, 'Curzon,' DNB.

22 Strachan, *Politics of the British Army*, p. 105.

23 Gopal, *British Policy in India*, pp. 290–1; Esher, Journals, II, pp. 84–5; G. H. Cassar, *Kitchener: Architect of Victory* (London, 1977), p. 153. Cf. Gilmour, *Curzon*, pp. 337–8 and Strachan, *Politics of British Army*, p. 108 that an important principle was involved.

24 Quoted Menezes, *Fidelity and Honour*, p. 237.

25 P. Boyden, 'Lord Roberts and the Kitchener-Curzon Debate,' pp. 17–21; Menezes, *Fidelity and Honour*, p. 252; R. Braddon, *The Siege* (London, 1969); C. Townshend, *When God made Hell: the British Campaign in Mesopotamia and the Creation of Iraq 1914–1921* (London, 2010).

26 Bobs, 122, letterbook no. 10, R. to Minto, 31 January 1907.

27 Accounts in *The Times*, 24 December 1907, *Daily Telegraph*, 31 January 1908, *The Sphere* (with sketch) 15 January 1908; *Punch*, 15 January 1908; all in Bobs, 139, vol. XVII. Old age pensions began the next year.

28 James, *Raj*, p. 423; Spear, *Oxford History of Modern India*, p. 328.

29 K28, 9 September 1907.

30 James, *Raj*, pp. 417–33; Gilbert, *Servant of India*, pp. 162, 164, 170.

31 K28, R. to K., 3 February 1909.

32 Fraser, *Lord Esher*, pp. 185–95 and for Roberts's agreement, pp. 196–7; Bowman and Connelly, *The Edwardian Army*, p. 107.

33 Bowman and Connelly, *The Edwardian Army*, p. 159.

34 A.J.A.Morris, *Scaremongers: the Advocacy of War and Rearmament* (London, 1984), pp. 235–8.

35 A.L. Friedberg, *The Weary Titan: Britain and the Experience of Relative Decline 1895–1905* (Princeton, 1988), pp. 60, 68, 85–6.

36 Clashes between Fisher and his disciples and opponents led by Lord Charles Beresford make differences between the 'Ashanti' and 'Indian' rings slight; *inter alia*, G. Penn, *Infighting Admirals: Fisher's Feud with Beresford and the Reactionaries* (London, 2000).

37 E. Talbot-Rice, 'Bobs', *Kipling Journal*, no. 252 (December 1889), p. 32.

38 See my article, 'Kipling and the South African War, "Dress Rehearsal for Armageddon"?' *Kipling Journal*, no. 344 (December 2011), p. 44.

39 Ensor, *England 1870–1914*, p. 526.

40 Adams, 'Field-Marshal Earl Roberts', pp. 61–3; Morris, *Letters of Repington*, pp. 6–11, 14, 28–9 and 111ff.

41 Adams, 'Field Marshal Lord Roberts', p. 65.

42 Ferguson, *Empire*, pp. 287–8; Morris, *The Scaremongers*, p. 156. P.G. Wodehouse lampooned the invasion genre in *The Swoop, or How Clarence Saved England*.

43 Morris, *Letters of Repington*, pp. 131–7.

44 *Hansard*, Lords debates, 23 November 1908, vol. 196, cc. 1679ff.; *The Times*, 24 November 1908, p. 6 and p. 11 for leader 'The Danger of Invasion'; *The Times*, 26 November 1908, pp. 5, 8 for foreign reaction.

45 Morris, *Scaremongers*, p. 230.

46 Hamilton, *The Happy Warrior*, p. 242.

47 Adams, 'Field Marshal Lord Roberts', p. 67; Liddell Hart Archives, Hamilton 5/1/32, Lady R. to H., 21 March 1912; he had been building bridges with a letter.

48 Morris, *The Scaremongers*, pp. 245–6.

49 Jeffery, *Henry Wilson*, pp. 60–1; quote in Callwell, *Wilson*, I, p. 94.

50 December 1910: Liberal 274, Unionist 271, Irish Nationalists 82, Labour 42.

51 Letter in James, p. 444.

52 *Hansard*, Lords debates 23 November 1908, vol. 196 column 1695 (debate on National Defence); Adams, 'Field Marshal Earl Roberts', pp. 66–7; Ensor, *England, 1870–1914*, pp. 417–30.

53 Feuchtwanger, *Democracy and Empire*, p. 352.

54 Quoted in James, pp. 451–4.

55 James, pp. 454–5.

56 J. Grigg, *Lloyd George: from Peace to War 1912–1916* (London, 1985), p. 161.

57 Oliver, *Ordeal by Battle*, p. 332.

58 *The Nation*, 26 October 1912.

59 Oliver, *Ordeal by Battle*, pp. 332–45; De Lisle, *Reminiscences of Sport and War*, pp. 207–8.

60 James, pp. 460–1; Strachan, *Politics of the British Army*, p. 110.

61 Morris, *The Scaremongers*, pp. 245–7, 309–36; N. Ferguson, *The Pity of War* (1998), Chapter 1.

62 Adams, 'Field Marshal Earl Roberts', p. 76, n. 58; Wood, *Winnowed Memories*, pp. 233–4, 236, 251, 267. Account of Roberts and the League largely based on Adams; Oliver, *Ordeal by Battle*; Morris, *Scaremongers*; R.T. Stearn, ' "The Last Glorious Campaign": Lord Roberts, the National Service League and Compulsory Military Training 1902–1914,' *JSAHR*, vol. 87, no. 352 (winter 2009), pp. 312–30.

63 Oliver, *Ordeal by Battle*, pp. 350–1.

64 M. Seligman, *Spies in Uniform: British Military and Naval Intelligence on the Eve of the First World War* (Oxford, 2006). Roberts with his War Office connections would have heard of these reports.

65 R. Shannon, *The Crisis of Imperialism 1865–1915* (St Albans, 1976), p. 429.

66 A different view: Bowman and Connolly, *Edwardian Army*, p. 218 point to weaknesses, some highlighted by Roberts, but doubt whether conscripts with the four months' training he advocated could have given much help to the BEF.

67 Esher, *Diaries*, II, p. 432; James, pp. 451–2, letter to Churchill; M. Paris, *Winged Warfare: the Literature and Theory of Aerial Warfare in Britain* (Manchester, 1992), pp. 128–9. Bobs, 52, 13 April 1909, Nicholson pooh-poohing aircraft.

68 Jeffery, *Henry Wilson*, pp. 39, 60–1.

69 Hamilton 3/5/128, 23 June 1928.

70   Lee, *Jean, Lady Hamilton*, p. 5.

71   Hamilton 4/1/2, both letters 18 November 1905.

72   Hamilton 5/4/3, 9 December 1910.

73   Bobs 61/38, 8 April 1911.

74   Morris, *Letters of Repington*, p. 78.

75   Cornwall Record Office, Pole-Carew papers, CO/F11/18/2–3, 6 January 1902.

76   Pole-Carew papers, CO/F11/18/2–3, 7 January 1902.

77   Pole-Carew papers, CO/F9/6, 20 February 1905.

78   Hamilton 2/4/12, N. Chamberlain for R. to Lansdowne, 28 August 1900.

79   Liddell Hart Archives, letters of 23 June and 29 October 1903. It appears from the papers that Adams wrote on his death-bed appealing for Pole-Carew.

80   Liddell Hart Archives, P-C. to Grenfell, 23 December 1905; see also his letter to Maurice, Liddell Hart Archives, Maurice papers, 4 October 1906. Pole-Carew was however a pall-bearer at Roberts's funeral.

81   Dolaucothi, L14289, 5 November 1902.

82   T. Travers, *The Killing Ground: the British Army, the Western Front & the Emergence of Modern War* (Barnsley, 2009), pp. 3–4, 26–7 and on Roberts, pp. 6, 8, 9, 10.

83   J. Hussey, 'Appointing the Staff College Commandant: A Case of Trickery, Negligence or Due Consideration,' *British Army Review*, vol. 114 (December 1996, pp. 99–106). Jeffery, *Henry Wilson*, p. 66.

84   Books on Hamilton and the Dardanelles are legion; the assessment by C.F. Aspinall-Oglander on Hamilton in the old *Dictionary of National Biography* is sound; for 'Rawly' see F. Maurice, *Lord Rawlinson of Trent* (London, 1928) and R. Prior and T. Wilson, *Command on the Western Front: The Military career of Sir Henry Rawlinson 1914–1918* (London, 1992).

85   Travers, *Killing Ground*; Travers, 'The hidden army: structural problems in the British officer corps 1900–1918', *Journal of Contemporary History*, vol. 17, no. 3 (1982), pp. 523–44; Bowman and Connelly, *Edwardian Army*, pp. 75–7.

86   Jeffery, *Field-Marshal Henry Wilson*, p. 66.

87   d'Ombrain, *War Machinery and High Policy*, pp. 141ff.

88   Holmes, *The Little Field Marshal*, pp. 40–2.

89   RAI, Woolwich, Parsons papers MD/1111/1, diary of service in Natal, 1 August 1900.

90   Bobs, 30/3, 10 May 1901. The sentiments are genuine, but French's words somewhat excessive.

91   Bobs, 122, no.150, 13 October 1901. He placed French above another fine fighting soldier, Archibald Hunter.

92   Bobs, 30, 22 September 1901.

93   K28, 24 September 1903.

94 Mead, *The Good Soldier*, pp. 105–6, 134, 189; Harris, *Douglas Haig and the First World War*, points to his capacity for intrigue.

95 Hamilton 20/Lady Hamilton diary, 20 June 1906.

96 K28, 11 August 1900.

97 Barrow, *Fire of Life*, p. 115.

98 IOL, Eur Mss. 951/3, Owen Tudor Burne papers, f.223.

99 *The Times*, 13 October 1913, 'The Farnborough Collision'.

100 Jeffery, *Field Marshal Henry Wilson*, pp. 60–1.

101 Information from Peter Boyden; the Liddell Hart Archives website; A. Neave, *The Flames of Calais* (London, 1972). Lt-Gen. Sir Euan Miller KCB, KBE, DSO, MC died in 1985. *The Times*, 5 September 1985 for his obit.

102 IOL, Eur Mss D166/18, f. 20.

103 *The Times*, 27 February 1913, p. 6, 'Marriage of Lady Edwina Roberts'. This third Fred was killed in Norway in 1940.

104 Jeffery, *An Irish Empire*, pp. 130ff. esp. n. 40 on p. 146.

105 Gilmour, *Long Recessional*, pp. 245–7. Carson was, like Roberts, a southern Unionist.

106 Westminster would retain control of defence and foreign affairs.

107 A.T.Q. Stewart, *Ulster Crisis: Resistance to Home Rule* (London, 1967), p. 73.

108 Jeffery, *Henry Wilson*, p. 115; I. Beckett, *The Army and the Curragh Incident 1914* (London, 1986), p. 49.

109 Bobs, 46/184, 19 September 1913; also, Jeffery, *Henry Wilson*, pp. 115–17; Strachan, *Politics of British Army*, p. 111. Dr Roger Stearn kindly assisted in recommending sources on Richardson. See T. Bowman, *Carson's Army: The UVF 1910–1922* (Manchester, 2012).

110 Quoted in R.R. James, *Churchill: A Study in Failure 1900–1939* (1970), p. 48.

111 James, p. 467.

112 Blunt, *Diaries*, p. 837, so inaccurate as to be worthless; Beckett, *Curragh Incident*, p. 5.

113 Ensor, *England 1870–1914*, pp. 453–4.

114 James, pp. 465–6.

115 Beckett, *Army and Curragh Incident*, pp. 109–10.

116 James, p. 468.

117 The account of Curragh based on Holmes, *Little Field Marshal*, pp. 166–94; Bobs, 202, 'Ulster and the Army'; Beckett, *Army and Curragh Incident*; Nicholson, *King George V*; Strachan, *Politics of the British Army*, pp. 111–17; Jeffery, *Henry Wilson*, pp. 121–6.

118 Adams, 'Field Marshal Earl Roberts', p. 72; James, p. 467 n 1. Papers are in Bobs, 204.

119 Bobs, 202. Cf. Strachan, *Politics of the British Army*, p. 114 that Wilson and Roberts suborned Paget.

120 Spiers, *Army and Society*, p. 283; Nicolson, *George V*, p. 239; Feuchtwanger, *Democracy and Empire*, pp. 341–5; F.S.L. Lyons, I*reland since the Famine* (London, 1986), pp. 309–10.

121 K. Jeffery, *Ireland and the Great War* (Cambridge, 2000), pp. 2–3, 5, 6, 10–12.

Epilogue: Armageddon

1 Bobs, 203–5, Lady [Aileen] Roberts's correspondence with Churchill, March 1930.

2 Bobs, 203–1, 'Draft papers . . . reference to probable German strategy and advance through Belgium.'

3 Cassar, *Kitchener*, pp. 184–93.

4 Esher, *Tragedy of Lord Kitchener*, p. 52. J. Bloch, *Is War Now Impossible* (Paris, 1898) and 'The Wars of the Future,' *The Contemporary Review*, vol. 80 (September 1901), pp. 305–32. Esher mistakenly calls Bloch Swiss; he was Polish.

5 Bobs, 205, Aileen's account of 1914.

6 Bobs, 205, Aileen's account of 1914.

7 Arthur, *Life of Lord Kitchener*, III, p. 266, n. 1.

8 James, p. 477.

9 Bobs, 205; K108, Lady (Nora) Roberts to Kitchener, 17 December 1914.

10 Bobs, 61/47, 5 January 1917.

11 Bobs, 203, 1914.

12 T. and V. Holt, *My Boy Jack: The Search for Kipling's Only Son* (Barnsley, 1998), p. 59. The Holts' book makes clear that John Kipling would have enlisted, with or without a commission from Roberts.

13 Hamilton, 16 November 1914, to E. Sellars.

14 Barnes and Nicholson, *Amery Diaries*, I, pp. 110–1; Maurice, *Rawlinson of Trent*, p. 116; Callwell, *Henry Wilson*, I, pp. 187–8; K51, Rawlinson to Kitchener, 18 November 1914; Bobs, 205.

15 Holmes, *Little Field Marshal*, p. 258.

16 D. Omissi, *Indian Voices of the Great War* (Basingstoke, 1999), pp. 100–10.

17 Churchill College, Amery papers, AMEL 8/66, Amery to wife, 17 November 1914.

18 Marling, *Rifleman and Hussar*, pp. 349–50.

19 IOL, Eur Mss F166/18, f. 52, 20 November 1914.

20 Imperial War Museum, *The 1912–1922 Memoirs of Captain M.D. Kennedy, OBE*.

21 *The Times*, 15 November 1914, p. 1.

22 V. Brittain, *Chronicle of Youth: Great War Diary 1913–1917* (London, 1981), p. 122.

23 Beckett, *The Army and the Curragh Incident*, p. 390, n. 18; *Hansard*, Commons debates, 17 November 1914, vol. 68, cc. 341–8. The memorial to Roberts was erected on Horse Guards in 1923, close to Wolseley's.

24 At Museum of the Welsh Soldier, Cardiff Castle (in Welsh).

25 M.C. Hendley, *Organised Patriotism and the Crucible of War: Popular Imperialism in Britain 1914–1932* (Montreal, 2012), p. 21 points to the patriotism of the occasion.

26 Arthur, *Life of Lord Kitchener*, III, p. 359.

27 *Hansard*, Lords debates, 17 November 1914, vol. 18, c. 61; also Lanceley, *Hall-Boy to House-Steward*, p. 61.

28 For many years the Lord Roberts Workshops (later Forces Help Society and Roberts Memorial workshops) continued to help disabled servicemen.

29 J.N. Horne and A. Kramer, *German Atrocities 1914: a History of Denial* (London, 2001); J. Black, *The Great War and the Making of the Modern World* (London, 2011), pp. 54, 89, 107–8, 168–9. Germany's First World War dictatorship was established under Hindenburg and Ludendorff.

30 Both speeches, *Hansard*, Lords debates, 17 November 1914, vol. 17, cc. 57–64. Despite her poor health, Countess Roberts outlived her husband by over six years, dying at the same age, eighty-two, on 21 December 1920.

SELECT BIBLIOGRAPHY

Bibliographical note

For a full list readers are referred to the notes. Below is a selection.

Manuscript and archival sources

National Army Museum: Roberts papers.
National Army Museum: Rawlinson papers.
National Army Museum: Haines papers.
Liddell Hart Archives, King's College, London: Hamilton papers.
British Library: Eur Mss F108 George White papers.
British Library: IOL, L/MIL/5/678–688 military correspondence, Second Afghan War.
British Library: IOL, L/MIL/17/5/1613. Short Report on the Important Questions dealt with during the tenure of Command of the Army in India by General Lord Roberts 1885–1893.
National Library of Wales, Aberystwyth: Hills-Johnes papers, 'Dolaucothi'.
The National Archives, Kew: WO108/408–411 and WO108/238–241 Roberts's correspondence and telegrams from South Africa.
The National Archives, Kew: WO138/53 Field Marshal Lord Roberts's service record.
The National Archives, Kew: Pro30/57 Kitchener papers.
The Royal Artillery Institute: the papers of Lt-Gen Sir Lawrence Parsons and Major-General Sir John Headlam.
The Royal Archives, Windsor: correspondence of the 2nd Duke of Cambridge.

Books and articles

Adams, R.J.Q., 'Field Marshal Earl Roberts: Army and Empire', in J.A. Thompson and A. Meija, *Edwardian Conservatism: Five Studies in Adaptation* (London, 1988).
Amery, L.S., ed., *The Times History of the War in South Africa* (7 vols, London, 1900–1909), esp. volumes III and IV.
Balfour, Lady Betty, *The History of Lord Lytton's Indian Administration, 1876 to 1880* (London, 1899).
Ballhatchet, K., *Race, Sex and Class under the Raj: Imperial Attitudes and Policies and their Critics, 1793–1905* (London, 1980).

Barnes, J. and Nicholson, D., eds, *The Leo Amery Diaries*, vol. 1 1896–1929 (London, 1980).

Barrow, General Sir George de S., *The Fire of Life* (London, 1942).

Beckett, I.F.W., 'Women and Patronage in the Late Victorian Army', *History*, 85 (2000), pp. 463–80.

Beckett, I.F.W., *The Victorians at War* (London, 2003).

Bourne, J.M., 'The East India Company's Military Seminary, Addiscombe, 1809–1858', *JSAHR*, 57 (1979), pp. 206–23.

Brackenbury, General Sir Henry, *Some Memories of My Spare Time* (London, 1909).

Brice, C.M., 'The Military Career of General Sir Henry Brackenbury 1856–1904: the Thinking Man's General' (unpubl. Ph.D. thesis, De Montfort University, 2009).

Buckle, G.E., ed., *The Letters of Queen Victoria*, third series (3 vols, London, 1930–2).

Chapman, General. E.F, 'Two years under Field-Marshal Sir Donald Stewart in Afghanistan 1878–80,' orig. publ in *Blackwoods Magazine* (Edinburgh, 1902), pp. 255–63.

Churchill, W., *Ian Hamilton's March* (London, 1900).

Cohn, B.S., 'Representing Authority in Victorian India', in E. Hosbawm and T. Ranger, *The Invention of Tradition* (Cambridge, 1983).

Corvi, S.J. and Ian F.W. Beckett, *Victoria's Generals* (Barnsley, 2009).

David, S., *The Indian Mutiny 1857* (London, 2002).

Diver, M., 'Bobs Bahadur', *The Cornhill Magazine*, 38 (January–June 1915), pp. 25–37.

Diver, M., *The Englishwoman in India* (Edinburgh and London, 1909).

Dufferin and Ava, Marchioness of, *Our Viceregal Life in India: Selections from my Journal 1884–1888* (2 vols, London, 1890).

Durand, M., *The Life of Field Marshal Sir George White, V.C.* (2 vols, Edinburgh and London, 1915).

Edwards-Stuart, Lt-Col Ivor, *A John Company General: the Life of Lt. General Sir Abraham Roberts* (Bognor Regis, 1983).

Elsmie, G.R., *Field-Marshal Sir Donald Stewart: An Account of his Life, Mainly in his own Words* (London, 1903).

Esher, *Journals and Letters of Reginald Viscount Esher*, ed. M.V. Brett (4 vols, 1934–1938).

Forrest, G.W., *The Life of Field Marshal Sir Neville Chamberlain* (Edinburgh and London, 1909).

Forrest, G.W., *The Life of Lord Roberts* (London, 1914).

Forster, R.F., *Lord Randolph Churchill: a Political Life* (Oxford, 1981).

Gopal, S., *British Policy in India 1858–1905* (Cambridge, 1965).

Gwynn, S., and Tuckwell, G.M., *The Life of the Rt Hon. Sir Charles W Dilke* (2 vols, London, 1918)

Hamilton, I., *Listening for the Drums* (London, 1944).

Heathcote, T.A., *The Afghan Wars 1838–1919* (London, 1980).

Heathcote, T.A., *The Military in British India: the Development of British land forces in South Asia 1600–1947* (Manchester and New York, 1995).

Hensman, H. *The Afghan War of 1879–80* (London, 1881).

Hibbert, C., *The Great Mutiny: India 1857* (London, 1978).

Hopkirk, P., *The Great Game: on Secret Service in High Asia* (Oxford, 1990).

James, D., *Lord Roberts* (London, 1954).

Jeffery, K., ed., 'An Irish Empire'? Aspects of Ireland and the British Empire (Manchester, 1996).

Jeffery, K., Field Marshal Sir Henry Wilson: a Political Soldier (Oxford, 2006).

Johnson, R.A., ' "Russians at the Gates of India?" Planning the Defence of India, 1885–1900', The Journal of Military History, LXVII (July 2003), pp. 697–744.

Judd, D., and Surridge, K., The Boer War (London, 2002).

Kandahar Correspondence: Sirdar Ayub Khan's Invasion of Southern Afghanistan, Defeat of General Burrows' Brigade, and military operations in consequence (2 vols, Simla and Calcutta, 1880–1).

Kipling, R., Something of Myself (London, 1937).

Lanceley, W., From Hall-Boy to House-Steward (London, 1925).

Low, C.R., Major-General Sir Frederick S. Roberts (London, 1883).

Lutyens, M., The Lyttons in India: an Account of Lord Lytton's Viceroyalty 1876–1880 (London, 1979).

Lytton, R., 1st Earl, Personal and Literary Letters, ed. Lady Betty Balfour (2 vols, London, 1906).

MacMunn, Major G.F., The Armies of India. With a foreword by Field Marshal Earl Roberts (London, 1911).

Marling, Colonel Sir P., Rifleman and Hussar (London, 1931).

Menezes, Lt. Gen. S.L., Fidelity & Honour: the Indian Army from the Seventeenth to the Twenty-First Century (New Delhi, 1993).

Midleton, the Earl of, Records and Reactions 1856–1939 (London, 1939).

Milner, Viscountess, My Picture Gallery 1886–1901 (London, 1951).

Miller, S., Lord Methuen and the British Army (London and Portland, 1999).

Nasson, B., The Boer War: the Struggle for South Africa (Stroud, 2011).

Pakenham, T., The Boer War (London, 1979).

Page, A.H., 'The Supply Services of the British Army in the South African War 1899–1902' (Unpubl. Oxford D. Phil. thesis, 1977).

Porter, B., The Absent-Minded Imperialists: Empire, Society and Culture in Britain (Oxford, 2004).

Porter, B. The Lion's Share: a Short History of British Imperialism 1850–1995 (3rd edition, London, 1996).

Preston, A., 'Wolseley, the Khartoum Relief Expedition and the Defence of India, 1885–1900', Journal of Imperial and Commonwealth History, VI (1978), pp. 254–80.

Preston, A., 'Sir Charles MacGregor and the Defence of India', The Historical Journal, XII, I (1969), pp. 58–77.

Preston, A., 'Frustrated Great Gamesmanship: Sir Garnet Wolseley's Plans for War against Russia 1873–1880', International History Review, 2 (1980), pp. 239–67.

Roberts, Field Marshal Lord, Forty-One Years in India: from Subaltern to Commander-in-Chief (London, 1897).

Roberts, Field Marshal Lord, Letters written during the Indian Mutiny by Fred. Roberts, afterwards Field-Marshall Earl Roberts, with a preface by his daughter Countess Roberts (London, 1924).

Robson, B., 'Maiwand, 27th July 1880,' JSAHR, 51 (1973), pp. 194–221.

Robson, B., 'The Eden Commission and the Reform of the Indian Army – 1879–1895', JSAHR, 60 (1982), pp. 4–13.

Robson, B., 'Changes in the Indian Army', JSAHR, 70 (1992), pp. 126–7.

Robson, B., ed., *Roberts in India: the Military Papers of Field Marshal Lord Roberts 1878–1893* (Stroud, 1993).

Robson, B., *The Road to Kabul: the Second Afghan War 1878–1881* (Staplehurst, 2003).

Robson, B., 'Frederick Sleigh Roberts, first Earl Roberts', *Oxford Dictionary of National Biography* (60 vols, Oxford, 2004).

Scholtz, L., *Why The Boers Lost the War* (Basingstoke, 2005).

Smith-Dorrien, General Sir H., *Memories of Forty-Eight Years' Service* (London, 1925).

Soboleff, Major-General L.N., *The Anglo-Afghan Struggle*. Translated, condensed and arranged from the Russian by Major W.E. Gowan (Calcutta, 1885).

Spenser Wilkinson, H., *Thirty-Five Years 1874–1909* (London, 1933).

Spiers, E.M., *The Late Victorian Army 1868–1902* (Manchester, 1992).

Spies, S.B., *Methods of Barbarism? Roberts and Kitchener and Civilians in the Boer Republics, January 1900–May, 1902* (Capetown, 1977).

Stanley, P., *White Mutiny: British Military Culture in India, 1825–1875* (London, 1998).

Stewart, A.T.Q., *The Pagoda War: Lord Dufferin and the fall of the Kingdom of Ava 1885–6* (London, 1972).

Stone, M.S., 'The Victorian Army: Health, Hospitals and Social Conditions as Encountered by British Troops during the South African War, 1899–1902' (Unpubl. Ph.D. Thesis, London University, 1992).

Strachan, H., *The Politics of the British Army* (Oxford and New York, 1997), Chapter 5.

Streets, H., 'Military Influence in Late Victorian and Edwardian Popular Media; the case of Frederick Roberts', *Journal of Victorian Culture*, VIII, pt II (2003), pp. 231–56.

Streets, H. *Martial Races: the Military, Race and Masculinity in British Imperial Culture 1857–1914* (Manchester and New York, 2004).

Surridge, K., *Managing the South African War, 1899–1902: Politicians v. Generals* (Woodbridge, 1998).

Travers, E.A. 'Kabul to Kandahar, 1880: Extracts from the diary of Lieutenant E.A. Travers, 2nd P.W.O. Goorkhas,' edited by Major General J.LO. Chapple and Colonel D.R. Wood, *JSAHR*, 59 (1981), pp. 207–28; 60 (1982), pp. 35–43.

Trousdale, W., ed., *War in Afghanistan 1879–1880: the Personal Diary of Major General Sir Charles Metcalfe MacGregor*, (Detroit, 1985).

Vaughan, General Sir J.L., *My Service in the Indian Army – And After* (London, 1904)

Vibart, Colonel H.M., *Addiscombe: Its Heroes and Men of Note*. With an introduction by Lord Roberts of Kandahar (Westminster, 1894).

Watteville, H. de, *Lord Roberts* (London and Glasgow, 1938).

Wessels, A., ed., *Lord Roberts and the War in South Africa 1899–1902* (Stroud, 2000).

Wessels, A., 'Frederick Roberts' in S.J. Corvi and I.F.W. Beckett, *Victoria's Generals*, (Barnsley, 2009).

Wilson, H.W., *With the Flag to Pretoria: A History of the Boer War of 1899–1900* (2 vols, London, 1900).

Wilson, H.W., *After Pretoria: The Guerrilla War: Supplement to 'With the Flag to Pretoria'* (2 vols, London, 1902).

Younghusband, Major-General Sir G., *A Soldier's Memories in Peace and War* (London, 1917).

INDEX

Italic page numbers indicate illustrations

Bolan Pass 14, 76, 113
Botha, Louis, Boer commander 183,
   208, 209, 210, 211, 214,
   218, 224
Bourchier, Brigadier 62–3
Brandwater Basin, capture of Boers
   (July 1900) 211
British Army 8; health in India 153–6;
   in South Africa 6, 181, 192;
   'enteric' epidemic 202–3; reforms
   6, 226–9, 233–4, 236; recruitment
   124; commander-in-chief *see under*
   Cambridge, Roberts, Wolseley;
   discipline and courts-martial
   156, 230–1; intelligence
   department 149, 169, 170,
   180, 221; in South Africa 192;
   intelligence memorandum on
   Transvaal 206, 209
British Army, guns: 40-pounders
   at Kandahar 109; floating
   batteries on the Irrawaddy 138,
   at Colenso 183–4; 12-pounders
   146; 18-pounders 226, 236;
   13-pounders 226; Lee-Enfield
   introduced 226, 236
British Army, units: 48th Regiment
   12; 60th Rifles 152, 162, 262,
   278n78; 101st (Royal Bengal
   Fusiliers) 150; CIV 208, 211, 214;
   Cheshire Regiment 155; Essex
   Regiment 201; 72nd Seaforth
   Highlanders 77, 79, 159; 92nd
   Gordon Highlanders 82, 84, 109,
   112, 130, 165–6, 208, 292n120,
   306n91; Cameronians 263;
   Grenadier Guards 209, 233;
   Household Cavalry 214, 260;
   King's Liverpool Regiment 40, 77,
   230; Northumberland Fusiliers
   158; East Surrey Regiment 158;
   Warwickshire Regiment 167;
   Worcestershire Regiment 156;
   Royal Scots Fusiliers 156; Royal
   Scots Greys 201; 6th Dragoon
   Guards 36; 9th Lancers 40; 10th
   Hussars 81; Royal Canadians 199;
   Mounted Infantry 143, 146–7,
   192, 194, 195, 200, 202, 205,

206, 209, 234; Queen Alexandra's
   Imperial Nursing Service 227;
   Royal Army Medical Corps 154,
   194, 202–3; Veterinary 192, 222,
   227; Remount 192, 227; military
   education and training 227; Staff
   College *see* separate entry
British Empire passim, 7, 10, 119, 124;
   Burma added 143, 158–9, 163,
   234; 'a life and death struggle'
   260; vanished 266; *see also* India,
   British rule; Ireland and Irish
   soldiers
Brittain, Vera, laments Roberts's death
   264
Brodrick, William St John Fremantle,
   Earl Midleton: 1898 Salisbury
   manoeuvres 181; Secretary of State
   for War 221–7, 229, 230–4, 235,
   238, 252; Secretary of State for
   India 238–9
Brownlow, Field Marshal Sir Charles:
   Lushai 62–3; Whitehall 133,
   144, 157
Brownlow, commanding officer of
   Seaforths 94, 109
Buller, General Sir Redvers 8, 9, 124,
   166, 167, 208, 214, 215, 218,
   221, 305n35, 311n190, 312n191;
   abuses Roberts 115, 174; beaten
   in manoeuvres 181; South African
   command 174, 176, 180, 182;
   Colenso 183–4; superseded 186–7;
   relieves Ladysmith 199; jealous
   of Roberts 206; meets Roberts
   at Pretoria 213–14; Amery and
   Cairns's views 219–20; relieved
   of command for speech 231–2;
   correspondence with Pole-Carew
   250–1; disbelieved at Royal
   Commission 312n200
Burma 21, 28, 51, 148, 202, 224; Third
   Burmese War 138–43, 146, 156
Burne, Owen 48, 53, 70, 82, 135
Burrows, Brigadier-General, beaten at
   Maiwand 102

Calcutta 20, 36, 43, 46, 49, 50, 57, 93,
   97, 120, 121, 144, 241